Dublin

Bristol London

Plymouth   Dieppe
        St Malo

La Rochelle

Bayonne

Seville

EA

7.22.80

THE WESTWARD
ENTERPRISE

The Westward Enterprise

English activities in Ireland, the Atlantic,
and America 1480–1650

EDITED BY
K.R.ANDREWS, N.P.CANNY
and P.E.H.HAIR

WAYNE STATE UNIVERSITY PRESS
DETROIT, 1979

Published in the United States and Canada, 1979, by
WAYNE STATE UNIVERSITY PRESS
Detroit, Michigan 48202

Manufactured in Great Britain

Library of Congress Cataloging in Publication Data
The Westward enterprise.
"The essays in this volume are offered ... in tribute to
D. B. Quinn to mark his retirement in 1976 from the Andrew
Geddes and John Rankin Chair of Modern History at the
University of Liverpool."
Includes index.
CONTENTS: Parry, J. H. Introduction: The English in
the New World.—Canny, N. The permissive frontier: social
control in English settlements in Ireland and Virginia, 1550–
1650.—Bottigheimer, K. S. Kingdom and colony: Ireland in
the westward enterprise, 1536-1660.—[etc.].
    1. America—Discovery and exploration—English—Ad-
dresses, essays, lectures. 2. Great Britain—Colonies—America
—Addresses, essays, lectures. 3. Great Britain—Territorial
expansion—Addresses, essays, lectures. 4. United States—
History—Colonial period, ca. 1600-1775—Addresses, essays,
lectures. 5. British in Ireland—History—Addresses, essays,
lectures. 6. Quinn, David Beers—Addresses, essays, lectures.
I. Andrews, Kenneth R. II. Canny, Nicholas P. III. Hair, Paul
Edward Hedley. IV. Quinn, David Beers.
E127.W47 1979   970.01'7   79-13801

ISBN 0-8143-1647-6

PREFACE

David Beers Quinn

The essays in this volume are offered by friends and admirers, colleagues and pupils, in tribute to D. B. Quinn to mark his retirement in 1976 from the Andrew Geddes and John Rankin Chair of Modern History at the University of Liverpool. While the occasion of the essays is the termination of David Quinn's distinguished career in university teaching, during which he has held one chair at Swansea for thirteen years and another at Liverpool for nineteen years, their theme is that wide area of historical interest to which he has chosen to devote his research career: a career which, if one may judge by the number of publications he is today actively preparing and the number of projects he is vigorously advancing, there is every prospect of his continuing for many years. It would be idle to pretend that the present volume matches in subject matter the extraordinary range of his historical interests—ships and maps, Basques and Bretons, English herbals, Dublin printers, North American languages and the many other topics his compulsive curiosity has drawn him to explore—but it does relate to the field of study that appears in retrospect to have come naturally to him.

Born in Dublin, and brought up in the little town of Clara in the Irish midlands and in Belfast, he graduated in 1931 from Queen's University, Belfast. For postgraduate study he moved to King's College, London, and learned the elements of his craft at the Institute of Historical Research, along with a group of contemporaries as distinguished as any that school has since produced. Curious as it must now seem, at Belfast he was taught neither British colonial nor Irish history, but wide reading developed interests in both. Two scholars who influenced him, J. E. Todd of Belfast and A. P. Newton of London, suggested he might pursue his overseas interests in postgraduate study; however he found it best to concentrate on Irish history, gaining his doctorate in 1934 with a study of early Tudor administration in Ireland. At a time of economic depression he was fortunate to gain a lectureship at the then tiny University College, Southampton, where he taught colonial history for the most part and began to publish his Irish material. Five years in this post focused his wider interests, so that he researched first on Southampton trade at the end of the medieval period, and then on Sir Humphrey Gilbert, who epitomized the dual Elizabethan involvement in plans to colonize Ireland and North America. In 1939 he was appointed to a special lectureship in Queen's University, Belfast, charged with the development of the study of Irish history, a subject recently introduced by T. W. Moody. During the early war years he retained a full teaching load at Queen's; and he served as a casualty officer in the air raids service and, for part of 1943, as an editor of the European programme of the B.B.C.

In 1944 he was appointed to the chair of history at University College, Swansea, and found the task of building the department anew arduous but exciting. Meanwhile his research interests in fifteenth- and sixteenth-century Irish history and in fifteenth- and sixteenth-century English nautical enterprise had finally coalesced and he was drawn, after the publication of his work on Gilbert in 1940, to an intensive and still-continuing study of English settlement in Ireland and North America in early modern times. Thanks to the generosity of his family (as he himself has observed), from Swansea, and after 1957 from Liverpool, he was able to visit London regularly to explore the archives and to work on documents. In his later years at Swansea he began those almost annual forays across the Atlantic to visit bibliographic and cartographic treasure-houses virtually fulfilling the vision of El Dorado: which led to his holding, at suitable intervals, library fellowships and a visiting professorship in the United States, and to his gaining a wide circle of friends and admirers throughout North America. Meanwhile in Britain and Ireland he has been active in many historical societies, but especially in the Hakluyt Society. First as a council member, then as a vice-president, he has been one of a remarkable group of men and women who have steered this invaluable society to new standards of success over a period of thirty years.

It was through his research and writing on early modern Ireland that David Quinn became interested in England's westward enterprise. The publications with which he launched his career were concerned almost exclusively with aspects of Anglo-Irish administration during the late fifteenth and early sixteenth centuries. This work was characterized by the patience with which he groped his way through material which had never hitherto been subjected to sustained historical investigation, by an imaginative yet faithful use of most unpromising sources, and by the lucid and elegant presentation of his findings.

Furthermore, David Quinn recognized from the outset that research on his chosen area of study was unlikely to flourish as long as the sources remained scattered and inaccessible, and he strove to remedy this by collecting and editing documents. In this endeavour he employed his palaeographic and linguistic skills to great effect. This massive output placed future generations of scholars, no less than his contemporaries, greatly in his debt; and all who have been students of sixteenth-century Ireland during the last half-century have not only had occasion to refer constantly to his published work but have always found him ready to give of his time and enormous erudition in providing advice, criticism, and suggestions.

David Quinn was one of the small band of scholars who, in the 1930s, did so much to professionalize Irish history when they formed the Irish Historical Society and the Ulster Society for Irish Historical Studies, and launched *Irish Historical Studies* as the joint publication of those two societies. The more prominent of this group received their historical training at London and, again like David Quinn, worked initially on the early modern period of Irish history, but the majority, having served their apprenticeship, shifted their interest to what seemed more relevant or exciting areas of study. Thus, in a sense, David Quinn's most vital contribution to the study of Irish history has been his persistence in the investigation of the sixteenth century, and his establishing a new relevance for the history of this century, by showing how events in Ireland impinged upon developments elsewhere in Europe while at the same time Ireland was being shaped by general European influences. It was, ironically, as a result of his discovering this broader context for Irish history that David Quinn was drawn towards the study of European expansion. But he never lost his interest in early modern Ireland, and each time he returned to it he brought new questions, fresh insights, and illuminating parallels, while his profound knowledge of events in Ireland equipped him to make a unique contribution to the study of Atlantic history. Much of his early work on Irish history has been revised and brought together by himself and appears in the second and third volumes of *A New History of Ireland* (Oxford, 1976–); and all Irish historians hope that he will, at some future date, assemble his many articles on English colonization in Ireland into one coherent statement and publish it as a companion volume to *England and the Discovery of America*. Meanwhile, the general reader can savour the quality of the man in his admirably detached study, *The Elizabethans and the Irish* (1966), perhaps the most civilized analysis of uncivil 'race' relations in earlier times yet produced.

Apart from his contribution to Irish history, David Quinn's main work has been concerned with the Atlantic enterprise of Englishmen, from the Bristol voyages of the late fifteenth century to the founding of Jamestown in 1607. It constitutes a massive demonstration of the power of modern scholarship to reconstruct the foundations of history. This he has achieved, not by the all-too-fashionable method of thinking up a bright idea and rummaging around for enough evidence to make it plausible, but by applying all the technical resources of research to clarify existing knowledge and supplement it with new, producing thereby a deeper and ultimately truer understanding of the past. For this task he found an appropriate vehicle in the Hakluyt Society editions of classic texts on travel and discovery, but his treatment of the Gilbert material (1940) established for these publications a new and higher standard, both in the rendering of the documents and in their annotation. Fifteen years later he proceeded to raise this standard yet again with the two-volume *Roanoke Voyages*. The most obvious distinguishing feature of these works was the precision of the editing, but what made them—and still makes them—the delight of students of the subject was the annotation, which superbly combined encyclopaedic knowledge with an acute sense of relevance. Nor did he ever stray in the direction of antiquarianism: when one has read with the alertness they deserve Quinn's studied presentations of Harriot's *Briefe and true report* or of the White drawings, for example, one comes away with an immensely enriched appreciation of what western planting really meant in terms of devoted effort, difficulties both physical and conceptual, the requirements of publicity and so forth; and one begins to look at other such texts with an altogether more creative view of their historical potential. Equally important in the making of these editions was the use of microscopic research to reconstruct missing or obscure episodes and persons in the story. The proper exercise of this craft requires command of a wide range of sources—legal, administrative, literary, national, local, foreign—and something that can only be described as *flair*. David Quinn's remarkable and continuing run of success in this type of work can be traced in a variety of journals and many of these articles were brought together recently in *England and the Discovery of America*. They are interesting in their own right and it would be difficult to find in historical literature a comparable series of original constructions by a single author, but essentially they are contributions to current discussion and stepping-stones towards those landmarks of the subject, the Hakluyt

Society editions. These include, of course, the facsimile edition of Hakluyt's *Principall Navigations* of 1589 with its fine critical and bibliographical introduction by Quinn and R. A. Skelton. This, together with the facsimile edition of *Divers Voyages* and Quinn's accompanying essay on Hakluyt as an editor, helped to prepare the way for the *Hakluyt Handbook*, inspired, produced, and largely written by David Quinn and his wife, Alison. The three works together constitute a great step forward in Hakluyt scholarship: the only major advance since G. B. Parks's *Richard Hakluyt and the English Voyages* was published in 1930.

David Quinn's contribution to what may be called the prehistory of British North America stands out as uniquely important in the historiography of the subject. Apart from the contemporary literature, what had been discovered about English enterprise in that direction from the Cabots to Christopher Newport appears now, in the light of Quinn's findings, surprisingly little, and the handling of that little surprisingly amateurish. Consequently his reputation already stands high in North America and will undoubtedly grow in course of time as the fundamental significance of his work gradually sinks in. He has also become widely recognized internationally as one of the leading authorities on the discovery of America, particularly since the publication of the brilliantly judicious 'argument for the English discovery of America' in 1961.

His reputation in this field rests and will endure on the solid basis of a large body of high-quality and significant research, but this does not mean that he has neglected to make his findings and views known to the wide public outside academic circles. *Raleigh and the British Empire* has been a steady seller since 1947 and has helped to form the opinions of many, perhaps most, younger people interested in the beginnings of English overseas expansion; and recently he has returned to the popular vein in several works, most impressively in the superb pictorial history done in collaboration with R. A. Skelton and W. P. Cumming.

A great deal of what D. B. Quinn has accomplished in the study of the history of 'the westward enterprise' may be called spade-work by those who have never done any to speak of. But it may more justly be compared to the patient labour of a skilful gardener who over the years comes to know the cumulative value of his efforts and deserves to know that others recognize it too. Elizabethan horticulture would in any case have been one of David Quinn's specialities, but he happened to be born the son of a gardener; which may add point not only to that particular interest but also to the suggested comparison.

Alison Quinn has contributed much more to David Quinn's career than the role conventionally and tactfully assigned to a wife in any tribute to a great yet happily married scholar. Her Scottish practicality and good humour have always tempered David's native qualities; and have made his odysseys possible, whether these were new voyages of discovery to the bibliographic and cartographic riches across the Atlantic or those long car journeys up and down Britain and Ireland which the two undertake on the slightest hint of a new reference, in a country house library or a provincial archive, to Eskimos at Bristol or Virginians on the Thames. In latter years, as their children left home, she has been able to contribute to Quinn publications at the level of higher scholarship. The 1965 facsimile reprint of the *Principall Navigations* was sandwiched between the learned introduction by Quinn and Skelton, and an index by Alison Quinn so detailed, knowledgeable, and systematic that it won her a professional award, the Wheatley Medal; and it may be claimed with some assurance that few among the scholars who have since consulted *PN* (1589) have not had cause to bless Alison for her index to the reprint. She continues indexing in many fields, and she worked with David in the assembly and arrangement of the elaborate detail presented in the *Hakluyt Handbook*. In the bibliography of D. B. Quinn's writings at the end of this volume some of Alison's contributions are specially noted.

At Liverpool, D. B. Quinn's achievements in the conduct of his department for nineteen years have been to widen its interests, spatially and chronologically, and to leave the School of History with the tradition that devotion to research and an impressive publications list can coexist with vigorous and conscientious teaching and with close attention to student needs and even student wishes. It is appropriate therefore to note that this volume was initiated and organized within the Liverpool department; and the Liverpool editor wishes to thank his colleague, Dr P. J. Buckland, senior lecturer in Irish history, for invaluable assistance and advice throughout the project, and his colleague, Dr W. J. Rowe, reader in American history, for his preparation of an index.

The three editors have worked together from the start but the Liverpool editor, non-expert in the theme, wishes to record that the academic editing was solely in the hands of Drs Andrews and Canny. All three thank Professor John Roberts of Laval University for his support when a wider project was discussed, and those other scholars who showed interest and were disappointed when this proved impracticable in difficult times. We further thank a large number of D. B. Quinn's oldest friends and admirers who gave us every encouragement even when their own circumstances or the theme we had chosen made it impossible for them to contribute. It is perhaps worthwhile adding that the essays which appear in this volume were completed by their authors during 1976. Finally the editors thank the essayists for their co-operation and understanding, and join them in wishing David and Alison Quinn long years of happy scholarship.

K.R.A.

N.P.C.

P.E.H.H.

CONTENTS

LIST OF PLATES

Between pages 200–203

I

Introduction:
the English in the New World

J. H. PARRY

It is natural that a collection of essays written in honour of David Quinn should reflect his major interests: principally the history of early English exploration and settlement in the New World. Quinn's latest major work, *England and the Discovery of America*, ranges geographically from Labrador to Virginia, and chronologically from the first vague intimations, in the 1480s, of English interest in distant lands in the North Atlantic, to the firm establishment of colonies in New England in the 1620s. The story is never told in isolation, but always as part of a wider European movement into the newly found Americas. *The Roanoke Voyages*, in particular, takes almost the form of a dialogue between English and Spanish sources. D. B. Quinn has done more than any other historian to explain and present the work of the younger Hakluyt to modern readers; appropriately, for Hakluyt also in his day used foreign sources to illuminate English achievements. These are the considerations which define the present collection. Most of the essays it contains are concerned with North America, though some range more widely. K. R. Andrews and Joyce Lorimer deal with events in the West Indies and Guiana, respectively; K. S. Bottigheimer and Brendan Bradshaw examine developments in Ireland. Nearly all are concerned with English ideas or endeavours; but most of the authors take account also of the presence of other Europeans—Frenchmen, Dutchmen, above all Spaniards—as neighbours, exemplars, or rivals. The question naturally arises, of what common features, if any, connected these different but related stories. What characteristics—other than obvious differences of time, place, and circumstance—distinguished the English way of doing things from that of Spaniards, Frenchmen, and the rest? In what did the Englishness of English oversea settlement consist?

The markedly commercial character of English colonies in America has often been noticed as a characteristic distinguishing them from other

European settlements, especially those of Spain. As Carole Shammas points out, however, this was a relatively late development. The English, in fact, were eclectic in their choice of aims and methods; at one time or another they tried almost everything. Late-comers to the New World, they had an abundance of precedents from which to choose. Throughout the sixteenth century their endeavours, like those of other northern Europeans, were inspired, defined, and of course limited, by the success which Spaniards had already achieved. The Englishmen who promoted American expeditions in Elizabeth's time—mostly gentlemen bred to arms, if not professional soldiers, rather than merchants or financiers— wished to emulate the *conquistadores,* by subduing native cities and king-doms, establishing personal lordships, and living upon rents and tributes. Estates and rent-rolls, however, could be acquired more easily and nearer home, in Ireland; Ireland is often cited as a precedent or training ground for American adventure, but it was also, as Shammas observes, a counter-attraction. In America, the Spaniards had pre-empted all the most desirable areas. Ralegh's Manoa was a figment of overheated imagina-tion, his own and Berrío's. Populous and productive provinces could be acquired only by conquest from Spain. Some Elizabethans contemplated this; it was probably among Ralegh's motives in promoting settlement at Roanoke, and certainly among the long-range objects of his enterprise in Guiana. The capture and retention of key harbours in the Caribbean was suggested to the Queen by Gilbert in 1577 and briefly attempted by Drake and Carleill in 1585. Nothing came of it all; the physical obstacles were too formidable, the Spaniards too strong, the Queen too cautious. It was not until the middle decades of the seventeenth century that Dutchmen and Englishmen succeeded in capturing and keeping Spanish territory, and then no more than thinly held scraps, remote Caribbean islands.

If the Spanish empire in America had to be accepted as a permanent fact, Englishmen could nevertheless profit by it, either by preying upon it as privateers in war or as pirates in peace, or by attaching themselves to it as parasites, by way of illicit trade. The two approaches were contra-dictory, since the predators weakened the body upon which the parasites would feed; but often the same people engaged in both, with damaging effect both on Spanish pockets and Spanish morale. Major English raids on Spanish harbours and shipping ceased in 1604, for fear of the King's displeasure, but smuggling, piracy, and petty raiding continued. K. R. Andrews traces the progress of this 'creeping invasion' of the Caribbean, and argues that it damaged Spanish interests far more severely, in the long run, than did the big semi-naval expeditions which Drake, Hawkins, Cumberland, and others had commanded in time of war. It virtually excluded Spanish shipping from the trade of many Spanish harbours in the Antilles and on the Main coast, and put Spain to crippling expense in protecting the main route of the treasure fleets against possible attack. Nevertheless, even from the point of view of its successful English and Dutch practitioners, piracy was self-defeating in the long run, and smuggling an unsatisfactory commercial expedient. Illicit trade was possible only in minor harbours, small places with restricted hinterlands; the main terminuses were too well guarded. It called for armed ships; business often had to be conducted at the pike's point, because of mutual distrust, and was always liable to interruption by Spanish cruisers. It could not provide an adequate and steady supply of the New World products most in demand in Europe.

The notion that these desired commodities might actually be produced in English colonies and that English settlers might earn a living by selling them to English traders, was curiously slow in formulation and acceptance. Some Elizabethan proponents of a 'forward' policy in America —Hakluyt among them—mentioned the supply of exotic commodities among the advantages to be expected from colonies; but often their suggestions amounted to no more than the wistful hope that gold or silver might be found in unoccupied parts of America. Frobisher's experience suggested that Englishmen—though they would vastly prefer, no doubt, to collect gold from Indians as tribute—might nevertheless be willing to work gold-mines themselves if they had to; but Frobisher's ore proved worthless, and few investors wished to finance random prospecting. Metals apart, the suggestions of the propagandists were usually perfunctory and vague. The commodities most commonly mentioned were wild products: timber, furs, and a small range of plants believed, on slender evidence, to possess medicinal properties.

Proposals to defray the cost of settlement by selling wild products were not wholly unrealistic. In Hakluyt's time cochineal, a wild product collected by Indians, was second in order of value, though a long way behind silver, among the exports of New Spain. Cochineal was exceptional, however, and did not occur in any territory accessible to Englishmen. The quantity of sassafras likely to be consumed in England would make no-one's fortune. In fact the only wild American plant product to be imported profitably into England in significant quantity in colonial times

was logwood; and most of that was cut surreptitiously in Spanish territory. Furs were a valuable commodity, in high demand in England; and
in favourable circumstances the fur trade could be very profitable. As an
economic base for a colony, however, it was unreliable, because European
settlement, unless very sparse and perilously scattered, drove fur-bearing
animals away. As for timber, it was plentiful indeed in coastal North
America; New England in particular had great stands of mast trees, which
old England urgently needed. Here, surely, was the basis of a valuable
trade; but once again events were to prove the propagandists wrong. The
transport of pine trunks across the Atlantic was expensive and troublesome. Transport from inland forests, where most of the 'great masts'
grew, down to the coast, presented even greater difficulties. In the early
years of settlement, the urgent demand for sawn timber for building took
precedence over other considerations, so that before an export trade
could develop, most of the streams, down which the masts might have
been floated to the coast, were blocked by sawmills. As an export crop,
timber was to defeat expectations for two hundred years.

The crop which first answered and exceeded them was tobacco. J.
Lorimer describes the successive attempts made by traders and planters
to satisfy the rapid rise in the demand for tobacco in England in the late
sixteenth and early seventeenth centuries: the early surreptitious trade,
first with wild Indians on the Guiana coast, then with Spanish planters
producing a better cured product in Trinidad; the early attempts of
English planters to grow tobacco in Guiana and on the Amazon; and the
emergence of Tidewater Virginia, with the support of the metropolitan
government, as the principal source of supply. Tobacco in Virginia
represented a 'break-through' in a number of ways. It was not a wild
product, but a cultivated one. It was not even native; *Nicotiana rustica*,
the species native to North America and used by Indians there, never
appealed to the European taste; *Nicotiana tabacum*, which appealed enor-
mously, was introduced into Virginia from South America. Its cultivation
made Virginia a market-oriented plantation settlement, the first English
colony to pay its way. Virginia, with tobacco, took a direction which
many other territories were to follow: the Carolinas with rice, the West
Indian islands successively with tobacco, cotton, indigo, above all with
sugar. This was the process which Shammas calls the commercialization
of English colonization. There was nothing peculiarly English about it.
Most European colonies in the Americas became commercially oriented, in
greater or less degree, in the seventeenth century. The English, indeed,

were conscious imitators: of the Spaniards in the growing and curing of tobacco, of the Brazilian Portuguese in large-scale sugar production, of the Dutch in the organization of an efficient carrying trade. In their choice of ends and means the English were as eclectic in the seventeenth century as they had been in the sixteenth, though the ends and means were different.

Perhaps the most striking characteristic of the English settlements in America was their diversity. No other colonial empire employed so wide a range of legal devices in establishing settlements, or allowed so many diverse forms of social, religious, and economic organization. Many factors contributed to this diversity: the habit of eclectic borrowing already noticed; differences in time, place, and circumstance; differences in personality and purpose; and the absence of sustained interest and continuous effective control by the central government. These factors interacted in complex and sometimes unpredictable fashion. Richard Dunn provides a striking illustration of differences in personality and purpose, contrasting John Winthrop, who went to New England to establish a godly commonwealth, and Sir Henry Colt, who tried to make his fortune by growing tobacco in St Kitts; yet there was no necessary affinity between puritanism and the rigours of New England, or between the West Indies and the desire to get rich quick. Some religious dissidents were attracted to the West Indies. The ill-fated Providence Company was organized by prominent puritans. Chance, not choice, deflected the Pilgrims from Virginia and landed them in New England, where they were soon joined by neighbours—Thomas Morton and his friends—who intended to make money by fur trading and had no interest whatever in a godly commonwealth. On the other hand, choice, rather than chance or necessity, governed the failure of New England to produce cash crops for sale in England. Sugar, it is true, will not grow there, but tobacco will; Massachusetts today produces great quantities of it. The technical difficulties inhibiting the export of timber could have been overcome, and the price in England in times of serious shortage could have rendered the trade profitable, if people in the colonies had been willing to take the trouble. The New Englanders' stubborn devotion to traditional English farming ways, and their initial indifference to cash crops, to export trade, and in general to the wishes of the metropolitan authorities, were by their own choice.

Hugh Kearney argues that historians of the English colonies in America have concentrated unduly upon New England; deceived by the intellectual pre-eminence of East Coast institutions in more recent times, they have attributed to seventeenth-century New England an importance it did not possess. No doubt the New England settlements, from the point of view of imperial administrators, were marginal and unsatisfactory outposts; and probably New England farmers and traders appeared uncouth and provincial in the eyes of successful planters further south. Yet New England did have a special significance, precisely because, in an empire of diversity, it provided the most striking example (except, perhaps, Port Royal and its buccaneers) of refusal to conform to a prescribed pattern.

New England was not unaffected by commercialization; but the change came late there, and took an unexpected direction. Though the region produced little that was marketable in England, it became in the later seventeenth century a major source of food and services for the booming plantations of the West Indies, and a significant market for sugar, molasses, and buccaneers' loot. Without this commercial partnership the New England settlements, despite their much recorded zeal for education, might have remained rustic Bible commonwealths based, as Professor Kearney puts it, on an idealized version of the gentry-cum-yeoman society already disappearing in England. Without it, certainly, the West Indians would have had great difficulty in feeding their slaves and themselves, and in barrelling their sugars for shipment. Thus the New Englanders, who refused so stubbornly to develop a docile, orthodox trade serving the direct needs of England, made a major indirect contribution to the prosperity of empire as a whole.

Administrators in England naturally did not see matters in quite this light. They thought of the metropolis as the hub of a commercial wheel, with colonial trade moving up and down the spokes rather than round the rim. They did not welcome nonconformity, whether economic, political, or religious; they learned, nevertheless, to tolerate it. Their attempts to enforce uniformity in these respects were occasional, somewhat half-hearted, and largely ineffectual. Inter-colonial trade, though some of it was taxed from 1673 onwards, was never prohibited, as it was, frequently and fairly effectively, in the Spanish empire. Religious separatists, though their doctrines were anathema to all the Stuart kings, on the whole had their way in New England; they would have had short shrift in New Spain or New France. The special rights, embodied in the charters by which many colonies had been founded, though they were sometimes modified, were not often challenged or abrogated. Some proprietary colonies, even —primitive relics—were allowed to survive into the eighteenth century.

In Spanish America the original *conquistadores* in the sixteenth century, if they survived their rivals' knives, had mostly been pushed aside by the officials of the central bureaucracy. The institutions they set up, *señorío*, *encomienda*, municipal *cabildo*, were always subject to change and regulation, even abolition, by central decree. The Spanish government, moreover, took firm and early measures to prevent the growth of anything resembling *cortes* in New Spain. In New France, apparently, no-one ever dreamed of such a thing. Government in England, by contrast, though it might disallow the enactments of colonial legislatures, did nothing to prevent the establishment of such bodies and only once (in 1683, briefly) suspended their sittings. Parliament very rarely legislated about the internal affairs of particular colonies, and even when legislating for the colonies in general usually confined itself to the regulation of trade and related matters. There was no general codification of statute law relating to the colonies, no English *Recopilación de Leyes de Indias*. Even Common Law, often loudly proclaimed as the palladium of English liberties overseas, was transferred to the colonies, as W. M. Billings amply demonstrates, in piecemeal and selective fashion. Different rules, different interpretations, were applied in different colonies, and then still further modified by local precedent as well as by local legislation. Finally, whereas the Spanish and Portuguese governments always retained the right to tax their colonial subjects, for colonial or metropolitan purposes, at will, the English government never attempted to do this. Its colonial revenue was indirect, arising from duties on colonial goods imported into England. Taxes raised in any English colony, usually by authority of the colonial assembly, were spent within that colony.

These characteristics set English colonizing activities in the seventeenth century apart from the activities of most other European groups. The differences should not be exaggerated; no European government at that time was strong enough to enforce its authority consistently over great distances—or even at home, often enough—and authoritarian formulas were not always to be taken literally. The Spanish government, for example, in practice and by convention, allowed its representatives in the Indies much greater latitude than their written instructions suggest. Nevertheless, the differences were real. English settlers in the Americas were, in general, left alone to manage their own affairs far more than were Spanish, Portuguese, or French. Government in England might react angrily to insolence or open defiance, particularly if the financial interests of influential people, the patronage of the Crown, or the defence of the colonies as a whole, appeared to be threatened; but otherwise it accepted patiently a great deal of discreet evasion and tactful dis- obedience. Its patience, no doubt, was in part the product of impotence; for long periods in the seventeenth century English governments were too preoccupied with troubles at home to deal firmly with colonial affairs. In part, it arose from indifference; in the estimation of most English statesmen, colonial affairs assumed urgent importance only when they impinged upon English politics. It may not be wholly fanciful, however, to regard this attitude of official England, this easy-going, tolerant (or merely lazy) live-and-let-live, as also, in part, a peculiarity of the English temperament at the time; or at the least as a very strongly ingrained habit.

This view is strengthened by consideration of English attitudes towards the natives of the Americas. There was no official policy, in the sense of a policy enunciated and enforced by government. Neither Crown nor Parliament accepted any responsibility in the matter. The Virginia Company initially proclaimed its intention of bringing the Indians to Christianity and 'civility', and as both L. E. Pennington and John Parker point out, propaganda on these lines in pamphlets and sermons was effective in attracting public support. After the massacre of 1622, how- ever, the spokesmen of the Company changed their tune abruptly, and proclaimed, as Captain John Smith had always done, that the only argu- ment savages could understand was that of force.

The inclination of most Englishmen actively concerned in the matter was, as far as possible, to leave the Indians alone. It was not possible to leave them alone entirely, of course. In the early years settlers were often dependent on Indians for food, and for information about native food plants, wild and cultivated. They sought to end this precarious depen- dence as soon as they could, by establishing their own cultivations, which necessarily encroached on Indian hunting grounds. In so vast a wilderness this seemed a small matter, and serious attempts were made to regulate it by treaty or purchase; but as settlement expanded, it aroused Indian fear and resentment, and sometimes savage hostility on both sides. Settlers could not avoid contact, whether friendly, indifferent, or hostile, with the Indians; but usually they preferred to keep it to a minimum, to keep the 'salvages' at arm's length. Once the initial food shortages were overcome, the Indians had little to offer the settlers. They were useless as a labour force. Wandering about the settlements, they were a nuisance and could be a danger. Nicholas Canny draws attention to the unsympathetic attitude of settlers towards those of their number who wandered off to live among the Indians. Such desertions were not infrequent in European settler communities everywhere in the Americas. It is of some interest to note that the Spanish colonial authorities also regarded them with displeasure, but on different grounds. They feared that Europeans who 'went native' would tyrannize and corrupt the Indians among whom they settled; whereas the English settler leaders feared that deserters would endanger the settlements by teaching the Indians European methods of fighting. Many accounts, written by Englishmen with American experience, give the impression that the authors would have preferred a New World without savages. Puritan writers in New England noted that the Indian population there had been thinned by pestilence shortly before the arrival of the English, and regarded this circumstance as a sign of divine favour; an attitude, one might say, of live and let die. Nevertheless, the Indians were there, and had to be accepted. Englishmen, for the most part, accepted them for what they were, as savages, and saw no point in trying to change them into something else.

English readiness to accept the savage on his own terms, as a savage, has often been remarked by historians, but has usually been defined in religious terms. Englishmen, it is often said, were indifferent to missionary endeavour, in contrast with (say) Spaniards, who were devoted to it. This is to over-simplify. Spanish proselytizing among Amerindians was certainly more effective than English, as was only to be expected. Spanish government in Church and State was devoted to the Christian mission and had money to spend on it; the kings of England acknowledged no such devotion and had no funds to spare. The regular orders in Spain formed a disciplined, mobile, spiritual militia, available for service anywhere, many of whose members had experience among the Moors of Andalusia; no such body of trained and dedicated men existed in England, or anywhere in Protestant Europe. The eastern woodland Indians, moreover, were much less promising neophytes than the settled people of, say, central Mexico. Ineffectiveness, however, does not necessarily imply indifference; the sermons preached at St Paul's Cross in support of the Virginia Company, and the pamphlets proclaiming the Company's spiritual mission, as Parker points out, were not merely exercises in public relations; missionaries such as Roger Williams and John Eliot, though few, were as zealous as any friar.

Nor was missionary fervour as general among the *conquistadores* as has sometimes been supposed. Historians of the Spanish conquests in America have concentrated unduly on Mexico and on the personality of Hernán Cortés, who alarmed his own companions by his pious belligerence. No considerations of prudence hindered Cortés from berating powerful Aztec rulers for their heathen superstition or from defacing the effigies of Mexican gods. Cortés, in the first flush of victory, requested the dispatch from Spain of the Franciscan mission, the famous Twelve, who with his support were to achieve rapid and dramatic success among the conquered Mexicans. Cortés was exceptional. Balboa's correspondence with the Crown hardly mentions missions. Pizarro was single-mindedly devoted to the political and financial advantage of himself, his family, and his friends and neighbours from Trujillo. For interests and considerations outside that narrow range he had only a bone-chilling indifference. In the surviving letters and recollections of those who accompanied him to the conquest of Peru there is only occasional and perfunctory mention of the hope and duty of winning souls for Christ. It is true that decrees emanating from Spain, and instructions to officials in the Indies, formally placed the Christian mission prominently among the purposes of administration; but for most lay Spaniards, official and unofficial, who thought of the matter, proselytizing was only part of the wider task of civilizing and Europeanizing the American natives. Responsible Spaniards wanted Indians to settle in properly organized towns and villages, wear proper clothes, go to church, seek regular wage-earning employment, pay regular tithes and taxes, as reasonable people ought to do. In part, of course, this attitude was self-interested; but in part it was didactic, and arose from a self-confident, conservative sense of the general fitness of things. This didactic urge—call it sense of responsibility, call it the irresistible itch to set the affairs of others to rights—has usually been characteristic, in greater or less degree, of all colonizing peoples. Among Spaniards it was intensely strong, among Englishmen, in the seventeenth century at least, relatively weak. That supremely arrogant phrase, *mission civilisatrice*, has no precise equivalent in English usage.

This is not to say that Englishmen in North America were indifferent to Indians; surrounded by them, they could not be indifferent. Some Englishmen developed a lively interest in the Indians with whom they came in contact, and wrote serious, often sympathetic, accounts of them. The very fact that they felt no particular didactic responsibility towards Indians enabled them to be more objective than Spaniards, for example, usually managed to be. Most of the early Spanish ethnologists were missionaries; of the two most conspicuous exceptions, Oviedo disliked

Indians and sought to justify the Spanish conquest by emphasizing Indian barbarity, irresponsibility, and idleness; Zorita depicted a nostalgic Utopia, contrasting the simplicity, the innocence, and the disciplined public spirit of pre-conquest Mexican society with the decadent greed and truculence of contemporary Europeans. *The Lords of New Spain* is certainly not an objective account of Indians as the author knew them. The ethnological work of missionaries was necessarily influenced by the nature of the authors' calling. Even Sahagún, most famous and most accomplished of the ethnologist friars, never forgot that his purpose in studying Indians was to convert them more effectively; that he studied Indian religious beliefs, the better to eradicate them. No English study of Indian life approached Sahagún's in its prodigious learning, its linguistic skill, and its sophisticated use of informants; but no Spanish account had the cool objectivity of Harriot's *Briefe and true Report*.

Among the few Spaniards and fewer Englishmen who wrote with understanding and sympathy of the Indians they knew, it is hard to find any who actually *liked* Indians as they were, who enjoyed their company without wishing to alter their behaviour. The Spaniard who came nearest to it was perhaps the Dominican Diego de Durán, who had been brought up among Indians in Texcoco, in his day the main centre of Mexican culture and repository of traditional learning, and who spoke Náhuatl as naturally as he spoke Spanish. His *Historia de las Indias de la Nueva España* is the most endearing of all books written by Spaniards about Indians, warmly affectionate, acutely sensitive, informed by a profound knowledge of Indian culture. Yet Durán was constantly torn between his liking for the Indians he knew and his concern for their spiritual well-being; between admiration for the beauty of their poetry and the ordered harmony of their social life on the one hand, and horror of their religious backsliding on the other. Even Durán could never forget that he was a missionary.

It is a far cry from the pious, if unorthodox, Durán to the unregenerate Thomas Morton; yet Morton, like Durán, had a real affection for his Indian friends. Morton's Indians, of course, were a far cry from Durán's. The bond which drew him to them was a common love of hunting rather than a common taste in poetry; but it was none the less genuine. He liked them, and they seem to have liked him. He found them more congenial, more hospitable, kinder than the sectaries who were his nearest European neighbours. Morton, no doubt, was an irresponsible, though amusing, rogue. He enjoyed carousing with the Indians, and (though he denied it) supplied rum for the purpose. As a fur trader, he bought the pelts they brought in and sold them guns to increase the efficiency of their hunting. Naturally Morton fell foul of his puritan neighbours, and the Massachusetts Bay authorities eventually arrested him, ostensibly, among other offences, for encouraging his companions to dance in a disorderly manner round a maypole. This confrontation of the Reformation with some of the more disreputable features of the Renaissance had its funny side; but for seventeenth-century puritans maypole-dancing, with its pagan associations, was no subject for humour, and fire-arms in the hands of Indians might be a very serious matter indeed. They burned Morton's house and shipped him off to England.

Morton's book, *The New English Canaan*, cannot compare with Durán's *Historia* as a serious account of an Indian society. The purposes of the two writers were different. Durán wrote to vindicate Indian culture against the calumnies of ignorant Europeans. Morton wrote to bring the New England puritans into ridicule, by comparing them, to their disadvantage, with the Indians. Durán's account was inevitably coloured by his missionary calling; Morton's, by his personal grievance and by an irreverent sense of humour. Durán wrote with deeply felt conviction, Morton with his tongue in his cheek. In discussing the origins of the Indian race, for example—a question of some moment theologically—Durán maintained, quite seriously, that they were the descendants of the lost tribes of Israel. This was a widespread opinion at the time, shared by many puritan writers. Morton, to whom the question of origins was a matter of indifference—he liked Indians as they were—seized an opportunity for satire upon puritan solemnity, by declaring the Indians to be the descendants of the defeated Trojans, and by inventing some preposterous but highly entertaining etymological arguments to 'prove' it. There is a good deal of this kind of thing in *The New English Canaan*; but there is also a good deal of valuable detail on Indian life, of an intimate kind unusual among writers on New England.

The chief value of Morton's book, however, lies in its descriptions of the natural scene. Morton was not a trained scientific observer, but he was a good field naturalist, the first to write in any detail about the wild animals, birds, and plants of New England; and he had a feeling for the right descriptive phrase. There is a convincing immediacy about his description of a wolf—'fearefull curre'—slinking away at a bank's end; or of a bear, 'a tyrant at a lobster', groping for them on the shore of a tidal estuary.

The puritans took wolves and bears seriously, but as troublesome vermin rather than as objects of interest; they did not for the most part observe them closely or write about them.

Morton was not, of course, an objective observer of wild life; like many good naturalists, he liked field sports and was a good shot. This probably explains why he and his companions apparently enjoyed their rough and raffish life, and kept in good health; they lived on the abundant wild game. The puritan settlers lived virtuous lives and attended to their cultivations; yet being inexpert in growing local crops, they died like flies. To some extent this was a question of numbers. Morton's people were a small party in an isolated place; the puritans were too numerous and too concentrated in their settlements to be able to subsist as he did. They same is true, *mutatis mutandis*, of the Spanish *conquistadores*; they entered the Americas in relatively large bands and settled in urban concentrations; they could not have maintained themselves on game, even where it was plentiful, had little skill in agriculture or inclination for it, and so had no recourse save commandeering food from the Indians. Wherever the Indians were few and primitive, the Spaniards suffered and died, as many of the puritans did. Apart from their numbers, however, the puritans seem to have been incompetent in their pursuit of game. Social origins may have had something to do with this. Morton described himself as a gentleman, and even his enemies did not deny his right to the title. Few of the puritan settlers were so described. John Winthrop was (and significantly liked to walk in the woods with his gun, though probably the anxieties of running the colony left him little time for shooting), but he was exceptional. Most of them came from small towns and villages in the more thickly populated parts of England, and were not of the class who preserved game in parks and chases for their own use and amusement; yet they were too respectable to be habitual poachers. They were not accustomed to the chase or to shooting, and had little skill in either. Morton has a hilarious description of the mishaps which befell 'Governor Bubble' (Bradford) when out in an Indian canoe on (literally) a wild goose chase.

Morton, with his interest in the natural scene and his delight in describing it, was unusual among the early settlers in New England; but a fair number of Englishmen in other parts of the Americas had similar interests. With those interests went a sensitive visual appreciation; and this too seems to have been characteristic of Englishmen—of some Englishmen at least—in the New World, whether or not they had any technical skill as artists. Nuño da Silva, the captured Portuguese navigator, describes Drake (rather surprisingly) as always having his sketchpad and water-colours by him. Whoever heard of a *conquistador* with a sketch-book? Spaniards in the New World were, on the whole, conspicuously insensitive to their visual surroundings. One thinks of Hernando Pizarro, most articulate of the Pizarro brothers and the only literate one, on his way to the spoil of Pachacámac, riding along the eastern rim of the tremendous chasm known today as the Callejón de Huaylas, with the towering spires of Huascarán on his left and the Santa River in its gorge far below him on his right; all he could find to say about it was that the snow made the going hard for the horses.

The New World Spaniards in general were more interested in the works of man than in the works of nature; more interested in cultivated fields than in forests; more interested in domestic animals than in wild ones; and more interested in the uses of things, than in what they looked like. Oviedo, comprehensive and conscientious, has excellent accounts of the principal Amerindian food crops, with crude but recognizable woodcuts, and gives an appreciative description of the Peruvian llama, an animal which greatly took the fancy of the *conquistadores*. On wild plants and wild animals he is much less convincing, even perfunctory. Presumably in many instances he relied on descriptions given by Indians rather than observing for himself. He rarely succeeds in conveying a clear impression of the appearance of the plant or animal he is describing. Nor have we, from Spanish writings, still less from Spanish drawings, clear visual impressions of the people of the New World. The ethnologist friars, Sahagún, Durán, and—most distinguished of all in this respect—Juan de Tovar, all employed Indian painter-scribes, *tlacuilos*, to illustrate their manuscripts. Well for us that they did so. It is odd that the only really lively and convincing drawings made by a European of Mexican Indians at the time of the conquest, were done by a German. Cortés, when he visited Spain in 1528, took with him several Mexican notables and a troop of acrobats and jugglers. The appearance of these people aroused great interest, and a series of water-colour drawings were made of them by Christoph Weiditz, medal engraver of Augsburg, who happened to be about the court on business unconnected with America. They are preserved in *Das Trachtenbuch des Christoph Weiditz*, in Nürnberg; odd again, that so valuable a record should be tucked away in a collection of drawings of costumes. Weiditz, incidentally, made a portrait medal of Cortés: the only portrait of an early *conquistador* known to have been done from life.

It shows him as a thin-lipped, twist-mouthed brigand, very different from the benevolent woolly-bearded knight-errant of later engravings.

The feature of Amerindian society which most impressed the invading Spaniards was the existence, in some areas, of large cities; and here one might expect Spanish powers of description to be exerted to the full. Bernal Díaz's excited account of his first sight of Tenochtitlán-Mexico has been quoted many times; it is indeed moving and evocative. Don Bernal describes the wide lake and the long straight causeways; but in describing the appearance of the city itself, he takes refuge in analogy with a popular romance. He does not really succeed in telling us what the place looked like, and to this day we have no clear picture of it, except for archaeological reconstructions. Similarly with Cuzco; there are a few early accounts of the architectural features of particular buildings, but apart from the fact that it had dressed-stone buildings, thatched roofs, and narrow streets we have no clear visual image, from contemporary sources, of the city as a whole, or of the mountains which rim the high valley in which it lies. Certainly there are no convincing drawings or paintings.

We have, in fact, a much clearer image of the primitive peoples of America, including Eskimos, and of the areas where they lived, than we have of the more sophisticated settled peoples and the cities that they built, and this is due in considerable measure to the ability of Englishmen to observe, describe, paint, and draw. Not entirely, of course. The delightful *Histoire d'un voyage fait en la terre du Brésil*, written by Jean de Léry, the protestant theological student who spent ten months with the unhappy Villegaignon colony in 1557, has admirable descriptions of native customs and, in its second (1580) edition, good illustrations; and the German mercenary Hans Staden did his amateur best to record the 'wild, naked man-eating people' by whom he had been captured and almost, so he said, cooked and eaten in Brazil. In a later generation both the wild people and the wild animals of Brazil were to receive distinguished attention from the artists and naturalists employed and encouraged by Prince Johan Maurits of Nassau, governor during the Dutch occupation of Pernambuco. Piso and Marcgrave, Frans Post and Albert Eckhout, provided the first full scientific and visual record of any part of America; Eckhout's paintings of Tapuya Indians, in particular, are remarkable for a detached, objective observation of primitive people. These men, however, came relatively late to an America already losing its maidenhead; coastal Brazil was already, in Johan Maurits's day, the principal producer of sugar for the European market, and the Tapuya

Indians, though wild enough, were already curiosities, in a country increasingly run by Europeans and dependent upon imported Africans for its labour. More significant for our purpose are the painters and observers who worked in parts of America only recently opened to Europeans, still new and strange; and most prominent among them Jacques Le Moyne in Florida and the incomparable John White in the West Indies, Carolina, and (probably) Labrador.

Paul Hulton, who edited, with Quinn, the splendid volumes of reproductions of White drawings which the British Museum published in 1964, here compares the two—inevitably somewhat to Le Moyne's disadvantage—considers the merits of each, and discusses the intricate relations between them. He points out that the recent discovery of fifty-nine hitherto unknown Le Moyne drawings has made a full critical treatment of Le Moyne's work a matter of urgency and says that such a book is, happily, nearing publication. He reminds us that White and Le Moyne were both practical colonizers—White as governor at Roanoke —as well as gifted artists. Both enjoyed the patronage of Ralegh, Le Moyne having removed to England 'for religion' about 1580. Both, but especially White, made important contributions to the spread of reliable knowledge of the New World. When Theodor de Bry was planning his *America,* he searched all over Europe for material on which to base the engravings for the work, and the ubiquitous Hakluyt brought the drawings of White and Le Moyne to his attention. So it came about that, in that vast and justly celebrated monument to European enterprise in the New World, the engravings of Mexican and Peruvian natives are based on written descriptions or hearsay, and present the features and attitudes of ancient Rome; but those of the North American natives, some of them at least, are after the work of artists who were familiar with their subject at first hand, who observed with a clear eye, and painted with cool, if sympathetic, fidelity. Sympathetic fidelity, cool judgement, close familiarity with the subject—these are the qualities which also, in a different context, have been chiefly characteristic of David Quinn's own work.

2

The permissive frontier:
the problem of social control in English
settlements in Ireland and Virginia
1550-1650[1]

NICHOLAS CANNY

Both politically aware contemporaries and subsequent generations of historians have recognized England's effort to subjugate Ireland and to establish colonies there and in North America as among her greatest undertakings and achievements during the early modern period. It is not generally appreciated, however, that contemporaries were dissatisfied with the outcome, since both government officials and promoters of colonial ventures saw their work as having fallen far short of what was intended. Their disappointment was caused both by the general failure of the colonists to assimilate the indigenous population in either Ireland or the New World, and by the total loss of or poor return on the money invested. These shortcomings stemmed however from the fundamental fact that the colonies that emerged were far from the models in civil living that had been intended, since the organizers had been forced by circumstances to accept patterns of settlement radically different from those originally envisaged. This paper will argue that the single most important factor that compelled this change in direction was the inability of organizers to maintain control over those to whom had been entrusted the task of colonization.

One factor that is frequently lost sight of is that the advocates of colonization did not consider it either possible or desirable in the short

1. Research on this paper was made possible by the award of a Senior Fulbright-Hays fellowship by *An Bórd Scoláireachtaí Cómalairte*, Dublin, for the academic year 1974-5. I also wish to thank the History Department of Harvard University, the Department of American Studies at Yale University, and the Institute of Early American History and Culture and the Colonial Williamsburg Foundation for acting as host institutions during my stay in the U.S.A. The criticism offered by Dr K. R. Andrews of Hull and Dr Paul Hair of Liverpool has done much to improve the paper.

term to reconstitute English society or legal institutions in an overseas setting.[2] The promotional literature emphasized, certainly, that no Englishman who ventured overseas would be deprived of his fundamental rights, but when it came to giving legal existence to colonies the charters were either evasive on the subject of extending common law procedures to the new settlements or else advocated a rigidly disciplined, tightly structured regime on military lines. Some adhered to a notion of relativism in legal matters and, therefore, did not think it possible to transfer English law to a new environment. Others, however, thought of colonization in classical terms and favoured the erection of authoritarian settlements based on what they understood to be Roman precedents.[3] Furthermore, the promoters of colonization had little confidence in those likely to present themselves as would-be colonists, and argued that such people would be useful only when subject to arbitrary rule.

Centrally planned and highly structured colonies on classical and military lines were first attempted in Ireland during the 1570s by Sir Thomas Smith and Walter Devereux, Earl of Essex, and the most coherent formula was that outlined by Smith. Those who joined Smith were advised that once they reached Ireland they would find themselves 'either wholly in the warre and half in peace' but they were, in any event, to proceed as if they 'were all in warre'. This justified granting to the principal officer of the colony the same powers as those enjoyed by a general of the army, and the only restrictions on his authority were that whenever he wished to amend the laws of the colony or levy taxes for its defence he should seek the advice and consent of 'the gravest and fathers of the colony' formed into a common council, and in selecting subordinate officers he was confined to this group. One of the officers mentioned was the marshal who was vested with wide discretionary powers, and considerable authority was also delegated to the principal colonists in the matter of administering justice. Every man who conveyed fifty footmen to the colony was designated lord of half a hundred, and after he had built

2. For an example of an assumption to the contrary see Peter Laslett, *The World we have Lost* (London, 1965), p. 253, where he asserts that English pre-industrial society 'can be studied not only *in situ* but also as it became when removed, it would seem almost for experimental purposes, 3,000 miles west across the sea into the American wilderness'.

3. On relativism in legal matters, see N. P. Canny, *The Formation of the Old-English Elite in Ireland* (O'Donnell lecture published by the National University of Ireland, 1975), pp. 17–18; 'Estate of the colony, 1620', in Samuel Purchas, *Hakluytus Posthumus, or Purchas his Pilgrimes* (Glasgow edn, 1906), vol. xix, p. 124. On classical precedents see N. P. Canny, *The Elizabethan Conquest of Ireland: A Pattern Established 1565–76* (Hassocks, Sussex and N.Y., 1976), pp. 128–32; Purchas, *Pilgrimes*, xix. 67–68.

a manor was to hold a court baron there at three-weekly intervals to decide on controversies involving copyholders and those with freeholds valued at less than forty shillings. Those who brought one hundred footmen were to become lords of a hundred and conduct, besides a court baron, a leet court once every six months to decide on controversies involving leaseholders, and also on felonies and breaches of the peace. All principal colonists were to combine their energies to build the central capital, *Elizabetha*, but it appears that Smith intended his colony to become a self-contained unit even in the matter of dispensing justice to fellow Englishmen: this despite the fact that machinery for the administration of the common law was readily available in Ireland.[4]

Neither this nor the Essex expedition, which was conceived on more purely military lines, met with success, and thereafter the government played a more active role in English colonization in Ireland. Nevertheless these efforts are significant because the authoritarian structure was acceptable to government officials in England; and all who subsequently undertook to establish plantation in Ireland presumed that they would be conceded substantial powers of martial law over their followers. In the light of this information it comes as no surprise that those entrusted with the management of an English settlement in Virginia at the beginning of the seventeenth century favoured the draconian system of martial law, known as the *Lawes Divine, Morall and Martiall*, introduced and implemented there between 1611 and 1618 by Thomas West, Lord de la Ware, by Sir Thomas Gates, and by Sir Thomas Dale.[5]

The principal reason given for such curtailment of Englishmen's rights was that most of those who ventured overseas came from the poorest elements of society, and were considered by their superiors to be incapable of self-discipline, to be barely civilized, and certainly not suitable instruments for transmitting civilization to others. Some writers, notably William Strachey, went further to suggest that the poorer elements in England were not only poorly motivated but were actually ideologically opposed to colonization. One of the two groups mentioned by Strachey as dissenting from England's westward enterprise was 'the meere ignorant

4. Orders of Sir Thomas Smith, 1 December 1573 (Essex County Record Office, D/Dsh 01/2); offices necessary in the colony of the Ardes (Essex County Record Office, D/Dsh 01/7).

5. *Lawes Divine, Morall and Martiall* (London, 1612) in Peter Force (ed.), *Tracts and Other Papers Relating Principally to the Origin, Settlement and Progress of the Colonies in north America* (Washington, 1836), vol. iii, no. 2; N. P. Canny, *The Elizabethan Conquest*, pp. 80–84.

(not only in *scientia scientiae,* as the scholeman saies, but including grosness and simplicity in any knowledge)'.[6]

No systematic work on English settlement in Ireland during the sixteenth century has yet been published, but contemporaries and historians are agreed that one of the chief factors operating against settlement was that those who actually came to settle were not suitable colonists. Those who organized plantations in Ireland were concerned that they should include a proper balance between servants, artisans, married men with previous experience in farming who would accept leaseholds, and single men from agricultural communities who would be satisfied with copyholds on the newly won Irish estates. This composition was not achieved in any plantation in Ireland prior to 1650, and certainly not in the plantation in Munster which was the only sixteenth-century settlement in Ireland that became a going concern (prior to its disruption in 1598 by insurrection). From the outset English merchants, especially those from the western ports, displayed interest in Irish plantations with a view to exploiting the natural resources, especially timber, of the country. It seems reasonable, therefore, to suppose that a substantial number of artisans were included among the possibly as many as 5,000 English who settled in Munster prior to 1598. The proprietors seem to have encountered greater difficulties in drawing suitable tenants to their estates, since those previously engaged in agriculture in England do not seem to have been convinced that they should abandon their holdings to gamble on a better future in Ireland. This cannot have been entirely unexpected as it was to overcome this difficulty that organizers of the earlier attempts at colonization, notably Essex, had convinced many substantial landowners, or their sons, to accompany him to Ireland, in the hope that they would transfer some of the tenants from their English estates to the colony.[7] The English noble families continued to provide financial support for colonial enterprises in Ireland and the New World, but few of them actually participated in the efforts subsequent to the Essex débâcle. Most of those who did offer their services as undertakers in Ireland lacked property, and hence tenants, in England, and had therefore to accept as tenants discharged soldiers and those of the unemployed and underemployed in England, particularly from the western counties, who

6. William Strachey, *The historie of travell into Virginia Britania* (London, 1612) ed. L. B. Wright and V. Freund (London, 1953), pp. 8–9.

7. N. P. Canny, *The Elizabethan Conquest,* pp. 66–92, esp. p. 83; D. B. Quinn, 'The Munster plantation: problems and opportunities', *Journal of the Cork Historical and Archaeological Society,* lxxi (1966), 19–41.

were attracted to Ireland by the intensive propaganda campaign, or were persuaded by their betters to go there. The information that is now available to us on social conditions in sixteenth-century England suggests that such people could have had little experience in intensive agriculture, and might well entertain an antipathy towards established authority; while some of them were not fully integrated into any organized religious system and might even identify with a counter-culture.[8]

The witness of contemporaries bears out the view that many of those who settled on English plantations in Ireland fitted this description. Fynes Moryson was satisfied that, with the exception of disbanded soldiers who were 'well knowne to be of good condition',

All the English in generall that voluntarily left England to plant themselves in Ireland, either under the sayd undertakers of Mounster, or upon the landes of any other English-Irish throughout Ireland, or to live in cittyes and townes, were generally observed to have beene eyther papists, men of disordered life, banckrots, or very poore ... by which course Ireland as the heele of the body was made the sincke of England, the stench wherof had almost annoyed very Cheapside the hart of the body.[9]

That Moryson's view was widely held in England is suggested by the fact that, in 1600, the author of a tract advocating further English engagement in North America cautioned that, without an assurance of mineral wealth, those with a secure position in England were unlikely to venture overseas, citing as evidence the 'too good experience by Ireland, which beinge neer us, a temperate and fertile contrye, subjecte to our owne lawes and halfe sivill, the ports and many places friendly inhabited, notwithstandinge many of good reputacon, [who] became undertakers there in the tyme of pease could not invite our people, neyther in any competent numbers, nor constantly in the action'.[1] The inconstant ones in Ireland must have been some of England's destitute, since the author categorically condemned the employment of 'the impotente' on the grounds that they were wont to complain of 'those most behovefull impositions which are layd upon them', but more especially because 'the poore man wants wealth to disburse any thinge, wants wisdom to foresee

8. Joan Thirsk (ed.), *The Agrarian History of England and Wales, 1500–1640* (Cambridge, 1967), pp. 71–80, 396–465, esp. p. 463; Keith Thomas, *Religion and the Decline of Magic* (London, 1971), pp. 179–206.

9. Fynes Moryson, 'The commonwealth of Ireland', in C. L. Falkiner, *Illustrations of Irish History* (London, 1904), pp. 259–60.

1. 'Proposition of planting an English colony in north west of America', anonymous, 1600: Public Record Office, London (P.R.O.), C.O. –1/1, no. 9, ff. 22–24.

the good and wants virtue to have patience and constancy to attend the reward of a good worke and industry'.

The continued British effort at colonization in Ireland during the first half of the seventeenth century gave commentators no reason to revise their opinion of those who ventured there as tenants. Munster did attract a substantial group of artisans who developed urban and manufacturing centres there in the early years of the seventeenth century, but those who went as tenants do not seem to have made any significant impact on social conditions since the various surveys show that pastoral farming remained dominant in the province.[2] The plantation in Ulster was organized on a much grander scale and we know that over 8,000 Scots males and slightly fewer English males had settled in the province by 1622. These large numbers of men, who may have been accompanied by substantial numbers of women, were required because of the relative underpopulation of the province in the aftermath of war. The addition of such numbers to the existing work force of the province certainly boosted the agricultural output, but the evidence suggests that those who settled there in the first half of the seventeenth century were neither equipped nor disposed to introduce any drastic social or economic change in Ulster. The leading authority on Scots migration to Ulster has established that they were drawn principally from some eight counties adjacent to the English border and up the west coast to Argyllshire, in neither of which areas can agricultural conditions have been significantly more advanced than those which had obtained in Ulster prior to the plantation. Nevertheless the new proprietors in Ulster were convinced that the Scots made better tenants than did their English counterparts, and it seems unlikely that either the Scots or English who migrated were the most successful at home.[3] The verdict of the various surveys and reports which monitored the progress of plantation in Ulster goes some way to upholding the near contemporary opinion of Andrew Stewart (an opinion naturally cited

2. D. B. Quinn, 'The Munster plantation', esp. pp. 36–38; *Cal. S.P. Ire., 1603–6*, pp. 472–3; T. O. Ranger, 'The career of Richard Boyle, first Earl of Cork in Ireland, 1588–1643' (Oxford, D.Phil. thesis, 1959), pp. 135–8, where he shows that Boyle was dissatisfied with those craftsmen who came from England to work in his manufacturing enterprises.

3. M. Perceval-Maxwell, *The Scottish Migration to Ulster in the Reign of James I* (London, 1973), pp. 228, 233–4, 250–1; see also the review of the above by N. P. Canny in *Irish Economic and Social History*, i (1974), 75–77. W. H. Crawford in 'Landlord–tenant relations in Ulster, 1609–1820', *Irish Economic and Social History*, ii (1975), 5–21, cites evidence that landlords in the early seventeenth century had to offer extremely attractive terms to lure 'good tenants'. See also T. W. Moody, *The Londonderry Plantation, 1609–41* (Belfast, 1939), and for an account of the unsettled conditions in the Scottish border counties T. I. Rae, *The Administration of the Scottish Frontier, 1513–1603* (Edinburgh, 1966), pp. 1–2.

with great relish by Irish nationalist historians), that those who migrated to Ulster before 1641 were 'generally the scum of both nations'.[4]

The scanty evidence that has so far come to light does not allow any generalizations about the attitudes and outlook of the new tenants in Ireland. Disbanded soldiers formed a conspicuous element among the settlers, and from what is known of the disposition of English soldiers in Ireland during the late sixteenth century, it must be considered extremely doubtful whether they proved successful agents of English civility. There had been a standing army in Ireland from 1534, and it provided a significant force from the commencement of the Leix–Offaly plantation in the 1550s until 1603 when peace was restored. The English soldiers in Ireland, like soldiers everywhere at that time, were notorious for acts of pillage, mutiny, desertion, and general insubordination, and it was with difficulty and sometimes only after liberal potions of alcohol that they were persuaded to face the enemy.[5] Much of their dissatisfaction stemmed from shortfalls in pay, but it appears also that the soldiers were often indifferent to the purpose which they were intended to serve. The garrisons introduced to the confiscated property in Leix–Offaly were intended to serve as soldier-cultivators, but they seem to have taken their role as farmers even less seriously than their military function. They idled in the forts, complained when pay and provisions were not forthcoming, and regularly pillaged the countryside. Some of the captains accepted native Irish as soldiers to make up their quota of men, while women from the surrounding countryside, who it was claimed acted as spies for the enemy, were entertained as mistresses in the forts. Even more alarming for the government was the fact that hungry, half-naked soldiers sold their weapons to the enemy, or themselves deserted to the Gaelic Irish.[6] Much of the propaganda which alleged the social inferiority of the Irish must have been intended to deter this trend, but it was to little avail. It was stated that when building up his army the Gaelic chieftain Shane O'Neill

4. Andrew Stewart, *The History of the Church of Ireland since the Scots were Naturalized*, ed. W. D. Killen (Belfast, 1866), p. 313; M. Perceval Maxwell, *The Scottish Migration*, pp. 274–89.

5. Richard Overton to Cecil, 17 March 1564 (P.R.O., S.P. 63, vol. 35, ff. 80–83); Sidney to Privy Council, 12 December 1566 (P.R.O. S.P. 63, vol. 19, no. 17, f. 140); 'Sidney's memoir', *Ulster Journal of Archaeology*, 1st series, vols iii–v (1855–7), iii. 348.

6. N. P. Canny, *The Elizabethan Conquest*, chap. 2, *passim*; book on garrison in Ireland, 22 March 1572 (Bodleian Library, Oxford, Carte MSS., vol. 57, no. 270, f. 521); Richard Overton to Cecil (as in note 5 above); Sidney to Matthew King, 7 March 1566 (P.R.O., S.P. 63, vol. 16, no. 49, f. 127); Fitzwilliam to Burghley, 19 August 1571 (P.R.O., S.P. 63, vol. 33, no. 35, f. 74); Sidney to Privy Council, 30 May 1566 (P.R.O., S.P. 63, vol. 17, no. 68).

'had his chief advantage by the service of discharged soldiers'; Shane's successor Turlough Luineach O'Neill likewise employed English soldiers; and the rebellion of the last of the great O'Neills, Hugh, Earl of Tyrone, was to a large extent made possible by English soldiers who had deserted to him and trained the native forces in modern methods of warfare. These deserters seem to have had no scruples about turning their weapons against their erstwhile comrades, and the ease with which they accommodated themselves to life in Gaelic Ireland is quite remarkable.[7]

In the light of this information it comes as no surprise that discharged soldiers were not considered to be particularly adept at turning swords into ploughshares. Furthermore, the evidence that is available suggests that those would-be tenants brought directly from England were drawn from the same background as, and most probably shared the same mental furniture with, their ex-military comrades. The experience of other plantations, Spanish as well as English, and our knowledge of English social organization, suggests that most settlers were single men, and until information to the contrary is produced we must assume that they were as likely to be assimilated through marriage into Irish society as they were to act as agents of change in an alien environment. This may explain why the promoters stipulated that the incoming tenants should be segregated from the indigenous population, and it is significant that in the conditions laid down by Sir Thomas Smith in 1573 tenants and soldiers were denied the right to marry Gaelic wives.[8]

Evidence on the behaviour of English soldiers in Ireland is also significant because it helps in the interpretation of some of the evidence relating to soldiers and common settlers in Virginia; while the Virginian material, in turn, tends to lend support to the hypotheses advanced concerning the mental outlook of English tenants in Ireland. In this context it is relevant to mention that some contemporaries were also of the opinion that ex-

7. Sidney to Privy Council (ibid.); 'Sidney's memoir', *Ulster Journal of Archaeology*, v. 310; G. A. Hayes-McCoy, 'Strategy and tactics in Irish warfare, 1593–1601', *Irish Historical Studies*, ii (1940–1), 262; Hayes-McCoy, 'The army of Ulster, 1593–1601', *The Irish Sword*, i (1949–53), 115–16. Hayes-McCoy stresses, correctly, that many of the captains and soldiers who fought with Hugh O'Neill had been assigned to him by the government in peace-time, but their failure to return to the English army when hostilities commenced can be seen as little short of desertion. Furthermore Hayes-McCoy implies that all who openly deserted to O'Neill were soldiers of Irish birth, but there is no evidence to sustain the point that only those deserted, and some of the material cited above establishes that even English-born captains were capable of 'turning native'.

8. Indenture of Frans Brunyngs, 16 December 1573 (Essex C.R.O., D/Dsh. 01/5); see also Moryson's warning on the danger of colonists 'mixing' with the Gaelic Irish, 'The commonwealth of Ireland', in C. L. Falkiner, *Illustrations of Irish History*, p. 298.

perience gained in one settlement could prove useful in the other. George Wyatt, sometimes a planter in Ireland, may well have been drawing on his experience in that country when he advised his son Francis, governor of Virginia 1621–6, 'to look with Janus two waies on your own contrime[n] Christians, and on the salvages infidels, . . . to the better cherishing of the former & to the wining of the latter. Yet so as you keepe Cesars rule to his Romans unto your memory, that you reccon more of the danger of one Christian your patriot, then of numbers of pagan infidels.'[9] We can speak with more certainty of the origins and attitudes of the lower social element who migrated to Virginia, principally because substantial court records have survived for which no counterpart exists for Ireland, and also because the general documentary evidence has been more fully exploited and catalogued. The earliest groups of settlers included soldiers; many craftsmen, some of them (for example, vine-dressers and pitch-boilers) specifically recruited on the continent; a significant number of footmen and other personal servants; and those, described as labourers, intended for the more menial work of clearing sites for fortifications and providing food for the settlement. It quickly became evident that the introduction of such a diversified group of craftsmen was premature. The efforts of the company were then directed towards the recruitment of more labourers to grow food for the colony and, after 1617, to engage in the cultivation of tobacco.[1] Most of those who crossed the Atlantic prior to 1650 set out from London, with significantly lesser numbers taking ship from the Isle of Wight, Plymouth, and Ireland, but the point of embarkation was not necessarily their place of origin. A group recruited in 1619 in Devon, Warwick, and Stafford were 'choice men borne and bred up to labour and industry' and were considered particularly admirable because they included 'about an hundred men brought up to husbandry'.[2] But mention was made of this fact because it was exceptional. Proprietors in Virginia, like their counterparts in Ireland, found it difficult to attract those with previous experience in agriculture, as is evident from their complaint in 1620 of 'a great scarcity, or none at all' of 'husbandmen truely bred'.[3] In desperation they sought after convicted felons and those of England's destitute who had drifted to the capital, either to search for employment or to escape from the rigours of the poor

9. George Wyatt to Francis Wyatt, undated (B.L., Wyatt MSS., no. 5).

1. Edmund S. Morgan, *American Slavery, American Freedom: The Ordeal of Colonial Virginia* (New York, 1975), pp. 82–88.

2. 'Estate of the colony, 1620', in Purchas, *Pilgrimes*, xix. 122–5.

3. Cited in Morgan, *American Slavery, American Freedom*, p. 87.

law. One element that was conspicuous among the new emigrants was a contingent drawn from the unemployed youths who congregated in bands on the streets of London. Many of these youths were rounded up at the direction of the corporation, which employed its charity fund to finance their passage to the New World, thus simultaneously ridding the city of those who were considered a threat to social order and supplying Virginia with a work force. Some may have been as young as 8 years old, but we cannot be certain that even these were born in London since they were described as vagrants without 'place of abode' or 'friends to relieve them'.[4] Generally speaking it is probable that a majority of those who took ship to Virginia were making the final of a series of moves in an unsettled and rootless existence. Those who arrived with Daniel Gookin from Ireland in 1621 did not bear Irish surnames, which suggests that these were in fact Englishmen whom Gookin had, some years previously, brought as tenants for his estate in Munster, and then transferred to his newly acquired property in Virginia.[5]

Few life histories of the poorer elements in Virginia can be pieced together. But exceptionally, indeed by a freak of nature, the court records of Virginia provide us with the details on the career of one Thomas or Thomasine Hall. This person was, or thought himself to be, bisexual, a condition which aroused the curiosity of his superiors who, in their effort to establish his true sex, hauled him before the court. The facts that emerged were that Hall was born in Newcastle upon Tyne, was christened Thomasine, and was dressed as a girl until the age of 12 when she went to live with an aunt in London. Employment must have been hard to come by in London because the resourceful Hall was forced to assume a male role in 1595 and enlisted in the English army then bound for Calais. At the cessation of hostilities, Hall returned to England, this time to Plymouth. Here female employment must have been more readily available, since our hero, or heroine, now 'made bone lace and did work with his needle'. However, 'shortly after' Hall again assumed a man's attire and took a passing ship bound for Virginia, where he would have disappeared into oblivion had it not been that, in 1629, possibly in response

4. Corporation of London, Record Office, Journal 30 (1618), f. 374; Journal 31 (1619), ff. 125–6; Journal 32 (1622), ff. 66–67; King James to Sir Thomas Smith, 13 January 1619 (Corporation of London, R.O., Remembrancia, v, letter no. 8).

5. A. L. Jester and M. W. Hiden, *Adventurers of Purse and Person, 1607–1625* (Princeton, 1956), p. 48; N. M. Nugent (ed.), *Cavaliers and Pioneers: Abstracts of Virginia Land Patents and Grants, 1623–1666* (Richmond, 1934), i. 78, 139–40; F. W. Gookin, *Daniel Gookin, 1612–87, Assistant and Major General of the Massachusetts Bay Colony* (Chicago, 1912), pp. 32–47.

to the disproportionate number of men in the colony, he took to wearing woman's apparel when in search of sexual adventure.[6]

Hall may have been eccentric in more ways than one, and it would be rash to assume that all servants in Virginia had led quite such a varied career prior to their arrival in Virginia. Nevertheless, his case does establish that somebody at the lowest level of society could be as mobile as the most venturesome of his superiors. The literary evidence certainly suggests that the poorer element in Virginia were widely travelled and it is likely that they came from more varied backgrounds than did their counterparts in Ireland. Otherwise they seem to have been not unlike those who migrated to Ireland and were frequently described in almost the same unflattering terms. We know that the vast majority were young single men, and indeed there was no serious effort to enlist women for Virginia prior to 1620.[7] We know hardly anything of what decided the would-be colonists to leave England. Convicted felons, unwanted vagrants, and other social undesirables had no choice in the matter. Some settlers may have been lured by the prospect of advancement highlighted in the propaganda campaign; but many of the unemployed in London must have drifted where opportunity beckoned, or looked to Virginia as an escape from the restraints of traditional society. We can be sure, however, that the majority were either ignorant or misinformed concerning conditions in the New World; and it is likely that they were both poorly equipped and poorly motivated for what lay ahead of them. It soon became evident that they had no intention of making extraordinary sacrifices for the advancement of civility, and they reacted quickly against the harsh laws, the privations, and the organized labour which they were called upon to endure. Almost every description of the work force in Virginia mentioned that they were 'full of mutenie and treasonable intendments',[8] and when we piece together the colonists' objections to the regime under which they were expected to serve, it falls little short of the counter-ideology which William Strachey thought to have been widespread among England's poor.

The most detailed account of popular opposition to the expansionist

6. *Minutes of the Council and General Court of Colonial Virginia*, ed. H. R. McIlwaine (Richmond, 1924), p. 194.

7. That frequent long-distance migration was not unusual among the poorer elements in early modern England has been established in Peter Clark, 'The migrant in Kentish towns, 1580–1640', in Peter Clark and Paul Slack (eds), *Crisis and Order in English Towns, 1500–1700* (London, 1972), pp. 117–63; see also Thirsk, *The Agrarian History*, pp. 396–465. On the scarcity of women in Virginia see Morgan, *American Slavery, American Freedom*, p. 111.

8. Sir Thomas Dale to Salisbury, 17 August 1610 (P.R.O., C.O. –1/1, no. 26, ff. 94–95).

effort comes from the self-same Strachey, when he discusses the colonists under the command of Sir Thomas Gates and Sir George Somers who were shipwrecked when bound for Virginia and marooned, from July 1609 until the spring of 1610, on Bermuda. Strachey's purpose in writing was to vindicate the actions of Gates whose leadership and actions were, in his own opinion, responsible for maintaining discipline while new craft were being constructed from fresh timber. Quite obviously Strachey had no sympathy for those who opposed Gates's leadership, but his narrative is important because it pinpoints the principal dissidents in the stranded colony and sketches the arguments formulated by them. 'The major part of the common sort', according to Strachey, accepted that 'they were (for the time) to loose the fruition of their friends and countrey', but in the circumstances preferred remaining permanently on the attractive and fruitful island to continuing the voyage to Virginia, where 'nothing but wretchedness and labour must be expected with many wants'. Dissatisfaction with the rule of Gates first became evident among the sailors, always a restless lot, who objected to work for which they had not contracted; but dissent also appeared among the landsmen. Those mentioned by Strachey as the chief conspirators, Nicholas Bennett and John Want, were both craftsmen but were also versed in scripture which they cited in support of their actions. This revolt achieved little but the leader of the second disturbance Stephen Hopkins was also 'a fellow who had much knowledge in the scriptures and could reason well therein'. Hopkins could also argue in secular terms and disputed the authority of Gates on the grounds that from the moment of shipwreck 'they were all then freed from the government of any man'. When this insurrection was suppressed the cause seemed hopeless but the rebels rose a third time, led by Henry Paine, described by Strachey as a gentleman, and withdrew into the woods rather than serve under Gates; and they proclaimed that 'they should happily suffer as martyrs' for their beliefs. This final outburst was also quashed and all but two of the dissenters had rejoined the main company when they sailed for Virginia.[9]

There exists no detailed account of the popular protests which occurred in Virginia, though the early years of the settlement were exceptionally turbulent. The visiting sailors, who were not subject to the jurisdiction of the government at Jamestown, were a truculent group and cared little

9. William Strachey, 'A true repertory of the wreck', in Purchas, *Pilgrimes*, xix. 5–72, esp. p. 28; for information on English sailors of the period see D. B. Quinn, *England and the Discovery of America, 1481–1620* (London, 1974), pp. 199–226.

for the welfare of the colony. From the beginning, the sailors pre-empted trade with the American Indians, but they also exploited the poor at Jamestown by denying them liquor and other desperately needed commodities 'unlesse [they] might have an East Indian increase, four for one, all charges cleared'.[1] Furthermore they were ready, probably at a price, to assist any dissatisfied group within the fort at Jamestown. Such opportunities must have been frequent since, according to one witness, 'the common sort . . . were active in nothing but adhearing to factions and parts, even to their owne ruine'.[2] Two popular insurrections known as 'Webbes and Prices design' occurred in the first year of settlement, and some years later one Jeffrey Abbot, a veteran of the wars in the Netherlands and Ireland, who up to that point had been an admirable worker, was driven by 'an unadvised passionate impatience' to foment an insurrection, probably because some 'of his farre inferiors [had been] preferred to over top him'. Five men deserted the colony in 1614 and sought to join a Spanish settlement which they believed to lie south of Virginia, while another group stole a boat and deserted to become pirates and freebooters 'with dreams of mountains of gold and happie robberies'.[3] The rulers at Jamestown were also under constant pressure to abandon the colony and return for England, and when Gates decided on this course of action in June 1610 he had difficulty in restraining some who wished to burn the fort, to ensure that they would never return.[4] One very dangerous action for the future of the colony was that taken in 1609 by some 'unruly youths' who stowed away on the same ships that had brought them to Virginia, having first 'bound themselves by mutuall oath' to discredit the colony. These on their return gave 'out in all places . . . (to colour their owne misbehaviour, and the cause of their returne with some pretence) most vile and scandalous reports, both of the countrey it selfe and the cariage of the businesse there'.[5]

There were more direct means available to the common settlers to register their dissent from the colony and its purpose. The most obvious way was to refuse to work, and many compounded this by drowning their sorrows whenever alcohol could be purchased from the sailors. To ensure

1. William Strachey, 'A true repertory', Purchas, *Pilgrimes,* xix. 50.
2. Alexander Brown, *The Genesis of the United States* (2 vols, Boston, 1890), i. 344.
3. Edward Arber and A. G. Bradley (eds), *Travels and Works of Captain John Smith* (Edinburgh, 1910), p. 508; Purchas, *Pilgrimes,* xix. 68, 98.
4. Lord de la Ware *et al.,* 'Relation of a voyage to Virginia', 7 July 1610 (B.L., Harleian MSS. 7009, ff. 58–61).
5. Broadside by the council of Virginia, 1610 (Society of Antiquaries, London, Broadside 122).

a regular supply some settlers bartered clothes, tools, and weapons to the Indians in return for skins and other commodities valued by the sailors. In this they were, whether wittingly or not we shall never know, following the example of the English soldiers in Ireland; and also as in Ireland some of the English at Jamestown deserted to the enemy, and these eventually integrated themselves into Indian society.

None of the contemporary commentators devote much attention to desertion, since mention of it would have countered their principal purpose in writing, which was to promote interest in the colony, or to vindicate their own actions. Captain John Smith, who is our chief informant on the early years at Jamestown, must have seen desertion to the Indians as an adverse reflection on his period of rule because he plays it down, and when he does refer to it, attributes responsibility to foreign artisans who would have appeared to his readers as less motivated and perhaps less civil than the native English. Even Smith revealed in his less guarded moments that Englishmen were among the deserters, and his, together with other corroborating evidence, suggests that there was a regular haemorrhage to the Indians from the moment of settlement in 1607 until the all but total breakdown in relations between English and natives following the 1622 massacre.

Smith in his account attributed the loss of weapons and tools from the fort to a conspiracy between the sailors, soldiers, and Indians, two of which groups were outside his control.[6] The first desertions he mentions occurred in his absence, and those who abandoned Jamestown were 'Dutchmen', by which he meant German craftsmen, lured by the prosperity evident among the natives and by the belief that the colony was about to be overthrown by Chief Powhatan. The Germans, however, according to Smith, were aided by six or seven confederates, 'expert theaves', within the fort who conveyed 'a good part of our arms . . . to the salvages', and who were themselves later discovered in the act of desertion. When William Volda, a 'Switzer', was dispatched by Smith to reclaim the fugitives, he too conspired with Powhatan to attack Jamestown. At this point in the narrative Smith acknowledged that not all who deserted were Germans, because Volda was commissioned to recall not only those but also 'one Bentley an other fugitive'.[7]

6. George Donne, 'Virginia reviewed', n.d. (B.L., Harleian MSS. 7021, ff. 9–10); *Minutes of the Council and General Court*, p. 5; de la Ware, 'Relation', 7 July 1610 (B.L., Harleian MSS. 7009, ff. 58–61); *Travels and Works of Smith*, pp. 128, 134.
7. *Travels and Works of Smith*, pp. 134, 139, 149, 158. But see James Axtell, 'The white Indians of colonial America', *William and Mary Quarterly*, 3rd series, xxxii (1975), 55–88.

The fact which Smith did not wish to reveal was that desertion to the Indians had been occurring almost from the moment of arrival. Edward Maria Wingfield, the first governor, mentioned his efforts in September 1607 to recall from the Indians 'a boy that was run from us' and also 'our men runnagates'.[8] The drift became more regular after the spring of 1609 when shortage of supplies compelled Smith to billet some of the colony on the native population. Thereafter 'divers of the soldiers ran away . . . [and] as many others . . . intended also to have followed them'. The attraction, according to Smith, was that they had been 'well treated', but the loosening of control with the dispersal of the settlement must also have been a factor. We cannot accept Smith's testimony that the drift ceased after he had punished those who were plotting to depart, since severe penalties for desertion were still thought necessary when in 1610 the *Lawes Divine, Morall and Martiall* were introduced.[9] Another authoritative source stated that the harshness of this regime 'forced many to flee for reliefe to the savage enemies', and of those who were afterwards captured in 1612 some were 'hanged some burned some . . . broken upon wheels, others staked and some . . . shott to death'. The justification given for 'all theis extreme and crewell tortures' was 'to terrify the reste for attempting the lyke'. This in itself is evidence that desertion to the Indians was a serious and persistent problem for the authorities.[1] Not all deserters were treated harshly because the government at Jamestown in its anxiety to elicit information about the Indians was willing to pardon some. Few returned under these conditions but at least one, Simons, was a persistent deserter 'who had thrice plaid the rennagate, whose lyes and villany much hindered our trade for corne'.[2]

The Spaniards, who did what they could to keep abreast of developments in Virginia during the early years, were of the opinion that 'a good many' had gone to the Indians, and that forty or fifty had actually married into Amerindian society.[3] Since the Spaniards were ill-disposed towards Virginia we cannot accept this evidence as final but it certainly does not conflict with what has been gleaned from the English sources.

The weight of evidence forces the conclusion that a significant number of the poorer elements at Jamestown saw desertion to the Indians as the

8. *Travels and Works of Smith*, p. lxxvii.
9. Ibid., p. 157; *Lawes Divine, Morall and Martiall*, p. 33.
1. Cited in Morgan, *American Slavery, American Freedom*, p. 74; *Journals of the House of Burgesses of Virginia, 1619–1659*, ed. H. R. McIlwaine (Richmond, 1915), pp. 21–22.
2. Purchas, *Pilgrimes*, xix. 104.
3. Brown, *Genesis*, ii. 572–3, 632–3, 648.

most extreme indictment of the colony and as the most effective means of winning freedom for themselves. Of those who were granted the opportunity of returning with pardon few accepted, and some went to great lengths by fleeing from one tribe to another to ensure that they would not be reclaimed.[4] There are also some references which suggest that the deserters were quickly absorbed into Indian society, assumed new names and a new appearance, and became virtually indistinguishable from their fellow tribesmen. One Robert Marcum who fled in 1616 was by 1621 known even to the English as Moutapass, and Ralph Hamor in 1614 encountered and reclaimed a fugitive who had by then spent three years with the Indians and had 'growne so like, both in complexion and habit like a salvage' that 'but by his tongue' he could not be recognized as an Englishman.[5] There are no references to English women having sought refuge with the Indians, but those who were captured in 1622 seem, at least, to have been accepted into Indian society. When Mrs Sarah Boyse, the most distinguished of the nineteen captives, was eventually returned she came 'apparrelled like one of their Queens which they desired wee should take notice of'. Another, Jane Dickenson, complained of the misery and slavery she had endured during her ten months with 'the cruell salvages', but this was no worse, she averred, than life as an indentured servant. A third woman, Anne Jackson, who returned to the colony in 1629, after a possible seven years with the Indians, seems to have caused a scandal since the court at Jamestown ordered that she 'be sent for England with the first opportunity', and her brother John Jackson was required in the meantime to 'give security for her passage and keep her safe till shee bee shipped abroade'.[6]

What we know of American Indian society suggests that it must have had considerable attraction for poor Englishmen, though hardly so for English women. The principal lure, according to Captain John Smith, was 'to live idle among the salvages', and this was most probably true since most work in American Indian society was done by women, while men

---

4. Purchas, *Pilgrimes*, xix. 104; *Travels and Works of Smith*, pp. 511, 513; S. Kingsbury (ed.), *The Records of the Virginia Company of London* (4 vols, Washington, 1906–35), iii. 74.
5. *Travels and Works of Smith*, pp. 519, 568.
6. Ibid., pp. 591–2; Christopher Best to John Woodall, 1 April 1623 (P.R.O., 30/15/2, no. 338, xxii); governor and council of Virginia to Southampton, 3 April 1623 (P.R.O., C.O. –1/2, no. 22, f. 128); *Records of the Virginia Company*, iv. p. 473; *Minutes of the Council and General Court*, p. 181. It may be relevant that, within English settlements in America, it was not unknown for settler wives to have sexual relations with Indians: a 1639 instance from New England is cited in Paul Hair, *Before the Bawdy Court* (London, 1972), p. 96.

fought and hunted.[7] It also seems likely that those confined in an almost completely male settlement at Jamestown hoped for some sexual release by fleeing to the Indians. In this context it is significant that when John Rolfe entered into a Christian marriage with Pochahontas he was accused by the 'vulgar sort' of 'wanting to gorge [himself] with incontinency'.[8] Whatever the attraction it seems that most Englishmen, and not all of them from the lower ranks, who came into close contact with Indian society were drawn towards it. Both Henry Spelman and Robert Poole, the first official interpreters, had spent a considerable time with the Indians to learn their language and they were thereafter suspect to the English. It was said of Spelman in 1619 that 'he had in him more of the savage than of the Christian', and Poole was described variously as being 'in a manner turned heathen', and 'even turned heathen'. No such accusations were brought against the third interpreter, who was inauspiciously named Thomas Savage, but it is significant that on accepting office he had to pay a bond of £200 'not to have any conference at all or familiaritie with the Indians'.[9]

Looked at from the other point of view we can be certain that the Indians welcomed deserters. American Indian society was accustomed to absorbing newcomers, to replace those of their ranks who had been killed in battle. The recent work of Francis Jennings has established that the Amerindian population had been greatly depleted before the arrival of the English at Jamestown, so local groups may well have been desperate for new recruits. This may explain the resentment of Powhatan at the efforts of the English to win back the fugitives.[1]

While we can understand the anxiety of the English to suppress information of desertion to the Indians they cannot have been surprised at that development. Many of the officers in the colony had seen service in Ireland and must have been familiar with the desertion of soldiers to the Gaelic Irish, an enemy represented as no less barbarous than the American Indians. Further, desertion cannot have been unexpected by those who had knowledge of earlier English reconnaisance in North America. It was generally accepted that some if not all, of the lost colony of 1587 had

7. *Travels and Works of Smith*, p. 157; Morgan, *American Slavery, American Freedom*, pp. 51–53.

8. L. G. Tyler (ed.), *Narratives of Early Virginia, 1606–25* (N.Y., 1907), p. 243.

9. *Travels and Works of Smith*, p. 542; *Records of the Virginia Company*, iii. 244–5; *Journals of the House of Burgesses of Virginia*, pp. 14–15; *Minutes of the Council and General Court*, p. 48.

1. Francis Jennings, *The Invasion of America: Indians, Colonialism, and the Cant of Conquest* (Chapel Hill, N.C., 1975), pp. 15–31; *Travels and Works of Smith*, p. 519.

survived by integrating themselves into Indian society, and one of the responsibilities of the Jamestown settlement was in fact to track down the survivors.[2] Again, it did not elicit any startled comment from the English to discover that other European settlers, such as the French at Port Royal and St Croix, would in emergency 'live among the salvages of those countries'.[3] The organizers of plantations must also have been well prepared for mutinous actions, since they were acutely aware of the rebelliousness of the English poor from whose ranks the settlers were drawn; and the overseas ventures of the sixteenth century gave no hope that this characteristic would change in an Atlantic crossing. Ralph Lane had complained in 1585 of the 'wyld men of myne owne nacione whose unrulynes ys suche as not to gyve leasure', and John Hawkins experienced the desertion of some of his company, who later aided the Spaniards in 'the murther and overthrow of their owne countrimen'.[4]

It has been necessary to elaborate in considerable detail the points made because, for the most part, neither the historians of colonial America nor those of early modern Ireland have seriously considered the possibility that significant numbers of the early settlers were so indifferent to the extension of English civility that they happily integrated themselves into the indigenous society. What has been said of the behaviour of English soldiers in Ireland during the sixteenth century lends extra authority to the argument that significant numbers of the English settlers in Virginia deserted to the Indians. On the other hand, the account of the attitudes of the English settlers in Virginia supports the hypothesis that the English and possibly the Scots poor who populated the various Irish plantations shared the mental world of the soldiers who had served in Ireland in the sixteenth century. Hence, the common settler outlook in Ireland cannot have been essentially different from that of the Virginian colonists. The evidence that has been cited suggests that the English poor did not accept the arguments of English social and cultural superiority that were expounded by their betters, and that their failure to do so had drastic consequences in a colonial setting. The massacre of 1622 in Virginia and the 1641 rebellion in Ireland must have forced the settlers in both cases to accept some part of what was being said of the native populations by their masters, although the resulting attitude seems to have been a simple

2. D. B. Quinn, *England and the Discovery of America,* pp. 432–81.

3. *Travels and Works of Smith,* p. 517.

4. Thirsk, *The Agrarian History,* pp. 396–465; Ralph Lane to Sir Philip Sidney, 12 August 1585 (P.R.O., C.O. –1/1, no. 5, f. 15); Brown, *Genesis,* ii. 792; Bernard Bailyn, *The New England Merchants in the Seventeenth Century* (N.Y., 2nd edn, 1964), p. 14.

one of hatred based on fear rather than one based on any sense of social superiority.[5] In Virginia, certainly, after English relations with the Indians had broken down, the poorer element showed themselves capable of accepting on equal terms another group who were portrayed by their superiors as social inferiors, that is black Africans. There are, for instance, many references in the local records to the existence of cordial, and even sexual relations between black and white servants in seventeenth-century Virginia, and some whites even combined with blacks against their masters.[6] When we piece everything together we still cannot say that the English poor in either Ireland or Virginia adhered to any clearly defined, well-articulated counter-ideology. But we can say with confidence that they were not imbued with any missionary zeal and that some approached the position of espousing the rights of the indigenous population against the intruder, a position which, as Christopher Hill has shown, was that taken by some radical spokesmen in mid-seventeenth-century England.[7]   2118800

The organizers must have been prepared for this type of colonist, but were confident that their efforts would succeed provided that all settlers were bound closely together under the watchful eye of the officers of the colony. There they would be subject to martial law, which was a feature of colonial settlement in Ireland and Virginia, and would also be exposed to a rigorous orientation programme. Those entrusted with the execution of such a programme were the ministers of religion, who were brought to the colonies perhaps largely for that purpose. There is some evidence that the ruling element both knew and was alarmed that the lesser colonists did not wholly share its religious and cultural outlook; but did not consider them beyond persuasion. Sir Thomas Dale deplored the fact that of those in Virginia 'not many give testimonie besides their names that

5. W. F. Craven, *White, Red and Black* (Charlottesville, 1971), pp. 51–56; G. B. Nash, 'The image of the Indian in the southern colonial mind', *William and Mary Quarterly*, 3rd series, xxix (1972), 197–230; K. J. Lindley, 'The impact of the 1641 rebellion upon England and Wales, 1641–5', *Irish Historical Studies*, xviii (1972), 143–76.

6. W. M. Billings, 'The cases of Fernando and Elizabeth Key: a note on the status of blacks in seventeenth-century Virginia', *William and Mary Quarterly*, 3rd series, xxx (1973), 467–74; Morgan, *American Slavery, American Freedom*, pp. 333–7; review of S. M. Ames (ed.), *County Court Records of Accomack-Northampton, Virginia, 1640–1645*, by E. S. Morgan in *Virginia Magazine of History and Biography*, lxxxii (1974), 191–3. The above together greatly modify the opinions on seventeenth-century Englishmen's antipathy for people with black pigmentation advanced in W. D. Jordan, *White over Black: American Attitudes toward the Negro, 1550–1812* (Chapel Hill, N.C., 1968). For evidence of black and white servants combining against their masters see *Minutes of the Council and General Court*, p. 467.

7. Christopher Hill, *The World Turned Upside Down* (London, 1972), pp. 271–2.

they are Christians'. But he seems nevertheless to have been confident that these backsliders, or even worse characters, might yet become useful instruments, because in the same letter he requested that the king 'banish hither all offenders condemned ... to die out of common Goales'.[8]

The educational process on which Dale obviously pinned such hope was that provided for in the *Lawes Divine, Morall and Martiall*, which prescribed compulsory sermons and prayers at 10 am and 4 pm daily, and services and sermons on Sunday. Much the same type of régime was enforced by Sir Thomas Gates among the stranded colonists on Bermuda, and Walter, Earl of Essex, instituted a somewhat similar programme among his followers in Ulster.[9] We cannot speak of the quality of the sermons, but William Strachey's description of Sunday service at Jamestown brings home to us the dramatic impact that such occasions must have had on the common colonist:

When the Lord Governor and Captaine Generall goeth to church he is accompanied with all the counsailers, captaines, other officers, and all the Gentlemen, and with a Guard of Holberdiers in his Lordships Livery, faire red cloakes, to the number of fifty, both on each side and behinde him: and being in the church, his Lordship hath his seate in the Quier, in a greene velvet chaire, with a cloath, with a velvet cushion spread on a table before him, on which he kneeleth, and on each side sit the counsell, captaines, and officers, each in their place, and when he returneth home againe, he is waited on to his house in the same manner.[1]

There is evidence from Ireland that the soldiers were exposed also to secular discourses by their commanders who reminded them as Englishmen of their superiority to their adversaries;[2] and it is possible that those at Jamestown fort were similarly treated to rousing speeches. None of this would have been possible in other than a closely bound settlement, but it was also hoped that the officers by their personal example would inspire their subordinates to higher things. Sir Thomas Smith in 1573 directed each captain to dine with his company, and enjoined on them to avoid 'superfluity of fare or delicatnes and excesse of apparell', because

---

8. Dale to Salisbury, 17 August 1610 (P.R.O., C.O. -1/1, no. 26, ff. 94–95).

9. *Lawes Divine, Morall and Martiall*, pp. 9–11; Purchas, *Pilgrimes*, xix. 28; Essex to the Queen, 2 November 1573 (P.R.O., S.P. 63, vol. 42, no. 64).

1. Purchas, *Pilgrimes*, xix. 56–57.

2. Edmund Tremayne, Notes and propositions, 1571 (P.R.O., S.P. 63, vol. 32, no. 66) which Tremayne mentions are based on speeches of Lord Deputy Sidney; 'Sidney's memoir', *Ulster Journal of Archaeology*, iii. 348.

their task was 'to laye the foundacion of a good and . . . an eternall colony for your posteritie, not a may game or stage playe'.[3]

All of this indicates that the promoters pinned their hopes on the officers in the colonies and especially on their ability to maintain discipline and supervise the educational programme. It was originally hoped that members of the nobility and gentry, or at least their sons, would act as officers in the colony. These, it was thought, were sufficiently independent financially to pursue the high ideals of the founders, and it was also assumed that they would be more easily able to maintain social control, since 'by nature everye man subordinate is ready to yeald a willing submission without comtempt or repyning' to those placed in the higher ranks of society.[4] The nobility and more affluent gentry did indeed contribute generously to all colonial ventures, but the only enterprise which actually employed substantial numbers from the upper ranks of English society was that of Essex in Ireland. That experience made clear that the special advantages with which those of elevated station were supposed to be endowed, were more than offset by their laziness and fondness for luxury, and by their inability to accommodate themselves to the rigours of life on the frontier. The failure of the exploit was, in fact, attributed to the lack of perseverance of 'our English gallant [who] will neither wett his foote nor want his fare'.[5] Such condemnation might explain why so few of noble birth took an active part in future plantation efforts in Ireland or Virginia, in the latter of which only one nobleman, Thomas West, Lord de la Ware, took an active role.

This failure to attract nobles as officers was the one single factor most responsible for the colonies following a pattern different from that intended by the original promoters. In the absence of officers of noble birth the managers had to make do with landless younger sons of minor gentry and discharged army captains who were noted neither for their honesty nor for their concern for the public good. Both groups were certainly sufficiently informed to echo the ideology of colonization favoured by their employers, but their chief interest in plantations was to achieve economic advancement commensurate with the social position which they enjoyed either from birth or from service. Many of the captains had been knighted for service on the field, and to this extent were gentlemen,

3. Orders of Smith, 20 December 1573 (Essex C.R.O., D/Dsh. 01/7).
4. Petition to Virginia Council, 1619 (P.R.O., 13/15/2, no. 247).
5. Leicester to Ashton, May 1575 (P.R.O., S.P. 63, vol. 51, no. 48, f. 134); N. P. Canny, *The Elizabethan Conquest*, pp. 88–90.

but they were so desperate for money in peacetime that it was feared that they might become pirates or offer their services to unfriendly powers.[6] Sixteenth-century Ireland had, in fact, provided examples of both courses of action. The most notorious case of treason by an officer in the army, and one considered worthy of dramatic presentation, was that of Sir Thomas Stukely, who when denied advancement by the Queen joined the Anglo-Irish rebel, Sir James Fitzmaurice Fitzgerald, and acted as his agent on the Continent to solicit support from the catholic enemies of Queen Elizabeth.[7] The most notorious case of a captain turning pirate was that of Sir Ralph Bingley, who in 1607, and seemingly with the knowledge of Sir Henry Bruncar, then Lord President of Munster, combined with one Arthur Chambers in deflecting a ship, the *Triall*, from its voyage to Virginia, and with Kinsale as a base used the ship for piratical exploits in alliance with two well-known pirates, Captains Isaack and Swedon.[8]

Incidents such as the above must have further convinced the authorities in England that it was wise to accept the offers from this restless element to act as undertakers and servitors in the Irish plantations, or as officers and subsequently planters in Virginia. Moreover the English experience in Ireland had shown this group to be, if not successful colonists, at least able conquerors. Some of the captains had admittedly sought to live off rather than destroy the Gaelic institutional system,[9] but generally speaking the officers of the army had forced the pace of conquest. Some, in their anxiety to acquire property in Ireland, deliberately fomented rebellion and eventually committed the government to bringing the entire country under its control. Much of what was achieved by such as Peter Carew in Leinster, Humphrey Gilbert in Munster, Richard Bingham in Connacht, and Captain Willis in Ulster was more characteristic of the action of frontiersmen than of responsible officers of the crown, but all were sufficiently informed to present plausible justifications for their use of extra-legal methods.[1]

6. Brown, *Genesis*, i. 50; Ro. Kayll, 'The trades decrease', undated (Cambridge University Library, Pepys MSS. 1477).

7. *The famous history of the life and death of Captain Thomas Stukeley* (London, 1605), in R. Simpson (ed.), *The School of Shakespeare*, vol. i (London, 1878).

8. Bingley was not actually convicted of piracy, but the evidence presented is convincing and the incident even caused embarrassment in England's diplomatic relations with Spain. See D. B. Quinn, 'The voyage of *Triall* 1606–7', *The American Neptune*, xxxi (1971), 85–103.

9. See for example the petition of John Rowe to the Queen, 1574 (Oxford, Carte MSS., vol. 56(2), f. 592); book on the garrisons in Ireland, 22 March 1572 (Oxford, Carte MSS., vol. 57, f. 521).

1. N. P. Canny, *The Elizabethan Conquest, passim*; Richard Bagwell, *Ireland under the Tudors* (3 vols, London, 1885–90), iii. 227–8.

The first group of officers appointed in 1607 to administer the affairs of the settlement in Virginia showed themselves by their actions to conform to the same type as the earlier adventurers in Ireland. Like those they purported to be primarily concerned with the advancement of English interests, but none was willing to accept direction either from London or from any superior within the colony. Captain John Smith eventually succeeded, by sheer force of personality, in winning the presidency for himself, but the other councillors, according to Smith, then allied themselves with the sailors and the dissidents within the colony 'to regaine their former credit and authority'.[2] When in 1609 it came to Smith's turn to be overruled by newly appointed officers of higher social standing than himself, he too 'to strengthen his authority, accorded with the mariners, and gave not any due respect to many worthy gentlemen that came in our ships'.[3]

The most revealing statement on this change of government came from Smith himself, who wished that 'they had never arrived, and we for ever abandoned, and we left to our fortunes'. By this he can only have meant that he could countenance a complete break with England, thus being left to reach some accommodation with the indigenous population as some of the English captains in Ireland had done. How far Smith would have gone we have no means of knowing, but when some of his adversaries 'calculated hee had the salvages in such subjection, hee would have made himselfe a king by marrying Pochahontas', Smith's only response was that such a marriage would not have entitled him to be a king under Indian law.[4]

The replacement of Smith by George Percy, brother to the Earl of Northumberland, who in turn was replaced the following year by Thomas West, Baron de la Ware, marks a renewed effort by the Virginia Company in London to institute the authoritarian system that had originally been intended for Virginia. This system, bolstered by the *Lawes Divine, Morall and Martiall*, does seem to have contained popular disturbance, although not flight to the Indians, but it met with continued opposition from army officers and freemen who sought greater autonomy. Some of these, such as Captain Brewster, who led mutinies successively against governors Sir George Percy, Sir Thomas Dale, and Samuel Argall,

---

2. Purchas, *Pilgrimes*, xix. 67; *Travels and Works of Smith*, p. 96.
3. Brown, *Genesis*, i. 328–32.
4. *Travels and Works of Smith*, pp. 479, 168.

solicited support from the discontented popular element and so threatened the very existence of the colony.[5]

Such challenges to authority were easily suppressed while the settlement was a small one, but after 1617 when the economic possibility of a tobacco crop had been recognized and labourers were required in ever-increasing numbers, the authorities in London saw that a broadening of the power base was necessary. Thus the dominant faction of the Virginia Company in London, who wished to profit from tobacco, introduced new institutions which transferred real power in Virginia to those already in the colony, and to any in England who wished to join them, for the sole motive of gain.[6] Once this devolution of power had taken place, English settlement in Virginia, which hitherto had been confined to Jamestown and a few outposts, spread itself in haphazard fashion along the banks of the James river, since every colonist with sufficient resources to convey indentured servants to Virginia took out a patent for land and launched himself as a private planter.

The pattern of settlement which emerged was shocking to all who cherished the high ideals of the founders. Instead of an ordered settlement the English in Virginia were by 1623 'planted dispersedlie in small families, far from neighbours ... covetous of large possessions (larger than 100 tymes their nomber were able to cultivate) ... like libertines out of the eye of the magistrate'.[7] The final point is the most telling one because it indicates that the central authority, like its counterpart in Ireland, no longer exerted any substantial influence over those who were theoretically subject to it. Likewise the instruments of social control were blunted because it was not 'fesible to governe a people so dispersed; especially such as for the most part are sent over', and neither was it possible to bring them together for divine service.[8]

Those who now shaped the settlement were the more successful tobacco planters, a few of whom were appointed governors, and who as a

5. Bill of complaint of Samuel Argall, 23 January 1622 (P.R.O., c. 2, Jas. I, A9/10); testimony of John Martin, 13 April 1622 (P.R.O., c. 24/486, pt. 1/12); testimony of John Waller, 11 May 1622 (P.R.O., c. 24/48/1); testimony of John Martin, 1 May 1622 (P.R.O., c. 24/489/1).

6. W. F. Craven, *Dissolution of the Virginia Company* (reprinted edition, Gloucester, Mass., 1964), pp. 47–104.

7. Morgan, *American Slavery, American Freedom*, pp. 108–30; George Sandys to Sir Miles Sandys, 30 March 1623 (*Records of Virginia Company*, iv. 70–72).

8. The parallel with Ireland is particularly evident from T. O. Ranger, 'The career of Richard Boyle', pp. 264–72 where the author shows that Boyle sought freedom for the planters to pursue their own policies without interference from either the Dublin or London governments; George Sandys to Farrer (P.R.O., 30/15/2, no. 318).

group controlled the council and the assembly. As councillors and jurors also, they determined the outcome of court proceedings before the general court at Jamestown, and as county commissioners and vestrymen they controlled local and ecclesiastical affairs. Their principal power lay, however, in their capacity as planters where they held sway over the dissatisfied indentured servants.[9]

This new power group did preside over the erection of legal, local, and ecclesiastical institutions, all of which were based on English models, but we should not lose sight of the fact that much of this was merely a polite veneer for an extremely brash society.[1] The very appearance of the settlement was offensive to English eyes, as was the disregard for human life and the brutal treatment meted out by the masters to their servants. The indentured servants who eventually poured into the colony at the rate of a thousand a year between 1625 and 1640[2] were certainly a potentially rebellious group, but one more easily controlled after 1622 when their escape to the Indians was cut off. Once they were dispersed through the scattered plantations they also had little opportunity to organize a concerted insurrection. The only means of protest now open to them were refusals to work, drunkenness, or attempts to flee to the Dutch settlement in the Hudson Valley.[3] Nevertheless the planters, who by this time had chief responsibility for discipline, were constantly alert to dissidence among the work force, and any servant who showed disrespect to his master or the government was hauled before the courts and severely punished. Laziness was reprimanded by whipping, and the courts were tolerant of masters who whipped their servants, female as well as male, to the point of death and even beyond.[4]

One gathers from the planters' concern to have ministers appointed that they saw the church as another instrument for keeping their servants in check or stimulating them to greater effort. They themselves were no religious enthusiasts, nor were they anxious to pay for the services provided, as is evident from the regular disputes, sometimes in most crude language, between ministers and planters over the paying of tithes.

9. Morgan, *American Slavery, American Freedom*, pp. 115–30.

1. Ibid., pp. 133–57.

2. Ibid., p. 159.

3. *Minutes of the Council and General Court*, pp. 105, 467; S. M. Ames (ed.), *County Court Records of Accomack-Northampton, Virginia, 1632–40* (Washington, 1954), pp. 120–1; Virginia State Library, county court records of Lower Norfolk county, 1637–46, ff. 7, 186.

4. *Minutes of the Council and General Court*, pp. 22–24; S. M. Ames (ed.), *County Court Records of Accomack-Northampton, Virginia, 1640–45* (Charlottesville, 1973), pp. 24–26, 266, 271; Morgan, *American Slavery, American Freedom*, pp. 126–9.

Nor did the planters finance any concerted effort to draw the Indians to Christianity.[5]

The masters were greatly concerned to prevent any moral turpitude among their servants, especially disrespect for authority, drunkenness, and sexual misdemeanours. They did not, however, establish very high standards in such matters themselves. In sartorial matters those from lowly backgrounds who made money as planters showed no regard for traditional deference to rank with the result that 'our cowkeepers here of James citty on Sundays goes accoutered all in fresh flaming silke and a wife of one that in England had professed the black art not of a scholler but of a collier of Croydon weares her rough bever hatt with a faire perle hatband, and a silken suite thereto correspondent'.[6] This behaviour seemed so erratic to English eyes that the 'two enormous excesses of apparell and drinking' were such that 'the infamie hath spredd it self to all that have but heard the name of Virginia'.[7] The principal information on sexual irregularities among the ruling element comes in fact from the charges brought against them by their servants. Some of these were motivated by revenge, especially by female servants who must have resented being governed by mistresses from the same background as themselves, but others were well founded and bear witness to much sexual exploitation of female servants by their masters.[8] All things considered, it appears that English society in Virginia not only fell short of the high standards expected by its founders, but was a fairly permissive society by any standard. As early as 1625 it could be said of Virginia 'that of a merchant-like trade there was some probabillitie at least for a while; but of a plantation there was none at all, neither in the courses, nor in the intencions, either of the adventurers here, or of the colonie there'.[9]

The behaviour of the New English proprietors in Ireland during the

5. *Minutes of the Council and General Court,* pp. 88, 105, and esp. p. 474 for the court order of 9 December 1640.

6. Letter of John Pory, 1618 (*Records of Virginia Company,* iii. 221).

7. Treasurer and council for Virginia to governor and council in Virginia, 1 August 1622 (*Records of Virginia Company,* iii. 668).

8. The records of each county bear witness to a 'permissive' sexual climate, and there appears to be a proportionally greater number of charges and convictions than in England. See especially the conviction for fornication of Matthew Phillips and Mary Rowge, 15 December 1641 (Virginia State Library, county court records of Lower Norfolk, 1637–46, f. 305). Philips was a county commissioner, a church warden and guardian to the orphans of Mrs Seawell and seduced Mary Rowge, servant to the orphans. There are also a few cases of mistresses having illicit sexual relations with their male servants; see *Minutes of the Council and General Court,* p. 475.

9. Discourse of the old company, April 1625 (*Records of Virginia Company,* iv. 521–2).

first half of the seventeenth century has been much less comprehensively studied, but from what is known it can be said that the plantations that emerged there were far from the models in civil living that had been intended by the promoters. Like their counterparts in Virginia the new landed proprietors gained control of the central government but used it as an instrument for their own enrichment rather than for the advancement of the interests of the monarch. This was certainly the verdict of Thomas Wentworth, Earl of Strafford, who assessed the achievements of the New English during his period as Lord Lieutenant of Ireland, 1638–41. Nor was Strafford convinced by the claims of the New English to be champions of protestantism, and one of his great concerns was to reclaim for the church that land which had come into the secular ownership of the grasping New English élite. The record of the New English as promoters of plantation was also dubious. Instead of being satisfied with and settling what had been granted to them, many of the New English proprietors sought after more land, either by purchase from their fellow countrymen or by prying into the titles of the indigenous landowners. Many ignored the conditions under which they had accepted land from the Crown, and neither constructed the defensible buildings which they had undertaken to provide, nor brought in British tenants in sufficient numbers to occupy their estates. Instead they retained many of the existing tenants, or else devoted themselves to making a quick return on money invested by denuding their lands of trees.[1] The plantation in Ulster was more comprehensive than elsewhere in the country, although not all the conditions were adhered to even in that province. For the remainder of the country during the first half of the seventeenth century we can with some justice speak of a 'moving frontier', for the new proprietors had hardly claimed ownership in one area before they sought more land in another plantation. In this respect their behaviour approximates to that of the planters in Virginia. The present state of knowledge does not permit any detailed account of the personal lives of the planters in Ireland, but it is quite evident that their demeanour was very different

---

1. T. W. Moody, *The Londonderry Plantation*, pp. 191–204, 331–41; H. F. Kearney, *Strafford in Ireland, 1633–41* (Manchester, 1959). See also T. O. Ranger's above-mentioned thesis, 'The career of Richard Boyle'; he agrees with Kearney on what Strafford thought of the New English planters, but shows (pp. 386–401) that Boyle built up a position in southeast Munster which resisted the onslaught of the 1641 rebellion. Boyle's earlier career down to 1614 certainly fits the general description of the grasping New English; see T. O. Ranger, 'Richard Boyle and the making of an Irish fortune', *Irish Historical Studies*, x (1956–7), 256–97.

from the public face which they presented. They were doubtful champions of both the crown and the established church, and some even seem to have succumbed to Gaelic practices which they decried in others.[2] Thus it could with exaggeration be said of them, as it was of the Virginia planters in 1641, that 'they themselves are become exceeding rude, more likely to turne heathen, than to turne others to the Christian faith'.[3]

The early promoters of colonization, both in Ireland and Virginia, expected so little of the common settlers that it was thought necessary to stipulate that the purpose of plantation was 'not to make savages and wild degenerate men of Christians, but Christians of those savage, wild, degenerate men'. The shortfall in expectations was, therefore, due to the officers and planters who placed short-term profit before high ideals, a point which was put most forcefully, in 1717, by Sir Robert Montgomery whose condemnation of the English planters in North America could be applied with equal justification to the New English proprietors in Ireland:

All our noble colonies ... have owed their disappointments to a want of due precaution in the forms of settling, or rather to their settling without any forms at all: the planters grasped at an undue extent of land, exceeding their capacity to manage, or defend: this scattered them to distances unsafe and solitary so that living in a wilderness incapable of mutual aid, the necessary artizans found no encouragement to dwell among them ... for want of towns, and places of defence, they suddenly became a prey to all invaders even the unformidable.[4]

2. Luke Gernon, a member of the council in Munster, displayed such a familiarity with the Gaelic practice of *cóisir*, long denounced by the English, that he himself must have participated in such festivities: 'A discourse of Ireland', in C. L. Falkiner, *Illustrations of Irish History*, pp. 360–2. There is also some evidence that New English proprietors acted as patrons to Gaelic *filí*, or poets.
3. 'A petition of William Castell exhibited to ... parliament, 1641', in Peter Force (ed.), *Tracts and Other Papers*, i. 1.
4. Purchas, *Pilgrimes*, xix. 222; Sir Robert Mountgomery, Bt, 'A discourse concerning the designed establishment of a new colony to the south of Carolina ...' (London, 1717), p. 4.

3

Kingdom and colony:
Ireland in the Westward Enterprise
1536-1660

KARL S. BOTTIGHEIMER

Where does Ireland fit into the story of English expansion? As recently as 1931 it was possible to answer 'nowhere', and to view English expansion as an exclusively transoceanic phenomenon in which, by definition, Ireland could serve only as agent, not object.[1] A long historiographical tradition sharply separated the extension of English power within the British Isles from English (*cum* Scottish, Irish, and Welsh) expansion overseas. This distinction was useful in many ways, and was based upon elementary facts of geography and chronology. But as the nationalist movements of 'the Celtic fringe' have obtruded more forcefully upon the historical perspective, it has become increasingly tempting to view English expansion within and without the British Isles as a single phenomenon. In some ways the pendulum has swung from the view of Ireland as an integral, albeit backward and provincial component of British expansion, to the view of Ireland as one of the earliest lands to feel the thrust of English expansion and conquest.[2]

The reference in the title to Ireland as 'kingdom and colony' is meant to suggest that the truth is hardly so simple as either of those extremes, and that there is a fundamental ambiguity which deserves exploration. The terms 'kingdom' and 'colony' are more emotive than precise. The first suggests, not altogether accurately, home rule. The second raises images of government from afar, exploitation, and subordination to interests nearer the seat of power. At first sight the two may appear

---

1. See A. D. Innes, *The Maritime and Colonial Expansion of England under the Stuarts* (London, 1931), p. 37.

2. A work which exemplifies this approach is Michael Hechter, *Internal Colonialism; The Celtic Fringe in British National Development, 1536–1966* (Berkeley, California, 1975); see also R. R. Davies, 'Colonial Wales', *Past and Present*, lxv (1974), 3–23.

incompatible; but where a monarch rules more than one kingdom, rarely will the inhabitants of each of them feel that they enjoy his favour equally. Existence as a kingdom does not preclude feelings of neglect or subordination, and it is but a short step from such feelings to resentment at colonial relegation, the keener if justified.

Nominally, Ireland was a kingdom of the English monarchy for nearly four hundred years, but unlike England and Scotland where the triumph of monarchy followed hard-won military and political consolidation, the promotion of Ireland to a kingdom in 1541 was little more than an over-zealous declaration of intent. It was a pledge, Brendan Bradshaw has written, 'to the political unification of Ireland under the jurisdiction of the Crown', a commitment into which Henry VIII was enticed by the Irish Council without 'adequate advertence to its implications'.3 However burdensome those implications subsequently became, the monarchy never abandoned them, and in the century and a half which followed, English arms and money were poured into Ireland on an unprecedented scale. By the end of the seventeenth century, the claim to dominion had finally been fulfilled.

Ironically, the hundred and fifty years in which Ireland was being brought into conformity with the concept of what a kingdom of the realm should be, were also the years of most palpable reduction to colonial status. The very means by which the kingdom was fulfilled were the means by which the island's indigenous organs were eradicated and an exogenous élite implanted. A growing body of historical literature is addressed to understanding that process, which was not necessarily the result of simple greed or ambition. The declaration of the kingdom in 1541 was not meant to signal a new English onslaught upon Ireland. Like Poynings' Law, it was intended to bolster those of English origin already there, not replace them.4 But time and time again the procedure of ruling through Dublin, the Pale, and the Anglo-Irish broke down, throwing Ireland into turmoil, and the Anglo-Irish into fury or despair.

Brendan Bradshaw provides a glimpse of this process on the very eve of the 1541 declaration. He shows how the dissolution of the religious orders in Ireland benefited new arrivals to almost the same degree that it

---

3. Brendan Bradshaw, 'The beginnings of modern Ireland', in Brian Farrell (ed.), *The Irish Parliamentary Tradition* (Dublin and New York, 1973), p. 76.

4. D. B. Quinn, 'The early interpretation of Poynings' law', *Irish Historical Studies,* ii (1941), 241–54; R. Dudley Edwards and T. W. Moody, 'The history of Poynings' law 1495–1615', ibid. ii (1941), 415–24. On the terms used to distinguish groups of English settlers, see p. 64.

enriched the Anglo-Irish who had a historic stake in the country. Of a total distribution of property valued at approximately £1,900, New English arrivals, including the lord deputy, received nearly £900.[5] Thus, the traditional ruling class in Ireland had less reason than that in England to believe that it would be the chief beneficiary of the redistribution of the wealth of the monasteries. This impolitic inclusion of the New English temporarily ended with the fall of Thomas Cromwell, and was generally resisted under the subsequent regime of Sir Anthony St Leger as lord deputy. But in the reign of Mary the influx of New English resumed and thereafter became an abiding feature of Tudor–Stuart rule in Ireland.

Some might argue that it matters little whether or not the Palesmen and Anglo-Irish lords succeeded in remaining the instruments of English rule; what matters is the oppression of the Gaelic nation by the English, whether old or new. The weakness in this argument is that it ignores the example of Scotland, Wales, and England itself. The triumph of the monarchy required essentially support from an effective élite. In this period there was nothing unusual in the culture and the language of a people differing from those of their monarch, so long as the kingdom responded to the authority of a ruling élite which, in turn, recognized the Crown. In Ireland, the aristocracy established by the Norman invasion never achieved effective authority over the island as a whole, and thus remained in grave danger of displacement whenever English aspirations expanded.[6] Had it instead succeeded, the eighteenth-century ascendancy would have been Old English rather than New, and the subsequent history of Ireland much more like that of Scotland. The kingdom might have been neglected and mistreated, but it would not have been subjected to the decades of disruption by newer, and hence more 'English' English immigrants. It is also likely that under such circumstances the Old English would have been no more resistant to religious reformation than were their kindred in England.[7] It is right and useful to concentrate on the Old English as the key to the failure of English rule in Ireland.

---

5. B. Bradshaw, *The Dissolution of the Religious Orders in Ireland under Henry VIII* (Cambridge, 1974), appendix 1.

6. This situation is cogently discussed in volumes vi and vii of the Gill History of Ireland: James Lydon, *Ireland in the Later Middle Ages* (Dublin, 1973); Margaret MacCurtain, *Tudor and Stuart Ireland* (Dublin, 1972).

7. Nothing is more notable about the progress of the reformation in Ireland than its failure among the Old English, that segment of the population from whom almost slavish obedience to English example was expected.

English (or more properly, Anglo-Norman) expansion, which occurred within a limited period in most other parts of the British Isles, occurred *repeatedly* in Ireland until, in the second half of the seventeenth century, the process was halted by an élite which refused to be displaced, and which transformed itself into what we know as the Ascendancy. Only when that occurred did Ireland cease to be a frontier capable of attracting and accepting new waves of planters. By the end of the seventeenth century those migrating to Ireland were mainly craftsmen, often Huguenot textile workers, or merchants relocating to serve the needs of prospering planters. A 'frontier' need not be a *terra incognita*, or even the *vacua loca* to which John Locke was ready to direct excess European population. It need be no more than the geographical locus of perceived (or supposed) opportunity. Ireland was such a place for much of the sixteenth and early seventeenth centuries, not because it was sparsely populated or possessed newly discovered treasures, but because in its turmoil lay glittering opportunity.

The root and cause of that turmoil lies outside the scope of this essay. What can be said here in summary is that the late medieval decline of effective English influence in Ireland intersected calamitously with the growing need of the early modern monarchy for strategic support in the western island. Irish support for the Yorkists demonstrated to the Tudors the dangers of an independent Ireland, and the events associated with 'the new monarchies' and the emerging European state system dramatized the importance of keeping England's enemies out of Ireland. With the expulsion of the English from the Continent at the conclusion of the Hundred Years' War, the nation was left with two 'pales': one around Calais and the other in Ireland. The limits of the first had been defined by nearly four hundred years of intermittent but vigorous struggle. But the limits of the second were the result of two centuries of only desultory English effort. The conscious English effort to probe the geographical and political limits of the Irish Pale, to revive its flagging authority, introduced a new and tumultuous era.

Many of the Anglo-Irish welcomed and encouraged the revival of English interest. Traditionally, they benefited from movements which enlarged their opportunities at the expense of their Gaelic neighbours. Despite their alleged 'degeneracy', their tendency to be assimilated into the Gaelic population, a substantial number of Anglo-Irish clung tenaciously to English culture, and insisted upon their primary English identity. In that manner they underlined their suitability to play the role of a ruling class in Ireland, and simultaneously portrayed Gaelic Ireland as barbarous, exotic, and implicitly subversive. A considerable part of 'the English image of Ireland' was thus manufactured in the Pale, and reflected less the ignorant prejudice of metropolitan Englishmen than the calculated snobbery of a struggling élite within Ireland.

The position of the Anglo-Irish was exceedingly hazardous, for it depended upon external forces over which they had very limited control. When the reins of military government fell into the hands of a man like Sir Thomas Radcliffe, Earl of Sussex and lord deputy under Mary, the campaign against the Gaelic Irish could get out of hand and end by undercutting Anglo-Irish interests as well. Nicholas Canny has commented of that episode, 'experience showed . . . [the Palesmen] that any increase in the size of the standing army entailed an extension of the practice of purveyance, and allowed the lord deputy to rely increasingly on London rather than Dublin'.[8] Purveyance was a disagreeable burden, but the real danger was the involvement of English soldiers and officers whom Sussex could reward with confiscated lands in his novel plantation of Leix and Offaly. Indeed, by 1563 the spoils of those two counties had been divided among 88 individuals 'half of whom had connections with the army and 29 of whom were native Irish, thus leaving only 15 Anglo-Irish who benefited'.[9] Expansion of the crusade against the Gaelic Irish carried with it the grave threat of fateful domination by the English ally.

Even when the crusade was cultural, legal, and educational, rather than military, the Anglo-Irish could suffer from their own propaganda. Their exaltation of English culture, and themselves as its propagators, could easily boomerang with the revival of the ancient charges of their degeneracy. And if Englishness was to be defined as a virtue in Ireland, who could be more English than the English-born newcomers? The Palesmen of the early Elizabethan period were misled, or deluded themselves, into believing that they might be found acceptable substitutes, but a dismal succession of denials after 1570 taught them otherwise.

The injection of Englishmen into situations of power and profit, a visible aspect of Thomas Cromwell's manipulation of Irish monastic possessions, and of the Earl of Sussex's plantation of confiscated lands in

8. N. P. Canny, *The Formation of the Old English Elite in Ireland* (O'Donnell Lecture, National University of Ireland, Dublin, 1975), p. 15.

9. D. G. White, 'The Tudor plantations in Ireland before 1571' (unpublished Ph.D. thesis, Trinity College, Dublin, 1968), chap. xii, cited in N. P. Canny, 'Glory and gain: Sir Henry Sidney and the Government of Ireland, 1558–1578' (unpublished Ph.D. thesis, University of Pennsylvania, 1971), p. 46.

Leix and Offaly, was continued under the deputyship of Sir Henry Sidney (episodically, from 1565 to 1578). The Palesmen had great hopes of Sidney before his arrival, but he himself was less struck by their professed Anglophilism than by their incorrigibly Irish ways. Not only did the Palesmen speak Irish ('the most part, with delight'), but they were 'spotted in manners, habit and conditions with Irish stains'.[1] By the mid 1570s Sidney's unshakeable prejudices were clear; but instead of denouncing the Crown, the Palesmen regrouped as 'commonwealth-men', defenders of 'Ireland as a commonwealth separate from that of England but enjoying the same monarch'.[2] They did not include the Gaelic Irish in this polity, but reserved to themselves the right and responsibility of drawing them to civility. They do not seem to have objected to the extension of English influence over Ireland as a whole, or to the presence of an English lord deputy and a large number of English officials. But they insisted upon a guiding role for themselves in the expansionary process, and repeatedly criticized what they took to be the ignorant, maladroit, and frequently excessive methods of interloping Englishmen. Rowland White, a Church of Ireland merchant but a Palesman none the less, urged in 1571 that the Queen's influence over the Gaelic Irish could better be widened 'by an amiable means of favorable reconcilement than by any other force of her power . . .'.[3]

From the 1570s onward, Palesmen began to turn away from aspects of English culture even though they continued to see the need to eliminate the Gaelic traits in their midst. Gradually, for instance, the English universities were forsaken for their counterparts on the Continent.[4] Prior to that watershed a certain number of Palesmen were sympathetic to the protestantizing Church of Ireland, and even demanded greater numbers of learned ministers to preach among the Gaelic population. The children who returned from continental universities looked upon the established Church with a more jaundiced eye. By the 1570s Lord Deputy Sidney was denouncing Palesmen as 'arrant papists', a further indication of the developing polarities.[5] Canny sees the eventual allegiance of the

1. N. P. Canny, *The Formation of the Old English Elite*, p. 20.
2. Ibid., p. 24.
3. Ibid., p. 26, quoting Rowland White, 'Book on the state of Ireland, 1571' (P.R.O., S.P. 63/31/32); I am indebted to Dr Canny for his helpful advice on these matters.
4. See Helga Hammerstein, 'Aspects of the continental education of Irish students in the reign of Queen Elizabeth I', in T. D. Williams (ed.), *Historical Studies VIII* (Dublin, 1971), pp. 137–57; Hammerstein sees the phenomenon as 'an increase in a well established trend' (p. 141), one with dire consequences for the reformation in Ireland.
5. N. P. Canny, *The Formation of the Old English Elite*, p. 29.

Palesmen to counter-reformation catholicism as a consequence of the political treatment to which they were subjected, and not as the cause of that treatment. In that, he is in accord with Bradshaw, who perceives sixteenth-century Irish catholicism as a feeble flower until it was invigorated by the heavy-handedness of English policy in the mid Elizabethan period.

The precise reasons for the eclipse of the Anglo-Irish remain obscure. In terms of land-holding some benefited while others suffered. By 1641 the Anglo-Irish (or 'Old English') held about a third of the profitable land in the southern three provinces, and a negligible amount in Ulster.[6] But the tide was running against them, as their displacement from positions of influence portended well before the close of the sixteenth century. Why, then, were they supplanted in office and in power? Bradshaw sees this mid Elizabethan transformation as an instance of that colonial *deus ex machina* which descends upon the Irish scene with little warning or reason. D. B. Quinn has explored a number of possible explanations of the phenomenon, perhaps most fruitfully the impact upon English statesmen of Spanish New World colonial rule both in theory and in practice.[7] Recently Canny has suggested that changing ideas about the educability of natural man laid the ideological groundwork for the seemingly novel English attitudes and practices in mid and late Elizabethan Ireland.[8] None of these scholars has found religious differences to be sufficiently explanatory, and they have acknowledged both the slowness with which counter-reformation catholicism took root in Ireland, and its relative inconsequence as a popular force until at least the closing years of the sixteenth century.

The removal of the Old English as a buffer had the palpable effect of exacerbating the clash of cultures. The 1570s opened a new age of Anglo-Irish conflict marked by unprecedented cruelty, barbarity, and bitterness. For instance, Sir Humphrey Gilbert made savagery into something approaching official policy in his Irish adventures. Thomas Churchyard, the chronicler of his campaigns, reported that on one occasion Gilbert arranged his encampment 'so that none could come into his tent for any

6. Aidan Clarke, *The Old English in Ireland, 1625–42* (London, 1966), appendix i, pp. 235–7.

7. D. B. Quinn, 'Ireland and sixteenth-century expansion', in T. D. Williams (ed.), *Historical Studies I* (London, 1958), pp. 20–32; ' "A discourse of Ireland" (*circa* 1599): a sidelight on English colonial policy', *Proceedings of the Royal Irish Academy*, xlvii, section C, no. 3 (1942), 151–66.

8. N. P. Canny, *The Formation of the Old English Elite*, pp. 17–19.

cause but commonly he must pass through a lane of heads [of slain Irish], which he used *ad terrorem*.[9] Canny contends that 'the Norman lords were not known to have committed such atrocities in Ireland, and there is no evidence that systematic execution of non-combatants by martial law was practised in any of the Tudor rebellions in England'.[1] If that is so—and the medievalists are perhaps yet to be heard—it is not difficult to accept the corollary that Elizabethan officers in the closing decades of the century 'believed that in dealing with the native Irish population they were absolved from all normal ethical restraints'.[2]

The history of Ireland in the sixteenth and seventeenth centuries is not merely a dismal continuation of the Middle Ages. There are at least three novel elements: cultural conflict of unprecedented bitterness; religious cleavage; and a palpable hardening of English administrative policy. Students of the period are inevitably drawn to the relationships between these elements in an effort to discover which, if any one, is ultimately causal. Brendan Bradshaw, for instance, would seem to be arguing that an inexplicable (and thus, primary) English policy of colonial advance in large part explains the success of the counter-reformation in Ireland. Nicholas Canny, in contrast, emphasizes cultural differences as the primary cause of this colonial advance, and implicitly, therefore, considers them a contributing cause to religious division. In such a view Ireland becomes a logical precursor to, and prototype for, the English subjugation of the Indian population of the American colonies. Numerous earlier historians have blamed Irish catholicism (or conversely, English protestantism) for the generations of hostility, as if the religious character of the two islands was, and had always been, the ultimate source of all conflicts.

The truth of the matter is not easily ascertained. If one examines Irish religious intransigence, for instance, it is necessary to ask at what point, and by what process, predilection for the old faith passed beyond what A. G. Dickens has called 'survivalism', in order to attain the inflexible, militant form which aroused the fear and detestation of generations of protestant Englishmen and Scots. In the light of recent regional studies of the progress or lack of progress of the reformation in England, it is no longer possible to view religious conservatism in Ireland as either peculiar

9. N. P. Canny, 'The ideology of English colonization: from Ireland to America', *William and Mary Quarterly*, 3rd series, xxx (1973), 581, quoting Thomas Churchyard, *A General Rehearsal of Wars* (London, 1579).
  1. N. P. Canny, 'The ideology of English colonization', p. 583.
  2. Ibid.

or shocking.[3] There may have been a more developed reform tradition in England than in Ireland in the early sixteenth century, but G. R. Elton has demonstrated that the reformation was painstakingly, even ingeniously, imposed upon English society, rather than enthusiastically clasped to its bosom.[4] It may not be far-fetched, therefore, to see the failure of the reformation in Ireland as merely a special case of the difficulties which it encountered in numerous parts of England.

The denunciation of early Irish recalcitrance has sometimes been given undue importance. An ardent reformer like John Bale (briefly Bishop of Ossory under Edward VI) could detect Rome on all sides in the Ireland of 1552, but his inflamed rhetoric provides little real clue as to the depth or width of the chasm opening between an England preponderantly protestant and an Ireland preponderantly catholic.[5] For Canny the religious factor becomes of critical importance only after the excommunication of Elizabeth, when it is reflected particularly in the actions and writings of Sidney as lord deputy from 1575 to 1578.[6] Although religious grievances were prominent in Fitzmaurice's rebellion of 1569, Canny follows F. M. Jones in discounting them as desperate efforts to incite a population for whom the uprising had little political or secular appeal.[7] By 1581 *The Image of Ireland* could include the popish religion as one of the many repellent and primitive customs of the island. 'The friars . . .', it observed, 'are the chiefest instruments of Irish disturbance.'[8] Even that was tame stuff compared to Barnaby Rich's observations of 1610:

It is popery that hath drawn the people from that confidence and trust that they should have in God, to believe in saints, to worship idols, and to fly from God's mercy to other mens merits, and to set up a pope-holy righteousness of their own works. It is popery that hath alienated the hearts of that people from that faith, fidelity, obedience, love, and loyalty that is required in subjects towards their sovereigns. It is popery that hath cost the lives of

3. See, for instance, A. G. Dickens, 'The extent and character of recusancy in Yorkshire, 1604', *Yorkshire Archaeological Journal*, xxxvii (1948–51), 24–48; other useful and recent studies of this subject include: K. R. Wark, *Elizabethan Recusancy in Cheshire*, Chetham Society, 3rd series, vol. xxix (Manchester, 1971); and Roger B. Manning, *Religion and Society in Elizabethan Sussex* (Leicester, 1969).

4. Of his many contributions see, in particular, G. R. Elton, *Policy and Police* (Cambridge, 1972).

5. 'The vocation of John Bale to the bishopric of Ossory in Ireland', *Harleian Miscellany*, vi (1745), 437–65.

6. N. P. Canny, 'Glory and gain', p. 294.

7. Ibid., p. 242; Frederick M. Jones, 'The counter-reformation', in Patrick J. Corish (ed.), *A History of Irish Catholicism*, iii (Dublin, 1967), 14.

8. Ascribed to John Derricke, Edinburgh edition (1883), p. 59.

multitudes, that hath ruined that whole realm and made it subject to the oppression of thieves, robbers, spoilers, murderers, rebels and traitors.[9]

But even 1610 may be too early a point at which to conclude that the die was cast in religious matters. We are not dealing with a steady, linear development, but rather with an erratic drift in which there were many perturbations, and which only eventually came to be regarded as permanent and irreversible. Even in the bitterest and most palpable phase of Elizabethan hostility to Rome, the 1590s, Pope Clement VIII refused to excommunicate 'that section of Anglo-Irish catholics who assisted Elizabeth during the war'.[1] However widespread and vigorous English dislike of Irish catholicism became, that revulsion never enjoyed the unambiguous support of any English ruler save Oliver Cromwell; and it encountered stiff, though sporadic, resistance from the first four Stuarts.

When we search for a turning point in the early modern religious history of Ireland, we find instead a sequence of swinging movements which gradually and almost unintentionally produce cleavage. The pace of change is much slower than the polemical statements of the sixteenth- and seventeenth-century disputants might make us suppose. H. F. Kearney reminds us, for instance, that it was only after 1618 that the Roman hierarchy began to be resident in Ireland, and only after 1624 that the dominance of the conservative Old English on the episcopal bench was diminished by appointments of pro-Spanish prelates from Ulster.[2] The feeble—though not always negligible—progress of the established protestant church in Ireland is easier to document than the enlistment of the mass of the Irish people into the ranks of the counter-reformation.[3]

It is hard, therefore, to argue that in Ireland religion explains all, when in reality it appears to be but one component of a complex picture. It is unlikely that at any precise point Irish catholicism became the express justification for English colonial activity. Even the displacement of Old English from positions of authority was accelerated, rather than initiated, by mistrust of their religion. But at the same time one must see changes in English policies towards Ireland as subtly, sometimes palpably, affected

9. Barnaby Rich, *A New Description of Ireland* (London, 1610), p. 90.

1. Frederick M. Jones, 'The counter-reformation', p. 48.

2. H. F. Kearney, 'Ecclesiastical politics and the counter-reformation in Ireland, 1618–48', *Journal of Ecclesiastical History*, xi (1960), 202–12.

3. The work of Emmet Larkin reveals how much of this 'enlistment' remained to be done in the nineteenth century; see, in particular, 'The devotional revolution in Ireland, 1850–75', *American Historical Review*, lxxvii (1975), 1244–76.

by the opening religious gulf. The religious difference reinforced at every point older conflicts of a political or cultural nature, and it must surely help to account for the rising incidence of massacres and atrocities in the warfare of the period.

Aidan Clarke expressed the complexity of the picture when he wrote that 'the lines of division in early Stuart Ireland were less clear and less rigid than an unqualified emphasis upon political and religious alignments might indicate. Men of sufficient property and station were within the pale of the gentry [despite their religion or culture].'[4] Specific evidence of this is the way 'the parliamentary opposition movement, in which catholics and protestants combined for more than a year, closed the ranks of the gentry against the common enemy, Thomas Wentworth, Earl of Strafford' in 1640–1.[5] The history of the confederates of Kilkenny, and of the restoration of Charles II, reveals the almost irrepressible tendency of the Old English to profess loyalty to the English monarchy and seek for avenues of accommodation in religious matters. It was a tendency which lingered for centuries, despite the treaty of Limerick and the penal laws.

The picture of Ireland as merely an eastern extension of the New World, with the Gaelic Irish cast as the local Red Indians, is accurate only up to a point. Fynes Moryson might refer to Ireland in 1617 as 'this famous island in the Virginian Sea',[6] but the island could never escape its legacy as a kingdom of the realm, or its long history of prior connections with England (and Scotland) and the English monarchy. In the reign of James I Ireland and America were linked in colonial propaganda as fertile areas for investment and adventure; but the proximity of Ireland to England was more than balanced by the ambiguity of its frontier, the cloudy and changeable status of its natives, and the numerous impediments created by generations of prior claimants to the land. Great colonial fortunes were amassed in sixteenth- and seventeenth-century Ireland, but the opportunities were recondite, fickle, and ephemeral. The careers of Richard Boyle, first Earl of Cork, and Sir John Clotworthy, first Viscount Massereene, illustrate the usefulness of guile, office, and place, in building an Irish estate.[7] Though many other examples could be found, Ireland must

---

4. A. Clarke, 'Ireland and the general crisis', *Past and Present*, xlviii (1970), 90.
5. Ibid.
6. Fynes Moryson, *An Itinerary* (1617, reprinted Glasgow, 1907–8), vol. iv, p. 185, as cited in D. B. Quinn, *The Elizabethans and the Irish* (Ithaca, New York, 1966), p. 122.
7. For Boyle see T. O. Ranger, 'Richard Boyle and the making of an Irish fortune', *Irish Historical Studies*, x (1957), 257–97; and 'The career of Richard Boyle, first Earl of Cork in Ireland, 1588–1643' (Oxford D.Phil. thesis, 1958). No adequate study of Clotworthy has been published.

have undone more men of 'the middling sort' than it raised to great wealth. As with so many sedulously promoted colonial ventures, for most of the participants the reality fell far short of the dream.

D. B. Quinn has stressed the importance of the English migrations to Munster and Ulster as 'amongst the largest population movements of their time'.[8] But the most notable, numerous, and enduring migration of early modern Irish history was clearly that of the Scots to Ulster. It began in the sixteenth century and at first lacked any religious justification, for the principal participants were catholics from the western isles. Perceval-Maxwell has recently provided an exhaustive account of the Jacobean phase of the Scottish movement.[9] The picture which emerges might well be called 'overflow' and notably lacks the studied and premeditated character of the Elizabethan enterprises of Thomas Smith or the first Earl of Essex. By 1630 the two Ulster counties nearest to Scotland, Down and Antrim contained 'more Scottish families than all six of the escheated [and officially planted] counties combined'.[1] This comparison leads Perceval-Maxwell to the conclusion that 'there would have been a natural flow of population from Scotland to Ireland even in the absence of any official planned migration'.[2] In both of the eastern counties 'the names of the chief landowners predominated among the tenants', suggesting not so much a new frontier for Scotland as a kind of re-settlement *en bloc*.[3] Although we find knots and clusters of related West Country Englishmen in Munster, there seems to be nothing in the English migrations as cohesive as the veritably tribal Scottish movement into Ulster.

The examination of the origins of Scottish settlers in Ulster reveals that 'the 14,000 or so adult Scots who populated Ulster during the Jacobean plantation came largely from the eight counties which lay either along the borders with England, or up the west coast to Argyllshire'.[4] By and large, 'immigrants with names associated with a specific district of Scotland very often settled near to one another'.[5] Although the nearer

8. D. B. Quinn, 'The Munster plantation: problems and opportunities', *Journal of the Cork Historical and Archaeological Society*, lxxi (1966), 19.

9. M. Perceval-Maxwell, *The Scottish Migration to Ulster in the Reign of James I* (London, 1973); Robert Hunter is working on a parallel study of the English settlement in Ulster, 1608–41, to complement T. W. Moody's now classic monograph, *The Londonderry Plantation, 1609–41* (Belfast, 1939).

1. M. Perceval-Maxwell, *The Scottish Migration to Ulster*, p. 251.

2. Ibid., p. 310.

3. Ibid., p. 288.

4. Ibid., p. 289.

5. Ibid., p. 286.

counties of Antrim and Down attracted the largest number of Scottish settlers, the more remote escheated county of Fermanagh had a distinct appeal for immigrants seeking to put as much distance as possible between themselves and the organs of Scottish justice.[6]

The growth of the Scottish colony in Ulster after 1630 is not well documented. Wentworth asserted that there were 100,000 'of the Scottish nation' in Ireland in 1639, but Perceval-Maxwell regards that figure as inflated, and questions whether the total colony was half that size a few years earlier, in 1630.[7] Equally unclear is whether Scottish movement to Ireland was a stimulus to transatlantic Scottish removal, or whether, quite the converse, 'Ulster tended to siphon off Scottish men and energy'.[8] The Ulster Scots were to play an active and important role in the North American colonies, particularly in Pennsylvania and the Piedmont; but their real impact would not be felt until the mid eighteenth century, a century and a half after their initial departure from Scotland.[9]

The Scottish migration to Ulster stands as a corrective to the view of Ireland as purely colonial, that is, as taken over *de novo* by a self-consciously separate and superior culture. Admittedly, massive confiscation of the six escheated counties of Ulster in 1609 facilitated Scottish settlement beyond Down and Antrim, the two counties so effectively colonized without benefit of official confiscation or plantation. It must also be conceded that many of the Scottish immigrants in the seventeenth-century phase were zealous Calvinists with no great love for popery, but those facts seem secondary to the basically internal and domestic nature of the Scottish encroachment. It was a 'natural' migration in the sense that populations had been spilling back and forth across the north channel since the Celts first inhabited the British Isles. It was 'internal' in the sense that 'James [VI & I] had established in one of the most vulnerable points in his three kingdoms a body of men who could quickly be turned into a formidable fighting force'.[1] It was a case of the 'excess' population of one kingdom being used by the monarchy to secure the doubtful loyalty of another.

6. Ibid., p. 287.

7. Ibid., p. 314, citing Westworth to Sir H. Vane, 30 May 1639, *H.M.C. Cowper*, vol. ii, pp. 229–30.

8. Ibid., p. 312; Perceval-Maxwell discusses both sides of this case but comes to no clear conclusion.

9. See R. J. Dickson, *Ulster Emigration to Colonial America, 1718–75* (London, 1966); and Maldwyn A. Jones, 'Ulster emigration, 1783–1815', in E. R. R. Green (ed.), *Essays in Scotch-Irish History* (London, 1969), pp. 46–68.

1. Perceval-Maxwell, *The Scottish Migration to Ulster*, p. 311.

Religion might, in a passive way, have helped to justify the Scots in their possession and enjoyment of what had been the land of Irishmen, but there is little evidence of their migration being intended as a religious crusade. On the contrary, there was considerable religious division among the Jacobean Scots in Ulster. According to Perceval-Maxwell:

Most of the immigrants were probably nominally protestant. Initially, certainly they do not seem to have possessed strong religious convictions. There is no evidence to show that in James's reign religion became a significant motive for leaving Scotland. Once the settlers had arrived in Ulster, what counted most in determining the religious complexion of the province was the nature of the leadership provided. In Donegal this leadership came from a bishop [Andrew Knox of Raphoe]; in the east, it was Robert Blair who provided it; in Strabane it was a Roman Catholic layman [Sir George Hamilton of Greenlaw] who seized the initiative. All these leaders, of whatever belief, promoted their ideas with vigour, thus introducing an element of division among the settlers which otherwise would not have been present.[2]

Did religious division give rise to 'colonialism'? Or did 'colonialism' give rise to religious division? There seems no satisfactory answer except that the processes became intertwined, constantly reinforcing each other. Although the Scottish incursion fell most heavily upon the Gaelic Irish of the north, it was not utterly without impact upon the Old English. Perceval-Maxwell brings to light an incident of 1611 in which a newly immigrated 'Scot and his wife who had gone to settle in Down' complained to the judges of assize that they 'had been beaten and stripped of all valuables by a band of Irishmen led by Rowland Savage, a descendant of the Norman settlement'.[3] Savage seems to have survived this accusation, for an inquisition of 1620 indicated that five Scottish settlers had leased land from him between 1611 and 1616.[4] Even when they did not take their land, the Scots were yet another affront to the Old English and another threat to their former hegemony in the island.

The barbarism and popery of the Gaelic Irish has in some ways served as a canard in Irish history, distracting attention from the more critical displacement of the Old English as a ruling class. Of course, the Old English publicized the canard in the first place to justify their short-

---

2. Ibid., p. 273.
3. Ibid., p. 153, citing *Register of the Privy Council of Scotland, 1610–1613*, pp. 597–8.
4. Ibid., p. 250, citing *Inquisitionum in officio rotulorum cancellariae Hiberniae asservatarum repertorium Ultonia*, Down, Jac. I, 9; and B.L., Add. MSS. 4770, ff. 204–14, 264–9.

comings as governors of Ireland, but barbarism and popery came to be used indiscriminately to characterize everything that was not protestant and New English. Clarke has sought to remind us, for instance, that the infamous conspirators accused of plotting the 1641 rebellion were not rude and shaggy Celts but 'socially and politically acceptable members of the propertied class', with numerous Old English connections.[5] The protestant propaganda of the time made almost no distinction and virtually assumed the complicity of 'the catholics of the Pale' [i.e., the Old English] in advance of its reality.

The injection of Scots into Ireland, like the injection of English, had inescapable colonial effects on that island. The Stuarts were the first English monarchs to have the three kingdoms of England, Scotland, and Ireland even nominally under their dominion. Their attempts to use them in concert were little short of disastrous, as the downfall of Strafford illustrated. Much of what seems 'colonial' in the sixteenth and seventeenth centuries is the result of the heavy-handed manipulation of the kingdoms in concert, so as to redress the deficiencies of one with the excesses of another. This could take a purely military form, in which case the impact of foreign soldiers, however disagreeable, was temporary. It could also take the form of foreign governors or officials, almost always English, and that was likely to be a more enduring intrusion. Most disruptive and least ephemeral was the arrival of planters, settlers, and other would-be permanent immigrants from another kingdom and culture. When employed, this last measure quite naturally adopted the rhetoric of overseas exploration and settlement and applied it to the intransigent Irish who were to be displaced.[6] True, some of that rhetoric was derived from early unfavourable accounts of Gaelic customs; but a distinction seems to have been retained between the barbarous state of affairs in the Irish hinterland and the much more remote and exotic barbarism of the New World. We know that Ireland became a refuge for a number of Englishmen disillusioned with conditions in the Americas but there is little evidence of Englishmen disillusioned with Ireland fleeing west across the Atlantic. They went to England instead.

The historiography of the British Isles has, understandably, been dominated by England, the preponderant constituent. The monarchy has often been treated as if it were not only originally, but also essentially,

5. Aidan Clarke, 'Ireland and the general crisis', p. 89.
6. See Margaret T. Hodgen, *Early Anthropology in the 16th and 17th Centuries* (Philadelphia, 1964).

English. Though true in large measure, this pervasive conception has sometimes obscured the respects in which the monarchy grew to be composite and polyglot. Certainly in the rest of early modern Europe the monarchy of many parts was the rule rather than the exception, and H. L. Koenigsberger has recently reminded us of the dynamics of such structures.

All the great monarchies of early modern Europe, with the arguable exception of France, were composite states, usually made up of one metropolitan and several peripheral kingdoms or principalities, with different laws, traditions, and often different languages ... Time and again, it was the attempt to extend royal power in an outlying kingdom which led first to rebellion and then to revolution or civil war; for it was precisely in these kingdoms that people were most touchy about any infringement, real or imagined, of their laws, traditions, or institutions and most willing to defend them against 'foreigners'.[7]

Koenigsberger is prepared to make an exception for Ireland and allow it 'colonial status', but it may be an unnecessary concession, courteously proffered to a tradition with which he would rather not tangle. Clearly his model makes more sense for Catalonia than for Ireland, but it should not be rejected out of hand. It describes an important aspect of the Anglo-Irish relationship which is vital to its intelligibility, and without which no picture of Ireland as 'Virginia writ nearby' can possibly be complete. Though seeming sometimes incompatible, the concept of colony and 'peripheral kingdom' are reconciled, in effect, by Hechter's thesis of 'internal colonialism'.[8] This is a provocative, sometimes pretentious, hypothesis which contends that colonialism begins at home, and that relationships which later characterized European rule in much of the overseas world were but extensions and adaptations of habits and institutions already well-established on European soil. It accords with the work of Charles Verlinden, a scholar who has laboured to reveal the Old World roots of what were once regarded as New World institutions, such as slavery or plantation sugar culture.[9]

Some, no doubt, will see the question of 'kingdom or colony' as frivolously taxonomic. Against that doubt may be urged the utility of breaking down the customary distinction between events 'at home' and those 'abroad'. The link between Ireland and America is not merely that

7. Review article in *Journal of Modern History*, xlvi (1974), 104.
8. Hechter, *Internal Colonialism*, p. 30.
9. Charles Verlinden, *The Beginnings of Modern Colonization* (Ithaca, New York, 1970).

dramatic events happened in each in the same period, nor is it limited to the fact that both were visited and settled by some of the same Elizabethan and Jacobean entrepreneurs, with the corollary that the English view of the 'wild Irish' resembled to some extent the English view of the American Indian. What Ireland and America shared was a vulnerability to conquest, though this occurred for different and unrelated causes. America was remote and unfamiliar. No loyalties were due to its natives. Ireland, by contrast, was cluttered with the remains of previous, uncompleted conquests. Its vulnerability was the result of the failure of any earlier invader, élite, or culture to gain and hold the whole island, either for or against the English monarchy. The displacement of the Old English created a power vacuum. The ambiguous result was that Ireland became simultaneously 'an island in the Virginian sea', that is, part of the colonizable periphery of the British Isles, while it remained a piece of the ancient main.

In the 1630s the flow of English emigrants to North America began to exceed that to Ireland, but it was the events of the 1640s and 1650s which effectively closed Ireland as a frontier rivalling the New World. Ireland did not simply 'fill-up'. It was not a matter of English and Scots settlers pouring into the island until there was no more room for them, whereupon they crossed the Atlantic. What ended opportunity in Ireland was the occurrence of an exception to the rule that each wave of immigrants displaced the one that had preceded it. The Cromwellians were that exception. Although they reduced Ireland to the most submissive state it had ever known, they failed (in part for lack of trying) to break the power of the Elizabethan and Jacobean planters. The soldiers of the Commonwealth and Protectorate succeeded in securing the protestant interest, but it was largely the interest of their predecessors which they served, and not their own plantation.

The Cromwellian conquest was aimed so narrowly against the catholic Irish (whether Old English or Gaelic) that it became in some respect the tool of protestants already established in Ireland. This was largely because the military triumph was not followed by a successful plantation. By the 1650s Englishmen were immensely reluctant to emigrate to Ireland unless there was specific and extraordinary inducement. The army of 30,000 which had carried out the reduction of the island was intended to be the chief source of colonists for the new protestant plantation there. Not more than a quarter of it appears to have remained. The hope for a protestant yeomanry was dashed. Permanent settlers came largely from

among the officers, most of whom were regarded for decades as par-
venus: eventually by marriage with older protestant families and sedulous
accumulation of estates, certain of them (for example, the Bowens and
Packenhams) joined the ranks of the ascendancy.[1] The adventurers for
Irish land were the civilian component of the Cromwellian plantation,
but they never numbered more than 1,500, and their reluctance to settle
the lands they had been awarded is well documented. By the mid 1660s
only some 500 had been confirmed in their estates and the number who
had crossed to Ireland before the Restoration must have been even
smaller. Adventurers' and soldiers' claims to Irish land became a commodity in which to speculate, rather than the hoped-for mechanism to
re-people the wasted land. The protestant land-holders who cut a figure
at the Restoration were not necessarily 'royalists', like Ormonde, but
they were almost exclusively 'old protestants', like Orrery, Coote,
Massereene, or Annesley, who had arrived before Cromwell, if only
narrowly.[2]

Of course, it was partly the Restoration itself which clipped the wings
of the Cromwellian settlement and renewed the fortunes of the old
protestants. But in fact the Cromwellians were all but ousted by the
old protestants in the later 1650s. The role of Henry Cromwell in Ireland
is the crucial factor, and working independently T. C. Barnard and I have
come to similar conclusions. In 1971 I wrote:

The significance of Henry Cromwell's regime is that it restrained and
delimited the nascent 'new interest'. It revived and restored to power the
'ancient protestants' who might otherwise have disappeared beneath the
tide of soldiery. In this way it laid the crucial foundations for the restoration
of Charles II which could thereafter be built upon the backs, as it were, of a
protestant Irish population which was arguably less guilty, in English
royalist terms, than either the Catholic Irish or Cromwellian protestants.[3]

Barnard in 1973 summed it up thus: 'A protestant ascendancy was
established in the 1650s; its core was not the adventurers or Cromwellian
soldiery, but the protestant settlers already in Ireland before 1649, the

1. For Colonel John Bowen see Elizabeth Bowen, *Bowen's Court* (London, 1942); for
photocopies of family manuscripts concerning Captain Henry Packenham I am indebted to
Lady Antonia Fraser and Thomas Pakenham.
    2. Karl S. Bottigheimer, *English Money and Irish Land; The 'Adventurers' in the Cromwellian
Settlement of Ireland* (Oxford, 1971).
    3. K. S. Bottigheimer, 'The restoration land settlement in Ireland: a structural view',
Irish Historical Studies, xviii (1972), 6.

"Old Protestants".'[4] Barnard's recent monograph on the government of Cromwellian Ireland fills out the argument with a mass of illustrative and corroborative detail.[5]

The Royalist versus Roundhead interpretation of seventeenth-century Irish history, an interpretation first aired at the time of the Restoration and later canonized by Thomas Carte in his mid eighteenth-century biography of the Duke of Ormonde, has now outlived most of its usefulness.[6] Instead, we are able to see that there was a subtle amalgamation of various conservative (i.e., landed) interests in the Ireland of Henry Cromwell, and that this grouping was incorporated at the restoration of Charles II. The New English were in future *not* crucially divided amongst themselves, instead they coalesced in opposition to catholic Ireland. By 1660 all but a small fraction of the profitable land belonging to catholics had been yielded up to protestant claimants.[7] Only if land could be wrested from protestants would there be a supply sufficient to make any large number of new Irish fortunes. At the Restoration many royalists hoped for precisely this outcome. If the Cromwellians could be denounced, condemned, and pried loose, their newly acquired lands might be reshuffled to compensate various royalists (some English, some Irish, some protestant, some catholic) for their losses. But the Cromwellian–Old Protestant alliance, tacitly maintained, dashed most of those hopes. Without royal favour, or without some extraordinary *entrée*, the prospects for cheap acquisition of Irish land diminished rapidly after 1660. Ireland did not cease to be a 'colony', as more than two centuries of subsequent commercial and constitutional conflict with England proved.[8] But with the closing of protestant ranks, it *did* cease to be a 'frontier'. A ruling class had been created, riddled with cultural, religious, and economic differences, but united against catholicism and Gaelic tradition. Five centuries after Strongbow, Ireland had finally been conquered. The full power of Britain had at last been brought to bear. The ascendancy to which it gave birth in Ireland no longer lacked the capacity to rule; only the freedom.

4. T. C. Barnard, 'Planters and policies in Cromwellian Ireland', *Past and Present*, lxi (1973), 33.

5. T. C. Barnard, *Cromwellian Ireland: English Government and Reform in Ireland, 1649–60* (Oxford, 1975).

6. Thomas Carte, *Life of James, 1st Duke of Ormonde* (Oxford, 1851).

7. J. G. Simms, *The Williamite Confiscations in Ireland* (London, 1956).

8. See Francis Godwin James, *Ireland in the Empire, 1688–1770* (Cambridge, Mass., 1973).

A NOTE ON NOMENCLATURE

Following Dr Canny I have used the term 'Anglo-Irish' to describe Norman, Anglo-Norman, and English settlers in Ireland (and their descendants) prior to the sixteenth century. Following Dr Clarke I have used the term 'Old English' for what is essentially the same population from roughly the Elizabethan period onwards, that is, from the time at which they must begin to be distinguished from the 'New English', the essentially protestant participants in the Elizabethan and subsequent plantations. A fourth term, 'Old Protestants', given currency by Dr Barnard, is useful to distinguish protestants who settled in Ireland prior to the Cromwellian campaign of 1649–50, from those who came during and after it. Finally, the term 'British Isles' is used without prejudice to mean Britain, Ireland, and the smaller islands which surround them.

4

Native reaction to
the Westward Enterprise:
a case-study in Gaelic ideology

BRENDAN BRADSHAW S.M.

Not the least contribution of D. B. Quinn to the historiography of sixteenth-century Ireland has been to pioneer the investigation of the intellectual history of conquest and colonization.[1] His lead was followed by Nicholas Canny in two important studies, one of which analysed the ideology of the new English colonists and the other the intellectual response of the old Anglo-Irish community to events which were as catalytic for them as for the indigenous Gaelic Irish.[2] The effect on the mentality of these last has received less attention.[3] What follows is intended as a contribution towards repairing the neglect.[4]

Lack of scholarly endeavour in the investigation of the political mentality of sixteenth-century Gaelic Ireland may be connected with discouragement about sources. The attitudes of the new English colonists and of the medieval Anglo-Irish settlers are reflected in a substantial body of surviving letters, speeches, and political tracts. Very little of this kind of material is available for the Gaelic Irish before the seventeenth century.

---

1. D. B. Quinn, 'Sir Thomas Smith (1513–77) and the beginnings of English colonial theory', *American Philosophical Society Proceedings*, lxxxix (1945), 543–60; idem, 'The Munster plantation: problems and opportunities', *Journal of the Cork Historical and Archaeological Society*, lxxi (1966), 19–40; idem, 'Ireland and sixteenth-century European expansion', *Historical Studies*, i (1958), 20–32; idem, *The Elizabethans and the Irish* (Ithaca, N.Y., 1966), *passim*.

2. N. P. Canny, 'The ideology of English colonization; from Ireland to America', *William and Mary Quarterly*, 3rd series, xxx (1973), 573–98; idem, *The Formation of the Old English Elite in Ireland* (O'Donnell Lecture, Dublin, 1975).

3. The subject was opened up, though necessarily in cursory fashion, in a comprehensive review of the changing cultural climate in Ireland in the sixteenth century by R. D. Edwards, 'Ireland, Elizabeth and the Counter-Reformation', in S. T. Bindoff *et al.* (eds), *Elizabethan Government and Society* (London, 1961), pp. 315–39.

4. A contribution is also made, though from the standpoint of the Celtic scholar rather than the historian, in J. Carney, *The Irish Bardic Poet* (Dublin, 1967).

Where, then, can the historian seek for a reflection of their outlook in the preceding century? In a lecture delivered to the British Academy in 1963, the distinguished Celtic scholar, Brian Ó Cuív, discussed the historical value of the considerable body of bardic poetry that survives from the late medieval period, including the sixteenth century.[5] The genre was highly political and historical in its orientation, since one of its major functions was to buttress the status of the dynastic kindreds of Gaelic society. While Ó Cuív stressed the need for caution in the use of bardic poetry as a source of hard factual information, Celtic scholars, including Ó Cuív himself, have always accepted it as a mirror of the outlook of the bards and of their patrons. In the same way as Celtic scholars have used bardic poetry to analyse social and, to some extent, political attitudes within Gaelic society, it is here proposed to examine the outward-looking ideological content of bardic poetry. Thus, it is proposed to approach the question of the ideological response of Gaelic Ireland to the initial phase of English conquest and colonization by analysing the only substantial body of contemporary documentary evidence available from inside Gaelic society: sixteenth-century bardic poetry.

Attention must here be drawn to the fact already indicated in the title that this essay offers a case-study, not an analysis of the whole range of bardic poetry throughout the phase of conquest and colonization. A general analysis would be well beyond the scope of a single essay. The conclusions that can be drawn from this study will, therefore, be limited. That is not to say that they will be without general significance. For instance, if it can be shown in this particular case, as I think it can, that a new self-conscious nationalism is articulated in the poetry, then this will be sufficient to explode the hypothesis that the Gaelic polity in the sixteenth century could not, or at least did not, generate a nationalist ideology. However, the extent to which such an ideology permeated the Gaelic community, and its impact on practical politics, are questions to which this study can only hope to provide the beginnings of an answer.

The happy coincidence of political interest and convenience of research indicated the choice of suitable material for investigation. The *duanairí* (poem books) of the O'Byrne sept of Colranell in County Wicklow were

5. Brian Ó Cuív, 'Literary creation and Irish historical tradition', *Proceedings of the British Academy*, xlix (1963), 233–62; for studies of the Irish bardic poet, see Osborn Bergin, *Irish Bardic Poetry*, ed. D. Greene and F. Kelly (Dublin, 1960); Carney, *The Irish Bardic Poet*; D. Greene, 'The professional poets' and B. Ó Cuív, 'An era of upheaval', in *Seven Centuries of Irish Learning* (Cork, 1971), pp. 38–50; E. Carwyn Williams, *The Court Poet in Mediaeval Ireland* (London, 1971).

edited and published in 1942 under the title of *Leabhar Branach* ('The Book of the O'Byrnes'). The poems span a period of some eighty years beginning in the middle of the sixteenth century.[6] Thus the bardic poetry relating to one of the most belligerent of the Leinster septs in the late sixteenth century can be studied on the basis of a definitive, printed text. This does not eliminate the headache of uncoiling the convoluted and highly stylized language of the verse, but it undoubtedly ameliorates the pain.

Before examining the verse, the historical context in which it was produced must be briefly sketched. The collection begins precisely at the stage when Tudor conciliation in Ireland—the policy that marked the closing years of the reign of Henry VIII—gave way to Tudor conquest. Although the inauguration of the classical strategy of conquest and colonization is to be associated with the administrations of Sir Henry Sidney during the years 1565–78, an aggressive militarist policy was in operation before then, having been initiated by Sir Edward Bellingham in 1549–50, and revived and developed by the Earl of Sussex. The collection closes in the period of the *pacata Hibernica*, when resistance to the Crown had collapsed and James I was applying himself to the task of securing the dearly won conquest.[7] The *Leabhar Branach*, therefore, spans one of the great cataclysms in Irish history. This was the period that gave birth to two issues that were to fuel the politics of dissent in Ireland up to and into the nineteenth century: land and religion. Though scholarship has yet to determine more precisely when and why religious attitudes in Ireland hardened against the English reformation, the catholic cause was invoked as early as the rebellion of the Fitzgeralds of Kildare in 1534. Very soon the Crown's policy of land confiscation and recolonization provided another source of alienation, beginning with Leix–Offaly in east Leinster in the 1550s. The attempted reformation of religion and society was accompanied by military conquest, which provoked violent rebellion within the indigenous communities, Gaelic and Anglo-Irish alike. Late sixteenth-century Ireland was notable for the incidence of major movements of disaffection—those of the O'Connors and the O'Mores in the

6. Seán Mac Airt (ed.), *Leabhar Branach* (Dublin, 1944); another case-study for this period, though more general and literary in its interests, has been made in relation to the poetry composed by Eochaidh Ó hEoghusa for the Maguires of Fermanagh, see Carney, *The Irish Bardic Poet*.

7. The best general survey of Crown policy in Ireland in the sixteenth century is now provided by G. A. Hayes-McCoy in T. W. Moody *et al.* (eds), *A New History of Ireland*, iii (Oxford, 1976), 39–141; see also N. P. Canny, *The Elizabethan Conquest of Ireland* (Sussex and N.Y., 1976).

1550s, of Shane O'Neill in the 1560s, of the Desmond Fitzgeralds in the 1580s, and the widespread upheavals known as the Nine Years War in the 1590s—these interspersed with outbreaks of a less momentous though by no means unsubstantial nature.

Such was the general political background against which the O'Byrnes of Colranell emerged into prominence for one turbulent half-century, from 1550 to 1600. In the 1540s they flit into government correspondence as the junior branch of a sept of the second rank accorded rather more than normal attention by the Crown because of their strategic location in the Wicklow hills, south of Dublin, blocking the English Pale from the colonial area in the south-east. By the 1570s, in contrast, they were at the centre of Leinster politics. Probably the enfeeblement by the Crown of more powerful neighbours westward—the Kildare Fitzgeralds in 1534–5, the O'Connors and O'Mores in the 1550s—was a factor in their rise. This removed inhibiting pressures and, according to Edmund Spenser, enabled the O'Byrnes to augment their military strength by recruiting from the followers of their expropriated neighbours. Another factor of importance was the successive emergence of two formidable leaders of the sept, Hugh McShane (1550–79) and Feagh McHugh (1580–97).[8]

A feature of the rise of the O'Byrnes of Colranell was the manifestation on their part of an increasingly aggressive attitude towards Crown government. They were associated with all the substantial gestures of rebellion in Leinster in the last four decades of the century, that is, with the rapparee activities of the expropriated O'Mores, and with the more formally mounted protests of the Butlers in 1569–70, of Viscount Baltinglass in 1579–81, and of the Ulster-initiated Nine Years War of the 1590s. It is not our purpose to analyse the political activities of the O'Byrnes in this period, but something must be said about the pressures which influenced their actions. One impetus was their determination to assert local hegemony to the full extent of their military capacity—an aspiration axiomatic in Gaelic politics. Hence there is evidence of friction with other branches of the sept, beginning as early as the 1540s and continuing throughout the period.[9] Also symptomatic of this local expansion is the

8. The history of the O'Byrnes in the sixteenth century has been treated by Liam Price in three useful essays in *Journal of the Royal Society of Antiquaries of Ireland*, lxiii (1933), 225–41, ibid. lxvi (1936), 42–66; *Journal of the Kildare Archaeological Society*, xi (1930), 134–75. On Spenser's treatment of the O'Byrnes, see *Leabhar Branach*, p. 350.

9. Aylmer to Bellingham, July 1548 (P.R.O., S.P. 61/1, no. 43); Alen to Bellingham, 28 September 1548 (S.P. 61/1, no. 101); Sutton to Bellingham (S.P. 61/1, no. 111).

extensive scope of their predatory operations and of their exaction of tribute, or black-rent as it was called when taken from Anglo-Irish settlements.[1] Inevitably all of this brought the sept into conflict with the Crown. Apart from the disruption of Anglo-Irish settlements, the government had an obligation to support the generally docile, senior branch of the O'Byrnes against their obstreperous juniors. One source from which the political activities of the O'Byrnes of Colranell derived was therefore an aggressive energy within the sept itself, expressing itself in a quest for local political dominance.

It seems certain, however, that the O'Byrnes were also responding to an external pressure. This was the Crown's policy of conquest and colonization. In fact colonization was not extended to the O'Byrne's own territories until the beginning of the seventeenth century. But the colonization of Leix and Offaly and the land-grabbing of Sir Peter Carew in south Leinster in the 1570s could not but generate insecurity among the great land-owning dynasties of Leinster generally. The sensitivity of the O'Byrnes in this respect is reflected in their repeated requests, urged even by the recalcitrant Feagh McHugh as late as the 1590s, for confirmation of their titles under royal patent.[2] The technique used to persuade the Crown to grant a patent varied from one dynastic kin to the next. Some, like the Cavanaghs and the senior branch of the O'Byrnes, used butter, demonstrating their innocuousness and malleability. Others, with disastrous consequences in the event, tried the clenched fist. Among the latter were the O'Byrnes of Colranell. Their belligerence can also be seen as a reaction to a more immediate and direct form of Crown government. In the 1560s Sussex and Sidney developed the seneschal system as a means of asserting the Crown's authority over the septs of south Leinster: the Cavanaghs, the O'Byrnes, and the O'Tooles. A number of English garrisons were established in the area and largely financed from the resources of the locality and these were designed to enforce civil obedience. Inevitably this intrusion was resented, more especially since the soldiers did not rise above the low level of conduct maintained by the English troops since the first permanent force arrived in Ireland in the

1. An incomplete list of the black-rents exacted by the O'Byrnes and the O'Tooles in the 1570s, devised by Thomas Alen, was edited by L. Price and published in *Journal of the Kildare Archaeological Society*, xi (1930), 134–75; see also the itemization of raids on royal settlements in Co. Kildare between May 1572 and October 1574 in P.R.O., S.P. 63/48, no. 43.

2. Price, *Journal of the Kildare Archaeological Society*, xi (1930), 154; on their initial overtures in the 1540s, see *State Papers, Henry VIII* (London, 1830), iii. 235, 251, 263, 266, 267, 272; for similar requests in the 1570s, see P.R.O., S.P. 63/31, no. 33.

1530s. It is easy to imagine the reaction of the aggressive O'Byrnes of Colranell to their seneschal Francis Agarde, when we learn that he was commended to the Queen in 1571 as 'a frowarde martiall man abrode'.[3]

The atmosphere of politics in south Leinster in the second half of the sixteenth century was volatile and menacing. English conquest had announced itself with the introduction of the seneschal system, and the spectre of colonization loomed large on the horizon. All of this conditioned relationships between the local septs and the Crown. In some cases it engendered a salutary fear and facilitated docility. In other cases it proved highly provocative. Among those who were provoked were the O'Byrnes of Colranell, whose emergence as a powerful force in local politics coincided with the new assertive presence of Crown government in the area.

Such was the political framework within which the O'Byrnes operated. What was the ideological one? That is the question which this study poses for itself. Before proceeding, however, an outline of the views expressed in the received historiography may help to provide a frame of reference for the discussion. Despite the lack of critical investigation mentioned at the outset there has been no lack of pronouncements on the subject, confidently based on the *a priori* assumptions of the various historical traditions from which they emanate. Thomas Davis in the mid nineteenth century and Patrick Pearse at the beginning of the twentieth century— one the prophet, the other the high priest of modern Irish nationalism— fixed the popular image of the sixteenth-century Gaelic rebel. He became identified with the revolutionary tradition inaugurated by the republican Wolfe Tone at the end of the eighteenth century. The whole was absorbed in a nationalist grand tradition stretching back to Brian Boru who repulsed the Norse at Clontarf in 1014, and to more shadowy figures still, to the Fíanna and Cúchulainn, those mighty heroes of the Irish sagas, the freedom fighters of that twilight age beyond the mystic space of twice a thousand years. What then did Gaelic dissent in the sixteenth century stand for? The ideal of the turbulent Shane O'Neill, Pearse assures us, was articulated for him by Tone over two centuries later in the formula 'to break the English connection'. And what Tone meant by that was elaborated, after the lapse of another century, in the philosophy

3. Sidney to Leicester, 1 March 1566 (P.R.O., S.P. 63/16, no. 35); W. St Leger to Cecil, 6 March 1566 (S.P. 63/16, no. 47); Sidney and Council to Privy Council, 13 April 1566 (S.P. 63/17, no. 8); Sidney to Cecil, 17 April 1566 (S.P. 63/17, no. 14); Lord Chancellor and Council to Queen, 23 March 1571 (P.R.O., S.P. 63/31, no. 33); for an account, from the native side, of the Gaelic political reaction to the English garrisons, see P.R.O., S.P. 63/1, no. 84. In general, see Canny, *The Elizabethan Conquest*, pp. 29–44.

of the Gaelic League, the authentic doctrine of which was summarized in Pearse's own famous dictum, 'Ireland not free merely but Gaelic as well, not Gaelic merely but free as well'. Over against this militant romantic nationalism may be set the scepticism of the rationalists. For these, the undeveloped and archaic nature of the Gaelic polity in the sixteenth century is axiomatic. In this view the aspirations and the political horizons of the Gaelic dynasts were so bound by the sept and the locality as to prevent the impingement of national issues and *a fortiori* of nationalism. The bulk of scholarly opinion has been associated with this view and hence has seen in the destruction of the Gaelic system at the end of the century an almost necessary precondition for the development of a national perspective in the political outlook of the Gaelic community. More recently, however, a scholarly interpretation has been proposed which is less radical in its scepticism. It assumes that, in the second half of the sixteenth century, attitudes within the Gaelic polity were not fixed, either in terms of modern romantic nationalism or in terms of primitive tribalism. Attitudes were in fact at the initial stage of a process of transition, under the traumatic impact of conquest and colonization combined with the counter-reformation. The latter was the modernizing influence that provided the impetus under which Gaelic Ireland groped towards a nationalist ideology of faith and fatherland, the ideology that was not to be fully articulated until the advent of the catholic confederates of the 1640s. Such are the hypotheses.[4] Our purpose now is to analyse the poems of the *Leabhar Branach* to see what they can tell us of the facts.

The first of the *duanairí* in the collection was compiled by Hugh McShane, under whom the O'Byrnes of Colranell came to prominence in the two decades or so before his death in 1579. No doubt the *duanaire* itself is a testimony to the growing prestige and assertiveness of the sept. Correspondingly the growing misgivings of the government are indicated in Lord Justice Fitzwilliam's description of Hugh in 1571 as 'that most wyle and subtell feloe' and of his son Feagh as 'very dangerous and

---

4. Pearse's exposition can be found in a fully developed form in his oration at the graveside of Wolfe Tone in 1913, *Collected Works* (Dublin, 1922 edn), pp. 53–63. Davis discusses the ideological outlook of Gaelic rebels in *Essays of Thomas Davis* (Dundalk, 1914 edn), pp. 160–3, 240–8, 344–8. He expresses some reservation about their nationalist outlook on p. 272. The classic exposition of the sceptical rationalist view is in D. Mathew, *The Celtic Peoples and Renaissance Europe* (London, 1933), *passim*. Edwards, 'Ireland, Elizabeth and the Counter-Reformation', explores the faith and fatherland view, but the fullest exposition is in P. J. Corish, 'The origins of Catholic nationalism', in P. J. Corish (ed.), *A History of Irish Catholicism* (Dublin, 1968), iii, fasc. 8.

garlus'.[5] Eighteen of the seventy-three pieces in the *Leabhar Branach* belong to Hugh's *duanaire*. Of these, three are non-political in character and do not come within the scope of our analysis.[6] The remaining fifteen are, on the whole, typical of the genre of medieval bardic poetry. Over the long length of twelve praise-poems, a victory roll and an elegy, hyperbole is piled upon hyperbole in praise of Hugh and his lineage, his prowess in battle, his success as a reiver, the extent of his tributes, the security of his territories, his liberality to poets—this last by no means least, indeed nauseatingly prominent, the intention being to shame Hugh into living up to an inflated reputation.[7] On the whole the poems reflect a political mentality as conventionally medieval as their structure. Their major function politically was to substantiate, in accordance with the norms of the Gaelic political system, those claims which Hugh's military strength enabled him to make and, at the same time, to provide polemic and propaganda for them. Thus the *duanaire* underscores Hugh's status as senior and best within the sept while at the same time it canvasses his claim to a special hegemony over east Leinster and even over Leinster as a whole.[8]

There is little in Hugh's *duanaire* that could be construed as a response to the political crisis precipitated by the Crown's policy of conquest and colonization. One encomium closes with a reference to forces coming to assist Hugh from further west. This seems to refer to his recruitment of disaffected members of the O'Mores and O'Connors, expropriated in the colonization of Leix and Offaly.[9] Two other pieces deal at length, one exclusively, with the decline of Gaelic culture, i.e. of patronage for bardic poetry, which is attributed to the policy of anglicization.[1] More important than the echoes of the implementation of specific aspects of the Crown's policy is the evidence of the attitude it elicited from Hugh, or perhaps the attitude towards it which certain of the bards attempted to elicit from him. Allusions to Hugh as the new Cúchulainn, the defender

5. Fitzwilliam to Privy Council, 12 April 1571 (P.R.O., S.P. 63/32, no. 9).

6. *Leabhar Branach*, nos 2, 10, 12.

7. For a treatment of the structure of encomiastic verse see E. Knott (ed.), *The Bardic Poems of Tadhg Dall Ó Huiginn* (London, 1922), i, pp. xxxiii–lxiv; Knott, *Irish Classical Poetry*, pp. 53–82.

8. The fullest assertion of Hugh's hegemony in Leinster was made in his victory-roll, composed after his death, *Leabhar Branach*, no. 18. Here his victories are listed proceeding in a clockwise direction from Wexford in south Leinster through five counties to Wicklow. This procedure recalls the ancient tribute-circuit of the Gaelic *rí*.

9. *Leabhar Branach*, no. 9 and note, p. 350.

1. Ibid., nos 5, 8; for a translation and commentary on no. 8, see P. Walsh, *Gleanings from Irish MSS* (Dublin, 1900), pp. 182–93.

of Colranell, of east Leinster and even of the whole province are, no doubt, to be set in the context of conquest and colonization.[2] Nevertheless the ideological concept they reflect is the conventional medieval one in which the dynastic lord figured as the defender of the local patrimony. In two cases something new seems to be emerging. Through the medium of the traditional forms the poet endeavours to advert to the national dimension. In the elegy composed on Hugh's death, one quatrain out of a total of twenty-nine contains a reference to the significance of the event in the context of the growing threat to the Gaelic polity as a whole. It laments that with the death of Hugh, succour for Ireland will no longer be found in the east and must be sought in the west.[3] More substantial evidence is provided by an encomium composed by the celebrated Tadhg Dall Ó Huiginn, probably towards the end of Hugh's career, when the signs of menace were mounting. (Indeed, the quatrain in the elegy just discussed might be regarded as a melancholy rejoinder to Tadhg Dall's encomium.) The poem begins with an admonition to Hugh not to neglect his lover, Ireland, thus presenting him as a national leader. The theme of war between the Irish and English races is introduced and Hugh is extolled as the banisher of foreign troops.[4] Due circumspection must be observed in interpreting the significance of such a piece. The theme of the dynast as spouse of Ireland and the theme of racial war were not new. In classical bardic verse these two concepts—that of the leader of the nation as *árd rí* (high king) or as spouse of Ireland, and that of the war of the Gael (Celt) against the Gall (foreign invader)—are found subsumed in an ideology concerned primarily with the sept and the locality. They function simply as poetic conceits, exploited to flatter the patron, neither intended nor taken seriously.[5] Nevertheless, in the menacing atmosphere of the 1570s, with conquest and colonization pushing steadily forward, it seems clear that such ideas, addressed to a dynast hostile to the government, were being translated from the realm of poetic fancy to that of political ideology. This poem is the only one in the collection in which it could be argued that the theme of national rebellion is prominent. However, the two poems already mentioned, which lament the decay of culture, can also be seen to have a special significance. More vividly than

2. The analogy with Cúchulainn is frequent. It is drawn in the first poem of the collection.
3. *Leabhar Branach*, no. 17.
4. Ibid., no. 16; for another edition of this poem, together with a translation, see Knott, *Tadhg Dall Ó Huiginn*, no. 35.
5. Knott, *Irish Classical Poetry*, pp. 70–72; see B. Ó Cuív, 'Literary creation and historical tradition', *Proceedings of the British Academy*, xlix (1963), 256–8.

anything else in the *duanaire* they give expression to a sense of alarm and peril. Even if they show a keener awareness of a national culture than of a national Gaelic polity, they implicitly identify both and draw attention to the attack being mounted against each.[6]

To summarize so far. The ideological outlook reflected in the *duanaire* of Hugh McShane is overwhelmingly that of the corpus of bardic poetry as a whole. Its focus is the dynasty and the locality. The leader within the sept, and the sept within the region, are the primary objects of devotion. This ideological outlook aptly corresponded to the political realities of late medieval Ireland. However, Hugh's *duanaire* also reflects in some measure the disintegration of the medieval political structure under pressure of Crown policy, and the efforts of certain of the bards to address themselves to the contemporary crisis. There is evidence of widening horizons, of the first stages of development of a national political consciousness, and of the creation of an image of the Gaelic dynast as a national rebel leader.

The seventeen years in the lordship of Colranell of Hugh's son, Feagh, coincided with the period of most dramatic development at the national level, the Desmond rebellion, the Munster plantation, and the emergence of a united front in Ulster against the government—the development that led to the final confrontation between the Crown and what might be called the political establishment of the traditional Gaelic system. The intensity of reaction to the government was correspondingly sharp within Colranell. The period began with the open rebellion of Feagh in association with Viscount Baltinglass. It closed with Feagh being cut to pieces in an ambush by Crown forces, after a concerted advance into the fastnesses of the Wicklow hills. As might be expected, this period produced a significant development at the ideological level.

Ten of the twenty-eight pieces in Feagh's *duanaire* are non-political in character and need not be considered here.[7] The five elegies that close the collection need not detain us either. Though they contain contemporary allusions, they present Feagh's death in personal and social terms, and are sparse in political comment. They are therefore of little value for the purpose of assessing ideological development in the period.[8] Eleven of the thirteen remaining pieces follow the traditional structure of the praise poem. It is a testimony to the conservatism of the bardic profession that

6. *Leabhar Branach*, nos 5, 8.
7. Ibid., nos 21, 22, 26, 29, 31, 33, 36, 37, 38, 40.
8. Ibid., nos 42–46.

six of them also adhere to the classical paradigms in their treatment. They reflect the ethos of late medieval Ireland, the world that bardic poetry was designed to serve, as if oblivious to the developments that were dramatically transforming that world.[9] A seventh poem shows signs of breaking out of this medieval mould. It alludes to the destruction of Ireland and envisages its restoration under Hugh. Nevertheless, the orientation of the piece is emphatically dynastic and provincial. It fails to give utterance to any clear concept of political nationality or of national struggle.[1] Finally, the remaining four encomiums are distinguished by providing evidence of just this crucial breakthrough.

In these four an obvious continuity can be observed with the encomium addressed by Tadhg Dall Ó Huiginn to Feagh's predecessor. On that occasion, as we saw, the traditional praise poem showed signs of developing into a vehicle for the expression of a national ideology. The local dynast began to be portrayed as a leader of national significance in the context of a struggle between the two historic 'races'. Two of the three pieces under discussion show this trend more clearly,[2] and in the third it has reached a fully developed form. Significantly, it would seem, the author of this last piece is also an Ó Huiginn, though he cannot be more clearly identified.[3] The manner in which he handles the traditional themes is striking. From the start, the perspective he provides is national. Feagh is presented as the new moon appearing in the east to whom the *Gaeil* look to redeem their rightful inheritance. This national perspective is retained throughout the poem. In traditional fashion, the poet's argument is developed by means of a historical analogy. Feagh is compared to Lugh Lámhfhada, who rallied the nation when it was threatened by the oppression of the evil-eyed Balor. The point is clinched by appeal to prophecy. Feagh is the one through whom the victory of the *Gaeil* over the *Gaill*, foretold from of old, is to be fulfilled. True, the structure and the themes of the traditional praise poem are here retained. The novelty lies in the way they are handled and the situation to which they address themselves. A pronounced shift has taken place from local and dynastic concerns to national issues. The poem centres on three themes of national significance, the historical claims of the *Gaeil* to the land of Ireland, the historic struggle against foreign bondage, and the need for Gaelic solidarity.

9. Ibid., nos 20, 25, 27, 28, 30, 34.
1. Ibid., no. 23.
2. Ibid., nos 19, 24.
3. Ibid., no. 32.

It is in relation to the national exigencies thus highlighted that the dynastic theme is presented and not, as hitherto, in relation to consideration of the aggrandizement of the dynasty itself. Set in the context of a very real threat to the Irish race and to its historic heritage, the portrayal of the dynastic lord in a role of national leadership against foreign oppression assumes dimensions of urgency and conviction which transform the flattering poetic conceits of bardic poetry into emotive ideological symbols. Thus the traditional themes are made to reflect a new ethos, the political nationality of Gaelic Ireland. The medieval tradition has been revolutionized. Devotion towards the sept and the locality are now subsumed under an ideology directed towards the Gaelic race and the Irish nation.

Three of the pieces in Feagh's *duanaire* remain to be examined. One of these belongs to a sub-category of the group just considered. Like them it adheres closely to the structure and themes of classical bardic poetry. However, the type to which this poem corresponds is not the straightforward encomium but the poem of council, in which the bard assumes his age-old function as councillor. There is no need to demonstrate again the process just described by means of which traditional themes are heightened and brought to bear on the contemporary political crisis. Suffice it to say that the advice offered in the poem does not concern the perennial topic of dynastic aggrandizement. Instead, the message is a warning against being deceived by overtures of peace from the Crown, since the Foreigner is bent on the total extermination of the Gaelic race.[4] A further point to be noted is the appearance of a new, passionate expressiveness in the language, to convey a new depth of emotional feeling. This can be simply shown by pointing to the opening word of the poem, the choice of which in bardic poetry was intended to provide a keynote to the whole of the poem. The theme is announced starkly with the opening word *hatred*. The poet then proceeds to give council in the context of inveterate war between the two races.

In the remaining two poems the metamorphosis of encomiastic verse is complete. The pieces are purely rebel songs. Indeed one of them discards the syllabic metres of bardic verse altogether, and is written instead in the popular rhythmic or song metre that was to be the medium of seventeenth-century rebel poetry. In content, the first is a stirring poem of incitement addressed to the warriors of the Gaeil, urging them to vindi-

4. *Leabhar Branach*, no. 39.

cate the race's reputation and its claim to the land of Ireland. The second celebrates a victorious assault upon an English garrison. In both poems the dynastic element is so entirely muted and incidental as to contain only the faintest echo of the traditional bardic encomium. In the first, only one verse out of fifteen devotes itself to saluting Colranell. In the second, the occasion for the poem is provided by Feagh's success, but the song is a celebration of a national victory, not of a mere dynastic success for Feagh and the O'Byrnes. Should the whole sept be wiped out tomorrow, exults the bard, still would their name live on because of this glorious deed in the national cause. This sentiment reveals a scale of priorities at which a traditional Gaelic Bard, for whom the sept was all, would certainly have looked askance. In another way also this song highlights the newly emerging political mentality of Gaelic Ireland: that is, in the passionate emotion it expresses on national issues. This can be shown by comparing the way the subject is handled here with corresponding references to similar assaults on Anglo-Irish settlements in the traditional encomiums. In the traditional pieces, no attitude to the inhabitants of the settlements is expressed, and the cause for celebration is the richness of the booty secured through the raid. Here, however, booty is hardly mentioned. Instead the author fondly dwells on the slaughter from which no non-Gael escaped, and he exults at the prospect of the warden's head displayed on a spike over the fortress. Under such bloody auspices was Gaelic nationalism born.[5]

It would serve no useful purpose to carry the analysis of the *Leabhar Branach* beyond this point. No further significant development of political themes can be discerned in the collections of Feagh's two successors,

5. Ibid., nos 35, 51; There can be no doubt that the author of both is Aonghus mac Doighre Ó Dálaigh, despite the slight confusion caused by the ascription of no. 41 in one of the two basic manuscripts to an otherwise unknown Aonghus Dubh Ó Dálaigh. The author contributed five other pieces to the *Leabhar Branach*, nos 43, 48, 65, 67, 69. These reflect the same ideological stance, though the subjects treated do not lend themselves to the same vivid expression of it as is found in the two here discussed. Ó Dálaigh belonged to a well-known bardic family of Co. Wexford, but practically none of the details of his life are known: ibid., p. 434. Poem no. 35 exhibits an important feature of the emerging Gaelic ideology that does not, however, become clearly defined in the *Leabhar Branach*. The racial prejudice which it fostered was directed against the English, not against the older, Anglo-Irish settlers. Translators have obscured this by translating the generic term *Gall* (foreigner) as 'English' even though its precise application depended on the context. In the medieval literature the specific term for the English was '*Saxain*'. From the seventeenth century the two colonial communities were distinguished as *sean-Ghaill* (old English) and *nua-Ghaill* (new English). Poem no. 35 was well known to nineteenth-century nationalists through a translation by Samuel Ferguson, in H. H. Sparling (ed.), *Irish Minstrelsy* (London, 1888), pp. 131–3. Though poem no. 41 accurately reflects the savagery of the warfare that developed in the later Tudor period, the Gaelic forces had no monopoly of atrocities.

Féilim and Brian. The reason is suggested in a long poem which occurs early in the *duanaire* of Feagh's son, Féilim. This enters into an elaborate argument on the futility of contending with the foreigner. History reveals, it is claimed, that the politically successful in Ireland have always invoked outside aid.[6] Thus, the bard in the role of councillor is once more called upon, this time to enable the O'Byrne rebel to come to terms with the government and to salvage something of the family fortunes, yet without losing his self-respect as a Gaelic lord. Thereafter the political content of the *Leabhar Branach* is muted and ambiguous, reflecting the actual political situation of the O'Byrnes themselves. The proud dynastic lord and the tradition-steeped professional poet were both casualties of conquest and colonization. But the new political verse which emerged from that *milieu* in the late sixteenth century burgeoned elsewhere in more popular form, despite, or perhaps because of, the demise of its creators.[7]

In summarizing the conclusions that can be drawn from an analysis of the ideological content of the *Leabhar Branach* it may be useful to set them in the context of the historiography discussed earlier. Despite the limited scope of the inquiry, it can serve as a critique of the general hypotheses there adduced. It indicates, for instance, that the hyper-sceptical view is certainly not wholly right and is likely on further investigation to prove substantially wrong. Despite a large element of archaism, despite being steeped in tradition and entrenched in the ancient system, the bards proved themselves to be neither oblivious nor uncomprehending in face of the contemporary crisis. The *Leabhar Branach* shows them gradually but increasingly addressing themselves to the new situation and moulding the traditional poetic forms to serve new purposes. The response took two main lines, each in its own way positive and progressive, not negative and reactionary as is often supposed. One was the attempt to mould a new national political consciousness and a nationalist ideology, the major theme of the present study. The second, quickly superseding the first when the futility of rebellion became apparent, was to help the dynasty to reconcile itself to the political realities and generally to create for it a satisfying public image within those limitations.

6. *Leabhar Branach*, no. 57. I wish to thank Sr Redempta of the Department of Irish at Mary Immaculate College of Education, Limerick, for help in unravelling the argument of this piece.

7. On this, see C. O'Reilly (ed.), *Five Seventeenth-Century Political Poems* (Dublin, 1952), *passim*, but especially the foreword, pp. vii–ix; also see P. de Brún *et al.* (eds), *Nua-Dhuanaire*, i (Dublin, 1971).

The proponents of the faith and fatherland hypothesis are not vindicated either. On the evidence of the *Leabhar Branach* the catholic nationalism of the 1640s does not find its ideological roots in the Gaelic dissent of the Tudor period. The verse gives no place to the theme of a holy crusade in defence of religion, despite the devotional sentiment of some pieces.[8] A second difference derives from the distinction between what may be called patriotic nationalism, based on devotion to the fatherland, and ethnic nationalism, in which the nation is identified with a racial group. The latter was the concept of the *Leabhar Branach*. Thirdly, the ideology which the bardic poetry expressed was emphatically that of rebellion. It was the ideology of an insurgent Gaelic race vindicating its historic rights. Not explicitly *pro Deo*, nor primarily *pro patria*, least of all *pro rege*, the nationalism of the *Leabhar Branach* finds no echo in the slogan of the confederates of 1641.[9] This suggests a further implication that would need further investigation. It is that Gaelic nationalism in the early modern period was a native product, deriving its elements from Gaelic history and culture, articulated first by native *literati* as a response to political developments within Ireland. This contradicts the accepted view of it as a continental import, part of the intellectual baggage of the counter-reformation. No doubt the latter impinged on the native creation but this seems to be an aspect of the intellectual history of the seventeenth century rather than of the sixteenth.[1]

Surprisingly, perhaps, the hypothesis that stands up best when set against the testimony of the *Leabhar Branach* is that of the amateur Celtic scholar, Pearse. Despite recent rebuttal, Pearse was certainly correct, as we have seen, in postulating a Gaelic nationalism in the sixteenth century. Furthermore, it seems that his claim of historical continuity between that nationalism and his own is substantially valid. As a succinct summary of the aspirations expressed in the nationalist verse of the *Leabhar*

8. It should be borne in mind that I speak about the ideology reflected in the *Leabhar Branach*. However, cursory investigation suggests that sixteenth-century bardic poetry reflects little concern about the religious reformation. The often quoted poem 'Fúbún fúibh, a shluaghadh Gaoidheal', dating from the mid century, which castigates the Gaelic lords for both political and religious betrayal, is probably untypical.

9. The confederation slogan has more obvious affinities with the nationalist ideology emerging within the Anglo-Irish community in the sixteenth century. See my unpublished doctoral thesis, 'The Irish constitutional revolution, 1515–57' (Cambridge, 1976). For a cursory treatment of the same subject, see my 'The beginning of modern Ireland', in B. Farrell (ed.), *The Irish Parliamentary Tradition* (Dublin, 1973).

1. An early example of the appearance of counter-reformation ideology in Irish bardic poetry is the poem 'Beannacht ar anmain Éireann', by Fear Flatha Ó Gnímh, composed in 1609—O. Bergin, *Irish Bardic Poetry*, ed. D. Greene and F. Kelly, no. 26.

Branach one could hardly cavil at the formula of Pearse, 'Ireland not free merely but Gaelic as well, not Gaelic merely but free as well'. No doubt the hyper-sceptics have better reason to scoff at the enlistment of the republican Francophile, Tone, under such a banner; as they have indeed at the enlistment of proud Gaelic dynasts behind the flag of the republic.

5

Bristol and America
1480-1631

PATRICK McGRATH

The interest which Bristolians showed in the New World varied considerably in the century and a half between John Jay's unsuccessful search for the Isle of Brasil in 1480 and Thomas James's equally unsuccessful search for a northwest passage in 1631. On occasion Bristolians were deeply concerned, but for long periods they ignored America. In some respects the story was one of high hopes which were not fulfilled and of enterprises which achieved little. It is possible that men from Bristol were the first to discover land across the Atlantic and kept quiet about it, or even lost it again. Some Bristolians gave support to John Cabot, but in the course of the sixteenth century his name was largely forgotten in Bristol. There was an intensification of effort in the first decade of the sixteenth century, but thereafter interest was rarely shown, and the city played only a minor part in Elizabethan explorations. In the seventeenth century there was a revival of activity both in exploration and in colonization, but in the end little was achieved. The voyage of Captain Thomas James in 1631 completed what was, from the point of view of investors, an unprofitable record.

A great deal has been written in recent years about various aspects of this subject, but it is worthwhile looking again at what was attempted by Bristolians. What they did has tended to be considered as part of the much larger story of English exploration, and so it is also desirable to examine, as far as the scanty evidence permits, the more limited problem of Bristol's financial involvement and to ask how many Bristolians actually contributed, what motives inspired them and what capital they invested in these hopeful but unsuccessful ventures.

The first known voyage from Bristol out into the Atlantic in search of 'the Isle of Brasil' was the venture of John Jay junior in 1480. The evidence for this is William Worcestre's *Itinerarium,* and Worcestre stated that the voyage was unsuccessful.[1] Another attempt was made in 1481. This expedition consisted of two ships—the *George* and the *Trinity*—and we know of it only because Thomas Croft, one of the Customers of Bristol, who owned a one-eighth share in each of the ships, was subsequently accused of engaging in trade, which he was not entitled to do while he held the office of Customer. The conclusion of the inquiry was that Croft was not engaged in trade and that the ships had been sent out 'to thentent to serch & fynde a certain Isle called the Isle of Brasile . . .'.[2] Whether or not the voyage of 1481 succeeded, we do not know.

After 1481, there is no evidence of any voyage from Bristol into the Atlantic until the 1490s, and what we have then is rather less satisfactory than the evidence for the voyages of 1480 and 1481. On 25 July 1498, after John Cabot's successful venture, Pedro de Ayala, the Spanish representative in London, reported to his sovereigns that 'For the last seven years the people of Bristol have equipped two, three [and] four caravels to go in search of the island of Brazil and the Seven Cities, according to the fancy of this Genoese'.[3] If he was right, then a really massive effort was being made by Bristolians in the 1490s, and it is possible to speculate, as does D. B. Quinn, on whether these ventures were voyages to the fishing banks off Newfoundland which had been discovered earlier and which were now being exploited by Bristolians, or whether, as Alwyn Ruddock suggests, they were desperate efforts to find again fishing grounds which had been discovered by chance before 1480 but the way to which had subsequently been lost.[4] When experts in the field have taken Ayala at face value, it may seem rash to question his reliability, but as a witness he is not quite in the same category as William Worcestre,

---

1. J. A. Williamson, *The Cabot Voyages and Bristol Discovery under Henry VII* (Cambridge 1962), pp. 19–20, 187–8 (hereafter cited as *Cabot Voyages*); D. B. Quinn, *England and the Discovery of America, 1481–1620* (London, 1974), pp. 7–8 (hereafter cited as Quinn, *Discovery*)

2. Williamson, *Cabot Voyages,* pp. 22–23, 188–9; Quinn, *Discovery,* pp. 54–58; W. E. C-Harrison, 'An early voyage of discovery', *Mariner's Mirror,* xvi (1930), 198–9; D. B. Quinn, 'Edward IV and exploration', ibid. xxi (1935), 275–84. For the licence to Thomas Croft, William Spencer, Robert Strange, and Willam de la Fount, merchants of Bristol, to trade for three years to any parts, except with staple goods, with two or three ships of 60 tons or under, see E. M. Carus-Wilson, *The Overseas Trade of Bristol in the Later Middle Ages* (Bristol, 1936), pp. 157–8. The licence is probably, but not certainly, related to the attempt at exploration.

3. Williamson, *Cabot Voyages,* pp. 228–9, 233–4; Quinn, *Discovery,* pp. 9–10.

4. Quinn, *Discovery,* p. 14; Alwyn A. Ruddock, 'John Day of Bristol and the English voyages across the Atlantic before 1497', *Geographical Journal,* cxxxii (1966), 225–33 (hereafter cited as Ruddock, 'John Day').

who knew Bristol and who was related to the Jay family, or the Bristol
jurors who, in answer to an Exchequer inquisition, stated that the voyage
of 1481 had been for exploration and not for trade.[5] Ayala, as far as we
know, had never been to Bristol, and it seems surprising that an effort on
the scale he suggests, spread over seven years and involving at least sixteen ships, and possibly well over twenty, should have left no mark on the
records. He may have simply been reporting what he had been told in
London, and what he was told may have been true, but his unsupported
testimony must be treated with some caution.

There may, of course, have been other voyages of which we know
nothing,[6] and we have yet to consider the evidence of John Day's letter,
but before doing so, it is worth commenting on what we know about the
extent to which Bristolians were involved. Only a handful of Bristol
merchants can be shown to be directly concerned. We know from William
Worcestre that John Jay the younger was associated with the voyage of
1480. Worcestre mentioned him because he was himself related to the
Jays. He appears to have left a blank for the names of other venturers, but
did not fill it in.[7] In the 1481 voyage, we know that Thomas Croft was
part-owner of the *Trinity* and the *George*, and it is a reasonable assumption
that Croft was associated in the venture with three Bristol merchants,
William Spencer, Robert Strange, and William de la Fount,[8] but these
are the only names for which we have direct evidence in the voyages of
1480 and 1481. There is nothing to support Williamson's conjecture that
'it is quite possible that this and other voyages of discovery may have
been financed by the greater part of mercantile Bristol'.[9] There is no
information at all about the men who backed the voyages which Ayala
alleges were sent out in the 1490s, but we can perhaps include in the list of
those who were involved in the later fifteenth century the merchants
Robert Thorne and Hugh Elyot, whom Robert Thorne the younger
claimed in 1527 to be 'the discoverers of the Newfound Landes . . .'.[1] The
circle could be widened a little if we included those involved in the

5. Quinn, *Discovery*, pp. 56–57.
6. We might never have heard of the voyage of 1480 if William Worcestre had not been
interested as a relative of the Jay family, and we would not know of the 1481 voyage if
Thomas Croft had not been a Customer of Bristol and laid himself open to the charge of
being engaged in trade.
7. Williamson, *Cabot Voyages*, pp. 19, 187–8.
8. See n. 2, p. 82.
9. Williamson, *Cabot Voyages*, p. 20.
1. Ibid., pp. 26–29, 202. It is not clear what Robert Thorne meant and when the discovery was supposed to have been made.

Icelandic and Iberian trades, those who traded to the Iberian islands in the Atlantic and those who may have been in touch directly or indirectly with the explorations being carried out from Spain and Portugal.[2] Now, the number of people who can meaningfully be described as merchants in Bristol in the later fifteenth century must have been well over 100, and many more were engaged in foreign trade at least part of the time. Between September 1479 and July 1480, for example, about 250 individuals traded with Gascony, Spain, and Portugal alone.[3] Thus, as far as voyages of discovery are concerned only a tiny fraction of the merchants can be shown to be involved and we cannot establish that the merchant community as a whole was deeply concerned about exploration.

How much capital was invested we do not know. The ship sent out in 1480 was one of 80 tons and it was away from Bristol for nine weeks. Two ships were sent out in 1481: the *Trinity* and the *George*. If they were sailing under the licence granted to Thomas Croft and his three associates in 1480, they should not have been of greater burden than 60 tons, and Quinn suggests that they were probably small fishing vessels. If the *Trinity* which went out in 1481 was in fact the *Trinity* on which John Balsall was purser, then the tonnage was between 300 and 360, and the investment would have been considerable, but there was more than one *Trinity* in Bristol at this time, and Quinn's argument that it is unlikely that the large vessel went out with the *George* carries conviction.[4] We have no evidence about the ships which Ayala alleges went out in the 1490s, and we cannot assert that Bristol merchants were investing on a major scale in exploration. It is possible that these ventures were probing voyages by small fishing vessels which a few Bristolians thought worth making but which did not involve great capital expenditure.

The voyages into the Atlantic required considerable, if not heavy, expenditure, and those who invested in them lost the opportunity to employ their capital profitably elsewhere. It is at least possible that moderate investment in exploration was one of the consequences of the prosperity which Bristol was enjoying in the later fifteenth century. As Sherborne has pointed out, 'during the last twenty years of the fifteenth

2. See Quinn, *Discovery*, chap. 3, 'England and the Atlantic'.
3. James Sherborne, *The Port of Bristol in the Middle Ages* (Bristol, 1971), p. 27 (hereafter cited as Sherborne). In 1545, 111 merchants and traders paid the subsidy, of whom about three-quarters paid on £10 or more (Jean Vanes, 'The overseas trade of Bristol in the sixteenth century', London Ph.D. thesis, 1975, p. 56: hereafter cited as Vanes).
4. T. F. Reddaway and A. A. Ruddock (eds), 'The accounts of John Balsall, purser of the *Trinity* of Bristol', *Camden Miscellany*, xxiii (1969), 1–26; Quinn, *Discovery*, pp. 54–55.

century Bristol exported more cloth, imported more wine and handled more goods subject to poundage than any other provincial port'.[5] The search for new markets and new sources of supply could sometimes be the consequence of a major disturbance in the traditional pattern of trade, but could also take place in circumstances of prosperity when money was available for risky, but possibly very profitable, ventures. Some of the Bristol merchants may have felt that it was worth making a modest investment on an outsider.

Another problem is that we have no direct evidence about the motives of those concerned. Some Bristolians were directly or indirectly in contact with Portuguese and Spanish thinking about exploration, but as far as we know the men of Bristol who sent ships out into the Atlantic were not trying to find a new way to Asia, still less to engage in exploration for its own sake.[6] One possible incentive was the need to find new fishing grounds for cod at a time when relations with Iceland were becoming increasingly difficult and Bristolians were finding it hard to obtain the stockfish which were so important in their Iberian trade.[7] It is relevant that some of the Bristolians who were involved in the Iceland–Portuguese trade were also involved, at least peripherally, in the voyages of 1480 and 1481.[8] It is, however, very difficult to say precisely how important the fisheries were in the total picture of Bristol's overseas trade in the later fifteenth century and to decide whether the decline and fall of the Icelandic trade really was the overriding and persistent motive which year after year led to men from Bristol 'launching voyages into the Atlantic wastes'.[9] If we accept the possibility that the fisheries had been discovered some time after 1480 and that Ayala's voyages of the 1490s were not voyages of discovery but 'annual fishing fleets on their way to and from Newfoundland waters',[1] it still remains surprising that Bristolians who had such an urgent need to exploit new sources of supply of cod were so slow to develop their interest in the Newfoundland fisheries in the later fifteenth and early sixteenth centuries.

The problem of the pre-Cabot voyages from Bristol is complicate by

5. Sherborne, p. 28.
6. See, however, Quinn, *Discovery*, p. 87.
7. Ruddock, 'John Day'.
8. For Bristol's relations with Iceland, see Quinn, *Discovery*, pp. 30, 47–50, 53–54, 56, 86, 105; E. M. Carus-Wilson, *Mediaeval Merchant Venturers* (London, 1954), chap. 2, 'The Icelandic Venture'.
9. Ruddock, 'John Day', p. 230.
1. Quinn, *Discovery*, p. 14.

John Day's letter which came to light in 1956.² The traditional story concerning John Cabot was that he came to Bristol in the 1490s because it was an obvious place to seek backing for his venture. Bristolians had already sent out a number of expeditions into the Atlantic. Their purpose may well have been different from Cabot's, since he was seeking a new way to the wealth of Asia and intended to take possession of whatever territories he found, but his purpose would not be incompatible with the discovery, or rediscovery, of rich fishing grounds. Moreover, if Cabot opened up trade with lands across the Atlantic, it was to be channelled through Bristol. This view was thrown into the melting pot by the publication of Day's letter, written in the winter months of 1497–8 to the Almirante Mayor, generally agreed to be Columbus himself. This letter not only provided new evidence about John Cabot's voyage in 1497 and about an unsuccessful voyage by Cabot, which was not previously known, but also referred to an earlier discovery by men from Bristol. Referring to Cabot's voyage of 1497, Day said: 'It is considered certain that the cape of the said land was found and discovered in the past (*en otros tiempos*) by the men from Bristol who found "Brasil" as your Lordship well knows. It was called the Island of Brasil, and it is assumed and believed to be the mainland that the men from Bristol found.'³

This letter, apart from an ambiguous statement made in 1527 by Robert Thorne about his father and Hugh Elyot,⁴ is the sole authority for the claim that men from Bristol had found land across the Atlantic before Cabot. It was therefore of vital importance to examine the credibility of the witness and he was eventually proved to be Hugh Say, mercer of London, who in the 1490s was operating from Bristol in the Iberian trade and who was in close touch with men who knew what was going on there.⁵

These revelations make him a better witness than he would otherwise have been, but do not necessarily mean that what he said was right. He

2. L. A. Vigneras, 'New light on the 1497 Cabot voyage to America', *Hispanic American Historical Review*, xxxvi (1956), 503–9 (hereafter cited as Vigneras [1956]) has the text in Spanish; L. A. Vigneras, 'The Cape Breton landfall: 1494 or 1497? Note on a letter by John Day', *Canadian Historical Review*, xxxviii (1957), 219–28 (hereafter cited as Vigneras [1957]) has an English translation. Another translation occurs in S. E. Morison, *The European Discovery of America: The Northern Voyages* (New York and London, 1971; hereafter cited as Morison).

3. Vigneras (1957), p. 228. The translation in Morison, pp. 208–9, reads: 'It is considered certain that this same point of land at another time was found and discovered by those of Bristol who found *el Brasil* as you are already aware, which is called Ysla de Brasil, and is presumed and believed to be the *tierra firma* which those of Bristol discovered.'

4. Williamson, *Cabot Voyages*, pp. 26–29, 202.

5. Ruddock, 'John Day'.

did not actually say that he himself knew that a discovery had been made or that he had talked to men who had been across the Atlantic before Cabot. He was apparently reporting what he had been told, and he did not say by whom 'it is considered certain'. Moreover, the statement would have carried greater weight if it had been made before and not after John Cabot's voyage of 1497. If, however, Day was right and there was a discovery before Cabot, questions naturally arise about when it was made and why it was not made public. Dr Ruddock argues that the discovery was made before 1480 but that the landfall was lost again in the Atlantic mist. Williamson thought it was made in the early 1490s but that it could have taken place in the early 1480s. He suggested that the reason why the discovery was not generally known was that until Cabot came home to announce that he had found a way to Asia 'few men outside Bristol were in the least interested in a new fishery worked from that port'. Quinn sums up his own careful examination of the evidence with the comment: 'an argument on the present basis indicates that the English discovery could reasonably have taken place between 1481 and 1491 . . . Further than this it would seem undesirable to go until something fresh can be adduced.' The case for a Bristol discovery of America certainly cannot be dismissed out of hand, but at present, in spite of John Day, it does not carry conviction.

There is very little information about the number of Bristolians involved in the Cabot voyages. According to John Day, Cabot made an unsuccessful voyage before 1497. Day wrote: 'he went with one ship, his crew confused him, he was short of supplies and ran into bad weather, and he decided to turn back'.[6] There is no other information about this early voyage, which may have taken place in 1496, and we do not know who put up the money for it or how much it cost. This is also true of the successful 1497 voyage. Cabot's patent entitled him to employ five ships of any tonnage,[7] but in fact he went in only one small ship with a company of eighteen or twenty people.[8] It is not unreasonable to assume that John Cabot would have preferred a larger expedition with two or more ships and that the reason why he did not get it was that insufficient funds were available. If this is so, it suggests that there was no rush among Bristolians to invest in the voyage. The patent had been granted to

6. Williamson, *Cabot Voyages*, p. 213; see also ibid., p. 54 for a suggestion that *la gente que llevaba le desconcerto* might mean 'he had a disagreement with his crew'.

7. Ibid., p. 204.

8. Raimondo de Raimondi de Soncino to the Duke of Milan, 18 December 1497, printed in Williamson, *Cabot Voyages*, p. 209. John Day gives the number as 20.

Cabot and his sons, and to their deputies. J. A. Williamson suggested that 'these may include the Bristol merchants known by other evidence to have been associated with them',[9] but this is only conjecture. It is not possible to name any Bristol merchant who can be clearly shown to have invested in the expedition. It was, in any case, a very small one, and the amount of capital cannot have been very large.

For John Cabot's voyage in 1498, larger resources were available, but this was not primarily because there were now many Bristolians ready to put their money into a project which looked very promising. The largest ship in the 1498 voyage was sent by the King himself, who provided the ship and the crew but not the cargo.[1] Williamson suggested that the King hired for the occasion a private merchantman belonging to Lancelot Thirkill and his partner, two London men, at a cost of £113 8s 0d, and that she was just under 200 tons in burden.[2] She was accompanied by four small ships from Bristol, and the cargo for the voyage was provided by 'dyvers merchauntes aswell of London as Bristow'.[3] It was, then, an expedition financed by the King and London merchants as well as some Bristol merchants, and this again may be an indication that Bristolians were unable or unwilling to make a really large-scale investment.

The Cabot voyages of 1497 and 1498 must have been very disappointing from the point of view of investors, and this may help to explain why even in Bristol the role which John Cabot had played in exploration was for a long time forgotten and his son Sebastian was able to take credit for his father's achievements. Nevertheless, at least a few Bristolians retained an interest in exploration in the first decade of the sixteenth century. This interest was closely related to the explorations being carried out by the Portuguese.[4] In 1501, a patent for exploration was granted to Richard Warde, Thomas Asshehurst, and John Thomas, merchants of Bristol[5] and to João Fernandes, Francisco Fernandes, and João Gonsalves of the Azores. Under this patent, there were voyages of exploration in 1501 and 1502. In January 1502 the King's Household Book records the following: 'Item

9. Williamson, *Cabot Voyages*, p. 51.

1. Ibid., pp. 91–92, 220–3.

2. Ibid., p. 92.

3. For the evidence of the London chronicles relating to this expedition, see ibid., pp. 220–3. Cabot's patent of 1498 entitled him to take six ships provided they were under 200 tons: ibid., pp. 226–7.

4. For the Portuguese explorations, see Williamson, *Cabot Voyages*, chap. 8, 'Bristol and the new found land', pp. 116–44; Quinn, *Discovery*, pp. 111–17.

5. The petition and grant are printed in Williamson, *Cabot Voyages*, pp. 235–47; see Quinn, *Discovery*, pp. 113–14, for a suggestion of why the Azoreans came to Bristol.

to men of bristoll that founde thisle, Cs',[6] and in September 'to the merchauntes of bristoll that have bene in the newe founde laund, xx li'.[7] Williamson pointed out that this group was not allowed to intrude on the discoveries made by the Cabot family, whose patent was still valid, and he suggested that there may have been another voyage in 1502 by Cabot's deputies, among whom may have been Robert Thorne and Hugh Elyot.[8]

Yet another patent was granted on 9 December 1502, this time to Thomas Asshehurst and Hugh Elyot, their heirs and deputies, and to João Gonsalves and Francisco Fernandes.[9] Williamson suggested that what may have happened was that the rights under the Cabot patent were now merged with the privileges granted to this new group in 1502.[1] The group came to be known as 'the Company adventurers in to the new fownde ilondes'.[2] Voyages were sent out in 1503, 1504, and 1505.[3] Williamson suggested that the purpose was to discover a northwest passage to Asia and that one or more colonial settlements were founded.[4]

In these ventures of the early sixteenth century others besides Bristolians were involved, including Portuguese from the Azores, William Clerk, a London merchant, and to some extent, Sir Bartholomew Rede, a London goldsmith.[5] The initiative may well have come from the Azoreans and some of the capital from London. Only about half a dozen Bristolians can be shown to have participated, and we do not know how much they invested.[6] As Williamson put it, 'the north-western push by the Bristol syndicate died out in the icefields. So also did that by the Portuguese. Later history shows that unless success came quickly, lack of money closed the effort.'[7]

As Quinn points out, these voyages are of considerable significance,[8]

6. Printed in Williamson, *Cabot Voyages*, p. 215.
7. Ibid., p. 216. See Quinn, *Discovery*, pp. 117–18 for these two voyages.
8. Ibid., pp. 131–2. There is, of course, no direct evidence to show that Asshehurst and Elyot were Cabot's 'deputies'.
9. Printed in Williamson, *Cabot Voyages*, pp. 250–61.
1. Ibid., pp. 133–4; Quinn, *Discovery*, p. 121.
2. Williamson, *Cabot Voyages*, p. 263.
3. Ibid., p. 134.
4. Ibid., p. 136; see also Quinn, *Discovery*, pp. 123–6.
5. Quinn, *Discovery*, pp. 122–3. The later history of the group was not happy and may have discouraged such associations in the future. See Williamson, *Cabot Voyages*, pp. 262–4.
6. In the conclusion to her thesis Vanes says that it is tempting to ascribe the decline in Bristol's trade in the first decade of the sixteenth century to 'the squandering of resources on voyages of exploration', but it cannot be shown that large resources were so squandered or that many Bristolians were involved.
7. Williamson, *Cabot Voyages*, p. 144.
8. Quinn, *Discovery*, pp. 129–30.

but they failed to produce dividends for the investors. It was not therefore surprising that although the little group of Bristol merchants associated during part or whole of the period 1480–1505 with western voyages had a long trading life, there is nothing to show that, from 1505 to 1525 at least, any of them had any concern with America or with voyages in that direction.[9] Merchants were not concerned with gaining a place in the histories of exploration, but with receiving a return on their capital. From this point of view, the early voyages of the sixteenth century must have been a complete loss.

It may be suggested that against this loss we should put on the credit side of the ledger the profits made from the Newfoundland fisheries. It has been argued that it was the need to find a new source of supply of cod that led Bristolians to cross the Atlantic in the first place, and the accounts of Cabot's voyage in 1497 stress the richness of the fisheries he discovered. Thus, in December 1497 the Milanese representative in England reported that those who had been on the expedition remarked that 'the sea there is swarming with fish, which can be taken not only with the net, but in baskets let down with a stone . . .';[1] and John Day reported that 'all along the coast they found many fish like those which in Iceland are dried in the open and sold in England and other countries'.[2] But if Bristolians discovered the fisheries, they did not apparently exploit them. S. E. Morison remarks that though Prowse, the historian of Newfoundland, asserted that West Country English were fishing off Newfoundland as early as 1498 this was pure conjecture.[3] Elsewhere, he writes: 'Bristol supported Cabot and the Anglo-Azorean syndicate, partly to find new fishing grounds; but when found, they were neglected. Rut found not one English fisherman in St John's in 1527; and Roberval, if any of the fishing fleets he encountered there were English, did not admit it.'[4]

---

9. Quinn, *Discovery*, p. 128.

1. Printed in Williamson, *Cabot Voyages*, p. 210.

2. Ibid., pp. 212–13.

3. Morison, p. 225.

4. Morison, p. 471; on the cod fisheries, ibid., pp. 225–8 and 470–8; also Quinn, *Discovery*, p. 144. In 1540–1, Roger Barlow referred to 'the new founde lande, which was fyrst discouered by marchantes of brystowe where now the bretons do trat thither everie yere a fyshing', Roger Barlow, *A Briefe Summe of Geographie*, ed. E. G. R. Taylor (London, 1932), p. 179 (hereafter cited as Taylor, *Barlow*). In 1576 it was estimated that thirty English ships went there, Gillian T. Cell, 'The Newfoundland Company: A study of subscribers to a colonizing venture', *William and Mary Quarterly*, 3rd series, xxii (1965), 612 (hereafter cited as Cell, 'Subscribers'): see also Gillian T. Cell, 'The English in Newfoundland, 1577–1660' (Liverpool University Ph.D. thesis, 1964), pp. 51–52 (hereafter cited as Cell, 'English in Newfoundland').

It may be that the Portuguese established themselves first and that, as a result, from the point of view of the English the need was less great than expected and the profit smaller. Bristolians and other Englishmen were to exploit the fisheries later in the century, as were the French and other nations, but this would not be of any great comfort to those who invested their money in exploration in the later fifteenth and early sixteenth centuries.

There remains for consideration one more voyage in the first decade of the sixteenth century about which there is a good deal of uncertainty, that of Sebastian Cabot in 1508–9. Morison thought that Sebastian Cabot's supposed voyage in 1508 in search of a northwest passage 'belongs in the doubtful class' and that the only voyage that Sebastian certainly commanded was in 1525–8 in the service of the King of Spain.[5] Williamson, however, maintained that the voyage did take place, and Quinn states that this is now generally accepted.[6] The question remains how far Bristolians were involved.

It is known that Sebastian Cabot was living in Bristol in 1505 when the King gave him a pension of £10 a year in consideration of diligent service in and about the town and port of Bristol,[7] but there is nothing to show that this had anything to do with exploration. Williamson pointed out that Sebastian and his brothers were inheritors of the Cabot patent, which was still uncancelled, and that the adventurers who got a patent in 1502 were also free to operate in the areas covered by the Cabot patent. He suggested that 'there may have been a fusion of interests between the Cabot patentees and the Company'. Although we lose sight of the Company after 1506, there is no proof that it ceased to operate. Williamson added: 'There is therefore a possibility that all this Bristol interest was behind Sebastian Cabot two years later. His voyage can have been an effort of the Company Adventurers. . . . It is a testimonial to Sebastian Cabot's reputation that Bristol and the King provided the money to equip him, for we may be certain that he did not find it all himself.'[8] This is going far beyond the evidence. Williamson himself must have had doubts, for he hastened to add: 'the above remarks on the Bristol support given to Cabot are speculative'.[9] In the present state of knowledge we cannot be sure

5. Morison, pp. 220–1.
6. Williamson, *Cabot Voyages*, pp. 145–72; Quinn, *Discovery*, pp. 131–59; see also D. B. Quinn, *Sebastian Cabot and Bristol Exploration* (Bristol, 1968).
7. Williamson, *Cabot Voyages*, p. 265.
8. Ibid., pp. 161–2.
9. Ibid., p. 162.

that Sebastian Cabot sailed from Bristol, or that whatever mercantile interests were involved were Bristol mercantile interests. Quinn sums up by saying: 'How much relevance Sebastian Cabot's voyage had for Bristol is not known.'[1]

From 1508–9 until Frobisher's voyages of 1576–8, there is very little evidence that Bristol was interested in voyages of exploration, although during his lifetime Cabot maintained connections with the city. He left Bristol and moved to London and then took service with the King of Spain, but in 1521 he visited England and secured the backing of Henry VIII, Wolsey, and the Council for 'a viage to be made into the newefound Iland'.[2] This was to be a London-based expedition, but 'as many Cites and Townes as be mynded to prepare any shipps forwardes for the same purpos & viage' might co-operate under the control of the City of London, and, according to the Drapers' Company records, 'the Towne of Bristowe hath sent up there knowledge, that they wyll prepare ij shipps . . .'.[3] It is reasonable to assume that Sebastian Cabot had been in touch with Bristol and may even have visited it. The plan met with opposition from some of the Londoners and in the end came to nothing. Quinn comments that 'there is nothing in the local records to show why this did not lead to an independent Bristol venture' and suggests that Cabot abandoned the idea because, after the major London companies showed their lack of enthusiasm, only a small London–Bristol venture was practicable, and this was not enough for him.[4] We do not know who in Bristol promised to provide the two ships or how serious they were. It is possible that there was in fact no great enthusiasm in Bristol, but that in reply to a pressing invitation from the king and council, the city government had expressed a willingness to co-operate without going into details about who was to provide the ships. When the grandiose scheme collapsed because of lack of large-scale support in London, Bristolians may well have been reluctant, in view of their previous experience, to go it alone.

Sebastian Cabot returned to England in 1549 and was for a time in Bristol, but he left for London in the same year, and was engaged in plans for the discovery of Cathay which led in 1553 to the voyage of Willoughby and Chancellor. This was a London-backed venture, and, as Quinn

1. Quinn, *Discovery*, p. 143.
2. For details of the proposed expedition given in the records of the Drapers' Company of London, see Williamson, *Cabot Voyages*, pp. 286–91.
3. Ibid., p. 288.
4. Quinn, *Discovery*, p. 147.

remarks, Bristol 'played no part in the northerly passage ventures with which Sebastian Cabot's English career reaches a late climax'.[5]

Bristol's lack of involvement in voyages of exploration in the second half of the sixteenth century cannot be explained solely in terms of the state of her overseas trade. She was not as prosperous as she had been in the later fifteenth century, but she was doing reasonably well and there were signs of expansion in the 1530s.[6] Part of the explanation for her lack of interest may be that her experience of overseas ventures in the later fifteenth and early sixteenth century had shown that such investments were not profitable. In addition, there is a possibility that some of the small groups of Bristolians who were interested in America found that they could best develop this interest not from Bristol itself but from Spain. Something must therefore be said about these men, even though what they did should be seen as the work of men who originally came from Bristol or who had Bristol connections rather than as strictly Bristol ventures.

A good deal is now known about the English merchants who resided in Spain in the first half of the sixteenth century.[7] The group included Robert Thorne the elder and his sons Robert and Nicholas, and Roger Barlow, who in 1533 became a freeman of Bristol by marriage.[8] Both Robert Thorne and Roger Barlow were keenly interested in exploration. They had been deeply involved in Sebastian Cabot's voyage of 1525–8 in the service of the King of Spain[9] and both had tried to arouse English interest in voyages of discovery.[1] Others who were Bristolians or who were connected with Bristol included Thomas Howell, William Ostriche, governor of the Andalusian Company, and Henry Patmer who accompanied Roger Barlow on the Cabot voyage in 1526.[2] The group of men with Bristol connections resident in Spain was admittedly very small, but it was influential, and under certain conditions these men were free to trade directly with the Spanish territories in the New World. E. G. R. Taylor noted that

5. Ibid., p. 151.

6. For Bristol trade in the sixteenth century, see Vanes.

7. G. Connell-Smith, 'English merchants trading to the New World in the early sixteenth century', *Bulletin of the Institute of Historical Research*, xxiii (1950), 53–67 (hereafter cited as Connell-Smith, 'Merchants'); G. Connell-Smith, *Forerunners of Drake* (London, 1954), hereafter cited as Connell-Smith, *Forerunners*). See also Taylor, *Barlow*; and Vanes, p. 347 ff.

8. Quinn, *Discovery*, p. 149, n. 2.

9. Ibid., p. 148.

1. Connell-Smith, 'Merchants', pp. 57–58; *Forerunners*, p. 10; see also Morison, pp. 233–7, for Robert Thorne's letter and John Rut's voyage.

2. Connell-Smith, *Forerunners*, pp. 10, 65, 66–68.

the generation reaching manhood early in the sixteenth century, who were the contemporaries and friends of the Barlow brothers, included Robert Thorne the younger and his brother Nicholas, both of whom had grown up in an atmosphere of adventure and high expectation. As children they must have seen John Cabot in their father's company, and they knew his son Sebastian first of all in Bristol and later in Seville, where they went to take over their father's business after his death in 1518–19.[3]

It is possible, then, that the more enterprising members of the small group of Bristol merchants who were interested in the New World decided that it would be better to leave Bristol and pursue their interest from London or from Spain itself, leaving their less adventurous brethren to continue with their customary trades.

Bristol's lack of involvement across the Atlantic continued to manifest itself during the age of Elizabeth I, and only on two occasions did the city show a flicker of interest. The three voyages of Martin Frobisher in search of a northwest passage between 1576 and 1578 aroused some excitement because some of the ships were fitted out in Bristol and some of the ore, which was thought to be gold-bearing, was brought back there and assayed.[4] In addition, Bristolians had an opportunity of seeing two Eskimos. A local chronicler noted:

They brought likewise a man called Callicho, and a woman called Ignorth: they were savage people and fed only upon raw flesh. The 9th of October he rowed in a little boat made of skin in the water at the Backe, where he killed 2 ducks with a dart, and when he had done carried his boat through the marsh upon his back: the like he did at the weir and other places where many beheld him. He could hit a duck a good distance off and not miss. They died within a month.[5]

The expeditions, however, were primarily London-based and London-financed, and the investment of Bristolians was minimal. C. M. MacInnes maintained that 'in the promoting of these voyages Bristol merchants were deeply concerned . . .',[6] but the only known Bristol investors were Thomas Chester, Thomas Kelke, Thomas Aldworth, and Robert Halton,

3. Taylor, *Barlow*, p. xxii.
4. For the expeditions, see R. Collinson (ed.), *The Three Voyages of Martin Frobisher* (London, 1867; hereafter cited as Collinson); V. Stefansson (ed.), *The Three Voyages of Martin Frobisher* (London, 1938).
5. Francis F. Fox (ed.), *Adams's Chronicle of Bristol* (Bristol, 1910), p. 115.
6. C. M. MacInnes, *A Gateway of Empire* (Bristol, 1939), p. 56 (hereafter cited as MacInnes, *Gateway*).

each of whom put up £25 for the second voyage.[7] Since the total investment in the three voyages was estimated to be £20,345,[8] the modest
£100 from Bristol does not suggest any deep commitment.

The only other occasion on which Bristolians showed an interest in
exploration and colonization across the Atlantic in the second half of the
sixteenth century was in relation to Sir Humphrey Gilbert's activities in
1582–3. In March 1583 Sir Francis Walsingham wrote to Thomas Aldworth, merchant and mayor of Bristol, referring to a letter which Aldworth had written to him in November 1582.[9] Walsingham wrote:

> Your good inclination to the Westerne discoverie I cannot but much
> commend. And for that Sir Humphrey Gilbert, as you have heard long
> since, hath bene preparing into those parts being readie to imbarke there 10
> dayes, who needeth some further supply of shipping then yet he hath, I am
> of opinion that you shall do well if the ship or 2 barkes you write of, be put
> in a readinesse to goe alongst with him, or so soone after as you may . . .,

and he asked Aldworth to confer with the bearers of the letter, Richard
Hakluyt and Thomas Steventon.[1] Thomas Aldworth replied on 27
March, saying that on receipt of these letters 'I presently conferred with
my friends in private, whom I know most affectionate to this godly enterprise, especially with M. William Salterne deputie of our company
of merchants'.[2] Since Aldworth himself was sick, Salterne had 'with as
convenient speede as he could . . . caused an assembly of the merchants
to be gathered'. Walsingham's letters were read out, and

> after some good light given by M. Hakluyt unto them that were ignorant of
> the Countrey and enterprise, and were desirous to be resolved, the motion
> grew generally so well to be liked, that there was eftsoones set downe by
> mens owne hands then present, and apparently knowen by their owne
> speach, and very willing offer, the summe of 1000 markes and upward:
> which summe if it should not suffice, we doubt not but otherwise to furnish
> out for this Westerne discovery, a ship of threescore, and a barke of 40
> tunne, to bee left in the countrey under the direction and government of
> your sonne in law M. Carlile . . .

---

7. Collinson, p. 109.
8. Ibid., p. xiii.
9. Aldworth's letter has not survived and we know of it only from Walsingham's letter.
1. Richard Hakluyt, *The Principal Navigations, Voyages, Traffiques and Discoveries of the English Nation* (12 vols, Glasgow, 1903–5), viii. 132 (hereafter cited as *Principal Navigations*).
2. This does not appear to be a reference to the Society of Merchant Venturers of Bristol. See Patrick McGrath, *The Merchant Venturers of Bristol* (Bristol, 1975), p. 21.

Aldworth asked Walsingham to send further instructions 'to my selfe, my brethren, and the rest of the merchants of this city, at your honors best and most convenient leisure, because we meane not to deferre the finall proceeding in this voyage, any further then to the end of April next coming'.[3]

There are a number of puzzling features about this episode which are discussed by Quinn. Walsingham's letter suggests that the first move came from the Bristol merchants, but there is a possibility that the initiative was in fact taken by Walsingham or Hakluyt or both.[4] It is also possible that Walsingham and Christopher Carleill were double-crossing Sir Humphrey Gilbert and withholding information about the Bristol offer in order that Bristol support should be channelled in the direction of a scheme proposed by Carleill which, it was hoped, would also be backed by the Muscovy Company. In the end, nothing came of Carleill's project, and Bristolians were not required to contribute the 1,000 marks or more which they had undertaken to find.[5]

A modest contribution of £100 towards Frobisher's second voyage and a declaration of intent to provide 1,000 marks for Christopher Carleill's proposed venture do not suggest that there was great interest among Bristolians in exploration and colonization during the Elizabethan period. Whether this was related to the prosperity of Bristol trade in general, we cannot say. Jean Vanes has suggested that, except in the mid-century and the 1560s, the economy of Bristol was not as depressed as used to be thought,[6] and the failure of the city to participate fully in Elizabethan exploration cannot be explained solely in terms of lack of resources.[7]

In the early seventeenth century, Bristol had a bigger contribution to make. How far this was due to a modest expansion in her overseas trade, to the enthusiasm of particular individuals or to pressure from outside is again difficult to say. A few days before the death of Elizabeth I, Martin

3. *Principal Navigations*, viii. 133–4.

4. D. B. Quinn (ed.), *The Voyages and Colonising Enterprises of Sir Humphrey Gilbert* (London, 1940), pp. 76–81 (hereafter cited as Quinn, *Gilbert*).

5. In May 1583, a committee of the Muscovy Company estimated the cost at £4,000 and reported 'One thowsande poundes whereof hathe ben verie readilie offered by the Cittie of Bristoll, the residewe beinge three thowsande poundes remaineth to be furnished by this Cittie of London', Quinn, *Gilbert*, p. 366.

6. Vanes, *passim*.

7. As Andrews has shown, some capital was available in Bristol for privateering, and some merchants got a satisfactory return on their capital, but this is at least partly to be explained in terms of employing in privateering ships which would in peace time have been used in the Iberian trade: K. R. Andrews, *Elizabethan Privateering* (Cambridge, 1969), pp. 32–33, 125–6, 141, 144, 146, 229, 258–61, 271.

Pring sailed from Bristol with the *Speedwell* of about 50 tons and a crew of 30, and the *Discoverer* of 26 tons with 13 men and a boy on a voyage to Virginia.[8] In his account of the expedition, Pring stated that it was 'a voyage set out from the Citie of Bristoll at the charge of the chiefest Merchants and Inhabitants of the said Citie with a small ship and a Barke for the farther discoverie of the North part of Virginia', and that it was undertaken 'upon many probable and reasonable inducements, used unto sundry of the chiefest Merchants of Bristoll, by Master Richard Hakluyt ... after divers meeting and due consultation'. Robert Aldworth and John Whitson, two of the leading merchants in Bristol, were the 'chief furtherers', and in all about £1,000 was raised. Robert Salterne of Bristol, who went with the expedition, had sailed from Falmouth to explore Virginia in the previous year. We do not know how many Bristolians put money into the venture or whether the bulk of the capital was provided by the 'chief furtherers'. Pring planted wheat, rye, and other crops, and carried out some exploration and trade in furs. At the end of July, the *Discoverer* was loaded with sassafras and sent home 'to give some speedie contentment to the Adventurers'.[9] She had been away $5\frac{1}{2}$ months. The *Speedwell* returned a fortnight later. Whether the adventurers did receive 'some speedie contentment' with the results of an expedition which had lasted six months, we do not know, but the venture cannot have been very profitable, and Aldworth and Whitson may have felt that they paid a high price for having their names given to a hill and a bay.[1]

The expedition of Martin Pring seems to have been a spontaneous Bristol venture, but the next occasion on which Bristolians were involved with America was the result of persuasion and pressure from outside. Sir Ferdinando Gorges and Lord Chief Justice Popham, who both had Bristol connections, were interested in settlement in North America at the time when the Virginia Company was in process of formation, and they endeavoured to get support from Bristol.[2] The initial response was not enthusiastic. The minutes of the Common Council of Bristol record that on 12 March 1606 the Lord Chief Justice's letter was read 'touchynge the

---

8. For this voyage, see Samuel Purchas, *Hakluytus Posthumus or Purchas his Pilgrimes* (20 vols, Glasgow, 1905–7), xviii. 322–9 (hereafter cited as Purchas); MacInnes, *Gateway*, pp. 69–70.

9. Purchas, xviii. 328.

1. For an account of the voyage, see Quinn, *Discovery*, pp. 423–7. Pring named a small bay Whitson Bay and one of the hills Mount Aldworth.

2. For Gorges, see R. A. Preston, *Gorges of Plymouth Fort* (Toronto, 1953); C. M. Mac-Innes, *Ferdinando Gorges and New England* (Bristol, 1965).

plantacion in Virginia' and that those present 'were all of opynyon not to adventure any thinge in that action unless yt shall please the Kinges Majestie to undertake the same and to Ioyne in that chardge. And then they will be contributory and adventure in some reasonable proportion.'[3] In April 1606, there was rather more enthusiasm. In the Common Council minutes for 1 April, there is a list of members of the Council who expressed willingness to make contributions for five years, and there is a memorandum that Thomas Hopkins and Thomas Aldworth, merchants, were appointed to confer with the inhabitants of Bristol and to certify what every man would advance towards 'this action of Virginia'.[4] Fourteen out of the forty-four members of the Council undertook to provide yearly contributions amounting to £90 for five years.[5] Whether any of the other inhabitants agreed to contribute, we do not know, nor have we any evidence that the members Common Council paid over the money. Expeditions were sent out in 1606 and 1607 and for a short time a colony was established in 'Northern Virginia', but it was not successful and the settlers returned home.[6]

A number of Bristolians were also concerned in the attempt to plant a colony in Newfoundland. In letters patent of 1610, James I established a company to be known as 'The Treasurer and the Company of the City of London and Bristol for the Colony of Plantations in Newfound Land'.[7] Of the forty-eight members named in the Charter, eleven, including John Guy, were Bristolians, and seven of these at various times held high office in the Bristol Society of Merchant Venturers.[8] It is not absolutely clear whether it was London or Bristol which took the initiative in establishing the Newfoundland Company. A Bristol chronicle with proper local pride stressed the role of the Bristol merchant John Guy:

3. Bristol Record Office: Common Council Proceedings 1598–1608, p. 114. Twenty-six members of the Council were present out of a total of 44.

4. Ibid., p. 115, 1 April 1606.

5. Thomas James, mayor, 20 marks a year for five years; William Hickes, 40s; William Ellis, £3; John Hopkins, £12 10s; John Rowbero and John Guy, 20 marks each; Robert Aldworth, £12 10s; John Boulton, William Cole, £5; Robert Rogers, £3; Arthur Needes, £3.

6. John Latimer, *Annals of Bristol in the Seventeenth Century* (Bristol, 1900), pp. 27–28.

7. The letters patent are printed in C. T. Carr (ed.), *Select Charters of Trading Companies* (London, 1913), pp. 51–62; for the formation of the company, see Cell, 'English in Newfoundland', pp. 123–5.

8. Patrick McGrath (ed.), *Records relating to the Society of Merchant Venturers of the City of Bristol in the Seventeenth Century* (Bristol, 1951), p. 199. The Bristol members were Matthew Haviland, Thomas Aldworth, William Lewes, John Guy, Richard Holworthy, John Langton, Humphrey Hooke, Philip Guy, William Meredith, Adrian Jennings, and John Doughty. There were twenty-five London merchants in the Company.

Also this year Mr. John Guy merchant (being one of the Councill of Bristoll) Intended a Plantation in the Newfoundland, and had gotten a Licence and Charter of the King for the same, having some Rich Merchants of London joined with him for the better Fraying of the charge and bringing it to Pass: and likewise many of this city did put in their Moneys hoping to reap Benefitt in the End, and so Mr Guy with some other Young Merchants (having fitted themselves with Men and other things necessary) took shipping for Newfoundland to make a Triale of the Place by staying there all the winter . . .[9]

Gillian Cell is also inclined to give Bristol the credit for the idea. She writes:

The Bristol subscribers could not but be aware that their city, traditionally linked with the island since the time of John Cabot if not before, now lagged behind the other lesser ports in the exploitation of the fishery. A chartered company, combining local know-how and London wealth, might be the means of restoring Bristol's lost eminence. Bristol's contribution, perhaps of inspiration and certainly of knowledge, was amply recognised in the Company's title which proclaimed the partnership of the two cities.[1]

T. K. Rabb calls the Company 'the one major undertaking of the period whose inspiration appears to have come from Bristol merchants'.[2] About the role of John Guy, there is, of course, no doubt, but the extent of commitment by Bristolians in general is less clear. The original forty-eight members subscribed £25 for a share, although it is possible that they could purchase more than one share.[3] The eleven Bristol subscribers would have bought themselves in by a total payment of £275,[4] and as Cell has shown, in the end 'most of the capital and the work of organisation' came from Londoners, and members of the Company's Council were required by the charter to reside in London.[5] It may be that the pioneer

9. Bristol Record Office: MS. Calendar no. 07831.

1. Cell, 'Subscribers', pp. 613–14.

2. Theodore K. Rabb, *Enterprise and Empire: Merchant and Gentry Investment in the Expansion of England, 1575–1630*, p. 23, n. 7.

3. Cell, 'Subscribers', p. 621.

4. In August 1610 it was discovered that some of the Bristol members, including Humphrey Hooke and William Meredith, had paid for only half their shares. It seems probable that by February 1612 the company had raised additional capital of £720 by further calls on all members, the Bristol members being presumably asked to participate in this (see Cell, 'English in Newfoundland', pp. 136–7).

5. For the history of the company, see Cell, 'English in Newfoundland'; D. W. Prowse, *History of Newfoundland* (n.p., 1895); Purchas, xix. 405 ff.; J. W. Damer Powell, 'The exploration of John Guy in Newfoundland', *Geographical Journal*, lxxxvi (1935), 512–18; *The New World: A Catalogue of an Exhibition of Books, Maps, Manuscripts and Documents* (Lambeth Palace Library, 1957), pp. 41–64.

work of the Bristolian John Guy has given to the merchant community as a whole a reputation which it did not deserve. The venture met with temporary success and resulted in settlement and exploration, but it ran into serious difficulties and there is no record of the settlement after the late 1620s.[6]

Related to the Newfoundland colony was another attempted settlement by Bristolians. The Newfoundland Company had insufficient funds and tried to raise capital by selling land to private developers.[7] Of the five grants which it made, one was to a group of Bristol merchants. The Society of Merchant Venturers Book of Charters records under the year 1618: 'Alsoe this yeere Divers particuler marchants of this Society Didd sett Forwardes the plantacion of a porcion of Land in the Country of Newfoundland called Bristolls Hope, which was graunted and confirmed vnto them, by the Treasouror and Company of the Cittyes of London and Bristoll For the Colonie or Plantacion in Newfoundland . . .',[8] but the settlement was abandoned after a few years.

Bristol was again involved in North America affairs between 1621 and 1623. In 1620 there had been incorporated a Company of New England governed by the 'Council established at Plymouth, in the County of Devon, for the planting, ruling, ordering, and governing of New England in America'. This Company tried to encourage various West Country towns to establish local groups for colonization, and it also had extensive control over the fisheries. On 18 September 1621, the Privy Council wrote to the mayors of Bristol, Exeter, Plymouth, and other West Country towns pointing out that although the Company had offered membership to merchants and others, some persons who had not joined were nevertheless continuing to go to New England to trade or to fish, and this practice was to stop. The mayor sent this letter to the Society of Merchant Venturers together with a letter from Sir Ferdinando Gorges concerning the proposed formation of subsidiary companies for colonization in Bristol, Exeter, and other towns. There was apparently no enthusiasm for the proposal in Bristol, but on the other hand the merchants were anxious that if any individual wanted to go on a fishing voyage, he should be allowed to do so on reasonable terms. A number of Bristol merchants wrote to the Bristol MPs, John Whitson and John Guy, asking them to

6. Guy broke with the Company in 1614: Cell, 'Subscribers', p. 623.
7. For these grants, see Cell, 'English in Newfoundland', pp. 193–6; D. W. Prowse, op. cit., p. 137; Purchas, xix. 445.
8. Society of Merchant Venturers: Book of Charters I, 57.

examine the Company's patent rights. If these were as wide as the Company claimed, then some Merchant Venturers would agree to accept the best terms they could get for licences to fish. In 1623 the Company once more tried to persuade West Country merchants to invest in colonization and the King wrote to the Earl of Pembroke asking him to use his influence. Pembroke sent a letter to the mayor of Bristol on 13 December 1623 urging him to be active in the matter, but there was apparently no enthusiasm in Bristol, whose merchants were concerned not with colonization but with getting the best terms they could for licences to fish.[9]

In 1631, the voyage of the *Henrietta Maria* in search of a northwest passage brought to an end the series of explorations backed by Bristolians which had begun over a hundred and fifty years earlier. The incentive was the fact that London merchants were preparing an expedition, and there was anxiety in Bristol lest Londoners should secure yet another monopoly. What eventually emerged in 1631 were two expeditions: that of Captain Luke Foxe in the *Charles* from London and that of Captain Thomas James from Bristol in a ship which was renamed for the occasion the *Henrietta Maria*. She was a ship of 70 tons provisioned for eighteen months.[1] The Society of Merchant Venturers of Bristol was very interested in the project, and a number of letters relating to it are found in its Book of Trade,[2] but the main cost was borne not by the Society, which had very limited funds, but by the individual merchants concerned in the voyage. The Society guaranteed the wages of all who went on the expedition and seems to have paid out £181 18s 1d.[3] We do not know the total cost, but in February 1631 a letter from John Barker, Richard Longe, John Tayler, and Giles Elbridge stated that about £800 had been subscribed to date.[4] Humphrey Hooke, Andrew Charlton, Miles Jackson, and Thomas Cole are also known to have been involved,[5] and there may, of course, have been others. The failure of the expedition meant that there

---

9. The documents from the Society of Merchant Venturers' Books of Trade relating to this affair were printed by Miller Christy, 'Attempts toward colonization: the council for New England and the Merchant Venturers of Bristol, 1621–1623', *American Historical Review*, iv (1898–9), 678–702. See also Preston, *Gorges of Plymouth Fort* and MacInnes, *Ferdinando Gorges and New England*.

1. Miller Christy (ed.), *The Voyages of Captain Luke Foxe of Hull and Captain Thomas James of Bristol in Search of a Northwest Passage in 1631–2* (2 vols, London, 1894); C. M. MacInnes, *Captain Thomas James and the Northwest Passage* (Bristol, 1967).

2. Printed in Miller Christy, op. cit.

3. Society of Merchant Venturers: Treasurer's Book I, 17.

4. Society of Merchant Venturers: Book of Trade, p. 186.

5. Ibid. :p. 194.

were additional names on the list of Bristolians who had burnt their fingers financing voyages of exploration.

Writing about investment in English overseas enterprises between 1575 and 1630, Rabb has commented on 'the sheer magnitude of popular involvement' and remarked that 'without the backing of thousands of obscure people the great successes could never have been achieved'.[6] Such comments could hardly be applied to Bristol in these years, and, indeed, as far as the whole period 1480–1631 is concerned, the admittedly limited evidence suggests that investment in such enterprises was the work of a very small number of men and that it was very modest. This does not, of course, mean that certain Bristolians do not deserve an important place in the history of exploration and colonization. It could also be argued that the contacts with America between 1480 and 1631 established traditions and attitudes which were helpful in the second half of the century when the city became the port of embarkation for thousands of Englishmen emigrating across the Atlantic[7] and built up a very important trade with the West Indies and America.[8] Although this, like the exploitation of the cod fisheries, might have been possible even if no explorers or settlers had sailed from Bristol in the period 1480–1631, it may be that the small band of pioneers and investors helped in the long run to win for their city dividends which they failed to obtain for themselves.

6. Theodore K. Rabb, 'Investment in English overseas empire, 1575–1630', *Economic History Review*, 2nd series, xix (1966), 70. For a detailed examination of investment, see Rabb, *Enterprise and Empire*, which stresses the overwhelming importance of London and concludes that 'it is impossible to ascribe more than minor importance to the role of other ports' (pp. 22–23).

7. For the passage of more than 10,000 emigrants through Bristol between 1654 and 1685, see *Bristol and America*, preface by M. Dermott Harding (Bristol, 1929); a new edition of the two volumes in Bristol Record Office relating to 'Servants to Foreign Plantations' is being prepared by Mr Noel Currer-Briggs.

8. In 1637–8, two ships from New England, three from Newfoundland, and two from the West Indies discharged cargoes in Bristol; in 1699–1700, 24 arrived from America, 50 from the West Indies, and 9 from Newfoundland: Patrick McGrath (ed.), *Merchants and Merchandise in Seventeenth-Century Bristol* (Bristol, 1955), p. 281.

6

The English in the Caribbean
1560-1620

K.R.ANDREWS

In the 1620s the planting of the first English settlements, coinciding with the formation of Dutch and French colonies, opened a new era in the West Indies. In examining English Caribbean activity in the preceding six decades it is impossible to ignore this sequel, to which the incursions of the Elizabethans may appear a prologue of doubtful relevance. That crabwise, scuttling motion of small groups taking precarious hold on unoccupied islands seems a far cry from Elizabethan sea-dogs commanding trade, ransom, or plunder, and conventional emphasis on the Hawkins–Drake saga tends to exaggerate the contrast, suggesting a marked discontinuity that demands explanation. Yet as long ago as 1913 James Williamson declared that the English tradition of maritime achievement rested 'not only upon the deeds of the great names which History records in her most lurid passages, but also upon the accumulated exploits of the infinite number of small men, but for whom the Drakes and the Hawkinses, the masters of the sea, would never have been'.[1] Since then we have learned much about the small men who in the sixteenth century opened up the Atlantic to English navigations and America to English colonization. The majority of their voyages were to the Caribbean, the history of which cannot be understood so long as these innumerable petty intrusions are either ignored or treated as footnote material to accounts of more famous expeditions. Conversely, the Caribbean significance of these few major ventures becomes clear only when they are seen in the context of the continuous erosion of Spain's position by a host of humbler men.

The more traditionalist version took definitive shape before the First World War on the basis of contemporary narrative matter from Hakluyt and other publications, some of later date, supplemented by some state paper and comparable documentation. Elizabethan publicity requires

---

1. J. A. Williamson, *Maritime Enterprise, 1485–1558* (Oxford, 1913), p. 122.

rather more than the pinch of salt the Victorians and Edwardians gave it. The prominence given to large expeditions was deliberate. Drake's 1585 West Indies raid, for example, was thought 'a very fit thing to be published, that they [the meaner sort of people] may see what victories a fewe Englishe men have made upon great numbers of Spaniardes'.[2] Like some other voyages of Drake and Hawkins, this was in part a political demonstration; its impact upon Spain's colonies fell far short of its success as a public relations exercise. Hero-worship also tended to inflate the importance of major ventures, though the idolization of Drake and Hawkins came later, reaching its height in the heady years of imperialism before 1914. Then too, strong views about naval strategy were in vogue. The Elizabethans cannot be held responsible for the grandiose notions of sea power thrust upon them by the disciples of A. T. Mahan. The former may have been given to fantasy, but their fantasies had little in common with the punditry of the Dreadnought age. Isolating English from French and Dutch activity obscured the international dimensions of Caribbean enterprise and reinforced the impression that the challenge to Spain consisted of occasional invasions, grand intentions, and minimal results.

The principal handicap of the earlier authorities was the paucity of accurate information available about the Caribbean in the later sixteenth century. The relevant Spanish source material in print amounted to little, nor did modern Spanish historians provide much help.[3] Research over the past fifty years has substantially improved the position. Haring and the Chaunu have used the Seville archive to demonstrate the workings of Spain's Atlantic system and studies of various parts of the Caribbean and of its defence have grown from the same rich soil.[4] At the same time

2. Walter Bigges, *A summarie and true discourse of Sir Frances Drakes West Indian voyage* (first issue by Richard Field, 1589, p. ii).

3. The classic Spanish histories such as Herrera are not of much use for this subject, nor are the nineteenth-century collections of *documentos inéditos*. Towards the end of the century valuable matter became available in Juan López de Velasco, *Geografía y Descripción Universal de las Indias* (Madrid, 1895; references herein are to the Madrid 1971 edition, cited as Velasco) and in E. Ruidíaz y Caravia, *La Florida, su Conquista y Colonización por Pedro Menéndez y Avilés* (2 vols, Madrid, 1893; hereafter cited as Ruidíaz). English historians relied heavily on C. Fernández Duro, *Armada Española desde la Unión de los Reinos de Castilla y de Aragón* (9 vols, Madrid, 1895–1903).

4. C. H. Haring, *Trade and Navigation between Spain and the Indies* (Harvard, 1918); H. et P. Chaunu, *Séville et l'Atlantique, 1504–1650* (11 vols, Paris, 1956–9; hereafter cited as Chaunu); A. Morales Carrión, *Puerto Rico and the Non-Hispanic Caribbean* (Puerto Rico, 1952, hereafter cited as Morales Carrión); F. Morales Padrón, *Jamaica Española* (Seville, 1952); I. A. Wright, *The Early History of Cuba, 1492–1586* (New York, 1916); P. Ojer, *La Formación del Oriente Venezolano* (Caracas, 1966); D. Angulo Iñíguez, *Bautista Antoneli: Las Fortificaciones Americanas del Siglo XVI* (Madrid, 1942; hereafter cited as Angulo Iñíguez); I. A. Wright, 'Rescates, with special reference to Cuba, 1599–1610', *Hispanic American Historical*

printed source material directly concerning English voyages has steadily accumulated, mostly quarried in Seville by Irene Wright, whose three volumes of translations and other works illuminated Spanish reactions in remarkable detail.[5] Much fresh English documentation has also appeared and above all the coupling of English and Spanish statements has borne fruit. David Quinn's *Roanoke Voyages* and more recent writings have shown how intensively this dialogue of evidence can be exploited to trace Spanish reactions to foreign enterprise with greater precision than was formerly possible and so to promote a more dynamic analysis of transatlantic rivalry. Moreover, in underlining the strategic interdependence of the southeast coast of North America and the Caribbean his findings have continually shed light on the latter region.[6] The advance of historical work on both fronts thus provides some encouragement and excuse for the following review.[7]

The slave-trade voyages of John Hawkins must have a certain prominence in any record of English Caribbean activity because they virtually began it. Nevertheless it was a false start. After the 1560s the English abandoned the slave trade for many decades and the events themselves do

Review, iii (1920), 333–61 (hereafter cited as Wright, 'Rescates'); E. Sluiter, 'Dutch-Spanish rivalry in the Caribbean area, 1594–1609', *Hispanic American Historical Review*, xxviii (1948), 165–96 (hereafter cited as Sluiter); R. Boulind, 'Shipwreck and mutiny in Spain's galleys on the Santo Domingo station, 1583', *Mariner's Mirror*, lviii (1972), 297–330 (hereafter cited as Boulind).

5. I. A. Wright (ed.), *Spanish Documents concerning English Voyages to the Caribbean, 1527–1568* (London, 1929; hereafter cited as Wright, *Spanish Documents 1527–1568*); *Documents concerning English Voyages to the Spanish Main, 1569–1580* (London, 1932; hereafter cited as Wright, *Documents concerning 1569–1580*); *Further English Voyages to Spanish America, 1583–1594* (London, 1951; hereafter cited as Wright, *Further English Voyages*); *Historia Documentada de San Cristóbal de la Habana en el Siglo XVI* (2 vols, Havana, 1927); *Historia Documentada de San Cristóbal de la Habana en la Primera Mitad del Siglo XVII* (Havana, 1930; hereafter cited as Wright, *Habana en la Primera Mitad*); 'The Spanish version of Sir Anthony Shirley's raid of Jamaica, 1597', *Hispanic American Historical Review*, v (1922), 227–48; further Spanish and English material on the voyages has appeared in K. R. Andrews (ed.), *English Privateering Voyages to the West Indies, 1588–1595* (Cambridge, 1959) and *The Last Voyage of Drake and Hawkins* (Cambridge, 1972; hereafter cited as Andrews, *Last Voyage*).

6. D. B. Quinn (ed.), *The Roanoke Voyages, 1584–1590* (2 vols, London, 1955; hereafter cited as Quinn, *Roanoke Voyages*); 'James I and the beginnings of empire in America', *Journal of Imperial and Commonwealth History*, ii (1974), 135–52 (hereafter cited as Quinn, 'James I'); 'An Anglo-French "voyage of discovery" to North America in 1604–5 and its sequel', *Bulletin de l'Institut Historique Belge de Rome*, xliv (1974), 513–34; 'The voyage of *Triall* 1606–1607: an abortive Virginia venture', *American Neptune*, xxxi (1971), 85–103.

7. I am of course much indebted to earlier surveys that have placed the English voyages in the context of Caribbean history, so correcting what I have called the 'traditionalist' interpretation, notably: A. P. Newton, *The European Nations in the West Indies, 1493–1688* (London, 1933); and J. H. Parry and P. M. Sherlock, *A Short History of the West Indies* (London, 1963).

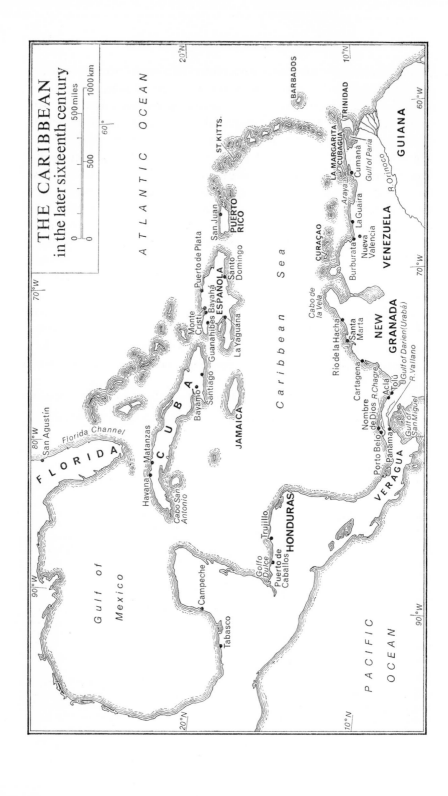

THE CARIBBEAN
in the later sixteenth century

500miles
1000 km
500
500
0
0

20°N

ATLANTIC OCEAN

60°

70°W

80°W

90°W

BARBADOS

ST KITTS.

San Juan
PUERTO
RICO

Puerto de Plata

Monte
Cristi
Guanahibes Bayahá
ESPAÑOLA
Santo
Domingo
La Yaguana

Santiago
Bayamo
CUBA

JAMAICA

Caribbean Sea

Havana
Matanzas
Cabo San
Antonio

Florida Channel

FLORIDA

San Agustin

Gulf
of
Mexico

Trujillo
Golfo
Dulce
Puerto de
Caballos HONDURAS

Campeche

Tabasco

PACIFIC

OCEAN

10°N

10°N

TRINIDAD

LA MARGARITA
CUBAGUA
Araya
Cumaná
Gulf of Paria

R. Orinoco

GUIANA

60°W

VENEZUELA

La Guaira
Nueva
Valencia

CURAÇAO

Burburata

70°W

Cabo de
la Vela

Rio de la Hacha
Santa
Marta
NEW
GRANADA

Cartagena
Tolú
Aclá
R. Chagre
Nombre
de Dios
Porto Belo
Panamá
VERAGUA

Gulf of Darien (Urabá)
R. Vallano
Gulf of
San Miguel

90°W

20°N

10°N

not, as is commonly assumed, explain this. The battle of San Juan de Ulúa had traumatic significance for national feeling in England, but its influence on the Caribbean was slight. The demand for slaves remained much the same and opportunities to pursue the trade there were not affected. The force that defeated Hawkins in 1568 did not stay in the Caribbean nor, had it done so, could it have stopped smuggling. Why then did not the English resume the trade? The Hakluyt account of the first voyage relates that Hawkins, assured by his Canarian contacts 'that Negros were very good marchandise in Hispaniola, and that store of Negros might easily bee had upon the coast of Guinea, resolved with himselfe to make triall thereof'.[8] The first venture had to be one of commercial reconnaissance and the whole series only makes economic sense as an exploratory speculation that proved disappointing and was consequently dropped.

The market for slaves probably proved less attractive than Hawkins initially hoped. The richest areas of Spanish exploitation, Mexico and Peru, were monopolized by the Seville fleets operating to Cartagena and Vera Cruz. Central America fell within the Mexican orbit, New Granada and the Panama Isthmus within Cartagena's. The market open to the interloper comprised the Greater Antilles and the settlements of Tierra Firme from the Gulf of Paria to Santa Marta. Since the collapse of their first boom the islands had developed exports of hides, sugar, and ginger and imports of black slaves to produce them. By 1570, according to Velasco, Española had 'more than twelve or thirteen thousand negroes', but suffered 'daily depopulation' because 'as gold is not mined, merchants do not frequent it, and so they cannot trade their produce'. Santo Domingo itself was 'diminishing, like the rest of the settlements of this island, because ships do not go there to trade'.[9] It was the same story in Puerto Rico. Ginger was widely cultivated and there were about twelve sugar plantations. About the end of the century ginger still flourished, but sugar production had slumped.[1] Cuba was a worse case in 1570: 'its citizens are all poor and this island, like Española, is losing its population day by day in the absence of gold', sugar having failed to develop to any comparable extent.[2] The islands were failing to realize their economic potential for lack of access to labour supplies and markets, both of which Hawkins, among others, could to some extent provide. But the trade was

8. R. Hakluyt, *The Principal Navigations* (12 vols, Glasgow, 1903–5), x. 7 (hereafter cited as *Principal Navigations*).　　　9. Velasco, pp. 51–52.

1. Ibid., p. 67; Morales Carrión, p. 36; cf. B.L., Sloane MSS. 3289.　　　2. Velasco, p. 58.

bound to be small in scale at first and its chances of growth were uncertain.

The coast of the Main offered no better opportunities for the present and foreseeable future. Trinidad was not yet colonized; the pearl fisheries at La Margarita and Cumaná were in decline; Cubagua was no longer inhabited; there was little business for slave traders in eastern Venezuela.[3] The vast area westwards to Cabo de la Vela contained about ten settlements of Spaniards with some 350 citizens, 'all very poor people', with the exception of those at Nueva Valencia who could pay in gold for wares, including slaves, brought to their harbour of Burburata.[4] Further west Río de la Hacha's pearl fishery prospered, but it was a small place of some fifty households and almost no hinterland. Santa Marta, having largely lost its hinterland of New Granada to Cartagena, was dwindling, depressed, and hard-pressed by warlike Indians throughout the later sixteenth century.[5] Spanish neglect of these ports increased in proportion to their distance east of Cartagena. The latter, a well-supplied base, did not afford much chance of trade to interlopers. The rest were accessible but not substantial markets. Unlike the plantations of the islands, moreover, most of these struggling townships had as yet little capacity for economic expansion even given improved outlets.[6] In sum the market available to Hawkins, as to other Caribbean interlopers in the period under review, was not a major field of commerce. Corresponding roughly to the amorphous *audiencia* of Santo Domingo, it was difficult of access from the main centres of Spanish wealth and power to the west by reason of the prevailing winds and starved of official favour as well as mercantile attention because it promised nothing like the rich returns of Peru, Mexico, or even Guatemala.

Even within this narrow scope Hawkins faced strong competition. The French were on the same footing but had more experience. The Portuguese had the advantages of easy access to supplies in Africa, familiarity with illicit commerce in the Indies, where not a few of the

---

3. Velasco, pp. 72, 78; S. A. Mosk, 'Spanish pearl-fishing operations on the Pearl Coast in the sixteenth century', *Hispanic American Historical Review*, xviii (1938), 392–400.

4. Velasco, pp. 73–75.   5. Ibid., pp. 77–78, 191–2.

6. Chaunu, viii (1), 613–79. Most of the foundations were of very recent date (for example, Caracas 1567) and frequently threatened by hostile Indians.

---

7. Jerónimo de Torres, 'Relación sobre cosas de la Isla Española' (1577) in E. Rodríguez Demorizi, *Relaciones Históricas de Santo Domingo* (Ciudad Trujillo, Dominican Republic, 1945), pp. 128–43 (hereafter cited as Rodríguez Demorizi) observes: 'the Portuguese fears the Frenchman and the Spanish fleet, goes more prudently and generally brings smaller ships, less well equipped than the French with munitions of war'.

merchants and planters were themselves Portuguese, and low shipping costs, since they spent far less on manning and arming their slavers than Hawkins did.[7] To the English interloper the Caribbean in Hawkins's time offered little more than a casual trade of scraps and pickings, suitable for a provincial shipowner seeking to employ a ship or two for windfalls of dubious origin, but scarcely worth the attention of big merchants. The Londoners who adventured with Hawkins were not interested in expanding the nation's cloth sales, as is sometimes assumed, nor did merchandise other than slaves play much part in Hawkins's transactions. What attracted their capital was the slave trade, with its prospect of high rates of profit. However, they must have over-estimated the size of the market, influenced presumably by vague reports of the scale of Spain's American trade. Hawkins's decision to switch his attention to the Main after the first venture (1562–3) suggests that the syndicate was not content with the Española market. In two of the three subsequent voyages the English failed to sell all their slaves. On the other hand outlays were naval rather than commercial in scale because Hawkins had to be equipped to overcome local resistance, 'trusting the Spaniards no further, then that by his owne strength he was able still to master them'.[8] For the game to be worth the candle the prizes had to be large; experience taught that they were small. After 1568 the Londoners withdrew their support for Caribbean venturing.

The collapse of the slave-trade project was due at least as much to difficulties in West Africa as to disillusionment with the West Indies. The Portuguese, strongly entrenched in the Guinea trade, made it hot for interlopers in the 1550s and 1560s. Lacking experience of the trade, local bases or connections with African dealers, the English tended to resort to piracy on Portuguese vessels and shore raids on African villages.[9] Escalating hostilities made each venture more difficult than the last and about 1568 the English apparently ceased to attempt trade. Spasmodic piracy persisted in the 1570s and early 1580s, but the commercial interest turned its attention elsewhere. In short, the risks and costs of operations at this corner of the triangle became prohibitive.

Commercially, therefore, the slave-trade initiative stood little chance of success and the fact that Hawkins did not turn to wholesale plunder in the Caribbean until after 1568 lends credence to Williamson's theory that

8. *Principal Navigations*, x. 8.

9. P. E. H. Hair, 'Protestants as pirates, slavers and proto-missionaries: Sierra Leone 1568 and 1582', *Journal of Ecclesiastical History*, xxi (1970), 203–24.

until then he hoped to ingratiate himself with the Spanish authorities so as to secure a privileged position as a licensed trader. This not unreasonable inference should be distinguished, however, from the claim that he planned to secure commercial dominance in the region by naval means, providing Spain with 'an armed force for the policing of the Caribbean' against the French, in return for the right to trade.[1] Such a view depends upon slight and dubious evidence, makes unwarrantable assumptions about Hawkins's attitudes to the French and Spaniards and implies that he failed to perceive the logistic facts that made his own operations possible. The notion that superior naval striking power conferred control of the sea upon the victor was foreign to that age and especially inapplicable to the Caribbean. No single force operating from Europe could police that vast sea. It could only be secured against intruders by an elaborate system of flotillas working from local bases. The Spaniards, with local resources beyond any that Hawkins could hope for, never achieved such a system. Can Hawkins have imagined that Spain would endow him with naval bases as well as rights of trade?

Nevertheless something more than commerce was probably contemplated. The connection of some of the partners with the royal navy, the involvement of the Queen's ships and the backing of such people as Leicester and Cecil inevitably gave the proceedings a political dimension. This is not to argue the existence of some grand strategic plan or objectives, for there is no evidence of any. The promoters were interested in Florida, but their intentions with respect to it were probably as obscure to themselves as they are to us. Of course they dreamed of breaching or even capturing the main trade of America, but that was an aspiration, not a guide to action. Hawkins and his partners were opportunists reconnoitring the fabled wealth of a strange region with all the optimistic vagueness typical of Elizabethan initiatives.[2] This gesture, tentative but undeniably aggressive, was denounced by Spain as a challenge to her sovereignty and rudely rebuffed at San Juan de Ulúa.

This and the next decade did, however, see critical events that shaped the structure of Caribbean rivalry for years to come. French raiding—a by-product of the Franco-Spanish wars in Europe—had begun to acquire strategic implications in the 1550s.[3] When the end of the war passed the

1. J. A. Williamson, *Sir John Hawkins* (Oxford, 1927), p. 77.

2. Richard Pares observed of Williamson's theory that it 'made more sense of Hawkins's voyage than Hawkins could have made of it for himself when he set out'—*War and Trade in the West Indies* (London, 1936), p. 6.

3. G. Marcel, *Les corsaires français au XVIe siècle dans les Antilles* (Paris, 1902); Ch. de la Roncière, *Histoire de la Marine Française* (6 vols, Paris, 1909-32), iii. 587–8.

initiative to the Huguenots, their attempt to occupy Florida (1562–5) was still essentially a move in the European struggle, directed at the supposed source of Spain's military power, American bullion. Jean Ribault's plan was to set up naval bases dominating the Florida Channel and northwest Cuba, so blocking the route of the plate fleets. The practical difficulties in founding such a base were great, but the greatest danger lay in giving Spain a fixed target on which to concentrate her considerable striking power. The unwonted speed and crushing effect of Spain's reaction proved the ability of Pedro Menéndez de Avilés, the commander of the force that destroyed French Florida in 1565; but it demonstrated equally clearly and even more importantly the Crown's prime concern for the safety of the treasure, its vital interest. This it was that gave Menéndez not only the strength he needed to destroy Ribault, but also effective backing for his subsequent drive to preempt Florida and the channel.[4]

At the same time the French were penetrating the West Indies at a different level, combining contraband trade and maritime plunder in small-scale ventures. Already in the 1540s they frequented Española, Cuba, and Puerto Rico,[5] while Burburata was so dominated by their shipping that its population was removed in 1553.[6] In 1577 Jerónimo de Torres described and analysed the phenomenon in detail.[7] The French and Portuguese usually, he said, came to the Main first, via La Margarita, but 'the Portuguese do not proceed from Río de la Hacha towards Nombre de Dios, nor do the French so-called merchants; those that do are robbers, who go on for plunder to the rivers of Chagre and Veragua'. The rest would cross to the large islands for trade, where the French, using stronger ships than the Portuguese, would at will supplement their return cargoes by looting Spanish and Portuguese vessels. *Rescates*—illicit transactions with foreign traders—began to reach deep into the economy of Española, involving not only the lesser settlements that handled the barter of hides and sugar for European manufactures and slaves, but also leading elements in the capital. The neighbouring islands and Tierra Firme were affected and since all were subject besides to the attentions of

4. Ruidíaz, ii, *passim*, especially pp. 90–95; Bartolomé Barrientos, *Pedro Menéndez de Avilés*, ed. A. Kerrigan (Gainesville, 1965); Gonzalo Solís de Meras, *Pedro Menéndez de Avilés, Adelantado, Governor and Captain-General of Florida*, ed. J. T. Connor (Deland, 1923).

5. Earlier visits appear to have been occasional raids rather than persistent frequentation, but the point is obscure. See, for example, Morales Carrión, p. 15.

6. Velasco, p. 76.

7. Loc. cit.

plain robbers, the local authorities developed an acute sense of insecurity. Río de la Hacha reported in 1568 that 'for every two ships that come hither from Spain, twenty corsairs appear. For this reason not a town on all this coast is safe.'[8] Smuggling was so prevalent in Española that Torres warned the King: 'if the citizens profit by this business, in effect your land is lost', for the French were driving Spanish shipping out of the trade.[9]

Menéndez, who held chief responsibility for West Indian defence until his death in 1574, was deeply concerned about the protection of the islands against these *cosarios*, as his letters and his own efforts to hound down the intruders show.[1] But with limited resources he had to give priority to defending the treasure and strategic points on its route. Therefore he made sure of the fleets themselves, the Florida Channel and Havana. Otherwise he had to be content with placing extra men and guns in Santo Domingo, Puerto Rico, and one or two lesser ports. The armada he designed and thereafter directed consisted mainly of galleons, which were primarily concerned with convoying the transatlantic fleets. Their various additional functions in the Carribbean, when not under repair, included occasional expeditions to clear the coasts of undesirable visitors. But chasing corsairs with galleons proved an expensive and rather unrewarding practice.[2] Thus Ribault's threat, though not really strong, unintentionally aggravated Spain's difficulties in other parts of the Caribbean. In the islands a predatory kind of commerce was at that juncture gathering dangerous momentum, setting in train a process of corrosion that soon became hard to arrest. And west of Cartagena a more urgent danger arose as the French corsairs, defeated in Florida, switched their attack to the equally vital and exposed Panama Isthmus, where the English now joined them.

In 1570 Velasco referred to Nombre de Dios as 'very subject to corsairs and without defence'. This was true of the entire coast from the Gulf of

8. Wright, *Spanish Documents 1527–1568*, pp. 118–19.
9. Loc. cit. The equally interesting *relación* by Diego Sánchez de Sotomayor in 1578 showed Trinidad and the neighbouring coasts and islands even more exposed to French shipping than Española, which was, he estimated, visited by ten or twelve large French ships each year: Museo Naval, Navarrete MSS., vol. 27, no. 51 (ff. 406–30), now available in the facsimile edition *Colección de Documentos y Manuscritos Compilados por Fernández de Navarrete* (32 vols, Nedeln, Liechtenstein, 1971; hereafter cited as Navarrete MSS.).
1. Ruidíaz, ii. 122, where Menéndez defines his task in terms of securing the ndies and Florida and ending the intrusion of corsairs and contrabandists, is typical; similarly ibid. ii. 160–9 and Barrientos, pp. 139, 142, 149.
2. Criticism of the galleons and preference for galleys for anti-corsair work were argued in a number of memoranda around 1580, e.g. Torres (loc. cit.) and Navarrete MSS., vol. 22, nos. 67 (1580?) and 87 (1584).

Darien to Veragua.[3] In 1569 the situation deteriorated sharply: French pirates seized vessels along the coast, raided up the Chagre and sacked Tolu. In the next four years French and English raiders focused on Nombre de Dios and the routes thither from Cartagena by sea and from Panama by sea, river, and mule-track. Though probably less numerous than panicky Spanish reports suggested, they caused substantial loss to the Crown and private merchants and jeopardized all trade at the heart of Spain's Indies. The Spaniards learned as early as 1571 that the French were making charts of the Isthmus and planning to attack Panama.[4] What made matters worse was the simultaneous menace of the two or three thousand *cimarrones*, whose aggressive bands inflicted 'heavy damage in robbery and death . . . daily, upon the highway from this city Panama to Nombre de Dios and the House at Cruces'.[5] Finally the colonists' fears materialized when the Negroes and corsairs united to develop the amphibious form of piracy-cum-banditry that culminated in Drake's capture of a pack-train of bullion in 1573.

Against these assaults the Spaniards had no adequate defence. As they realized, 'all this kingdom and the country of Darien, Acla and Veragua is little explored and dominated'.[6] Panama and Veragua together had but seven Spanish settlements with eight hundred households in all.[7] Their inland expeditions against the *cimarrones* achieved little in the face of the rebels' guerrilla tactics and in that land of mountain and jungle they could hardly prevent a corsair making a temporary base in a remote harbour, entering the unprotected Chagre or moving across country with Negro help. When the fleet came to Cartagena galleons went in pursuit of the pirates, but all observers agreed that they proved useless for the purpose.[8] The events of 1572–3 introduced a new note of desperation into official reports: 'if remedial action be delayed disaster is imminent . . . the principal design of these English is to explore and study this land, and what strength there is in it, in order to come from England with more people to plunder and occupy it'.[9] Three years later, when Oxenham resumed the

3. Velasco, p. 174. A report of 1575 said that letters received showed that 'in these last four years in this area it has been impossible to live with security on the entire coast of Tierra Firme, Santa Marta, Cartagena, Veragua and Honduras for the many English corsairs' (Navarrete MSS., vol. 25, no. 36, f. 145). Very few of the English pirates in the West Indies in the 1570s (Andrew Barker and Gilbert Horseley, for example) have been identified.
4. Navarrete MSS., vol. 25, no. 25 (ff. 110–13).
5. Wright, *Documents Concerning 1569–1580*, p. 33; pp. 24 and 72 for Spanish estimates of their numbers.
6. Ibid., p. 17.   7. Velasco, p. 171.
8. Wright, *Documents Concerning 1569–1580*, pp. 18, 32, 63, 66, 109–10, 151.
9. Ibid., pp. 49–50; and for a similar statement, p. 66.

Negro alliance, crossing from Acla to the Pacific and using the Pearl Islands as a base for the seizure of treasure ships, the colonial government was again worried that the English meant to return in greater numbers, settle among the *cimarrones* and infest the Pacific.[1] The Vallano country east of the upper Chagre and the land-and-water routes from the Acla coast to the Gulf of San Miguel looked very insecure and it was feared that the enemy, once established there, would become 'masters of the Pacific, which God forbid, for this is the key to all Peru'.[2]

The danger was potential rather than actual, for neither Drake's nor Oxenham's strength was sufficient for more than marauding. Their secret harbours could not become firm bases without continuous support from England, which in these years was never at all likely.[3] But the strategic implications of these episodes and the continuance of piracy on the north coast did alarm the Spaniards into action. Prompt moves by sea and land from Panama broke Oxenham's force in 1577 and in the next few years military aid from Peru brought about the settlement of the *cimarrones* in two villages under Spanish tutelage.[4] In 1578 the Crown, responding to repeated pleas, sent two galleys to Cartagena to protect the Isthmus coast. They proved their worth within a year by taking six or seven French corsairs and in consequence, as Irene Wright observed, 'such enemies preferred for the next few years to prey on shipping along the undefended coasts of the Antilles'.[5] The two galleys sent to Santo Domingo in 1582 did not suffice to police the Antilles and their inadequacy appeared immediately, when in 1583 the wreck of one and mutiny aboard the other effectively put the whole force out of action.[6] Here and on the Venezuela coast French interloping flourished in the late 1570s and early 1580s, again with some English accompaniment, notably the fleet of seven sail led by William Hawkins in 1583, that poached pearls off La Margarita and Puerto Rico, sold contraband in both areas and possibly gutted a treasure ship to make the voyage.[7]

Neither in Florida nor in the Isthmus was the strategic threat to

1. Ibid., pp. 113, 122, 130–1, 135, 138, etc.   2. Ibid., p. 142.

3. The actual level of planning is suggested by Henry Killigrew's letter to William Davison in August 1577: 'ther is one oxenden now in perow that hath 150000 li. in gold but he hath no shipping nor meanes to bring yt thence. Ser Umphery Gylbert som think wyll Relyve hem'—D. B. Quinn, *The Voyages and Colonising Enterprises of Sir Humphrey Gilbert* (2 vols, London, 1940), p. 169 (hereafter cited as Quinn, *Gilbert*); there appears to be no evidence of links between the Barker, Horseley, and Oxenham ventures.

4. *Principal Navigations*, xi. 234; Wright, *Documents Concerning 1569–1580*, pp. 223–41. The villages were Santiago del Principe, near Nombre de Dios, and Santa Cruz la Real, on the Río Vallano (now the Chepo)—see Andrews, *Last Voyage*, pp. 207–12.

5. Wright, *Documents Concerning 1569–1580*, p. lxiv.   6. Boulind.

7. J. A. Williamson, *Hawkins of Plymouth* (London, 1949), pp. 220–5.

Spanish America a powerful one. Neither in Florida nor in the Isthmus was Spain's reaction strong enough to secure a firm hold on the area— Menéndez and his successors had a hard struggle to maintain a Spanish presence in Florida, while the Isthmus appeared almost as vulnerable in 1607 as in 1572.[8] But in both cases the measures taken were sufficient for the time being to withstand and divert enemy pressure to areas of less vital concern to the Crown.

Drake's West Indies raid of 1585–6 accentuated this pattern of challenge and response. Although the strategic thrust was now more pronounced than in former English enterprise, which had seemed more concerned with private profit than with breaking Spain's New World monopoly, Drake was not primarily concerned with English prospects in or near the Caribbean. It was the armed confrontation of Spain and England in Europe that generated this expedition and determined its principal aims: to acquire booty for Elizabeth's war chest, to weaken Spain's military capacity by disrupting her transatlantic trade, and to damage her politically in Europe by exposing the vulnerability of the empire that was generally supposed to be her main source of strength. Essentially Drake's plan was to sack various centres, particularly Santo Domingo, Cartagena, Panama, and Havana. At this last, it was thought, 'If he find the place tenable and s [. . .], he will leave a company of soldiers [there]'.[9] This and other reference to settlement suggests tentative discussion of various possibilities rather than the formulation of any clear plan. Certainly no question arose of permanent colonization within the Caribbean. The most that was envisaged was short-term military occupation of a base to exert pressure on the enemy until he yielded on the main issues. Humphrey Gilbert had shown the intention of such projects in 1577, when he advocated the occupation of Cuba and Española to divert the King of Spain's energies and convince him 'that any kind of peace shalbe better for him then warres with England'.[1]

Ralph Lane's letter to Sir Philip Sidney suggests that some such scheme was originally contemplated for 1585, the assumption being that Sidney would command an occupying force and so 'gaulle ye king of Spayne, as yt wolde dyverte hys forces'. Sidney's absence, however, implied the relegation of this project from a high to a low priority[2] and Spanish

8. D. B. Quinn, *England and the Discovery of America, 1481–1620* (London, 1974), pp. 264–81; Manuel Serrano y Sanz (ed.), *Relaciones Históricas y Geográficas de América Central* (Madrid, 1908), pp. 137–218 ('Descripción de Panamá . . . 1607: 3.—Que pertenece a lo militar').

9. J. S. Corbett (ed.), *Papers Relating to the Navy During the Spanish War, 1585–1587* (London, 1898), p. 73.

1. Quinn, *Gilbert*, pp. 176–80.   2. Quinn, *Roanoke Voyages*, pp. 205, 250.

material shows that Drake's intention at Cartagena in February 1586 was merely to use it as a temporary base to launch and cover a raid on Panama. The stated reason for giving up the place was that with manpower reduced by sickness 'the keeping of the towne against the force of the enemy' involved risking the fleet. The Spaniards for their part thought Drake could not afford the time to attack the Isthmus for fear the expected armada would catch his fleet undermanned.[3] It is not surprising that discretion proved the better part of Drake's valour here and at Havana. One Spaniard maintained, 'I am quite certain that he will not attack Havana because there was great dissension among them and they could agree on nothing'.[4] No doubt some of the English had reasonable misgivings about plans that assumed the sustained logistic effort and political commitment necessary to hold a base within the Caribbean. The less accessible colony at Roanoke was of course a different matter, for the Spaniards could not immediately locate and destroy it, whereas Drake was able to demolish San Agustín. Though possibly not a major object of the expedition, this blow did reduce Spain's chances of scotching what was essentially a threat to the treasure fleets. But the advantage was lost as soon as gained, for the Spaniards in Florida speedily rebuilt their base, while Drake found himself ironically obliged to evacuate Lane's entire colony.

Drake's raid, therefore, did not produce any tangible gain of a strategic order in the Caribbean. The dramatic news of a virtually unopposed tour of pillage no doubt shook Philip II's prestige and credit in Europe, but the damage done at Santo Domingo, Cartagena, and San Agustín was merely tactical, for the light fortifications and the three galleys Drake destroyed were soon replaced. Even the returns in plunder where disappointing, for they apparently failed to meet the charges of the venture. The influence of the raid on the fortunes of Spain and England in the Caribbean was oblique: on the one hand Drake's example stimulated English privateering; on the other, heavy private losses and an exaggerated sense of peril reverberated from the Indies to Spain and moved the Crown to stronger measures of defence.

The *avería*, the tax levied mainly on return cargoes to pay convoy costs, was raised substantially in 1587 and ran at two or three times the former rate for the rest of the war.[5] The Crown financed the building of fast war-frigates—an expensive policy designed not so much to secure the Caribbean or the general merchant fleets as to maintain the flow of treasure, a

3. Wright, *Further English Voyages*, pp. 44–45, 52; *Principal Navigations*, x. 121.
4. Wright, *Further English Voyages*, p. 145.   5. Chaunu, i. 208–9.

function these busy and efficient vessels performed admirably. In 1586 the Crown also instituted a new fortification programme by sending out Bautista Antoneli, one of the leading engineers of the day, together with the soldier Juan de Tejeda, to survey the key sites: Vera Cruz, Porto Belo, Cartagena, Havana, Santo Domingo, and Puerto Rico.[6] But it was not until 1595 that Antoneli's plans for the Isthmus were implemented: work then began at Porto Belo, while Nombre de Dios, Panama, and the mouth of the Chagre remained practically defenceless. Progress was also slow at San Juan de Puerto Rico, where the building of the Morro started about 1590 and was thereafter retarded by lack of labour and materials. Cartagena, Vera Cruz, and Havana fared better because they were more conveniently situated for supplies and, as nodes of the treasure route, ranked higher in the Crown's priorities. In the long run these defensive works served to protect the centres of most strategic concern to Spain against occupation by major forces, but they did not in fact have much bearing upon the defeat of the next large-scale English offensive in 1595–6: the last voyage of Drake and Hawkins. Their repulse at Puerto Rico was due less to the new fortifications than to the somewhat fortuitous presence of five well-armed frigates and large numbers of men and guns, without which help the island would undoubtedly have fallen. At the Isthmus disease and reinforcements from Peru stopped the English, who actually razed the only long-term works to be found there—at Porto Belo. The course of this expedition proved Spain's maritime communications and naval forces to have grown more capable of resistance to a major invasion since 1586, but the essential cause of its failure lay in weaknesses of planning, organization, and leadership on the English side.[7]

Moreover Spain's defence drive, which was mainly concerned with treasure, with fleets and with the bases that served them, did not considerably impede the growth of privateering and smuggling throughout the Caribbean in the two decades of Anglo-Spanish hostilities. Nor indeed did the defeat of Drake and Hawkins set back the mounting campaign of pillage. Alongside and largely independent of the fumbling fits and starts of the strategic war there proceeded a little war of trade and plunder, a continuous exertion of economic and naval pressure by individuals and groups acting for private gain. Such incursions increased from 1585 to reach unprecedented and, to the Spaniards, well-nigh disastrous volume in

6. Angulo Iñíguez; Navarrete MSS., vol. 27, no. 37 (ff. 309–12).

7. Andrews, *Last Voyage*. The original object of the voyage was probably the occupation of Panama for a limited period to force Spain to terms, but before the outset the project had already been reduced to a raid for plunder only.

the years 1598 to 1605. The colonials flooded the Council of the Indies with desperate protests and appeals for galleys, frigates, men, munitions, and money, but the Crown's practical response fell far short of their real needs. The protection of the Caribbean against creeping invasion on this scale presented problems that were insoluble given the limited resources Spain could make available.

On the Spanish Main the two Cartagena galleys that replaced those destroyed by Drake in 1586 effectively shielded the traffic westwards to the Isthmus for some years, but by 1600 the task of maintaining this force with men and supplies proved too much. Thenceforth it could not operate at full strength.[8] When William Parker, after his audacious seizure of Porto Belo in 1601, returned past Cartagena plundering local frigates, the governor thought better of venturing a galley and let him pass unmolested.[9] In July he thought it advisable, because 'this coast is so threatened by the continuation of the corsairs', to send a galley to scour the Gulf of Urabá and the Acla coast.[1] Nor did Cartagena's protective rôle extend very far to the east. Río de la Hacha, some two hundred miles away, suffered continually and increasingly.[2] Dutch, English, and French shipping came to dominate eastern Venezuela, the pearl islands, Trinidad and the Wild Coast. From 1598 to 1605 hundreds of hulks descended on the salt pans of Araya, La Margarita's pearl fishery was paralysed and foreign smugglers monopolized the ports from Cumaná to La Guaira, developing a prosperous tobacco export trade.[3] Although the English took a minor share in the commercial penetration of this area, they contributed vitally to the process by plundering Spanish shipping and driving it off the sea. Cumaná, for example, was 'barred from trade and Intercourse with all places because noe ship nor frigett of Trade dare not Come hither'.[4] It was because they could neither protect their own merchantmen nor damage the enemy's that the colonies of the eastern Main came to depend on foreign trade, while Dutch, English, and French adven-

---

8. Chaunu, viii (1). 1042–7.

9. S. Purchas, *Hakluytus Posthumus or Purchas His Pilgrimes* (20 vols, Glasgow, 1905–7), xvi. 297.

1. Archivo General de Indias (A.G.I.), Santa Fe, *legajo* 38, Gerónimo Çuaço to the Crown, 26 July 1601.

2. A series of raids is mentioned in K. R. Andrews, 'English voyages to the Caribbean, 1596–1604', *William and Mary Quarterly*, xxxi (1974), 243–54 (hereafter cited as Andrews, 'English voyages'); by the end of the war the place had been thoroughly impoverished by 'the many English corsairs who ordinarily come to it and prevent fishing, rob and plunder the canoes'—A.G.I., Santo Domingo, *legajo* 202, 3 April 1603.   3. Sluiter.

4. P.R.O., S.P. 94/7, ff. 136–41: a contemporary translation of an intercepted letter from Diego Suárez de Amaya, governor of Cumaná, to the Crown, dated 14 November 1600.

turers without let or hindrance probed the Guiana coast for trade and explored the possibilities of settlement.

Havana also received two galleys in 1586, but these were less successful than those of Cartagena. Corsairs infested the Havana coast from Cape San Antonio on the west to Matanzas on the east for the next eighteen years. In the early 1590s they not only took valuable prizes near Havana but at certain periods controlled the approaches and even bottled up the main fleets in harbour. Later the Spaniards somewhat reduced the pressure by using local-built frigates in addition to galleys and galleons, but they failed to eliminate privateering even here at the hub of their commercial system and could do almost nothing to check it in neighbouring areas. On his appointment as governor of Havana in 1600 Pedro de Valdés pleaded for armed vessels to deal with corsairs and to escort Honduras, Española, and Puerto Rico merchantmen to Havana 'so that enemies should not take them on the way as they do every day'.[5] Repeatedly French and English raiders pillaged Puerto de Caballos and the Golfo Dulce in Honduras and in 1603 combined to launch a devastating attack led by Christopher Newport. In the end the Spaniards had to move the town. From 1596 English privateers extended their raiding into the Gulf of Mexico, sacking Campeche and Tabasco and plundering local trade. As for Cuba itself, Valdés on his arrival found smuggling rife in all its southern ports, where alien men-of-war also resorted to sell their booty.

In Puerto Rico the gradual advance of the defences of San Juan did not protect the rest of the island nor its shipping from privateers and finally in 1598 the Earl of Cumberland's raid, following fast upon a severe epidemic, left the town and the island utterly impoverished.[6] As usual, however, it was in and around Española that trade and plunder flourished most. Already in 1590 the governor thought the island too weak to resist any attack. 'This winter', he wrote, 'there have been many corsairs in the island and on the northern coast; it cannot be prevented because, knowing the galleys are out of action, they proceed very freely.' He explained that the two replacement galleys of 1586 had proved impossibly expensive and practically useless.[7] Throughout the war raiders swept the southern coast, keeping Santo Domingo blockaded for much of the time: 'Coming or going, we always have a corsair in sight. Not a ship coming up from the outside escapes them; nor does any which leaves the harbour get

5. A.G.I., Indiferente General, *legajo* 1866, 2 April 1600.

6. Morales Carrión, pp. 27–30; H. P. Biggar (ed.), *The Works of Samuel Champlain* (8 vols, Toronto, 1922–36), i. 14 (hereafter cited as Biggar).

7. Rodríguez Demorizi, pp. 147–8.

past them. If this continues, either this island will be depopulated or they will compel us to do business with them rather than with Spain.'[8] The stranglehold of the privateers so reduced Spanish opposition and competition that by 1600 contrabandists dominated Española's outports and controlled a large share of its trade. In this context plunder and trade were never separate occupations and towards 1600 they became even more interwoven as Dutch and English merchant cruisers took up smuggling in earnest. These ships were, in Champlain's words, 'fitted out, half for war, half for trading',[9] but commerce now became their main concern. At the same time privateers interested chiefly in pillage collaborated closely with the merchantmen, exchanging crew, trade-goods, and prize-goods with them and using the same harbours, like La Yaguana and Guanahibes, as bases for increasingly powerful raids on other parts of the West Indies.[1]

In the years about the turn of the century reports from the Caribbean began to convince the government of the gravity of the situation. Neglect of the naval and commercial security of the Antilles and eastern Venezuela had given Spain's enemies maritime dominance over those parts, threatening not only her sovereignty locally but also her major interests in the New World. The danger was clearly outlined by Juan Maldonado Barnuevo, recently returned from Havana, in 1604.[2] 'He who is master of the sea will be master of the land', he wrote. Henceforth the corsairs would not be content with the limited trading and raiding of earlier years; they would attack fleets and treasure galleons and if successful would not hesitate to attempt conquest. He noted that the advent of the Dutch had transformed the scale of the invasion and stressed the immensity of the space to be protected by a mere six fortified places incapable even of assisting each other, the absence of any naval force for the defence of the lesser settlements, and the unreliability of the population, many of whom were Negroes, *mestizos,* and mulattoes, though these were not peculiar in preferring *rescates* to officially approved trade.

Over a period of years the endless discussion of remedies for such parlous conditions did eventually result in certain plans and even practical steps to deal with the crisis. By 1600 it was clear that in the Antilles galleys were as unsuitable for suppressing corsairs as judges for suppress-

8. A.G.I., Santo Domingo, *legajo* 81, Diego Ibarra to the Crown, 14 October 1595.
9. Biggar, i. 26.
1. These features were marked in, for example, the operations of the *Archangel, Neptune, Phoenix, Vineyard, Mayflower, Elizabeth and Cleeve,* and *Dorothy* in 1603–4—Andrews, 'English voyages', pp. 251–4.
2. A.G.I., Indiferente General, *legajo* 1867, 12 December 1604 (a copy lies in B.L., Add. MSS. 36318, ff. 308–23).

ing *rescatadores* and that the situation demanded concerted action by land and sea: vigorous police measures against *rescates* within and systematic pursuit of the enemy without by an *armada del barlovento* based in the Caribbean for the purpose. Such a windward squadron was to have accompanied Pedro de Valdés and Antonio Osorio, the new governors of Cuba and Española respectively, when they went out to take up their posts in 1602, armed with special orders to root out *rescates*. But in the event the money and supplies needed for such a force could not be found and they sailed without it.[3] At Havana Valdés had to use local resources to create *armadillas*: *ad hoc* squadrons of limited size, range, and effect. Instead of the *armada del barlovento* a special armada sailed under Luis Fajardo late in 1605 to attack the large concentrations of salt-laders and smugglers at Araya and elsewhere in east Venezuelan and Antillean waters. In the first area Fajardo succeeded in dispersing the enemy, capturing considerable numbers of them, but in the second he and his vice-admiral achieved nothing of importance before their return to Spain in 1606.

The punitive campaign against *rescates* had similarly mixed results. In Cuba the violent efforts of Valdés led only to frustration and ended with the issue of a general pardon in 1607. In Española in 1605–6 Osorio undertook, on the Crown's orders, the draconic depopulation of the north and west coasts, transporting the settlements by force to the south, which was indeed an effective answer to smuggling, but incidentally ruined the island's economy and left a wilderness that soon became the breeding ground of a new and worse generation of predators. A comparably negative policy was applied in Venezuela, where Nueva Ecija de Cumanagoto, the chief smuggling centre, was depopulated and tobacco-growing prohibited, though the equally drastic proposal to inundate the salt pans of Araya was abandoned for lack of the resources to see it through.[4]

That the Spanish government paid serious attention to the problem of Caribbean contraband in the first decade of the seventeenth century cannot be doubted, and although those responsible for executing the various measures were inclined to magnify their own achievements, their efforts, including frequent hangings of captured foreigners *pour encourager les autres,* must have helped to diminish the volume of *rescates* in the short run. But it was probably not so much the devotion of officialdom as the

3. A.G.I., Indiferente General, *legajo* 747, 'La orden que se deve dar al armada de la guarda de las Indias', 17 February 1602; *legajo* 1866, *consulta* del Consejo de Cámara, 12 April 1602 (a copy lies in B.L., Add. MSS. 36318, ff. 100–7).
4. Rodríguez Demorizi, pp. 195–296; Wright, 'Rescates'; Sluiter.

advent of peace between the European powers that arrested the progressive deterioration of Spain's Caribbean empire at this time. Peace made the drive against smuggling possible and gave it some chance of success, whereas with continued war commitments Spain could hardly have spared the strength necessary for such an offensive. James I's accession quickly stopped the mounting campaign of privateering on both sides of the Atlantic, relieving naval pressure in the Caribbean itself while enabling Spain to mobilize a striking force against the contrabandists. At the same time James's open disapproval also broke the impetus of the commercial push into the Caribbean that had developed towards the end of the war with Sir Robert Cecil's discreet favour. From the first the Spaniards were not slow to exploit the new king's foreign policy and clearly perceived the advantage of supplementing physical measures in the Caribbean by diplomatic pressure in London.[5] The practical cessation of Dutch–Spanish hostilities in 1607 greatly reduced the Dutch Caribbean presence also, particularly since they then returned to the Iberian coast for their salt. The Caribbean, still a minor market for the merchants of Normandy, London, and the Netherlands, lost some of its attraction when peace gave them renewed access to Seville.[6] For the time being Spain kept the Caribbean more or less intact not so much by her own exertions as by default, her enemies lacking the desire or the need to exploit their opportunities and her weakness any further at this stage.

In fact the fundamental economic and defence problems of the West Indies had not been solved. The methods adopted in Española and Venezuela aggravated rather than cured the disease in the long run, while the abandonment of the construction of the *armada del barlovento* at Havana in 1609 left the Caribbean without regular naval defence. The decline of the flota trade and its revenue hindered policies requiring extra money and Spain's initial burst of defence energy was soon spent. She did not succeed in cleansing the sea of corsairs and contrabandists. In 1609 the *Junta de Guerra de Indias* advised the Crown that the shores of the islands, Tierra Firme and Araya were not clear.[7] Three years later the governor of Cuba reported his coasts infested with pirates who were 'becoming as attached to *rescates* as to pillage'.[8] In 1615 Española was said

5. K. R. Andrews, 'Caribbean rivalry and the Anglo-Spanish peace of 1604', *History*, lix (1974), 1–17; Quinn, 'James I'.

6. The guild of Seville merchants argued that English, French, and Dutch participation in the flota trade gave those nations a certain interest in its security—Navarrete MSS., vol. 24, no. 49, *consulado* memorandum of 29 December 1615.

7. A.G.I., Indiferente General, *legajo* 1867, 7 September 1609.

8. Wright, *Habana en la Primera Mitad*, p. 103.

to be likewise infested by French and English vessels, against whom, in the absence of powder supplies, the Santo Domingo authorities admitted themselves incapable of action.[9] In 1618–19 pirates took nine of the frigates that plied the ports of eastern Cuba in a period of ten months.[1] The anti-contraband measures at Cumaná and thereabouts had the effect of focusing smuggling upon Trinidad and the Orinoco, where the English and Dutch then developed a substantial trade for tobacco. Robert Harcourt observed the trade already well established in 1609 and in the next few years it increased remarkably, reaching its maximum in 1611–12. Trinidad at that time was said to be the outlet for the tobacco of all Venezuela and the inlet for European wares that reached Cartagena and beyond.[2] As Joyce Lorimer relates elsewhere in this volume, the tobacco trade declined after 1612, but English, Dutch, and French shipping did not cease to frequent the area, nor did the local authorities cease to complain that those coasts were infested with enemies and without effective defence.[3]

Thus alien activity persisted in the Caribbean all through the interval between the Treaty of London in 1604 and the landing of English settlers on St Kitts in 1622. The latter event resulted immediately from the failure of one of the repeated attempts to found plantations in Guiana, but in broader perspective it may be seen as the final outcome of a long period of penetration of the Caribbean region by the contrabandists, pirates, and privateers of France, England, and the Netherlands. This largely spontaneous and international movement created a parasitic presence which continuously distressed and endangered the body politic of Spain's West Indies as much as it gratified their body economic. Until the 1620s the strategic assaults of the French and English, occasional and feeble as they were, assisted this process only indirectly and unintentionally. Eventually, however, when the parasites passed from mobile contact to sedentary attachment, from haunting by sea to planting by land, they did so in the shadow of a new offensive that at last co-ordinated strategic and economic ends and means: the work of a mercantile state and its instrument, the Dutch West India Company.

9. B.L., Add. MSS. 36319, ff. 281–2, Diego Gómez de Sandoval to the Crown, 30 March 1615.

1. I. A. Wright, *Santiago de Cuba and its District, 1607–1640* (Madrid, 1918), p. 44.

2. B.L., Add. MSS. 36319, ff. 268–71 (London intelligence, 1611).

3. B.L., Add. MSS. 36320, ff. 154–9, 209, 263–5; and 36321, ff. 12, 122.

7

The English contraband tobacco trade in Trinidad and Guiana 1590-1617

JOYCE LORIMER

The tobacco trade of the Spanish colonies in Trinidad and Guiana between 1590 and 1617 constitutes a little-studied example of the persistence of English commercial invasions of the Spanish American empire after the Anglo-Spanish peace of 1604. More significantly the history of this trade, particularly of the political and economic reasons for its gradual disappearance by 1617, illustrates how that peace affected the development of English interest in Trinidad and Guiana as a whole.

It is not known exactly when English ships first began to bring tobacco back from Trinidad and Guiana. The trade developed, as did all other English activities in the region, out of Elizabethan privateering. English interest was drawn first to Trinidad by the convenience that the island, not permanently occupied by the Spaniards until 1592, offered as a way-station for shipping bound for the Tierra Firme and the Caribbean.[1] The first definite evidence of an English presence there dates from 1569.[2] The incidence of English vessels in the Gulf of Paria steadily increased during the next twenty-three years.[3] It was only when Trinidad was settled by the Spaniards in 1592, however, that English activities there

1. For a discussion of English privateering contacts with Trinidad see J. Lorimer, 'English trade and exploration in Trinidad and Guiana, 1569-1648' (unpublished Ph.D. thesis, University of Liverpool, 1973), pp. 53–85 (hereafter cited as Lorimer).

2. Juan Troche Ponce de León, commissioned by the Spanish crown to settle Trinidad, complained of the French corsairs and English Lutherans who haunted its shores: see P. Ojer, *La formación del Oriente Venezolano* (Caracas, 1966), p. 268 (hereafter cited as Ojer, *La formación*).

3. For the history of English contacts with Trinidad to 1593 see Lorimer, pp. 53–85.

came under close scrutiny and evidence of their traffic with the Indians for tobacco came to light.[4]

The earliest allusion to English traders importing tobacco from Trinidad is contained in a letter written to the Spanish government by its governor Antonio de Berrío in November 1593. Berrío reported, 'English ships resort here very commonly ... it was four months ago that two English ships cruised off here trading for tobacco with the Indians, which I myself went out against and captured a captain and five Englishmen. ...'[5] From the tone of his letter it would seem that the English had begun to resort to Trinidad, and some years before 1593, as much for its tobacco as for its convenience as a privateering haven. Berrío's lieutenant, who left Trinidad in 1593, told officials in Spain in 1595 that, in addition to the usual English and French privateers who haunted the island, there were 'Englishmen who went there solely to trade for tobacco and they took Indians to England and taught them the language and brought them back'.[6] By 1595 the words Trinidad and tobacco were interchangeable in English common usage.[7] It is clear that the tobacco traffic was established some years before Ralegh published the legend of Manoa to lure English investment to the Guiana mainland.

It is also evident that by the mid 1590s the tobacco trade at Trinidad had come to be more than merely part of the general barter with the Indians for victuals and necessities. It provides some of the earliest evidence of a growing trend amongst English privateers at the turn of the seventeenth century to combine their reprisals with illicit trade at the ill-supplied Spanish outposts and unguarded Indian and slave settlements of the Antilles, the eastern Tierra Firme and Honduras. The development of the tobacco traffic out of privateering contacts with Trinidad is merely one indication amongst many that English promoters had begun to see the advantages of devoting the capital and organizational expertise gained

4. On Antonio de Berrío's expeditions in search of El Dorado and his settlement of Trinidad see Ojer, *La formación*, pp. 467–582. Reports of clashes between English and Spaniards at Trinidad can be found in Antonio de Berrío to Philip II, 27 July 1592: B.L., Add. MSS. 36315, f. 251; Henry May, 'A briefe note of a voyage to the East Indies, begun the 10 of April 1591', printed in R. Hakluyt, *The Principal Navigations* (12 vols, Glasgow, 1903–5), x. 194–203 (hereafter cited as *Principal Navigations*).

5. Antonio de Berrío to Philip II, 24 November 1593: B.L., Add. MSS. 36315, ff. 233 et seqq.

6. Domingo de Vera Ibarguen to Philip II, 1595: ibid., ff. 264 et seqq.

7. For the usage of the word 'Trinidado' to denote tobacco in the 1590s see the literature quoted in S. A. Dickson, *Panacea or Precious Bane* (New York, 1954), pp. 184, 186, 202–3.

in reprisals to commercial enterprise, and of establishing a strong claim to free trade in the Indies as the war entered its closing stages.[8]

Moves to end the hostilities between England and Spain got under way by 1602. Andrews has made the interesting suggestion that the build-up of English privateering and trade in the Caribbean and Guiana at the time may well have been encouraged by Secretary Cecil and the Lord High Admiral, Lord Charles Howard, not merely for personal profit, but in hopes, if not of pressing the Spaniards to grant free trade in the Indies, at least of forcing them to grant concessions elsewhere to protect their imperial monopoly.[9] These aims, if they existed, were dashed by the accession of James I, who was both determined to avoid the financial drain of continued war and genuinely desirous of acting as an arbiter between protestant and catholic Europe. The King declared an end to hostilities, and showed himself willing to allow Spanish suits for restoration of prize goods taken after the ceasefire. Whilst upholding the important principle that Spain might rightfully claim a monopoly of trade only in those areas it effectively held, James I at the same time removed official backing for enterprises into the occupied Caribbean, just when the assaults of the last few years had left the Spaniards determined to rid the area of interlopers by forceful means. In the treaty of London signed in August 1604 no mention was made of the West Indies, since the Spaniards were not prepared to concede any part, occupied or unoccupied, of the exclusive empire granted by Alexander VI's papal donation. In James I's interpretation Englishmen might lawfully colonize regions not settled by any other Christian prince. The question of contraband trade with Spanish colonies was left to adventure. Englishmen might trade there, but the consequences of their activities lay upon their own heads. The Crown disclaimed any obligation to defend its subjects and held them criminally responsible should they engage in hostilities with the Spaniards. Those sailing to the Caribbean, therefore, found themselves liable to the double jeopardy of Spanish assault and charges of piracy at home should they retaliate.[1]

8. For details of English participation in the contraband see K. R. Andrews, *Elizabethan Privateering* (London, 1964) (hereafter cited as Andrews, *Elizabethan Privateering*); Andrews, 'English voyages to the Caribbean, 1596 to 1604: an annotated list', *William and Mary Quarterly*, 3rd series, xxxi (1974), 243–54; and Andrews, 'Caribbean rivalry and the Anglo-Spanish peace of 1604', *History*, lix (1974), 1–17 (hereafter cited as Andrews, 'Caribbean rivalry').

9. Andrews, 'Caribbean rivalry', p. 10.

1. R. D. Hussey, 'America in European diplomacy, 1597–1604', *Revista de Historia de America*, xli (1956), 1–30; Andrews, 'Caribbean rivalry', pp. 1–17.

The peace treaty had a momentous effect on the direction of English overseas expansion in the next two decades. English smuggling in the Caribbean continued, as Spanish complaints and cases in the English High Court of Admiralty indicate. Nevertheless the risks of suffering rough justice from the Spaniards in the Indies, and charges of piracy at home, diverted the greater part of English investment in the Americas to Virginia and other areas on the east coast of the safer, unoccupied North American continent.[2] Guiana also, to a lesser extent, benefited from this deflection of attention from the Caribbean. Yet the impediments that made ventures in the latter area so hazardous ensured that English enterprise in Guiana, although potentially and immediately more profitable than that in the North American colonies, would remain small in scale. Those interested in the commercial possibilities of the Americas showed themselves reluctant to invest their money in Guiana enterprise because they lacked both the secure right to defend themselves and the assurance of support from their government. Cautious city and gentry investors put their capital into North America instead, and by the mid 1620s the priority of those colonies over the ill-financed and shaky ventures in Guiana had been established.[3] The history of the English tobacco trade in Trinidad and Guiana after 1604 reflects the uncertain climate of Anglo-Spanish relations during the reign of James I, which discouraged English investment in the area as a whole. The profits of a small but lucrative contraband trade in tobacco with the Spanish settlers on Trinidad and the Orinoco had to be abandoned under the combined pressures of half-hearted resistance from the Spaniards in the Indies, which made peaceful trade impossible, and diplomatic pressures at home, which made anything but peaceful trade unthinkable.

Contemporary references indicate that tobacco smuggling got seriously under way in or about the year of the conclusion of the peace. It is true that the crew of a Dutch vessel, which visited the Orinoco and Trinidad in 1598, found the Spaniards there friendly and willing to trade.[4] It is

---

2. Andrews, 'Caribbean rivalry', p. 17; D. B. Quinn, 'The voyage of *Triall* 1606–7', *American Neptune*, xxxi, no. 2 (1971), 85–103; and Quinn, 'James I and the beginnings of empire in America', *Journal of Imperial and Commonwealth History*, ii (1974), 135–52 (hereafter cited as Quinn, 'James I').

3. For the history of English investment in Guiana see Lorimer, *passim*; J. A. Williamson, *English Colonies in Guiana and on the Amazon, 1604–68* (Oxford, 1923), *passim*.

4. A. Cabeliau, 'Account of a journey to Guiana and the island of Trinidad . . . 1599', *Venezuela-British Guiana Boundary Arbitration*, 'British case' (12 vols, London, 1898), app. I, no. 8, pp. 18–22 (hereafter cited as *V.B.A.*).

probable that Dutch, French, and English ships visited the settlements at
the turn of the seventeenth century, unnoticed and unrecorded. Nevertheless, Spanish settlers at Trinidad in 1612 confessed to have been
seriously involved in trading with foreigners for only about eight years.[5]
The first evidence of an English ship acquiring tobacco from them dates
from 1605.[6] One C.T., the author of *An Advice How to Plant Tobacco In
England*, written in 1615, reckoned that Englishmen had been importing
'Spanish' tobacco from the Orinoco for seven or eight years. Ralegh, in
1618, echoed his conclusions, estimating that English vessels had
frequented the river for the last ten or twelve years.[7] However willing
the Spaniards may have been to trade, it is unlikely that their new plantations had sufficient tobacco before 1604–5 to distract many northern European traders from the fine tobacco which could be acquired from the
settlements on the coast of Venezuela and New Andalucía. Reports from
the Spanish authorities in Venezuela in the last years of the war manifested
growing alarm about the dominance of tobacco cultivation over all other
forms of agriculture and about the increasing numbers of French, Dutch,
and English pirates the commodity attracted to the province. By 1605
tobacco smuggling there had reached such proportions that the *cabildo* of
Caracas petitioned that its cultivation be suspended. A royal *cédula* of
1606 forbade all tobacco growing in Venezuela for the next ten years.
Officials in New Andalucía renewed their efforts to stamp out tobacco-
running in their jurisdiction.[8] It was the increasing difficulty of acquiring
supplies of tobacco from the Spaniards of the eastern Main that turned
north European traders to the small and as yet unguarded Spanish settlements in Trinidad and the Orinoco. There they found ill-supplied
colonists anxious for their custom.

Antonio de Berrío and his heirs had been vested in 1595 with the
government and captaincy-general of the 'provinces and kingdoms of
Dorado, Guayana and the great Manoa which is between the two rivers

5. Sancho de Alquiza's report on his *residencia* in Guayana, 14 June 1612: B.L., Add.
MSS. 36320, ff. 285–9.
    6. See below, p. 131.
    7. 'Sir Walter Raghley's large appologie for the ill successe of his enterprise to Guiana',
in V. T. Harlow (ed.), *Ralegh's Last Voyage* (London, 1932), p. 323 (hereafter cited as Harlow,
Ralegh's Last Voyage).
    8. E. Arcila Farias, *Economía Colonial de Venezuela* (Mexico City, 1946), pp. 80–86;
Bernardino de Cevallos to Philip III, 9 December 1605, B.L., Add. MSS. 36319, f. 58;
Andrés de Rojas y Guzmán to Philip III, 16 December 1605, ibid., ff. 63, 69; Pedro Suárez
Coronel to Philip III, 28 April 1607, ibid., f. 74; Sancho de Alquiza to Philip III, 15 June
1607, ibid., ff. 141 et seqq.

Pauto and Papameme which by other names are the Orinoco and Marañon and the island of Trinidad'.[9] The province, generally referred to as 'Trinidad y Guayana', had been incorporated in the belief that the interior reaches of the Orinoco would soon yield up the wealth of the lake kingdom of El Dorado. Ralegh's expedition of 1595 had convinced the Spanish crown of the urgency of settling the river and in the following year between one and two thousand immigrants were dispatched to the new government. Arriving at Trinidad, they rebuilt San Josef de Oruña, the small town first established by Berrío on the highlands of the river Caroni, in the northwest of the island, in 1592. Others crossed to the Orinoco to the small hamlet of San Tomé de la Guayana, founded by Berrío in late 1595 on the south bank of the river, three miles east of the confluence of the Caroni. The latter tributary Berrío believed was the gateway to the rich civilization in the interior. Berrío died in 1597, his hopes of discovering it unfulfilled. His son and successor Fernando de Berrío allegedly sent out eighteen expeditions in search of El Dorado during his first period of government in the province, 1597–1612, with the same lack of success. Long marches through the arduous interior brought nothing better than a few gold trinkets retrieved from Indian huts. Prospecting in the vicinity of San Tomé revealed no gold-mines apart from small pockets of alluvial gold panned from the ever-changing margins of the Orinoco. Disease, desertion, and Indian assaults wrought havoc among the new arrivals from Spain. By 1597 only 300 men remained in the jurisdiction. The soldiers from New Granada, cattle ranchers from Venezuela, and general riff-raff from New Andalucía, who trekked south to San Tomé in the first ten years, when hopes of finding El Dorado remained alive, left again when disillusionment set in. By 1609 the male population of San Josef had dropped to 40 and remained at approximately that figure until the 1640s. The stockade of San Tomé held some 160 souls in 1598, but its population declined rapidly thereafter, to remain during the next forty years slightly less than that of San Josef.

Realizing that they could not live on visions of El Dorado, the residents of the two outposts began very quickly to develop a plantation economy. Those at San Josef raised some sugar and ginger. The planters on the Orinoco grew cotton and indigo and ranched substantial herds of cattle. Tobacco cultivation, however, was the chief commercial livelihood of

9. Governor Fernando de Berrío, son and successor of Antonio de Berrío, referred to his jurisdiction thus in a letter of 3 November 1601: B.L., Add. MSS. 36318, f. 85.

both communities.¹ None of these commodities was of any interest to the Spanish crown. Once hope of discovering Manoa had faded, it afforded 'Trinidad y Guayana' the same minimal attention as the other marginal plantation colonies in the Antilles and the outer perimeter of the Main. They were valued only as defence and supply posts along the land and sea routes to the vital mining provinces and as symbols of Spain's effective occupation of the territories apportioned to it by Alexander VI.² Like other insignificant outposts in the Indies, San Tomé and San Josef were left for the first eighteen years of their existence without any direct contact with Spanish markets. They received goods at second-hand from coastal traders dispatched either from the official ports-of-call of the annual convoys or from colonies privileged to receive special trade vessels from Spain.³ The high costs and shortages of such a system were alone enough to induce the colonists of 'Trinidad y Guayana' to involve themselves in contraband trade with north European intruders. It is likely, however, that the tobacco plantations at San Tomé and San Josef were developed from the beginning with an eye to the possibilities of illicit traffic. Fernando de Berrío, unlike his visionary father, was an opportunist whose activities in Guayana were directed essentially to serve his own interests and gain some profit from the territory which had eaten up the lives and fortunes of his family.⁴ His friendly reception of a Dutch trader in the Orinoco in 1598, the first year of his governorship, indicates that he had early recognized that the discovery of El Dorado was not an immediate prospect and that contraband would provide much surer returns.⁵ Those who stayed with him in the jurisdiction appear to have been a dubious mixture of adventurers and drifters. His government was described in 1608 as full of 'soldiers who without spiritual or temporal yoke, run headlong into every kind of vice . . . the chosen resort of secular

1. For the history of the El Dorado expeditions, the creation of the province of 'Trinidad y Guayana', and the establishment of the settlements of San Josef and San Tomé see Lorimer, pp. 38–49, 295–303; and J. A. de Armas Chitty, *Guayana su tierra y su historia* (Caracas, 1964), i, *passim*.

2. For Spain's policy to its marginal colonies see H. et P. Chaunu, *Séville et l'Atlantique* (11 vols, Paris, 1956–9), viii, pt i (hereafter cited as Chaunu); J. Lynch, *Spain under the Habsburgs* (Oxford, 1969), ii, chap. 8.

3. Trinidad was granted one licensed trading ship a year in 1614, see below, p. 147.

4. Nothing has been written on Fernando de Berrío apart from the articles by K. S. Wise, 'Don Fernando de Berrío as Governor of Trinidad'; 'Tobacco cultivation in Trinidad 1600–14'; 'Don Fernando de Berrío and the Residencia 1611–14'; and 'The final efforts of Don Fernando (1618–22)', in *Historical Sketches of Trinidad and Tobago* (Trinidad, 1936), ii. 7–37, which greatly romanticize his undertakings. The records of his activities throughout B.L., Add. MSS. 36318–21 are open to a less favourable interpretation.

5. See n. 4, p. 127.

criminals, irregular priests and apostate friars, and in general a seminary of rascals'.[6] Tobacco had drawn foreigners to Trinidad before Antonio de Berrío had settled it. The harvest of the Venezuelan and New Andalucian plantations proved a magnet for north European interlopers. San Tomé and San Josef, tucked quietly to the windward of the Tierra Firme, could also hope to participate in the lucrative contraband trade. The destruction of the Venezuelan plantations in 1606 and the increasing vigilance of officials on the Main benefited the residents of San Tomé and San Josef considerably in the short term, making their settlements the only relatively secure source of good 'Spanish' tobacco for English, Dutch, and French traders.

It is not possible to assess exactly how many English ships visited San Tomé and Port of Spain (Trinidad) annually whilst the contraband trade lasted. The data for it are miscellaneous and one can only compare records of specific English ventures with contemporary estimates of the total numbers of English, Dutch, and French ships involved. Evidence for the first years of the commerce is very scanty, since it was not until the illicit trade on the Main had been suppressed that Spanish officials there began to take note of the activities of the residents of 'Trinidad y Guayana'. The first record of English merchants trading with them for tobacco dates from November 1605, when 'Joice Waus owner of a ship called the Delight of Apsham, with certain merchants traded to Trinidado ...'.[7] John Scott noted in his 'Discription of Trinidada' that Dutch merchants sold slaves to the residents of San Josef in that year,[8] an indication that the foreign presence at the island was becoming increasingly common. In 1606 a Dutch ship commanded by an Englishman, John Sims, called at Trinidad for tobacco, after trading in the rivers of the mainland.[9] Another Dutch ship, under one Isaac Duverne, carried slaves to Port of Spain that year.[1] According to Spanish observers tobacco-smuggling was in full swing by 1607. The governor of Cumaná complained in December

6. Juan de Borja to Philip III, 20 June 1608: *V.B.A.*, 'British counter-case', app., pt i, no. 2.

7. 'Instructions for your Lordship to entitle the Queen to the tobacco at Apsham in Devon ... 1606', *Cal. H.M.C. Hatfield House*, xviii. 448–9. Two English ships, the *Castor and Pollux* and the *Pollux and Castor*, backed by French merchants and manned by an Anglo-French crew called at Trinidad for tobacco in 1604, see Quinn, 'James I', pp. 141–4.

8. John Scott, 'The discription of Trinidad', in V. T. Harlow (ed.), *Colonizing Expeditions to the West Indies and Guiana, 1623–67* (London, 1924), p. 125.

9. 'Relation of Master John Wilson of Wanstead in Essex, one of the last ten that returned into England from Wiapoco in Guiana, 1606', in Samuel Purchas, *Purchas his Pilgrimes* (20 vols, Glasgow, 1905–7), xvi. 351.

1. Scott, 'The discription of Trinidad', loc. cit., p. 125.

of that year, 'now tobacco is cleared from all these provinces except San Tomé and the island of Trinidad where Don Fernando Berrío de la Hoz is governor. They tell me, on good security, that in Trinidad a great quantity of goods is smuggled and that English and Dutch ships are never lacking there.'[2] In that year the *Royall Marchant* of London, commanded by Robert Thornton, visited the island in the last stages of a reconnaissance voyage of Guiana commissioned by the Duke of Florence.[3] In 1608 the governor of Santa Fé complained that 'the trade with the enemy pirates' at San Tomé and Trinidad was 'so extensive and continual that the merchandise comes as far as this kingdom through the licence of the same Don Fernando . . .'.[4] Thomas Hickory, an English captain who traded annually there from 1608, told his Spanish captors at Santo Domingo in 1611 that it was usual for foreign shipping to visit Trinidad and the Orinoco between about October and March.[5] They thus avoided the 'many calmes . . . outrageous gustes, foule weather, and contrarie windes', which Ralegh had learned in 1595 were common during the heavy rains of April to late July.[6] Hickory estimated that twenty vessels in all had called at Trinidad to pick up tobacco during these months in 1608–9.[7] Although specific details are scanty, it is likely that English ships constituted at least one-third of this total. Contemporary English descriptions of the traffic imply that interest and participation in it was well established by 1608. One of two other English ships definitely known to have sought tobacco at Trinidad in that year, in addition to Hickory's vessel, was the *Ulysses* of London, sent forth by the merchant Richard Hall. The crew of the *Ulysses*, present at Port of Spain in late August or September, was joined by the company of the *Primrose* 'belonginge to one Master Harwood of London' and 'shipped by Sir Walter Rawleghe', which called at the island for tobacco after trading with the Indians on the mainland.[8] The *Wilmott* of Topsham owned by Lewis Plumley also set

---

2. Pedro Suárez Coronel to Philip III, 18 December 1607: B.L., Add. MSS. 36319, f. 149.

3. *A true relation of the travels of William Davis Barber-Surgion of London, under the Duke of Florence* (London, 1614).

4. Juan de Borja to Philip III, 20 June 1608: *V.B.A.*, 'British counter-case', app., pt i, no. 2.

5. Deposition by Thomas 'Icurri' [Hickory/Curry?] made in Santo Domingo, 26 June 1611: B.L., Add. MSS. 36319, ff. 294 et seqq.

6. Sir Walter Ralegh, 'The discoverie of the large, rich, and beautifull Empire of Guiana . . . Performed in the yeere 1595', *Principal Navigations*, x. 427.

7. Deposition by Thomas 'Icurri': B.L., Add. MSS. 36319, ff. 294 et seqq.

8. For references to the voyages of the *Ulysses* and the *Primrose* see depositions by William Hill, 1 May 1609, Public Record Office, London (P.R.O.), H.C.A. 1/47, ff. 4–5; William Longecastle, ibid., f. 56; William Tavernor, ibid., ff. 56–57; John Moore, 20 November 1609, ibid., f. 59; Peter Cannon, 21 November 1610, H.C.A. 13/41, f. 110; and letters of the

out for 'Trinidado and Guana' in the summer of 1608, but was cast away in Barbary.[9]

The months between summer and spring of 1609–10 witnessed the arrival of thirty foreign vessels at Port of Spain, according to Thomas Hickory's reckoning.[1] In addition to the latter's own ship at least six of these were English. Spanish officials at La Margarita learned of the presence of five vessels trading at Port of Spain in October 1609.[2] Two of these were commanded by Robert Harcourt, who had anchored at the island in hopes of acquiring a saving cargo of tobacco on the way home from his newly established colony on the Wiapoco. He encountered there the *Diana*, under Master William Thorne, trading for three Flemish merchants resident in London: Arnold Lull, John Abealls, and Joos Croppenbury.[3] Also present was the *Penelope* and her pinnace the *Indevor*, sent out once again by Richard Hall.[4] Some time in late 1609 or early 1610 John Moore sailed the *Archangell* of London to Trinidad and the Orinoco, bringing back a cargo of tobacco for Sir John Watts and partners in July 1610. Lull, Croppenbury, and Abealls also adventured in the ship.[5]

A dispatch to Spain from La Margarita dated 16 July 1610 reported that there were then eleven foreign ships trading at Trinidad.[6] A memorial presented in Seville in May 1611 asserted that some thirty ships had

---

Mayor of Chichester to the Earl of Nottingham, 11 March 1609, Bodleian Library, Oxford, Clarendon Papers, i, no. 39; W. Roscarack to the same, 24 March 1609, ibid., no. 41; Sir William Monson to the same, 3 April 1609, ibid., no. 44; Richard Hall to the same, 3 April 1609, ibid., no. 45.

9. Evidence of John Elliott, 9 June 1610: P.R.O., H.C.A. 1/47, f. 132.

1. Deposition by Thomas 'Icurri': B.L., Add. MSS. 36319, ff. 294 et seqq.

2. Francisco Manso de Contreras to Philip III, 22 October 1609: B.L., Add. MSS. 36319, f. 194.

3. Robert Harcourt, *A Relation of a Voyage to Guiana*, ed. C. A. Harris (London, 1928), pp. 121–3; and the entry concerning the *Diana* in the London port books for 21 June 1610: P.R.O., E.190/15/5.

4. Harcourt, *A Relation of a Voyage to Guiana*, pp. 121–3; evidence of Augustine Phillipps, 17 November 1610, P.R.O., H.C.A. 13/41, ff. 101–4; Israell Dale, 19 November 1610, ibid., ff. 104–7; Lucas Pinchback, 21 November 1610, ibid., ff. 108–10; Peter Cannon, 21 November 1610, ibid., ff. 110–13; William Warner, 21 November 1610, ibid., ff. 113–16; Richard Bracey, 26 November 1610, ibid., ff. 117–19; the *libel* submitted by Richard Hall against the Spanish ambassador, H.C.A. 24/75, nos 170–3; and letters from Ellis Fludd to the Earl of Nottingham, 25 August 1610, Bodleian, Clarendon Papers, i, no. 49; Richard Hall to the same, ibid., no. 50; Sir Richard Cooper to the same, 28 August 1610, ibid., no. 51.

5. Appraisement of tobacco on board the *Archangell*, 14 July 1610: P.R.O., H.C.A. 24/74, no. 31; entry concerning the *Archangell* in the London port books for 7 July 1610, P.R.O., E.190/15/5.

6. Warrant from Philip III to Sancho de Alquiza, 31 July 1611: B.L., Add. MSS. 36319, f. 236.

visited Trinidad during the 1610–11 season.[7] Hickory stated that eight or nine ships called at San Tomé between October and December of 1610, that to his certain knowledge thirteen had anchored off Port of Spain and that there had probably been more than he himself knew of. Hickory was captured off Santo Domingo *en route* for England in the following June.[8] John Moore returned to San Tomé for Watts and company in the *Archangell* alias *John* of London in autumn 1610. He loaded tobacco and quickly departed, making arrangements to return in the following season. He left a factor John Brewer behind as a guarantee for an outstanding debt. He carried back with him to London a Portuguese merchant, Francisco Carnero, who had been slave-trading illegally at La Margarita, Trinidad, and San Tomé.[9] Carnero testified to the English High Court of Admiralty that whilst he 'was at Gwyana aforesyd, there was divers english, french, and dutch merchants there also, and the sayd Fernando de Bareo governor of St Thome aforesyd did trade and traffique with them . . .'.[1] A Spanish agent in London, who reported Moore's return, noted that two Dutch and three English ships were in the Orinoco when Moore left it late in 1610, and that there were four or five other unidentified vessels at Trinidad.[2] Sir Thomas Roe, who reached the island in February 1611 after exploring the Guiana coastline, noted fifteen vessels there, English, Dutch, and French, 'freighting smoke'.[3] One of them would appear to have been a Dartmouth vessel captained by an Irishman, Philip Purcell.[4] The *Lyons Clawe* of London also appears to have been at the island at this time.[5] Letters written to Spain in March

7. Memorial of Gregorio de Palma Hurtado, 28 May 1611, in Chaunu, iv. 346–8.

8. Deposition by Thomas 'Icurri': B.L., Add. MSS. 36319, ff. 294 et seqq.

9. See the examinations of John Curtis and Giles Hawkins, 5 February 1612; Francis Wright, 23 March 1612; John Hedland, John Johnson, and Robert Adams, 26 March 1612; William Wigg and Henry Carnaby, 28 March 1612; John Fludd, 30 March 1612, all in P.R.O., H.C.A. 13/42, ff. 18–20, 23–36; Articles on behalf of Francisco Carnero, H.C.A. 24/75, no. 65; *libels* submitted by Robert Brooke, ibid., nos 67, 150; *libel* submitted by the Spanish ambassador, ibid., no. 239; entry in the Act books, 3 April 1611 (N.S.), H.C.A. 3/28; 'Information as to the great trade in tobacco, carried on by the Dutch and English in Trinidad and on the Orinoco, 28 March 1611', B.L., Add. MSS. 36319, ff. 268 et seqq.; Ralegh to the Privy Council, 1611, B.L., Harleian MSS. 39, ff. 350–1.

1. Articles on behalf of Francisco Carnero: P.R.O., H.C.A. 24/75, no. 65.

2. 'Information as to the great trade in tobacco': B.L., Add. MSS. 36319, ff. 268 et seqq.

3. Sir Thomas Roe to the Earl of Salisbury, 28 February 1611: P.R.O., C.O. 1/1, no. 25.

4. 'Relacion de la navegacion y poblacion y trato que Irlandeses y Inglesses han hecho en el rio de las Amazonas, 1621': Archivo General de Simancas, Estado 7031, lib. 374, ff. 162–3.

5. See the examinations of Robert Tottle, 13 August and 7 October 1611, P.R.O., H.C.A. 13/41, ff. 240, 255; William Harte, 7 October 1611, ibid., ff. 255–6; John Wightman, 8 November 1611, ibid., f. 267; and the responses of William Stannard, Peter Sohier, and Emmanuell Exall, H.C.A. 24/75, no. 70.

1611 by the Spanish ambassador in England mentioned that three ships had recently arrived in London carrying tobacco acquired at Trinidad. One of them was doubtless Moore's ship. The ambassador and the agent who had observed Moore's return both reported that four other ships were preparing in March 1611 to leave for the tobacco plantations.[6] It is known that Moore's ship, the *Archangell,* returned to the Orinoco in the spring of 1611 under Master William Little to pay the debt left by Moore and to bring back more tobacco for Arnold Lull.[7] The governor of Cumaná complained in June 1611 that the coast of his jurisdiction was infested with foreign vessels coming from Trinidad.[8]

The letters of Ambassador Velasco and the anonymous 'Information as to the great trade in tobacco, carried on by the Dutch and English in Trinidad and on the Orinoco', dispatched about the same time from London, stressed the ever-increasing numbers of English ships involved.[9] The trading season of 1611–12 saw the climax of the lucrative traffic. Alarmed members of the Spanish Junta de Guerra reported in March 1612 that 'great quantities of enemy ships of different nations, particularly Dutch and English, resort to the island of Trinidad to contraband with the residents for the fruits of the soil and above all tobacco . . . and all this is done so freely that ordinarily there are ten or twelve ships there'.[1] Amongst the English ships which picked up tobacco there during that season were the *Little John* of Sandwich, John Johnson master, trading for Robert Brooke and associates of London; the *Amity* alias *John* of London commanded by John Moore for Sir John Watts and numerous partners; and two other vessels under a master Thorne and a 'Captain Rider'.[2] The ships all loaded tobacco at San Tomé in October 1611. Doubtless numerous others followed their example. Sancho de Alquiza, commissioned by Philip III to investigate and put an end to the illicit traffic, picked up certain information that eighteen, and perhaps as many as twenty-seven ships, were in the Gulf of Paria between late December 1611 and February

6. Consejo de Indias to Philip III, 13 May 1611, B.L., Add. MSS. 36319, ff. 277 et seqq.; 'Information as to the great trade in tobacco', ibid., ff. 268 et seqq.

7. See the testimony of Thomas Ford, 25 October 1611, P.R.O., H.C.A. 1/47, ff. 244–5; and Francis Wright, 23 March 1612, H.C.A. 13/42.

8. Dispatch from Pedro Suárez Coronel, 20 June 1611, B.L., Add. MSS. 36319, f. 285.

9. See note 6 above.

1. Consulta of the Junta de Guerra, 11 March 1612, B.L., Add. MSS. 36320, f. 4.

2. See the sources listed in n. 9, p. 137, together with the examinations of William Wigg, 28 March 1612, P.R.O., H.C.A. 13/42; Samuel Skelton, ibid., William Wigg and Samuel Tickenor, 14 June 1612, ibid., f. 60; and the depositions of Dudley Hawkes, 25 March 1612, H.C.A. 1/47, f. 274; John Hedland and Otwell Johnson, 9 April 1612, ibid., f. 277.

1612. He encountered four in his outward and return journey between San Josef and San Tomé in February and April. On his return to Trinidad in mid April he discovered an English vessel trading at Port of Spain and laid a successful ambush for its company. His captives said that they had come from an Anglo-Dutch settlement on the Wiapoco and that they expected five more ships and a patache to follow them to Trinidad at the end of May. The alarmed residents of San Josef kept watch for the intruders, but they had not appeared before Alquiza left the island in June. The latter reported, however, that he had sighted some thirty ships off the coast of Trinidad between mid April and the end of May.[3] Another eighteen passed out of the Gulf of Paria to cruise off the pearl fisheries during the next three months.[4]

The alarming reports of 1612 were not repeated in following years. As we shall see, the investigations of Sancho de Alquiza marked the beginning of the end of the thriving tobacco traffic. The numbers of English, Dutch, and French ships visiting San Tomé and Port of Spain fell off sharply after 1612 and dwindled into insignificance by the end of the decade.

The Trinidad and Orinoco plantations produced approximately 200,000 pounds of tobacco each year for trade.[5] No series of figures exists to indicate exactly how much of this was imported into England each year while the contraband lasted. A Spanish observer in 1611 asserted that England consumed 100,000 pounds of tobacco yearly, of which only 6,000 pounds was acquired from Spain. If his computations, which approximate to other contemporary estimates, were correct, then a substantial part of the tobacco not acquired in Spain must have come from Trinidad and San Tomé.[6] Virginia and Bermuda had not yet begun to export tobacco, full-scale cultivation had not yet been resumed in Venezuela and imports from the English colonies in Guiana and other Spanish colonies in the Indies are unlikely to have been large. Such

3. Sancho de Alquiza to Philip III, 11 February 1612, B.L., Add. MSS. 36320, f. 298; 13 June 1612, ibid., ff. 294–5; 14 June 1612, ibid., ff. 287–95.
4. Bernardo de Vargas Machuca to Philip III, 16 August 1612, B.L., Add. MSS. 36320, f. 32.
5. Chaunu, iv. 577.
6. 'Information as to the great trade in tobacco': B.L., Add. MSS. 36319, ff. 268 et seqq. Other contemporary records place the total imports between 50,000 and 75,000 pounds per annum, and much entered the country which did not show up on the customs' records: S. Gray and V. J. Wyckoff, 'The international tobacco trade in the seventeenth century', *Southern Economic Journal*, vii, no. 1 (July 1940), 18; A. Rive, 'The consumption of tobacco since 1600', *Economic Journal*, supp. i (1926–9), 57–59, 71.

details for incoming cargoes as do survive indicate that English traders may have acquired some 60,000 pounds or more of tobacco annually through contraband at Trinidad and San Tomé in the boom years before 1612.[7]

The quantity imported reflects both the demand and the profitability of the product on the English market. English smokers showed a marked preference for 'Spanish'-grown tobacco, which between 1605 and 1612 retailed at 30s to 40s per pound.[8] At these prices it constituted a highly lucrative merchandise. Nevertheless it is clear that only a small number of those English promoters actively engaged in American trade in the early seventeenth century were prepared to participate in the contraband trade to secure it. The hazards of adventuring either purse or person, in peacetime, into a region where Spanish resistance might be expected and any retaliatory show of force was prohibited were sufficient to discourage interest. The sources for the traffic, although fragmentary and incomplete, yield the names of only thirty-eight merchants and ships' masters who participated in it. Twenty-seven of these individuals were merchants, but only five of them were men of real substance, London merchants with considerable resources and multifarious interests.[9] Nineteen

7. John Moore brought back 16,000 pounds of tobacco in the *Archangell* in 1611, 'Information as to the great trade in tobacco', B.L., Add. MSS. 36319, ff. 268 et seqq. For figures for the purchases of individual traders, usually between 2,000 and 4,000 pounds, see the evidence from English depositions quoted in earlier notes.

8. Purchases recorded in the household accounts of the Manners family and the account rolls of the Duke of Northumberland demonstrate its retail value: *Cal. H.M.C. MSS. of the Duke of Rutland, Belvoir*, iv, *passim*; *Cal. H.M.C. Sixth Report*, app., pp. 226–31.

9. On the careers of three of them, Sir John Watts, his son Captain John Watts, and Captain Michael Geare (*Amity* 1611) see Andrews, *Elizabethan Privateering*, pp. 87–88, 104–9, 121. On Richard Hall of London, grocer, who invested in privateering, and in contraband in the West Indies, and traded to Venice, Leghorn, Barbary, and Virginia see Guildhall Library, London, Grocers' Company, Orders of the Court of Assistants, 1591–1616, pp. 64–65, 82, 116–17, 157–60, 170, 206, 210, 223, 254, 262, 284, 300, 305–6, 349, 447, 453, 472–3; 'Examination of certain Barcelonans', 15 August 1599, P.R.O., H.C.A. 24/67, no. 7; Edward Collyns and Richard Hall to Sir Robert Cecil [1598–9], *Cal. H.M.C. Hatfield House*, xiv. 105; Andrews, *Elizabethan Privateering*, pp. 184–5, 269; Examinations for 24 and 25 May, 9, 18, 19, and 21 June, 13, 14, 18, and 21 July, 4, 22, and 30 August 1604, 19 March 1604–5, 4 April 1605, P.R.O., H.C.A. 13/37; 'A note of the merchants and marryners names taken in the West Indies in the ship called the *Aide* belonging to John Eldred and Richard Hall in July 1605', P.R.O., S.P. Span. xi. 21; Depositions concerning the voyage of the *Ulysses*, 1606, P.R.O., H.C.A. 24/73, pt ii, nos 126, 160, 161, 260, 371, 376, 414, 453, 454; S. R. Gardiner, *History of England* (London, 1883), i. 347–57; Privy Council, 9 March and 1 June 1617, P.R.O., P.C. 2/28, pp. 581–2 and 2/29; will, 6 June 1622, P.R.O., P.C.C. 10 Swann; S. M. Kingsbury (ed.), *The Records of the Virginia Company of London* (Washington, 1906–35), iii, doc. xiii. Details of the career of Robert Brooke, grocer (of the *Little John*, 1611), can be found in Guildhall Library, Grocers' Company, Orders of the Court of Assistants, 1591–1616, entries for 8, 29 June 1608; T. K. Rabb, *Enterprise and Empire* (Cambridge, Mass., 1967), p. 254.

others were also London men, seven of them grocers.[1] Four were foreigners resident in London, one a Portuguese, and three Flemings.[2] The three remaining merchants were outport men, two trading with unknown associates out of Topsham and the other, an Irishman, operating out of Dartmouth.[3] Of the total of thirty-eight individuals who were involved in the contraband at least 43 per cent had been previously engaged in privateering or *rescates* in the West Indies.[4] They were clearly men who were interested enough in maintaining English claims to free trade in the region to continue barter and piracy there after 1604, as long as they could do so at a reasonable risk.

The chances of being prosecuted at home for misdemeanours in the Indies were less if a vessel could operate out of an obscure harbour. The evidence probably under-represents the strength of outport involvement in the Trinidad and Orinoco trade. A. P. Newton, writing in 1914, asserted that many small vessels from the southwest and Irish ports engaged in the traffic. Whilst I have yet to find the evidence on which he based his statement, I have no doubt that he was correct in his appreciation of the role of the outports in this risky business.[5] Whether the Flemish and Portuguese merchants, who might claim to be Spanish subjects, served as frontmen to mask the dubious activities of their English associates is not clear. The three Flemings, Arnold Lull, Joos Croppenbury, and John Abealls, adventured in Sir John Watts's ships and one of the latter's vessels carried the Portuguese slave trader Carnero back to

1. Little is known of fifteen of them beyond their names; Robert Sharpe (*Penelope*, 1609); John Wightman grocer, Robert Tottle grocer, Peter Sohier, William Harte, Robert Smith, and William Stannarde (*Lyons Clawe*, 1611); Giles Hawkins (*Archangell*, 1610; *Amity*, 1611); Andrew Miller (*Archangell*, 1611); Benjamin and Emmanuell Finch, Captain Merricke, William Wigg grocer (*Amity*, 1611). William Wigg also associated with William Dodson and Dudley Hawkes, both grocers, in the *Little John*, 1611.

2. See above, pp. 133–4. For references to the activities of Francisco Carnero the Portuguese merchant see nn. 1, 9, p. 134 above. On the activities of the Flemings, Arnold Lull, Joos Croppenbury, and John Abealls see *Aliens in London, 1523–1625* (Huguenot Society of London, x, Aberdeen, 1900–8), ii. 212, 240, 315, 321, 389, 402, 428, 442, 464, 466; iii. 6, 9, 60, 63, 109, 124–6, 128–9, 131–2, 150–2, 165, 184–5, 237, 278; P.R.O., H.C.A. 13/32, ff. 232–3, 237, 240, 361; H.C.A. 13/33, ff. 195–6, 273; H.C.A. 13/34, ff. 52, 171, 364; H.C.A. 24/65, nos 1, 249; H.C.A. 24/67, no. 111; H.C.A. 3/25, ff. 32, 37–38, 40–41, 45–52, 61, 71.

3. See above, pp. 131, 132, 134.

4. Amongst the merchants Sir John Watts, Captain John Watts, Richard Hall, Michael Geare, Benjamin and Emmanuell Finch, Dudley Hawkes, Robert Sharpe; among the ships' masters William Longecastle, William Warner, John Moore, Andrew Miller, Robert Adams, John Johnson, William Thorne.

5. A. P. Newton, *The Colonizing Activities of the English Puritans* (New Haven, 1914), chap. 1.

London from the Orinoco in 1611.[6] It is possible that Watts's dealings with Carnero are the earliest indication of what was to become a well-developed fraud. After 1612 licensed Portuguese slave traders acting for syndicates of Dutch and English merchants picked up tobacco for them at 'Trinidad y Guayana' and other marginal plantations in the Indies because direct trade had become too risky.[7]

Such was the situation by 1612. The relative isolation which had made the plantations in 'Trinidad y Guayana' such a secure source of good tobacco, after commerce in Venezuela and New Andalucía became too hazardous, could not last. The Spanish government, informed of the thriving illegal barter at the two obscure settlements, moved to suppress it. The circumstances which, since the peace treaty of 1604, had left English intruders in the Spanish Indies liable both to Spanish assaults and to legal charges at home now served to put an end to direct English involvement in the lucrative tobacco trade at Trinidad and San Tomé. Both the Spanish and the English participants in the commerce were victims of the policies of their respective governments. The residents of San Tomé and San Josef were anxious to engage in smuggling, but were obliged to abandon it without any alternative means of subsistence. While the Spanish settlers were forced into hostile action against their north European customers, the English at least had to maintain a pacific stance, which effectively ended any possibility of continuing the barter at reasonable risk and profit.

Until 1606 the tobacco smuggling in Venezuela and New Andalucía had provided an effective smoke-screen behind which the inhabitants of San Tomé and San Josef could pursue their illegal activities unnoticed. Harassed authorities on the Main were therefore enraged to discover that the north European interlopers they had driven from their provinces now resorted to 'Trinidad y Guayana' for tobacco. As the governor of Cumaná complained to Philip III, in a letter of 18 December 1607, 'tobacco is now cleared from all these provinces except in San Tomé and the island of Trinidad ... and if Your Majesty does not remedy the contraband in tobacco there, neither in Santo Domingo, Caracas, nor here shall we have achieved anything'.[8] For the remainder of the decade the Crown was bombarded with reports from officials in New Granada, Venezuela, New Andalucía, La Margarita, and Santo Domingo detailing Berrío's corruption.

6. See above, p. 134.
7. See below, p. 150.
8. Pedro Suárez Coronel to Philip III, 18 December 1607: B.L., Add. MSS. 36319, f. 149.

Their dispatches stressed the possibilities that Trinidad might become a dangerous privateering base if it fell to foreign interlopers and that the Orinoco might become a route via the Meta and the Casanare to the rich mining provinces of New Granada. Faced with such reports of the potential consequences of Berrío's crimes, the Crown exhorted its officials in the Indies to do their utmost to put an end to them.[9]

While the unwelcome surveillance by his neighbours could not persuade Fernando de Berrío to forswear the profits of the tobacco trade, it was sufficiently unnerving to oblige him to mount occasional attacks on visiting merchant vessels to maintain a façade of legality. Thus it was in autumn 1608 after the *audiencia* of Santa Fe had commissioned one Fernando de Mendoza to look into his government,[1] that English vessels trading at Trinidad suffered one of Berrío's demonstrations. Witnesses in the English High Court of Admiralty testified that Berrío had lured twenty-seven men ashore from Richard Hall's *Ulysses* and Ralegh's *Primrose* and imprisoned them, demanding a ransom of 20,000 ducats worth of goods. When a ransom was paid he hanged the captives. This information, supplied as an excuse for the later capture of a Spanish prize by Hall's men in the Indies, might be taken with a pinch of salt were it not confirmed by Ralegh, who declared in 1618 that 'those verye Spaniards which were encountred att St Thome did, of late yeares, murder 36 of Mr. Hall's men of London, and myne, who landed without weapon upon the Spanishe faithe to trade with them'.[2]

Berrío's action did not discourage the trade, but he resorted to similar attempts to blind outside Spanish authorities in the following autumn (1609),[3] while an *oidor* of Panama was in La Margarita making inquiries about his jurisdiction, and once again the demonstration was at Richard Hall's expense. The crew of the *Penelope* and the *Indevor* declared that the Spaniards had, under cover of friendly trade at Port of Spain, sent messages to La Margarita informing its governor that the English in-

---

9. These reports are to be found in B.L., Add. MSS. 36319, ff. 104, 155, 193, 202, 207, 229–31, 236, 240, 250, 287.

1. Juan de Borja to Philip III, 20 June 1608: *V.B.A.*, 'British counter-case', app., pt i, no. 2.

2. The examination of Peter Cannon, 21 November 1610, P.R.O., H.C.A. 13/41, ff. 110–11; 'A declaration of his Highness, by the advice of his council; setting forth, on the behalf of this Commonwealth, the justice of their cause against Spain, 26 Oct. 1655', in G. K. Fortescue (ed.), *Catalogue of the Pamphlets collected by George Thomason, 1640–1661* (2 vols, London, 1908); E. Edwards, *The Life of Sir Walter Ralegh* (London, 1868), ii. 375–80 (hereafter cited as Edwards).

3. Francisco Manso de Contreras to Philip III, 22 October 1609: B.L., Add. MSS. 36319, f. 194.

tended to cut wood at Cape Tres Puntas and advising him to set an ambush. Forewarned by a friendly Indian, Hall's men beat off the attack. Later, to add to the trials of the voyage, the *Penelope* and *Indevor* clashed with three Spanish men-of-war off Cuba, and after this the *Indevor* was captured while trading at that island. In retaliation the company of the *Penelope* seized and brought back to England a Spanish prize, allegedly the very ship which had taken the *Indevor*.[4] A stern reprimand from the King and new inquiries initiated at Santo Domingo tightened the noose round Berrío in 1610.[5] He continued to welcome foreign traders although growing tension in the province rendered his treatment of them increasingly unpredictable.

Sir Thomas Roe, who reached Trinidad in February 1611, found relations between the planters and visiting traders increasingly strained, as the Spaniards awaited the arrival of a judge appointed to inquire into their activities. The settlers were in a disturbed and seditious mood at the prospect of losing their trade, wishful to maintain it as long as possible, and yet, at the same time, anxious to impress neighbouring officials with their loyalty by hostile confrontations with those who supplied their livelihood. Roe 'had some question with them on land . . . concerning the Trade of our Countrymen whom they used woorse then Moores'.[6] A sign of the general alert in the Caribbean against the trade was the careful questioning of Thomas Hickory, captured off Española in June 1611.[7] A pinnace sent off by Watts's *Archangell* to trade at the latter island was taken in the summer of 1611.[8] The jittery settlers at Trinidad continued to harbour foreign vessels, although the arrival of the official investigator was hourly expected. Governor Berrío, determined to continue his profits until the last possible moment, contracted with his usual foreign customers at the beginning of the new tobacco season, in autumn 1611. He was, however, determined that all the inhabitants of San Tomé should stand together to face the royal judge when he descended upon them. The *Little John* of Sandwich took aboard, in October 1611, a Portuguese named Camacha, who wished to leave the Orinoco whilst the going was good. Berrío immediately seized Dutchmen then present in San Tomé and threatened to hang them unless the Portuguese was put ashore. The

---

4. See n. 4, p. 133.
5. Royal warrant to Fernando de Berrío, 27 February 1610, B.L., Add. MSS. 36319, f. 227; Royal warrant to the *audiencia* of Santo Domingo, 3 July 1610, ibid., ff. 229–30.
6. Sir Thomas Roe to the Earl of Salisbury, 28 February 1611: P.R.O., C.O. 1/1, no. 25.
7. Deposition by Thomas 'Icurri': B.L., Add. MSS. 36319, ff. 294 et seqq.
8. Deposition of Thomas Ford, 25 October 1611: P.R.O., H.C.A. 1/47, ff. 244–5.

master of the *Little John,* pressed by the companies of English and Dutch ships in the river, complied with Berrío's demands. The unfortunate Camacha was hanged.[9] After the investigating judge, Sancho de Alquiza, arrived at Trinidad in late December 1611, Berrío coolly sold the last of his tobacco harvest, doing business at night after pretending to fight with the visiting traders all day.[1]

The arrival of the Spanish judge at San Tomé in February 1612 heralded, for the English, the beginning of the end of a profitable commerce. It was not the physical hazards now involved in the traffic which deterred them. Such encounters were part and parcel of trade within the bounds of the Spanish empire. It was rather their inability to defend themselves, or to take compensation for losses, which made the returns of the contraband no longer worth the risk.

The end of peaceful traffic at Port of Spain and San Tomé enmeshed the English who had participated in it in the tangled web of Anglo-Spanish diplomacy, and after 1604 English presence in the West Indies became one of the counters in an equivocal English foreign policy aimed at holding the balance between catholic Spain and the rest of protestant Europe. Hopes for establishing a closer alliance with Spain through a marriage alliance were doomed from 1605 on as exchanges between the two powers became increasingly strained. Spain kept the negotiations alive only as a means of lessening English support for the Dutch and was offended by English activities in the United Provinces and the Indies. The English government's intentions were soured by the Spanish crown's connivance in treasonous conspiracies against it and by the frequent losses and harassment suffered by English subjects trading lawfully in Spain and the Mediterranean. The Spanish crown and its law courts were slow to respond to English merchant grievances.[2] To the long list of complaints continually presented to the Spanish authorities by Ambassador Cornwallis, during his tenure of office, 1605–9, was added the vicious treatment meted out to English subjects unlucky enough to be captured in the Caribbean after the peace.[3] This, however, the English government

9. See the High Court of Admiralty evidence listed in n. 1, p. 134, and n. 2, p. 135.

1. Sancho de Alquiza to Philip III, 13 June 1612: B.L., Add. MSS. 36320, f. 292.

2. J. R. Jones, *Britain and Europe in the Seventeenth Century* (London, 1966), pp. 14–20; C. H. Carter, *The Secret Diplomacy of the Habsburgs, 1598–1625* (New York, 1964), pp. 47–60; G. D. Howat, *Stuart and Cromwellian Foreign Policy* (London, 1974), pp. 13–24 (hereafter cited as Howat).

3. Records of Cornwallis's representations are to be found throughout P.R.O., S.P. Span., xii–xv; and E. Sawyer (ed.), *Memorials of Affairs of State . . . Papers of the Right Honourable Sir Ralph Winwood* (London, 1725), ii and iii (cited hereafter as Winwood).

did not see as contrary to the terms of the peace treaty. The Earl of Salisbury informed Cornwallis in August 1606: 'as for all those particular Cruelties used in the Indies, we said we would not object them as Injuries to the Treaty, because we had agreed to leave them to adventure; but only to let them see that in the Forme of punishment there appeared more Bitterness and Indignity than if they had sunk them in the Sea'.[4] Unprepared to take strong action to defend its subjects who were foolhardy enough to trade in the Indies, the English government nevertheless would not admit their presence there to be illegal. In November 1607 Salisbury informed Cornwallis that any steps to relieve English prisoners taken in the Indies and held in Spain were to be informal. The Crown wished, at all costs, to avoid using any means to gain their freedom which could be construed as requesting a special favour from the Spanish government. The English government's position was that the men had been imprisoned without reason and should be free by right.[5] While upholding the right of his subjects to enter the Indies, James I was not prepared to take responsibility for their actions. Cornwallis established his position when he informed the Duke of Lerma, in March 1607, 'those voyages into ye Indies, were neyther with ye permission, or pruyty of ye king my soverayn; that Marchants being once at sea were lyke byrds out of hand; if so adventurous they would be of theyr own lives, and fortunes, yt was not in his Maiesties poure to restraine them . . .'.[6]

Allowed to resort to the Indies, yet left to their own fate if they ran into difficulties, English traders were also prohibited from retaliatory measures which might breach the problematic peace. At the conclusion of the latter, James I had declared that any of his subjects that 'hence forwarde shall goe to sea with intention to take anye shippes or goodes from subiects of Princes with whome we hould Freindshippe . . . shalbe declared and accompted off as Pirates and . . . shall suffer . . . death with confiscation of all their goods . . .'.[7] There was no hope that bellicose behaviour in the Caribbean would pass unnoticed. Lacking the financial resources to defend its marginal colonies adequately, the Spanish crown used all the diplomatic levers at its disposal to make English activities there more difficult. Its ambassadors and agents in England kept West

---

4. Earl of Salisbury to Sir Charles Cornwallis, 17 August 1606: Winwood, ii. 251.
5. Earl of Salisbury to Sir Charles Cornwallis, 18 November 1607: Winwood, ii. 359.
6. Sir Charles Cornwallis to the Earl of Salisbury, ult. March 1607, P.R.O., S.P. Span. xiii, f. 202.
7. P.R.O., S.P. Span. xi, f. 272.

Indies ventures under constant surveillance and, where the opportunity offered, ships returning from the region were attached with charges of piracy and representations made to James I.[8] The activities of the tobacco traders were closely watched. Richard Hall's ship the *Penelope* and the prize it brought back from the West Indies were arrested by Admiralty officials at the suit of the Spanish ambassador in 1610.[9] The dealings of Francisco Carnero on the Orinoco were similarly contested in the High Court of Admiralty in 1611, and in 1612 Robert Brooke was sued for tobacco which had belonged to the unfortunate Portuguese Camacha.[1] Such cases were inconvenient and often costly in terms of cargo spoiled by overlong storage.

Nevertheless as Anglo-Spanish relations worsened before 1610 the English courts showed themselves just as dilatory and partial as did those in Spain. The English government's reaction to the exploits of its subjects operating in the Indies was conditioned by the temperature of the exchanges between the two crowns. It found the threat of unleashing its subjects on the Indies at times a useful lever to bring Spain to a more reasonable posture in European affairs. Such considerations influenced its dealings with the London merchant and tobacco trader, Richard Hall. Hall's vessel the *Ulysses*, outward bound for Trinidad in 1608, took a Bristol ship laden with Portuguese goods off the Barbary coast.[2] News of the piracy reached the English community in Madrid with the rumour, as an informant wrote to Salisbury, that the *Ulysses* had been set 'forth by order with a letter of marte'.[3] The gossip was not true and the ship's master William Longecastle was hanged for piracy when he returned to England.[4] Nevertheless Richard Hall was able to avail himself of the influence of the Earl of Nottingham to secure the tobacco and goods from the voyage, which his unruly company had tried to smuggle into Chichester. James I, on the recommendation of Salisbury as Lord Trea-

8. Quinn, 'James I and the beginnings of empire in America', pp. 135–52.
9. See the High Court of Admiralty evidence quoted in n. 4, p. 133.
1. See the High Court of Admiralty evidence quoted in n. 9, p. 134. The Spanish ambassador addressed petitions to James I for the arrest of Francisco Carnero, 16 April 1611, P.R.O., S.P. Span. xviii, f. 63; and to Sir Robert Cecil, 4 May 1611, ibid., f. 71.
2. See the depositions of William Longecastle, November 1609, P.R.O., H.C.A. 1/47, f. 56; William Tavernor, ibid., ff. 56–57; John Moore, 28 November 1609, ibid., f. 59; John Paine, 28 November 1609, ibid., ff. 59–60; Edmund Willoughby, 14 December 1609, ibid., ff. 69–70; Samuel Cade, 27 March 1610, ibid., ff. 90–93; Anthony Wye, 1610, ibid., f. 150; and the examination of Anthony Wye, 21 March 1609–10, H.C.A. 13/40, ff. 99–100.
3. John Jude to the Earl of Salisbury, 27 July 1608, P.R.O., S.P. Span. xv, f. 90.
4. Deposition of Roger Hurrell, 7 June 1610: P.R.O., H.C.A. 1/47, ff. 126–8.

surer, remitted all customs owing on the tobacco.[5] Furthermore, when Hall's ship the *Penelope*, returning from Trinidad and the Caribbean with a Spanish prize in 1610, was arrested on suspicion of piracy, it was freed on the receipt of a letter from the Lord Admiral. It was only re-arrested when the Spanish ambassador began a legal suit against it.[6] Hall acknowledged to the Earl of Nottingham how much he 'depended upon your honours Favor and the Lord Tresorer my much respected Lord'.[7] Indeed such were his connections that he was awarded the Spanish prize in the High Court of Admiralty. Hall's influence at court was not the result of Salisbury's and Howard's long-standing interest in West Indian ventures,[8] nor was it, as the fraternity of West Indian traders thought, a sign of the government's intention to reopen privateering. The Crown's treatment of Hall aroused expectations amongst the merchant community out of all proportion to its intentions. The favour shown to him was a much more obvious message to the Spanish government. Hall's losses at the hands of the Spaniards had become a *cause célèbre* in the English merchant community. He claimed to have lost seven ships since the peace.[9] While some of them, taken in the Caribbean, might be dismissed as the unavoidable risks of such a trade, the arrest of the *Triall*, in the course of peaceful commerce in the Mediterranean in 1605, was a flagrant example of Spanish maltreatment of English merchants since the peace. In default of redress in Spain, the capture of the *Triall*, a symbol of all other such losses at the hands of the Spaniards, roused the House of Commons to demand the issue of letters of marque in 1607.[1] The concessions made to Hall for the tobacco of the *Ulysses* and the favourable decision on the matter of the

5. Richard Hall to the Earl of Nottingham, 3 April 1609, Bodleian Library, Clarendon Papers, i, no. 45; Sir William Monson to the same, 3 April 1609, ibid., no. 44; Warrant from James I to the Lord Treasurer, 7 February 1610, P.R.O., S.P. Dom., Jas. I, lii, no. 54.

6. Richard Hall to the Earl of Nottingham, 27 August 1610, Bodleian Library, Clarendon Papers, i, no. 50; Sir Richard Cooper to the same, 28 August 1610, ibid., no. 51.

7. Richard Hall to the Earl of Nottingham, 27 August 1610, Bodleian Library, Clarendon Papers, i, no. 50.

8. On the involvement of Sir Robert Cecil and Sir Charles Howard in West Indies ventures see Andrews, 'Caribbean Rivalry', pp. 5–17; *Elizabethan Privateering*, pp. 89–90, 236–8; L. Stone, 'The fruits of office', in F. J. Fisher (ed.), *Essays in the Economic and Social History of Tudor and Stuart England* (Cambridge, 1961), pp. 89–116; R. W. Kenny, *Elizabeth's Admiral: The Political Career of Charles Howard Earl of Nottingham, 1536–1624* (London, 1970), *passim*.

9. Richard Hall to the Earl of Nottingham, 27 August 1610; Bodleian Library, Clarendon Papers, i, no. 50.

1. The case of the loss of the *Triall* set forth to the Mediterranean in 1605, by Richard Hall and John Eldred, and the political furore it raised is fully described in Gardiner, *History of England*, i. 347–57; ii. 134–40.

Penelope's prize served as palliatives to a House of Commons once more clamouring for war in 1610 and as warnings to Spain of the possible consequences of continued intransigence. Yet the Crown had no intention of issuing general licences for privateering or countenancing warfare in the Indies. The behaviour of the Spanish crown might induce James I to disregard Spanish protests about the settlement of Virginia, but it could not persuade him to allow the resumption of hostilities beyond the line.[2]

The confusion of hope and uncertainty raised by the government's dealings with Hall was further deepened in 1609–10 by the manoeuvrings of the Earl of Salisbury. Moved by the increasingly aggressive posture of Spain in Europe to seek a counter-alliance with France, he was beginning to use his contacts with Guiana venturers and tobacco traders to explore the possibility of striking at the Spanish Empire should war break out. Sir Thomas Roe sailed for Guiana in 1610 to discover whether it contained an Indian civilization in the interior, or gold-mines on the Orinoco rich enough to warrant and to finance armed intervention in the Spanish Indies. His mission was one of extreme delicacy. Openly provocative behaviour in the Spanish-occupied territory of the Indies would arouse a predictably hostile reaction from Spain and enrage James I by aggravating Anglo-Spanish relations. Thus Sir Thomas Roe was warned to pursue his relations with the Spanish settlers at Trinidad and San Tomé with great caution, and to avoid hostilities.[3] Roe's letter to Salisbury from Trinidad in February 1611 illustrates well the feelings of frustration, confusion, and constraint experienced by the English involved in the tobacco trade there.

The Spaniards here are equally proud, insolent, yet needy and weake: theyr force is reputation, and theyr safety opinion: yet dare they use us whose hands are bound with any contumely and treachery: . . . I hope your Noble disposition will not take it ill that we defend ourselves and the Honour of our Nation: I will not exceed your Honorable caution your Lordship gave me, nor stoope to so wretched an enemy (for so he is here) nor synke under injuryes I am able to repulse. I have had some question with them on land, but it is ended with quiett, concerning the Trade of our contrymen, whom they used woorse than Moores. All seamen here bless your Lordship, and wish that the State would not be offended if they made themselves recompense, and have gotten a rumor, or made one, of Lettres of Mark, because Mr. Halls prise hath beene admitted: If the example were sure, we could second yt, but we dare not handle fyre, nor cannot take fast hould of ayre.[4]

2. Quinn, 'James I'.
3. Harlow, *Ralegh's Last Voyage*, chap. 1.
4. Sir Thomas Roe to the Earl of Salisbury, 28 February 1611: P.R.O.,C.O. 1/1 ,no. 25.

Their caution was understandable. Salisbury, similarly fearful of taking any action in the region which might tip Anglo-Spanish relations towards war, before it had been shown to contain anything more remunerative than 'smoake', dropped his scheme. The Crown might ignore Spanish claims to unoccupied North America, but Guiana was another matter. The definite possibility of gold might compensate James I for the consequent deterioration of relations and the loss of the Spanish dowry, but not the abominable weed tobacco.[5] Ralegh was to find this out to his cost in 1618.

After 1612 the Spanish plantations in Trinidad and the Orinoco ceased to be a secure source of tobacco for north European traders. The Spanish investigator, Sancho de Alquiza, forbade the cultivation of tobacco at the settlements in 1612, so that there was no crop available for the 1612–13 season.[6] He did not completely succeed in putting an end to the traffic, however. When he departed the province in June 1612 he left behind law-abiding deputy administrators in each settlement, governing planters who bitterly resented the loss of their former livelihood. Not until 1614 was provision made for the despatch of one licensed trading ship a year from Seville to Port of Spain.

San Tomé had to wait until 1619 for a similar concession.[7] It is not surprising, therefore, that some disaffected planters were willing to carry on clandestine trade with foreigners prepared to run the risk of discovery by the authorities.

It would appear, however, that in the two or three years immediately after 1612, only the Dutch were willing to do so. Spanish sources record that one foreign ship went up-river to San Tomé in 1613. It was driven off by the inhabitants but remained down river for several days, raising suspicions that somebody was trading with its company.[8] The residents of Trinidad were harassed by Dutch pirates, accompanied by Carib war canoes, in 1613. They believed the Dutch ships to be supply vessels, which had discovered, and were out to revenge, the loss of their tobacco factory in the Corentine, destroyed earlier that year by Spaniards from Trinidad.[9] The possibility of being visited by Dutch vessels, homeward

5. Harlow, *Ralegh's Last Voyage*, chap. 1.

6. Sancho de Alquiza to Philip III, 13 June 1612: B.L., Add. MSS. 36320, f. 292.

7. Chaunu, iv. 4; Philip III to the Casa de Contratación, 18 February 1620, B.L., Add. MSS. 36321, f. 138.

8. Philip III to Diego Palomeque de Acuña, 8 November 1615: B.L., Add. MSS. 36319, f. 240.

9. Memorial on the state of Trinidad sent to the Consejo de Indias, October 1614, B.L., Add. MSS. 36320, ff. 154–8; 'Informacion de la despoblacion de los flamencos que estavan el rio de Corentin y Marataca, 16 Feb. 1614', ibid., ff. 44 et seqq.

bound from plantations in southern Guiana, continued to worry officials at San Josef through the next two years. The lieutenant-governor of Trinidad captured the crew of a Dutch ship at the island in 1614. He claimed that foreigners had virtually ceased to call there for fear of reprisals, but that they still found a welcome in the Orinoco.[1] Three ships, nationality unspecified, were seen in the latter river in 1614.[2]

The year 1615 saw the arrival at San Tomé of the new governor who was determined to stamp out the last vestiges of the contraband.[3] It is paradoxical, therefore, that his assumption of office seems to have coincided with a slight revival of English interest in the Orinoco traffic, after one or two years of virtual cessation of contact. Sir Walter Ralegh informed Lord Carew that 'Mr. Thorne alsoe, of Tower Street in London, besids many other Englishe, was in like sort murdered [by the Spaniards of San Tomé], the yeare before my delivery out of the Tower'—1615.[4] The reappearance of the English on the river was an indication of a changed climate of Anglo-Spanish relations and of reviving English designs on Guiana. Ralegh's scheme for the opening of alleged gold-mines on the Orinoco, dropped by Salisbury as too dangerous in 1611, had been resurrected. The increasing dominance of the anti-Spanish party at the court after 1614 made James I willing to entertain it as means either of replenishing his depleted treasury or of pressing the Spanish crown to the desired marriage alliance by aggressive manoeuvres in the Indies.[5]

The English traders, probably two or three in all, who entered the Orinoco to trade clandestinely for tobacco in 1615, were also commissioned to scout the Spanish positions and pick up information on possible gold-mines. Some of the victims of the Spanish attack in 1615 probably belonged to a ship sent out by Ralegh to reconnoitre the river in that year.[6] One or two more ships may have entered the Orinoco in 1616. Ralegh noted in the journal of his last voyage, for February 1618, that one of the men on Sir John Pennington's ship saw an Indian 'who two

1. Memorial on the state of Trinidad: B.L., Add. MSS. 36320, ff. 154–8.
2. Philip III to Diego Palomeque de Acuña, 8 November 1615, B.L., Add. MSS. 36319, f. 240.
3. Ibid.
4. Sir Walter Ralegh to Lord Carew, 1618, in Edwards, ii. 375–80.
5. Harlow, *Ralegh's Last Voyage*, chap. 1; Howat, pp. 22–24.
6. Sir Walter Ralegh to Lord Carew, 1618, in Edwards, ii. 375–80; Laurence Keymis to the same, 1615, New York Public Library, Arents Collections, MS. Acc. 6044; Reports dispatched by a Spanish agent to Madrid, 1614, Biblioteca Nacional, Madrid, 18184/18.

yeere before he had seene in Orenoke'.[7] It does seem that English as well as Dutch traders kept up contacts with dissident Spaniards and Caribs on the Orinoco up to 1617. Ralegh claimed to have acquired from the sack of San Tomé a letter of the late governor's 'to the kinge of Spaine, dated July the eighteenth which . . . complained . . . that even those Indians that live under their noses, doe in despite of all the kings edicts trade with Los Flamingos et Anglesos Enemigos . . .'.[8] A good proportion of the 'masters' and 'maryners' who sailed in Ralegh's fleet for the Orinoco in 1617 'had traded there 10 or 12 yeares for tobacco'.[9] Many of them showed more interest in acquiring tobacco from Trinidad and San Tomé than in discovering gold-mines.

Any hopes that the expedition would give the English control of the rich plantations on the river were dashed by its failure to find gold. James I's wrath and Ralegh's consequent execution only served to drive home the considerations which had curtailed interest in the tobacco traffic after 1612. In the delicate balance of Anglo-Spanish diplomacy hostilities in the Indies would be tolerated only if they could provide something of material benefit to make up for the breach of the peace. Tobacco was not enough. The events of 1618 put the finishing blow to English interest in acquiring tobacco directly from San Josef and San Tomé. Two English ships turned up in the Orinoco delta in March 1620 demanding tobacco as a ransom for Spaniards captured on the Essequibo. They withdrew when the settlers refused to deal with them.[1] This is the last discoverable reference to English traders seeking tobacco from the Spanish plantations. Their participation in the direct barter, sharply curtailed after 1612, had dwindled into insignificance by the end of the decade.

Any tobacco entering England from the plantations of San Josef and San Tomé thereafter was received at second or third hand. The planters on Trinidad and the Orinoco, cowed into outward obedience by Ralegh's expedition and yet still without an adequate market for their produce, turned increasingly after 1612 to Portuguese traders. By 1620 the Spanish

7. Sir Walter Ralegh's journal of his last voyage to Guiana, 1617–18, B.L., Cotton MSS., Titus B. VIII, ff. 153 et seqq., printed in R. H. Schomburgk (ed.), *The discovery of the large, rich and beautiful empire of Guiana* (London, 1848), p. 206.

8. Ralegh's 'appologie' in Harlow, *Ralegh's Last Voyage*, p. 334.

9. Ibid., p. 323.

1. Pedro Fernández de Pulgar, 'Fragmentos referentes a la historia de Peru y Chile', Real Academía de Historia, Madrid, Muñoz A/66, f. 144 et seqq.; Consejo de Indias to Philip III, 1620, B.L., Add. MSS. 36321, f. 4.

crown had become more worried about the activities of its Portuguese subjects in its marginal tobacco colonies than about the intrusions of north Europeans. The tobacco trade had become virtually a Portuguese monopoly. Portuguese ships, licensed to carry slaves to the mining provinces in the Indies, carried them instead to the tobacco plantations, where they exchanged them for tobacco. The tobacco was transported directly either to England or the United Provinces, or else transhipped to Dutch or English vessels in the Canaries or on the coast of Portugal. All participants involved thus avoided paying customs. An attempt by the Spanish crown in the early 1620s to end this fraud by creating a royal tobacco monopoly was thwarted by planter resistance and insuperable organizational difficulties. After a very few years control of the trade of the tobacco-producing colonies returned to the hands of the Portuguese.[2]

The pressures which led to the end of direct English trade at San Tomé and San Josef were the same as those which had from the beginning discouraged English investment in the region as a whole. The profitable contraband trade at the tobacco plantations of Trinidad and the Orinoco and indeed the opportunity to take possession of these were abandoned because they threatened the achievement of the Anglo-Spanish marriage alliance. The same considerations hindered colonial interest in Guiana, deflecting it to Virginia and Bermuda, thus establishing their priority and guaranteeing them, after 1620, the monopoly of the increasingly glutted domestic tobacco market. The breakdown of Anglo-Spanish relations after 1624 only produced the new West Indian colonies as rivals for investment capital and tobacco production. The effect of Anglo-Spanish diplomacy on the direction of English colonial developments in the two decades after 1604 worked to ensure that 'Virginia' rather than 'Trinidado' or 'Orinoco' became synonymous with tobacco for the English consumer.

2. Chaunu, iv. 572–8.

8

English commercial development and American colonization 1560-1620

CAROLE SHAMMAS

The colonization of America was a long and drawn-out process for the English. As early as the end of the fifteenth century English adventurers and seamen were participating in New World voyages and exploring coastal areas. Attempts to colonize, however, only began in the 1560s and though interest in founding settlements continued throughout the Elizabethan period, none of the projects resulted in lasting colonies.[1] Not until the second decade of the seventeenth century, when Virginia planters started to send regular shipments of tobacco back to the mother country, could the English be sure of a permanent New World settlement. During this period of over a century there were major internal changes within England which altered perceptions about both the New World and colonization and which ultimately made possible the establishment of a network of settlements in America. Specialists on exploration and discovery and colonial and economic historians have all contributed towards identifying these changes and assessing their effect on westward expansion.

Recent research on the early seventeenth-century Chesapeake and West Indies settlements has underlined the commercial character of the earliest successful plantations and the role marketable commodities played in making them a success. Neither extremely high mortality rates nor abysmal living conditions could discourage men from pouring into these areas once a profitable crop had been developed. In hot pursuit of quick rewards, these planters devoted themselves almost entirely to the cultivation of the staple crop and they largely neglected public projects, defence, town building and, in some cases, food production. As one historian has phrased it, settlements such as Jamestown resembled boom

1. The best discussion of the early English voyages to America is in D. B. Quinn, *England and the Discovery of America* (London and New York, 1974).

towns more than ordinary English villages. They were socially primitive but commercially sophisticated, possessing close market ties with the metropolis, London, and enjoying, by pre-industrial standards, a high per capita output.[2] Colonies founded by religious dissidents usually took on a more traditional appearance, yet ultimately these communities would have had difficulty in surviving if plantation colonies had not existed for the inhabitants of these less hectic settlements to service.

The formation of relatively high-powered mercantile entities was a new type of colonial experience for the English, and for most other western European nations as well. Charles Verlinden has pointed out that in the medieval period Italian city states set up plantations and communes in the Near East which functioned much like the American colonies of the seventeenth and eighteenth centuries. Yet it is clear that during the Middle Ages less commercialized areas, such as England, were accustomed to practising a very different type of territorial domination, one which reflected their own feudal forms of organization. Lords or knights who subdued native populations on the Continent, in the Near East, and in Ireland lived off tributes and dues and seldom attempted to integrate the economy of the conquered land with that of the homeland for the benefit of the latter. Moreover, while the lord might owe allegiance to a European king, that king had often very little political control over the newly annexed territory.[3] Although by 1500 England had developed both a fairly complex mercantile community and a moderately centralized government, expansion at first was more of a reaction to than a direct manifestation of these elements and Elizabethan attempts to claim New World land, like the early Spanish conquests in the Americas, continued in many ways to bear the marks of the type of domination prevalent in earlier centuries.

Nearly all the papers and documents of the principal Elizabethan colonizing enterprises have now been collected and published, many by the Hakluyt Society. These volumes contain information about the scope of sixteenth-century planting attempts, the men who participated and the nature of their aims and plans. There were about a dozen projects, but

2. E. S. Morgan, 'The first American boom: Virginia 1618 to 1630', *William and Mary Quarterly*, 3rd series, xxviii (1971), 169–98; R. Menard, 'The demography of Somerset County, Maryland: a preliminary report' (paper presented to the Stony Brook Conference on Social History, Stony Brook, New York, June 1975); and R. S. Dunn, *Sugar and Slaves: Rise of the Planter Class in the English West Indies 1624–1713* (Chapel Hill, 1972).
3. C. Verlinden, *The Beginnings of Modern Colonization* (Ithaca, 1970), pp. 3–32; J. Prawer, *The Crusader's Kingdom* (New York, 1972), pp. 85–93 and 482–503.

only nine of them succeeded in sending out ships bound for America—at an estimated cost of £75,000 and involving about 4,600 seamen and colonists.[4] In view of the corresponding figures for privateering activities during the peak period of Anglo-Spanish hostility, these totals of money and people seem small indeed.[5] Clearly New World colonization appealed to a very narrow segment of the Tudor population. Merchants played a limited role in these early colonization efforts, as did the country squire, the religious dissident, and the ordinary labourer. Those who became enthusiastic about claiming American territory in this period were the same men who pushed for action against the Spanish, wanted the Crown to extend protection to the Low Countries, and fought in Ireland and France, men such as Walter Ralegh, his half-brother Humphrey Gilbert, Henry Knollys, Philip Sidney, Ralph Lane, Richard Grenville, and Christopher Carleill. Some quickly lost interest in America and went on to further martial adventures; but others actually organized expeditions staffed by friends from court and county, relatives, servants, and seamen. Whether well placed or mere hangers-on, these gentlemen tended to frequent the court and chose military rather than administrative tasks as a means to advance themselves. As the Crown furnished neither enough opportunities nor the kind of service to satisfy the ambitions of these men, they organized private expeditions to Europe, Ireland, and America. They grasped at opportunities as they emerged and there was no real pattern in their choice of destination. Some went to Ireland before they became interested in America while others did the reverse.

The object of this form of expansion was the acquisition of an area which would provide economic rewards in the form of revenues, tributes, rents, and offices that could be parcelled out to followers. Europe was of course the most desirable area, but it had a growing nation-state system which was rapidly making such private military adventuring an anachronism. This development, together with the growing rivalry between England and Spain, turned men's eyes to the Americas. The most appealing territory in the New World, however, was also protected by the system. English adventurers had elaborate schemes for taking over the

4. Figures for each of the projects and the method used to calculate them can be found in C. Shammas, 'The gentleman adventurer and Elizabethan western planting' (unpublished Ph.D. dissertation, Johns Hopkins University, 1971), chap. 4. My figures are much lower than those estimated by T. K. Rabb, *Enterprise and Empire* (Cambridge, Mass., 1967), pp. 57–68 (hereafter cited as Rabb, *Enterprise and Empire*).

5. K. R. Andrews, *Elizabethan Privateering: English Privateering during the Spanish War 1585–1603* (Cambridge, 1964), pp. 127–8; and Rabb, *Enterprise and Empire*, p. 61.

ready-made empires of Spain: for example Ralegh, in founding Roanoke, evidently hoped to use it to attack Spanish colonies. Later, in his second New World enterprise, Ralegh hoped not only to conquer Guiana but also to continue and take over the rest of Spanish South America. Gilbert had tried to convince the Queen in the late 1570s that she should allow him to execute an assault on the West Indies, conquering Santo Domingo and Cuba and making them bases for an invasion of New Spain. Christopher Carleill, as land commander of the 1585 Drake expedition to the West Indies, managed for a brief time to seize several port towns.[6] But any conquest of Spanish possessions needed the support of the Crown, and Elizabeth, fearing Philip II's wrath, hesitated to give either aid or approval for a permanent capture. As a result, the adventurers had to find other lands to subdue.[7]

Examination of the reading of the Elizabethan adventurers and of the interviews they conducted with foreign soldier-seamen in the months before they made their plans indicates that most of them were looking for Indian cities and that they usually had a particular place in mind when they began to organize their enterprises. We know Thomas Stukely learned about opportunities in America in 1562 from the Frenchman Jean Ribault while the latter was visiting the English court. Ribault had just returned from helping to found a Huguenot-sponsored colony in what is now Port Royal Island, South Carolina, which he referred to as Terra Florida. The account of his voyage circulated at court before it was published in 1563. It indicates that Ribault had not only been concerned with esablishing a base for intercepting Spain's treasure fleets,

---

6. Roanoke was to be a scheduled stop for the privateering fleets of Sir George Carey and Sir Francis Drake, and a military expert drew up plans for a fort there. Ralegh's soldiers were supposed to be prepared to deal with both 'naked men' and Spaniards: D. B. Quinn (ed.), *The Roanoke Voyages 1584–1590* (London, 1955), pp. 32, 63–64, and 130–9 (hereafter cited as Quinn, *Roanoke Voyages*). Hakluyt hinted that the settlers were to aid in the interception of treasure fleets and to join up with Florida Indians in an invasion of Spanish territories: E. G. R. Taylor (ed.), *The Original Writings and Correspondence of the Two Richard Hakluyts* (London, 1935), pp. 240–3 and 323 (hereafter cited as *Writings* [1935]). For plans by Ralegh to rid South America of the Spanish, see 'Of the voyage for Guiana', written by or on behalf of Ralegh for the Queen, in V. T. Harlow (ed.), *The Discoverie of Guiana* (London, 1928), pp. 139–48 (hereafter cited as Harlow, *Discoverie of Guiana*). For Gilbert see 'A discourse how hir majestie may meete with and annoy the King of Spayne' in D. B. Quinn (ed.), *The Voyages and Colonizing Enterprises of Sir Humphrey Gilbert* (London, 1940), pp. 170–80 (hereafter cited as Quinn, *Gilbert*). On Carleill, see Irene Wright (ed.), *Further English Voyages to Spanish America 1583–1599* (London, 1951), pp. lvii–lviii.

7. The adventurers were encouraged to think that new lands in America, unlike other places, were in the reach of 'pryvat men' because of the example of the *conquistadores*: Cambridge University Library, untitled manuscript Dd. 3.85, and George Peckham, 'A true report of the late discoveries' in Quinn, *Gilbert*, p. 471.

but had also been interested in finding Cibola (the legendary Seven Cities of Gold). Ribault reported that the Indians had told him that Cibola lay only twenty days from the place where the French had made their settlement. The narrative also noted that these Indians were willing to obey, and content to serve, white men who treated them well.[8]

Richard Grenville, a friend and distant relative of Stukely, probably first heard about New World opportunities from the French pilots who were to have led Stukeley to Terra Florida. Grenville had these men in his custody for a few months in 1564.[9] Later Grenville learned more, this time about an area around the River Plate in South America, from some French mariners involved in Villegaignon's Brazilian colony who spent six months in his household.[1] These reports led to his abortive 1573 venture.

Rumours of a legendary Indian city called Norumbega, located somewhere on the northeast coast of America along an important river, seem to have been the inspiration for Gilbert's 1583 journey to America and later for Gosnold's voyage to New England. The French, drawing on accounts of Verrazzano, Gomes, and Alfonce, first popularized the story of this city which was supposedly inhabited by highly civilized natives, rich in precious metals and furs. The myth caught on enough for Mercator to put Norumbega on his widely circulated and copied 1569 map and to draw a large castle by the name, signifying the presence of a big Indian society there.[2] Originally Gilbert had a prejudice against the northern parts of America (probably because it was believed gold was only found in warm regions) but Norumbega was not thought to be far north and was reputed to have a wonderfully temperate climate.[3] John Walker, an Englishman who had journeyed to the coast of North America, told Gilbert that there were silver mines along the Norumbega River. Gilbert also learned about the alleged wealth of Norumbega from David Ingram,

8. The manuscript report of Ribault's journey is printed in H. P. Biggar, 'Jean Ribault's discovery of Terra Florida', *English Historical Review*, xxxii (1917), pp. 253–70. For information on the origins of the legend, see G. Buker, 'The seven cities: the role of a myth on the exploration of the Atlantic', *American Neptune*, xxx (1970), 249–59.

9. J. Izon, *Sir Thomas Stucley* (London, 1956), p. 50.

1. B.L., Add. MSS. 48151; and Zelia Nuttall (ed.), *New Light on Drake* (London, 1914), pp. 6–10.

2. See S. Diamond, 'Norumbega: New England Xanadu', *American Neptune*, xi (1951), 95–107.

3. Edward Hayes's narrative in Quinn, *Gilbert*, p. 390. From the tract and petitions he wrote in the 1560s concerning a voyage to Cathay, which included a plan to receive 'captenshippe' over New World land, we know Gilbert had read widely in the literature of overseas expansion: ibid., *passim*.

an English seaman, who reported among other things that its inhabitants lived in domed houses of crystal and silver.[4] Gilbert was eager to believe these stories, fantastic though they were, and the discovery of Norumbega became the object of his second expedition.[5] Twenty years later Bartholomew Gosnold, using Verrazzano's account as his guide, went to America to search for the same locality.[6]

Another series of rumours, this time concerning Guiana, attracted the attention of the most famous of the adventurers. Ralegh, while active in privateering, was never completely satisfied with the kind of hit-and-run exploit conducted by Drake, feeling that 'it had sorted ill with the offices of Honor, which by her Maiesties grace, I hold ... to run from Cape to Cape ... for the pillage of ordinarie prizes'. He had greater ambitions. In 1586 Ralegh had the opportunity to talk with Don Pedro Sarmiento de Gamboa, a Spanish adventurer captured by the English, who may have told him about the fabulous golden land of El Dorado, inhabited by runaway descendants of the Emperor of Peru. When he arrived in Guiana, Ralegh heard more from Don Antonio de Berrío, who had been a relentless pursuer of El Dorado for many years and knew about the many previous attempts made by Germans and Iberians to locate it.[7] Ralegh publicized the legend in England, so that by the time Charles Leigh organized his voyage, Guiana was 'reputed to be the chiefest place for golde Mines in all the West India'.[8]

The Elizabethans assumed that when they got to these golden Indian cities, the treasure would be there waiting for them to claim. Thus Ralegh told his gentlemen associates: 'Those commanders and Chieftaines, that shoote at honour, and abundance, shal find there more rich and bewtifull cities, more temples adorned with golden Images, more sepulchers filled with treasure than either Cortez found in Mexico or Pazzaro in Peru: and the shining glorie of this conquest will eclipse all those so farre extended beames of the Spanish nation.'[9] Frobisher's *Meta Incognita* project in the

---

4. 'Sondrie reports of the contrie which Sir Humfrey Gilbert goeth to discover': Quinn, *Gilbert*, pp. 287 and 309.

5. 'Things knowen by experyence to be in the contryes about the Ryver of Norrinberge': Edward Hoby's Commonplace Book, B.L., Add. MSS. 39823; and Quinn, *Gilbert*, pp. 378 and 423.

6. 'Gosnold to his father, 7 September 1602', in Samuel Purchas, *Purchas his Pilgrimes* (20 vols, Glasgow, 1905–7), xviii. 300–2 (hereafter cited as Purchas, *Pilgrimes*).

7. Walter Ralegh, 'The discoverie of the large and bewtiful empire of Guiana' in Harlow, *Discoverie of Guiana*, p. 4.

8. John Nicholl, *An houre glasse of Indian newes* (London, 1607), sig. Blv.

9. Ralegh, 'Discoverie of Guiana' in Harlow, *Discoverie of Guiana*, p. 71.

mid 1570s showed that Englishmen when forced by circumstances would search out and mine metals themselves, but generally speaking the adventurers expected to obtain gold from the Indians. Any reader of the histories of the Spanish in America translated into English at this time might conclude that a small band of valiant white men could with relative ease seize Indian cities and collect princely tributes of gold, silver, and jewels from the awed inhabitants in exchange for a promise of protection.[1] The Spaniards, following the custom within Europe, imposed tribute on conquered Indian cities and English adventurers planned to do the same in their ventures.[2] One author, writing on behalf of Ralegh's Guiana enterprise, even told the Queen that the Indians might voluntarily become tributaries of the English, in exchange for help in ridding South America of the Spanish. No harsh conquest or inhumane treatment of the natives would be necessary, yet England could gain lordship over all the treasures on the continent and deal a severe blow to Spanish power.[3]

When the adventurers landed in the New World they immediately began to search out Indians who could recount stories of gold, and to sample rocks that showed promise of containing precious metals. Interest in other commodities was low. True, the colonizers often praised the areas they discovered, mentioning the abundance of flora and fauna, but this was primarily to show that the land could sustain life. It was not simply personal greed for gold that made them so eager to find Indians with precious metals, but also the necessity of providing an economic foundation for their domain that would attract men to follow them to America. In an age when the Crown had control over so many offices and privileges, the comparable patronage that would flow from the claiming of New World territories was supremely attractive to private gentlemen. Yet privileges had to be worth something, had to make some discernible difference to the fortunes of the recipient. Petitions for projects, therefore, invariably promised 'great treasures and richesse' and promotion tracts

1. See E. Arber (ed.), *The First Three English Books on America* (Birmingham, 1885); Francisco López de Gómara, *The conquest of the Weast Indies* (London, 1578); and Augustín Zarate, *The strange and delectable history of the discoverie and conquest of the provinces of Peru, in the South Sea*, trans. T. Nicholas (London, 1581). John Chilton's relation, B.L., Add. MSS. 22904, outlines the tribute system of the Spanish empire in America. Chilton's relation was printed in Richard Hakluyt, *The principall navigations, voyages and discoveries of the English nation* (London, 1589), pp. 487–94, and again in the second edition, but much of the tribute information was omitted.

2. C. G. Cruickshank, *The English Occupation of Tournai 1513–1519* (Oxford, 1971), pp. 1–12, discusses tribute, ransoms, and plundering in early modern Europe.

3. On tribute, see 'Of the voyage for Guiana' in Harlow, *Discoverie of Guiana*, p. 146; and Quinn, *Gilbert*, p. 403.

told the common soldier that in America he would 'fight for gold, and pay himselfe in steede of pence, with plates of halfe a foote brode, wheras he breaketh his bones in other warres for provant and penury'.[4]

The patents awarded the adventurers gave them extensive powers and privileges over land and men, more than they would have obtained in any of the Queen's other dominions, including even Ireland.[5] The grantee usually had power over defence, government, justice, land distribution, and trade; in return the Queen required only that he reserve for the Crown one-fifth of all precious metals found and that he govern his settlements in general conformity with the laws of England, a provision which was vague enough to give the leader a great deal of latitude.

D. B. Quinn has found and published an interesting document drafted by Humphrey Gilbert just before his second voyage to America in 1583. In it Gilbert gave a detailed picture of what he intended his settlement to be like.[6] He saw himself and his heirs ultimately ruling over an agrarian society peopled by settlers of all sorts, from gentlemen bringing tenants with them to the poor sent over at the charge of the realm. The latter, along with volunteers, who paid their own way, would become Gilbert's tenants and receive 60 and 120 acres respectively for the term of three lives. In return, they were to pay rent, relief, and heriot. Gentlemen who became adventurers 'in the next two voyages' would receive 1,000 acres or more of land, depending on the number of men they brought over, and were to pay entry fines as well as yearly rents. A tenant with more than 4,000 acres was required to build a townhouse. Each of Gilbert's younger children, as well as Gilbert's wife when widowed, was to receive the profits from a 'seignorie', together with the benefit of special privileges and duties. Each settler had to furnish military equipment, pay 1*s* 2*d* per annum after ten years on every acre of land and woods 'possessed and manured', for the maintenance of the army and navy, and give two-fifths of all gold, silver, and precious stones, as well as one-tenth of all other metals acquired, to Gilbert's heir. Estates were to be set aside for ministers, bishops, and an archbishop. Land was to be divided into parishes and there were to be tithes. For the support of maimed soldiers,

---

4. R. Pease-Chope, 'New light on Sir Richard Grenville', *Reports and Transactions of the Devonshire Association*, xlix (1917), 241–5; Walter Ralegh, 'The discoverie of Guiana' in Harlow, *Discoverie of Guiana*, p. 71.

5. See for example Quinn, *Gilbert*, pp. 188–94 and *Roanoke Voyages,* pp. 82–89.

6. 'Grant of authority by Sir Humphrey Gilbert, regarding his rights in America, to Sir John Gilbert, Sir George Peckham, and William Aucher' in Quinn, *Gilbert*, pp. 266–77. Two of Gilbert's grantees, Sir George Peckham and Sir Thomas Gerrard, drew up a similar plan for government with themselves as 'Lords Paramount': ibid., pp. 257–60.

lecturers, scholars, and learning in general, the landlords were to reserve the profits from one-fortieth of their land and ministers were to set aside one-twentieth of their livings. Gilbert's heir was in charge of defence and the maintenance of order and the inhabitants would choose thirteen counsellors for martial and marine causes. But beyond the statement that there were to be 'chiefe magistrates and lawe makers' his plans contained no specific measures for government and the administration of justice.

This, then, was the dominion Gilbert hoped to see established in the New World. He or his heir would be a practically autonomous lord of a vast tract of land. Having no specific plan for the development of marketable commodities and showing the proper indifference of a gentleman to the mechanics of mercantile activity, he turned over the monopoly of trade to a group of Southampton merchants in exchange for a sizeable cut of the customs on goods and membership fines.[7] The principal profit on this kind of monopoly was presumably thought to arise from the supply of the settlement, not from the export of New World products. The production of a surplus for market arising from the farming of the land by the inhabitants was not referred to by Gilbert. There is no indication, therefore, that the dominion was conceived as a unit for producing special marketable commodities which would further the commercial aims of the mother country and the private gains of the planters.

On this last point, Gilbert's outlook seems to have been fairly typical of that of the adventurers generally. They expected to use martial rather than entrepreneurial skills to get the wealth and status they and their followers wanted. When in search of merchant investment, the expedition leaders would sometimes discuss trade, but generally on a very superficial level. They would tell the merchant that America and perhaps its native inhabitants could provide ready commodities (such as wood and sassafras) for which they could trade their cloth, thus replacing lost or allegedly declining markets in France, Spain, and other places. They promised the nation a reduction in 'idleness' as well as a stimulus to shipping.[8] But they did not suggest any plan for engaging settlers or American Indians in large-scale production of agricultural commodities for the market nor did

---

7. 'Agreement between Sir Humphrey Gilbert and the Merchant Adventurers of Southampton [November 2, 1582]', and 'Additional Articles . . .' in Quinn, *Gilbert*, pp. 313–35. The monopoly on trade was also the first thing Ralegh alienated in his Virginia enterprise, Quinn, *Roanoke Voyages*, pp. 569–78.

8. Two examples that illustrate these attitudes are Christopher Carleill's 'A Briefe and Summary Discourse . . .' in Quinn, *Gilbert*, pp. 351–64, and the sections on trade found in the pamphlet on America by Gilbert's associate, George Peckham, ibid., pp. 460–7.

they suggest that the trade between America and England would be anything more than the simple exchange of goods.[9] The peculiar commercial arrangement that was eventually to develop between 'mother country' and 'plantation' was not foreseen by the leading adventurers.

The most advanced commercial thinking about America in the sixteenth century was done by servants or minor associates of the major figures—men such as Thomas Hariot, John White, and Edward Hayes, whose professional interests or trading backgrounds and more modest social status made them less concerned about equalling the achievements of a Cortés. The Hakluyts also fell into this category, the elder Richard Hakluyt being a lawyer and his younger cousin a clergyman. Unhampered by the special concerns of the gentleman soldier, they were mainly interested in getting Englishmen planted in the Americas before the area was entirely occupied by the Spanish. Consequently they gave consideration to any possible way America could support a population and be made of value, including the growing of marketable commodities on New World soil. They argued that America could provide a market for English goods, particularly cloth, could employ the idle, and could supply England with commodities she currently had to obtain at high prices from foreigners. Although the Hakluyts certainly went further than almost any other writer of the sixteenth century in pointing to the economic possibilities of the Americas, there were limits to what they could foresee and argue convincingly. On the carrying trade and the role American raw materials could play in expanding England's foreign commerce, a major pre-

---

9. Gilbert's failure to mention Indians in his plan, despite the fact he was heading for a supposed Indian city, indicates he assumed land to be so plentiful that the English could have their lands separate from those of the native inhabitants. This was perhaps also Ralegh's plan in Guiana, for the tract written to the Queen about the project specified that in addition to tribute the Indians were to allot some 'large fruitful countryes' for the planting of Englishmen, implying the English would not displace the natives: 'Of the voyage for Guiana' in Harlow, *Discoverie of Guiana*, p. 146. Charles Leigh had wished to settle separate from the first Guianians encountered (who obviously had no riches), but they insisted the English had to be near them to give military aid against their enemies. Also Leigh needed the houses and gardens they provided: Public Record Office, London, SP 14/8/87. Having no real plans for developing marketable commodities and being over-sanguine about the prospects of getting gold or some form of tribute, the Elizabethans wrote little about demanding direct agricultural labour from the Indians. At Roanoke, when Francis Drake delivered some Indians and Negroes purloined from the Spanish West Indies, this labour supplement did nothing to deter the English from abandoning the settlement, Quinn, *Roanoke Voyages*, p. 32. The discussions about using natives for labour that E. S. Morgan notes in 'The labor problem at Jamestown, 1607–1618', *American Historical Review*, lxxvi (1971), 598–9, mainly occurred later, when it had become obvious that Jamestown had to find a mercantile base to be successful and the settlers therefore started planting tobacco.

occupation of seventeenth-century writers, they were almost silent.[1] Nor did the writings of the Hakluyts exactly represent the attitudes of the promoters. Ralegh and others encouraged them to write tracts for purposes of information and promotion, but often, as happened in Virginia, the adventurers in practice ignored the Hakluyts' suggestions regarding the prompt development of trade in commodities. The families John White recruited to settle and farm in Roanoke received little attention, either from Ralegh, who contributed only a small amount to their migration, and then transferred the responsibility for the settlement to London merchants, or from the merchants who in the busy Armada period never followed through the agreement.

When the adventurers were unable to find Indian societies sufficiently developed economically to be worth conquering, they were often at a loss to know what to do instead. The reaction of Ralph Lane, captain of Ralegh's Virginia colony, was probably typical. Lane had exhausted himself on excursions searching for Indians reputed to have a special kind of copper. Finally in disgust he abandoned the settlement, declaring that only the discovery of precious metals or possibly a route to the East 'can bring this country in request to be inhabited by our nation'. Without such benefits, those commodities that could be collected such as sassafras, roots, and gums (he did not even consider commodities that would have to be cultivated) 'of themselves will not bee worth the fetching'.[2] Almost twenty years later many Englishmen still shared Lane's opinion. Charles Leigh, in 1604, after searching in vain for El Dorado in Guiana, attempted to save his enterprise by growing flax. His company, however, would have none of it. They forced him into another campaign against the Caribs who were rumoured to have gold. That operation failed and his men grew unruly, claiming that there were not 'any commodities the Country yeelded which would afoord them present benefit'. When a Dutch ship arrived with black slaves, the settlers chose to sail home with the captain rather than stay and buy his merchandise. Bartholomew Gosnold, who had set out to find Norumbega around the same time and

---

1. Richard Hakluyt the elder, 'Notes framed by a gentleman heretofore to bee given to one that prepared for a discoverie, and went not' in *Writings* (1935), pp. 116–22; 'Pamphlet for the Virginia enterprise': ibid., pp. 327–38; and Richard Hakluyt the younger, 'Discourse of western planting', ibid., pp. 211–324. These are probably the most revealing statements they made on Elizabethan colonization. In the two Taylor volumes, there are only three brief references to possible markets for American goods outside England: American commodities might replace Spanish ones in Ireland, 'adjoining realms' might buy wood and soap ash, and Flanders might buy hides: ibid., pp. 267, 281, and 331.

2. 'Discourse of the first colony' in Quinn, *Roanoke Voyages*, pp. 272–3.

ended up trying to settle men in New England, had a similar experience with his followers.[3] During the first few years, Jamestown also had its fair share of settlers who were obsessed with discovering precious metals and refused to consider any other alternatives. All of this is reminiscent of those Spanish *conquistadores* in Mexico who, after exhausting the Indians' supply of gold, considered abandoning the country. It was useless, they thought, to try and merchandise New Spain's cotton goods, cacao, or maize in Castile, since ships would not come from the mother country to collect such products.[4]

The Elizabethan adventurers who appeared so insensitive to the commercial potential of the Americas and turned a cold shoulder to the recommendations of the Hakluyts, Hariot, and other advocates of economic development had, of course, little experience with conquest in lands markedly less developed than their own. In countries with which they were familiar, especially Ireland, Englishmen tended to blame their failure to obtain the kind of rewards they sought on the inherent rebelliousness of the populace rather than on economic conditions. Furthermore, and most significantly, the Elizabethans belonged to a society which was still uncertain about the role of trade in the economy.

In the past few decades the work of economic historians has discredited the idea that the Elizabethan period was a time of great expansion in trade. Instead the English nation was essentially 'straddling the fence' in commercial matters throughout the Tudor period.[5] Traditionally commerce had been viewed mainly as a process whereby a nation, through a small discrete group of merchants, vented its surplus, in England's case wool and cloth, and received in exchange commodities which it did not possess. Gentlemen on the whole did not specifically connect trade with the national or their own prosperity; while the Crown only became interested when trade seemed to be responsible for a gold outflow or for unemployment, and at such times protection of cloth manufacturing

---

3. Charles Leigh to Sir Oliph Leigh, 2 July 1604, Purchas, *Pilgrimes,* xvi. 316–23, and 'The relation of Master John Wilson of Wanstead in Essex . . .': ibid., pp. 338–43. Leigh had observed Dutch ships coming into Guiana to get flax. John Brereton, *A briefe and true relation of the discoverie of the north part of Virginia* (London, 1602), p. 12, and Gabriel Archer, 'Relation of Captaine Gosnols voyages to the north part of Virginia . . .' in Purchas, *Pilgrimes* xviii. 311–12.

4. E. Chevalier, *Land and Society in Colonial Mexico* (Berkeley, 1970), pp. 37–38, quoting from an account of an *encomendero*.

5. I. Wallerstein, *The Modern World-System: Capitalist Agriculture and the Origins of the European World-Economy in the Sixteenth Century* (New York, 1974), pp. 274–5. See also L. Stone, 'Elizabethan overseas trade', *Economic History Review,* 2nd series, ii (1949), 30–58.

tended to have priority over protection of English traders. Even so prescient an official as Thomas Cromwell felt that the way to aid a stagnant economy was less by encouraging English merchants to seek out new foreign markets and more by reducing the duties alien merchants had to pay, thereby improving their access to the commodities marketed by English wool producers and weavers. During the Elizabethan period the government did indeed enter into commercial affairs more widely: it licensed trade to new areas and discouraged foreign merchants. Yet behind these measures, which were significant steps forward though by no means coherent enough to be considered a programme, one perceives motives of balance and self-sufficiency rather than a commitment to enlarge the commercial sector. New direct markets for cloth were sought to replace the old entrepôts, but the importance of the carrying trade in elevating England's position in the world was not widely appreciated. In fact the solution to the balance of trade problem which was most often suggested involved a ban on trade in new 'luxury' products and not an increase of English overseas commerce.[6] Moreover when mercantile endeavours seemed to threaten political aims, the Elizabethan government still proved capable of arguing that trade led to the neglect of tillage and made men more difficult to govern.[7]

Public discussion on the increase of trade was extremely limited and when occasional tracts on the subject did appear they tended to play down the commercial aspects of the project being put forward. For instance, in 1580 Robert Hitchcock published a pamphlet containing a plan for the establishment of a trade in herring. It was a very ambitious economic venture involving a system of national financing and the development of new markets at home and abroad; but Hitchcock completely subordinated his claims about an increase in trade and exports which the project would produce to the argument that the enterprise would rid the realm of vagabonds and beggars. In a society still confused about the ethics of increased mercantile activity and sceptical about its ultimate profitability to the public, Hitchcock was understandably reluctant to stress the wealth that could be gained from opening new markets. One

6. See G. R. Elton, *Reform and Renewal: Thomas Cromwell and the Common Weal* (Cambridge, 1973), p. 115; L. Stone, op. cit.; F. J. Fisher, 'Commercial trends and policy in sixteenth century England', *Economic History Review*, 1st series, x (1939–40), 95–117; and V. Ponko, 'The Privy Council and the spirit of Elizabethan economic management, 1558–1603', *Transactions of the American Philosophical Society*, N.S., lviii, part 4 (1968).

7. 'Memorandum by Cecil on the export trade in cloth and wool, 1564(?)', *Tudor Economic Documents*, ed. R. H. Tawney and E. Power (3 vols, London, 1924), ii. 45–47.

also finds that merchants who had managed to secure monopolies over specific foreign markets often tried to minimize the profitability of the trade in order to keep down the number of those who might attempt to enter it and reduce their share.[8] It may seem peculiar that a society which complained constantly about being plagued by too many people possessing too few opportunities for self-support did not assume a more vigorous posture in regard to commerce. However, Englishmen preferred to direct their excess capital and manpower into military pursuits.

It was not until the turn of the century that an important shift in activities and attitudes occurred. First, the merchant community became much more speculative and aggressive. In the early years of the seventeenth century, amid a flurry of bulletins and newsletters concerning its first fleets, the East India Company launched its Asian trade.[9] It was not only the huge ships, the long distance, and the numerous stockholders which made this trade unique, but also the lack of connection with cloth exporting. Many contemporaries criticized the outflow of bullion that such commerce entailed; yet the London-based concern continued its operations. In the following years, particularly the first fifteen years of James I's reign, there was an unprecedented boom in joint-stock company shares, and project requests poured into the Privy Council.[1]

At the same time an alteration in attitudes towards the role of commerce in society became noticeable in significant non-mercantile groups, not least the group of gentlemen in contact with London and the court, the men who formed the most cosmopolitan element in the nation. This growing realization among the gentry of the importance of mercantile

8. Robert Hitchcock, 'A politic plat for the honour of the prince . . . [1580]', *Social England Illustrated* (New York, n.d.), vi. 55–94. The terms 'trade' (in the general sense) and 'commerce' seldom appear in sixteenth-century tracts when the exchange of wares between countries is being discussed: 'merchandize' is the word most frequently employed. L. Muchmore, 'The project literature: an Elizabethan example', *Business History Review*, xlv (1971), 474–87, has noted the lack of printed tracts on economic projects in this period. Those that did appear, according to Muchmore, stressed employment and self-sufficiency rather than more ambitious economic goals. For an example of merchants trying to minimize trading possibilities, see R. Brenner, 'The social basis of English commercial expansion 1560–1650', *Journal of Economic History*, xxxii (March–June 1972), 370.

9. See J. Parker, *Books to Build an Empire* (Amsterdam, 1966), pp. 255–7, for pamphlets reporting the progress of the Dutch and the English in reaching the East Indies, put out by the English company between 1598 and 1606.

1. Rabb, *Enterprise and Empire*, pp. 71 and 77. For a useful critique of Rabb's book, see John J. McCusker's review in *Historical Methods Newsletter*, ii, no. 3 (1969), 14–18. McCusker suggests that Rabb's handling of missing data results in the small merchant being underrepresented in the percentages for each class of investor. Muchmore, 'Project literature', p. 475, notes that in 1609 a Privy Councillor listed 105 projects being considered by the Council.

activities manifested itself in the 1604 session of the Commons when Edwin Sandys, later a leader of the Virginia Company, presented two bills: 'For all merchants to have free liberty of Trade into all Countries, as is used in all other Nations', and 'For the Enlargement of Trade for his Majesty's Subjects into Foreign Countries'. The report issued with the two bills made constant reference to the accomplishments of the Dutch and argued that the monopolies of the merchant companies unnaturally restricted both the size of the merchant community and the volume of goods traded. When the bill came to a vote, the Journal records that it 'passed with great consent and applause of the House (as being for the exceeding benefit of all the land) scarce forty voices dissenting from it'.[2] Historians have drawn attention to the interests, principally the outport merchants and the prospective investors in joint stock companies, that were behind the passage of the measure.[3] But preoccupation with the interests involved should not distract attention from the assumptions behind the legislation, namely, that a great expansion in foreign trade was possible and that this expansion must occur if England were to prosper in its competition with other nations. Likewise those who launched the attack on monopolies in the law courts during this period defended their position on the grounds that Crown favours might discourage enterprise and hamper the growth of the commercial sector. Thus they rejected the argument that such items as playing cards were 'things of vanity' rather than significant trading objects and that royal privileges in this sphere did no harm. The notion of what constituted an important commercial commodity was enlarged as the variety of consumer items increased.[4]

Although fiercely protective about its prerogatives, the Crown was not completely oblivious to the spirit of the times. King James, while by no means as sensitive to the commercial situation as were some gentry groups, delivered public speeches on the importance of increasing trade. The government in this period did not inaugurate any major mercantile

2. The titles of the bills, the accompanying report, and comments are contained in *The Journal of the House of Commons* (London, 1803), i. 218–22. The report has been reprinted in A. E. Bland, P. A. Brown, and R. H. Tawney (eds), *English Economic History: Select Documents* (London, 1914), pp. 443–53. W. Notestein, *The House of Commons 1604–1610* (New Haven, 1971), pp. 106–25, has a description of the full proceedings in the House of Commons.

3. See A. Friis, *Alderman Cockayne and the Cloth Trade* (London, 1927); T. K. Rabb, 'Sir Edwin Sandys and the Parliament of 1604', *American Historical Review*, lxix (1964), 646–70, and R. Ashton's comment on Rabb's article in 'The Parliamentary agitation for free trade in the opening years of the reign of James I', *Past and Present*, xxxviii (1967), 40–55. A rejoinder by Rabb was published in xl (1968), 165–73.

4. Concerning the attack on monopolies see D. Little, *Religion, Order, and Law: A Study in Pre-Revolutionary England* (New York, 1969), pp. 167–219 and 238–46.

programme nor erect any elaborate administrative apparatus to deal specifically with trade as was done later in the century, but the early Stuarts were more careful than their predecessors to make sure that in their search for stability they did not regress in industrial or commercial affairs.[5]

By 1615 the 'mercantilization' of English society had progressed to the point where special interests frequently debated purely commercial questions in print. Robert Hitchcock's pamphlet on the fishing trade had several Jacobean successors, Tobias Gentleman's *England's Way to Wealth* (London, 1614), E.S.'s *Britain's Busse* (London, 1615), and Robert Kayll's [?] *The Trade's Increase* (London, 1615);[6] and these authors displayed less hesitancy about exhibiting mercantile ambition than had their Elizabethan counterparts. Others in this period published pieces on behalf of the East India trade. For example, when Kayll in the process of promoting his project attacked the East India Company, it prompted Dudley Digges, one of the gentlemen investors, to reply in a tract entitled *A Defense of Trade* (London, 1615). Six years later, Thomas Mun undertook the same task in his *Discourse on Trade* (London, 1621). His pamphlet, heavily laced with the detailed figures on costs and profits which were to become a trademark of the political arithmeticians, was a plea not just for the survival of the Asian trade but for an exploitation of all possible sources of commercial products. The avowed purpose of these writings was educational. Critics of the new enterprises were 'led away in ignorance; not having as yet, discerned the mysteries of such waightie affaires'. People were confused because in 'strict tearmes of need' England had sufficient 'food and rayment' to take care of its population. Why then should the mercantile community expand and attempt to find new superfluous commodities? Would not this benefit 'onely the merchants'? The answer to these questions was stated simply in the opening sentence of Mun's tract. 'The trade of merchandize', he declared, 'is not onely that laudable practize whereby the entercourse of nations is so worthily performed, but also (as I may terme it) the very Touchstone of a kingdomes prosperitie. . . .' England could become powerful and rich if she would

5. B. Supple, *Commercial Crisis and Change in England 1600–1642* (Cambridge, 1964), p. 251. See the Chamberlain letter of 7 April 1614, on a speech made by James I, in A. Brown, *Genesis of the United States* (2 vols, Boston, 1890), ii. 686. James became particularly interested in the production of goods within England for export. On this see his prefatory letter in William Stallenge, *Instructions for the Increasing of Mulberie Trees, and the Breeding of Silkewormes* (London, 1609).

6. 'The Trade's Increase' was also the name of an enormous East India Company ship which was wrecked almost immediately after being built.

'multiply the Arts at home' (develop commodities for export) and 'increase and guide the Trades abroad' (engage in the carrying trade). In other words, trade was more than just supplying necessities to consumers and exporting surplus cloth. It was a service industry which, at the expense of other nations, could expand and employ more people, bring in enormous profits, and enlarge Crown revenue. The defenders of the East India Company especially stressed the profits to be made from the carrying trade because their commerce did not involve home-produced commodities. Only by emphasizing the opportunities for re-export could the company escape the charge that they were flooding the country with unnecessary items and draining England's store of gold.[7]

To support their arguments and accentuate the link between an increase in trade and an increase in national power, all the tracts cited the example of the Dutch states. The mercurial rise of this small country with few natural resources to a place of some prominence in Europe amazed and puzzled Englishmen. The only explanation seemed to be commercial acumen, their ability to penetrate new markets and capture the carrying trade. The Dutch, lamented one pamphleteer, had made such a name for themselves in mercantile affairs that foreigners in distant ports asked whether the king of England or the king of Holland was the greater monarch.[8] The query might indeed jolt Englishmen, considering that only a few decades earlier the Dutch, that nation of crafty merchants, had offered their Crown to one of Elizabeth's courtiers in exchange for aid against the Spanish. The success of the Netherlands proved that national power could rest almost entirely on a mercantile base: this made a deep impression on the English, gave incentive to English merchants and raised the stock of the commercial sector among the non-merchant elements in English society.

What lay behind this new preoccupation with trade? The answer continues to be a subject for debate. Certainly England's growing demographic problems were creating an environment essentially favourable to some form of economic change. We know that in the sixteenth century English population accelerated its recovery from the low level at the end

---

7. Mun, *Discourse*, pp. 1, 3, 12, 27, 49–50, 57; and Digges, *Defense*, pp. 41–42.

8. Kayll, *Trade's Increase*, p. 48. For other comments on the Dutch, see E.S., *Britain's Busse*, sigs E2–E4^v; Gentleman, *England's way, passim*; Digges, *Defense*, p. 18; and Mun, *Discourse*, pp. 37, 41. According to R. Davis, *The Rise of the English Shipping Industry in the Seventeenth and Eighteenth Century* (London, 1962), p. 9, the Dutch were not seriously cutting into any traditional English markets. It seems, therefore, that the English were concerned about the new markets the Dutch had created for themselves.

of the Black Death period and probably passed the four million mark. 'Enclosure' and new methods of agrarian organization which accompanied it probably made farming more efficient and market-oriented, but they also reduced the number of persons needed on the land. Unless the society could find profitable ways to utilize this superfluous manpower, per capita output would decline. Complaints about rogues and vagabonds and the restless migration of people into and out of towns, documented by recent research, testify to this unemployment and underemployment problem.[9] This situation did not necessarily produce economic innovation. Most pre-industrial societies simply allowed living standards to decline until mortality and fertility intervened to recreate homoeostatis. This indeed is exactly what one demographer believes happened in England and he argues that comparison of population and wage levels shows that labour demand remained relatively constant throughout the seventeenth century. His figures, however, suggest only that there was no rise in the wage rates of workers. They do not show shifts in the percentage of time worked, nor the benefits derived by capitalists from an enlarged trading sector.[1]

Proponents of the new economic history have recently suggested lower 'transactions costs' and the emergence of a set of efficient and impersonal property rights as the precipitants of the new interest in trade.[2] Although their suggestions are not completely new, the terminology they employ is useful and provides a more systematic language for classifying the economic phenomena of the early modern period. At present, however, the impact of the elements they focus upon remains hypothetical because of insufficient research. In any case, one cannot, it seems, completely rely on these elements to explain the situation in the early seventeenth century. Both lower transactions costs and new property rights arrange-

9. See L. Stone's introduction to the reprint of R. H. Tawney, *The Agrarian Problem in the Sixteenth Century* (New York, 1967), pp. vii–xviii; Wallerstein, *Modern World-System*, pp. 249–54; P. Clark, 'The migrant in Kentish towns 1580–1640', in P. Clark and P. Slack (eds), *Crisis and Order in English Towns 1500–1700* (London, 1972), pp. 117–63.

1. R. Lee, 'Population in pre-industrial England: an econometric analysis', *Quarterly Journal of Economics*, lxxxvii (1973), 581–607.

2. C. G. Reed, 'Transactions costs and differential growth in seventeenth century Western Europe', *Journal of Economic History*, xxxiii (March–June 1973), 177–90; and D. C. North and R. P. Thomas, *The Rise of the Western World: A New Economic History* (Cambridge, 1973). Also see D. R. Ringrose, 'European economic growth: comments on the North–Thomas theory', *Economic History Review*, 2nd series, xxvi (1973), 285–92. Reed (pp. 180–1) includes under transactions costs the expenses involved in obtaining information about market opportunities, making contract negotiations, securing contract enforcement, and transporting the goods. North and Thomas (p. 93) do not include transportation costs.

ments often appear to be the companions rather than the instigators of new trade patterns. Even if one assumes that much of the decrease in transactions costs occurred because of growing domestic demand, this demand largely resulted from urbanization, which in turn had to a great degree occurred because of stimulation from the foreign trade sector.[3] Likewise some highly unfavourable property rights arrangements persisted until the merchant community and its supporters gained enough influence to have them changed.[4]

Rather than trying to explain England's eventual commercial supremacy solely by factors which made trade more efficient, one should also look at factors which made other methods of advancing both individuals and society less efficient. In previous centuries, success in war had brought direct economic benefit to the victors in the form of land, rents, tribute, booty, and ransoms. The economic benefits of the new state-sponsored warfare were less direct (mainly government offices supported by taxation of the conquered) but still significant. By the end of the Elizabethan period, however, Englishmen might quite properly question the viability of this method of expanding their resources. Fifty years of intermittent conflict on European soil had shown that neither private adventurers nor Crown forces, nor any combination of the two, could any longer compete with the expensive nationally recruited armies, backed by professional mercenaries, which protected valuable continental land, goods, and taxes.[5] It was the growing impossibility of realizing meaningful returns in European wars which had originally attracted some adventurers to the Americas, where, for different reasons already explained, martial activities also proved unrewarding. Only privateering had been profitable, but in the early seventeenth century it too presented problems, not simply because the Crown opposed its continuance, but because large numbers of contestants had entered the field and the defence mechanisms of the victims had improved. Furthermore privateering gave ambitious gentlemen no permanent power over men and land. By the Jacobean

3. Comment on Reed article by R. Roehl, in *Journal of Economic History*, xxxii (March–June 1973), 230–1.

4. Despite their argument, North and Thomas seem to recognize this, for they state that 'the detailed political history of the first forty-one years of the seventeenth century, like that of the sixteenth century, provides, aside from the Statute of Monopolies, little indication that a set of impersonal and efficient property rights was emerging': *Western World*, p. 148.

5. R. Bean, 'War and the birth of the nation state', *Journal of Economic History*, xxxiii (March–June 1973), 203–21 discusses the changes in early modern warfare which led to a military stalemate. His explanation of the relationship between these military developments and economic growth is, however, incomplete.

period English enthusiasm for military confrontations had noticeably fallen off, as is evident in the generally pacific foreign policy of the first forty years of the seventeenth century and in the reduced interest members of the upper classes evinced in martial roles.[6] Merchants of course had never been eager supporters of armed conflict. Even if relations between the Crown and the political nation had been good enough to permit the formation of a standing army, it is not clear what that army would have been able to accomplish in Europe. In contrast, the high transactions costs and uncertain property arrangements which might be involved in overseas commerce now tended to seem less formidable, particularly since the protective apparatus of the Iberian powers over world-wide markets turned out to be not well developed, as the Dutch had proved. Privateering eased the transition. Elizabethan sea marauding had aided navigation, kept shipping healthy, and demonstrated through the privateers' sale of contraband what markets were available for sugar, tobacco, and other exotic commodities.[7] Consequently many Jacobeans came to see long-distance trade as the panacea for both unemployment and national impotence. When the martial spirit revived later in the century, warfare was completely state-sponsored and principally directed toward controlling overseas markets.

The new mercantile fever did not necessarily alter the personal motives of the various groups that pushed for overseas colonization, but it did affect their approach. Gentlemen who became deeply involved in expansion during the early Stuart period still saw western planting as a way to establish new bases of power over men and land. Churchmen, fearing a completely papist America, had their own reasons for supporting English settlements. Whatever economic function colonies might or might not serve, these groups supported plantations overseas; but to get commoners to emigrate and live in 'due subjection' to their superiors and the church, some credible advantage to them had to be offered.[8] After so many failures, potential emigrants and investors could no longer be expected to believe in the old vision of New World El Dorado. What the new emphasis on markets did for American colonization was to restore its plausibility and underline its desirability. Jacobean organizers of projects now told prospective participants that men would be planted and the

6. On the unprofitability of Elizabethan warfare and the aristocracy's failure to assume martial roles in the early seventeenth century, see L. Stone, *Crisis of the Aristocracy* (Oxford, 1965), pp. 199–270, 454–8, and 583.

7. See Andrews, *Elizabethan Privateering*, pp. 200–38.

8. R.J. [Robert Johnson], *The new life of Virginea* (London, 1612), sig. E3.

gospel spread in the New World by way of 'merchandizing and trade' rather than by 'conquest' and denied that there was any similarity in 'ends' or 'managing of meanes' between their ventures and those of the Elizabethans. After 'some planting and husbandry' the Americas could supply not only England's needs but those of other nations as well. 'The generall sort that shall goe to be planters', stated one Virginia Company pamphlet, 'bee they never so poore so they be honest, and painefull, the place will make them riche . . .'9 The old practice of addressing discussions of 'merchantable commodities' to merchants alone was dropped, for such information, at this point, had become of wider interest. Although in many cases the leaders had little idea what the successful commodity or commodities might be—wine, sugar, and naval stores received the most frequent mention—they could draw attention to current trade developments which supported their argument.

First they pointed to the great alteration in England's commercial standing in the recent past. 'What a novice our nation was', wrote one spokesman for the Virginia Company, Robert Johnson, in 1609, 'within these six score yeeres, in case of forrane trade, not knowing whence to fetch, nor which way to transport, but onely to some mart or staple towne, within two dayes sailing and that was counted so great a matter then, that therefore they were called Marchant adventurers. . . .' It was the 'great hulkes of Italie' and the ships of other nations which brought in rich goods and 'fed us as they listed'. Happily things had changed, and, in retrospect, Johnson could see the turning point as occurring in the Elizabethan period. Now England had control of its own merchandising but much remained to be done before 'this little Northerne corner of the world' could be 'the richest Store house and Staple for marchandize in all Europe'. The overseas settlements were portrayed as being a crucial part of the general effort that was already clearly under way to expand English commerce. Although each individual colonizing group claimed that its trade showed more promise than any other, it generally took care not to belittle the East India, Muscovy, and Levant enterprises, partly because some of the leading merchant members of the colonization companies also directed these trades. But also it was self-defeating to point out the risks and hazards of eastern commerce because this would undermine arguments about the feasibility of merchandising in so remote a western region

9. *A true declaration of the estate in Virginia* (London, 1609), pp. 6–9 and 58; Robert Gray, *A good speed to Virginia* (London, 1609), sig. D1; R.J. [Robert Johnson], *Nova Britannia* (London, 1609), sig. D3.

as America. Thus the promotional writers tended to use the eastern trades for support, as evidence proving that long distance should not be a discouragement and that great rewards could be obtained if men were patient.[1]

Supporters of colonization could also now point to an international situation in which trade in far-flung areas of the globe was becoming increasingly competitive. Echoing the arguments found in the strictly commercial pamphlets, they warned that England ran the danger of being 'eaten out of all profitt of trade' by 'more industrious neighbors' and could ill-afford to neglect any opportunity for commercial gain.[2] While the Iberians still merited mention as pioneers (though now more in connection with their New World 'navigation' than with the actions of the *conquistadores*) and while Spain still posed the greatest military threat to English expansion, the Netherlanders received the most attention in mercantile writings because they appeared to be new entrants in the American sweepstakes and exhibited vigorous commercial skills which Englishmen thought worthy of emulation. They possessed little wealth in land or natural resources and a century earlier they had been 'poor and servile', but now they exceeded the English in 'plentie of coine and shipping'. England could not stand by and watch another European nation, one of essentially 'lesser meanes', take over what remained of America, particularly when England was at peace and could not rely on wars to check population and employ men.[3]

The response of the mercantile sector to colonization was considerably more enthusiastic in the Jacobean period than it had been in the previous

1. Johnson, *Nova Britannia*, sigs C4 and D4. On eastern trades as proving the feasibility of the Virginia trade see ibid., sig. D3v; William Crashaw, *A sermon preached in London* (London, 1610), sig. E1–E1v; *A true declaration*, pp. 56–57; and Alexander Whitaker, *Good newes from Virginia* (London, 1613), p. 32. Almost all the Virginia tracts stressed the profits of the carrying trade as did Richard Whitbourne (*A discourse and discovery of New-foundland*, London, 1620, p. 44), who argued for a Newfoundland colony on the grounds that it would aid the English in the fish trade, cause other nations to drop out, and thus result in England supplying those nations.

2. In early 1611, the Virginia Council sent out circulars with this warning to a number of county leaders. Examples can be found in Brown, *Genesis*, i. 463; and Circular letter to Deputy Lord Lieutenant of Leicestershire, Huntington Library, San Marino, California, Hastings MSS. 4117.

3. Mention of the Dutch example in colonization tracts can be found in Johnson, *Nova Britannia*, sigs C4 and D1; *A true declaration*, pp. 58–60; Crashaw, *A sermon*, sig. G1; Whitaker, *Good newes*, p. 37; Whitbourne, *Discourse*, sigs B1–B2 and p. 49. In the first two decades of the seventeenth century, lack of war rather than enclosure is most often cited as the cause of the growing number of idle people: Gray, *Good speed*, sig. B2–B2v; *A true declaration*, p. 60; Johnson, *New Life*, sigs F3v–F4; and Brown, *Genesis*, ii. 756. Jacobeans possessed a good understanding of the social functions of armed conflict.

one, when gentry–merchant partnership was mainly confined to privateering ventures. Many of the merchants who made the first large investments had a strong interest in other long distance trades and seemed to be aiming at a monopoly of all these new markets. When, after a time, some of these leading merchants lost interest, or as in the case of the Virginia Company, were forced out of the projects, the greatly expanded trading community provided lesser merchants as replacements.[4]

The majority of the people who emigrated to America in the first two decades of the seventeenth century came almost certainly from about the same social class as those who had accompanied Gilbert, Ralegh, and Leigh. The principal difference was not their class or status but the role they expected to fulfil. In the Elizabethan period they had left England hoping for some kind of conquest which would bring them easy wealth. In the Jacobean period, as the purposes and images of the settlements gradually changed, so too did ideas concerning the types of opportunity available in America which could better a man's station in life. Settlers were willing to undertake agriculture provided this meant a connection with the English market economy. After twelve years of effort at Jamestown, the English could boast of their first New World personal success story. A Virginia Company official reported in 1619 that a settler 'by his owne labour' had cleared in one year £200 from the cultivation of tobacco. 'Rags to riches' tales like this, however exaggerated or untypical the case, helped to attract new people to a colony, and without them it is unlikely most settlements could have survived.[5]

The process I have attempted to describe might be best termed 'the commercializing of colonization'.[6] The type of expansion eventually engaged in by England and other western European countries in the Americas was new, because it involved the integration of the New World economies with those of the homelands. This enabled the former to fulfil a special mercantile function, a function which also gradually placed these settlements in a special and inferior political category *vis-à-vis* the mother country. For this type of expansion or colonization to occur, the homeland itself had to place a high value on commercial development. In England this emphasis does not become evident until the early seventeenth century when an appreciation of three factors, first, the ultimate profitability

---

4. Brenner, 'Social basis', pp. 374–84, discusses these 'new men' in the colonial trades.
   5. 'Letter of John Pory, September 30, 1619' in S. M. Kingsbury (ed.), *The Records of the Virginia Company of London* (Washington, D.C., 1933), iii. 221.
   6. For a general discussion of market economy development see J. Hicks, *A Theory of Economic History* (Oxford, 1969).

of a world-wide carrying trade, second, the variety and volume of goods home consumers might learn to need, and third, the link between commerce and national power, clearly emerged in important sectors of the country beyond the traditional merchant community.

The Elizabethans who led expeditions to America came mostly from the court and received little merchant support. To these court gentlemen the western hemisphere was primarily a place where one created dominions built on the gold and silver tributes of conquered Indians. Experience demonstrated the bankruptcy of that concept, and at the very end of the Elizabethan period one or two colonizers tried to redirect their enterprises into commercial activity. But their followers exhibited little enthusiasm. About the time James I succeeded to the throne and the Spanish war ended, however, a new awareness of the role of commerce in society surfaced, and overseas colonization benefited from it. Colonization became identified with the general effort to build up English trade, hence attracting not only widespread public support but also the financial backing of merchants. Settlers in fair numbers began to go to America as planters rather than as soldiers. While the new colonization projects experienced great problems, constantly having to make adjustments in order to cope with the economic situation that confronted them in the New World, and while the majority of them failed to establish permanent settlements, the most ambitious undertaking, Virginia, had by 1620 found a commodity which offered returns sufficient to ensure the continuing migration of labour and capital to America. Reflecting the economic changes going on within English society, a plantation settlement of the type described at the beginning of this essay had evolved, so that eventually the term 'colony' came to imply a highly market-oriented overseas settlement.

9

The Amerindian in English promotional literature
1575-1625

LOREN E. PENNINGTON

About 1517 the London printer John Rastell published his well-known cosmographical play, *A New Interlude and Mery of the Nature of the iiii Elements*. It contained the first English statement of what might be termed the white man's burden as it applied to the American Indian. In the description of the New World which he included in the work, Rastell suggested '. . . What a great merytoryous dede / It were to have the people instructed / To lyve more vertuously / . . . And also to knowe god theyr maker / . . . For they nother knowe god nor the deveil / Nor never harde tell of hevyn nor hell.'[1] Even though his play contains not a trace of any real understanding or sympathy for the Amerindian, Rastell's simple proposal for civilizing and Christianizing the native was to become a principal philosophic justification for English colonization in America.

Historians of the twentieth century have expressed varied opinions regarding the importance and sincerity of the missionary motive in Elizabethan and Jacobean overseas expansion. Most have regarded it as of lesser importance or as mere cliché.[2] A few, notably Louis B. Wright, have seen it as both sincerely held and important.[3] Francis P. Jennings,

1. J. Rastell, *New interlude*, sig. Cii[r].
2. As examples, see G. L. Beer, *Origins of the British Colonial System* (New York, 1908), pp. 27–30; E. A. J. Johnson, *American Economic Thought in the Seventeenth Century* (1932; reprinted, New York, 1961), pp. 35–60; J. A. Williamson, *The Ocean in English History* (Oxford, 1941), p. 123; and J. H. Parry, *Europe and a Wider World* (London, 1949), pp. 106–7. D. B. Quinn, in his 'Prologue' to part iv of *England and the Discovery of America, 1481–1620* (New York, 1974), calls conversion 'a weak motive with limited drive' (p. 312).
3. L. B. Wright, *Religion and Empire: The Alliance between Piety and Commerce in English Expansion, 1558–1625* (Chapel Hill, N.C., 1943), pp. 4–6, *passim* (hereafter cited as Wright, *Religion and Empire*); Wright, *Gold, Glory, and the Gospel: The Adventurous Lives and Times of the Renaissance Explorers* (New York, 1970), pp. x–xii. See also C. R. Lucas, *Religion, Colonizing and Trade: Driving Forces of the Old Empire* (London, 1910), pp. 1–35; W. F. Craven, 'Indian

the latest writer on the subject, agrees as to its importance, but finds it totally hypocritical.[4] This essay eschews all these positions in an attempt to show that the English colonial movement for America in the beginning was not particularly sympathetic towards the Amerindian, and that when the English proponents of American colonization did develop such a sympathy, it was only temporarily, and more a response to necessity than to philosophic commitment.[5] This is neither a denial of the view that men are moved by ideas nor an acceptance of the Beardian assumption that ideas are mere rationalizations of the real world; it is only to say that men's ideas are seldom created in a vacuum; immediate circumstances are almost always important in their creation.

The best and almost the only materials which render an extended impression of English thinking on the Amerindian in the period to 1625 are those writings published to promote English overseas exploration, trade, and colonization in the New World. America occupied a place in a number of chronicles, histories, geographies, and literary works during this period, but virtually all of these, from Archbishop George Abbot's *Briefe description of the whole world* to William Shakespeare's *The Tempest*, took their cues from what has been termed the promotional literature.[6] But when one attempts to use propaganda as an index of ideas some caveats must be kept in mind. There are always doubts about the sincerity of the writer and about the influence of his ideas, to which in a period so

policy in early Virginia', *William and Mary Quarterly*, 3rd series, i (1944), 65–68 (hereafter cited as Craven, 'Indian policy'); and R. P. Beaver, *Church, State, and the American Indians: Two and a Half Centuries of Partnership between the Protestant Churches and Government* (St Louis, 1966), pp. 7–13.

4. F. P. Jennings, *The Invasion of America: Indians, Colonialism, and the Cant of Conquest* (Chapel Hill, N.C., 1975, hereafter cited as Jennings, *Invasion*).

5. The modern writer who is closest to paralleling this view is R. H. Pierce in his *Savages and Civilisation: A Study of the Indian in the American Mind* (rev. edn, Baltimore, 1965), pp. 3–16 (hereafter cited as Pierce, *Savages*).

6. For extended discussions of English promotional literature for America through the Virginia Company period, see B. Penrose, *Travel and Discovery in the Renaissance* (Cambridge, Mass., 1952), pp. 312–25; L. B. Wright, *Middle Class Culture in Elizabethan England* (1935; reprinted, Ithaca, N.Y., 1968), pp. 508–49; H. M. Jones, 'The image of the New World', *Elizabethan Studies and Other Essays in Honor of George F. Reynolds* (Boulder, Col., 1945), pp. 62–92 (hereafter cited as Jones, 'Image'); Jones, 'The colonial impulse: an analysis of the "promotional literature of colonization" ', *American Philosophical Society Proceedings*, xc (1946), 131–61; Jones, *O Strange New World. American Culture: The Formative Years* (New York, 1964), *passim* (hereafter cited as Jones, *New World*); L. E. Pennington, 'The origins of English promotional literature for America, 1553–1625' (unpublished Ph.D. dissertation, University of Michigan, 1962); and especially J. Parker, *Books to Build an Empire: A Bibliographical History of English Overseas Interests to 1620* (Amsterdam, 1965, hereafter cited as Parker, *Books*).

early must be added doubts about the effect of the printed page upon a relatively unlettered public. In this class of propaganda there is the added problem of considerable inconsistency. Although the early promotional literature of English colonization does represent a conscious effort to manipulate public opinion, it is also revealing of ideas and interests. As Gordon Wood has put it in another context, propaganda may not be factually true, but is always psychologically true in that it represents the thought of the time,[7] if not the writer's, at least what he believes to be the reader's. The influence of the colonial propagandists' ideas we may judge by the extent to which their views entered into other literature of the day. As to the value of the printed page in the sixteenth and seventeenth centuries, this was an age in which America came to be defined in print,[8] and the evidence suggests that by this time there existed in England a truly national reading audience.[9] Finally, the inconsistencies of the promotional line we may partly regard as the inefficiencies of writers who were not professional propagandists, and partly ignore in favour of discerning the general trend.

About the middle of the sixteenth century the English began to take an ever-increasing interest in the prospects of overseas expansion in Asia, Africa, and America; and there began to emerge a literature aimed at promoting this expansion. In much of it the native races were a major theme. This was only natural in a day which thought of geography as the history of travel,[1] and in human rather than physical terms.[2] The interest in the American Indian was especially intense because in America it was proposed to put down in the natives' midst substantial groups of Englishmen. This raised the whole question of the right of displacement, a right which, considering the age, could be framed only in philosophic and religious terms, and specifically in this, the last age of the world before the Second Coming, in terms of native conversion. That the idea of conversion was closely tied to displacement is best proved by the English literature of this same period for Asia and Africa. There the English intended trade rather than extended settlement and displacement, and in

7. G. Wood, 'Rhetoric and reality in the American revolution', *William and Mary Quarterly*, 3rd series, xxxiii (1966), 31.

8. R. Slotkin, *Regeneration through Violence: The Mythology of the American Frontier* (Middletown, Conn., 1973), p. 15.

9. Parker, *Books*, pp. 8–9; E. H. Miller, *The Professional Writer in Elizabethan England* (Cambridge, Mass., 1959), pp. 32–41, 59–62 (hereafter cited as Miller, *Writer*).

1. E. G. R. Taylor, *Tudor Geography, 1485–1583* (1930; reprinted, New York, 1968), pp. 40–41.

2. Ibid., pp. 23–24; Jones, 'Image', pp. 66–67.

that literature the conversion argument was very seldom used.[3] This is not to argue an insincerity in the English conversion motif, but only to indicate that in an age when Machiavellianism was a well-accepted principle of statecraft,[4] promotional writers dealt with the question of native races in terms of the logic of the entire colonial effort within a given area, and not as a question of over-all principle.[5]

The English propagandists soon found a further problem in regard to the Amerindian. Because settlement was the intent, it was necessary to make the native a part of the attraction of the New World—to make sure that he was a propaganda asset rather than a liability.[6] But in the effort to sell books, the writers found it difficult to resist the temptation of the shocking and sensational, of native savagery, treachery, and cannibalism, even though such accounts might have an unfortunate effect on potential investors or, more especially, settlers. What the propaganda writers faced, then, was a dilemma. Indian barbarism attracted the reading public, sold books, and might be used to justify displacement, but implied the great difficulty of conversion. On the other hand, portraying the American native as civilized or benign increased hopes for conversion, but made it difficult to justify the seizure of his lands and the uprooting of his society.

3. Even the most cursory reading of the promotional works of the East India Company reveals the lack of the conversion argument. The main concern of English clergy in the East Indies was not the natives, but Englishmen making the voyage, according to Wright, *Religion and Empire*, p. 57. On the lack of English missionary interest in Africa, see W. D. Jordan, *White over Black: American Attitudes toward the Negro* (Chapel Hill, N.C., 1968), pp. 20–22, and in the abridgement, *White over Black, The White Man's Burden: Historical Origins of Racism in the United States* (New York, 1974), p. 14; and H. Baudet, *Paradise on Earth: Some Thoughts on the European Images of Non-European Man* (New Haven, Conn., 1965), pp. 19–25, 29–31 (hereafter cited as Baudet, *Paradise*), which suggests possible reasons for the differing European views of the Negro and the Amerindian.

4. Jones, *New World*, pp. 114–52; and G. L. Mosse, *The Holy Pretence: A Study in Christianity and Reason of State from William Perkins to John Winthrop* (1957; reprinted, New York, 1968), pp. 1–33.

5. For an interesting analysis of how the Amerindian fitted into various Euramerican views of America, and was seldom considered as an issue in himself, see B. W. Sheehan, 'Paradise and the noble savage in Jeffersonian thought', *William and Mary Quarterly*, 3rd series, xxiii (1969), 328–9, 346, 357–8. For other views on the development of European thinking in regard to the American native, see J. H. Elliott, 'The discovery of America and the discovery of man', *Proceedings of the British Academy*, lvii (1972), 110; W. E. Washburn (ed.), *The Indian and the White Man* (New York, 1964), introduction, p. xii; Baudet, *Paradise*, pp. 9–49; and H. N. Fairchild, *The Noble Savage: A Study in Romantic Naturalism* (1928; reprinted, New York, 1961), *passim*, but especially pp. 1–22.

6. G. B. Nash contends that it was trade possibilities which demanded that the Amerindian be portrayed in a favourable manner; only the good Indian would be a trading Indian. See his 'The image of the Indian in the southern colonial mind', *William and Mary Quarterly*, 3rd series, xxix (1972), 205–6 (hereafter cited as Nash, 'Image'). There is no necessary connection between trade and a favourable view of the natives, as the English literature on Africa testifies.

A possible solution to this dilemma would have been to regard the Amerindian as a total savage without hope of redemption and therefore a non-person with no more title to the land than the beasts of the forest.[7] But this view the English settlers adopted only after years of contact, and even then rather haphazardly.

The origins of English ideas on colonization provided a matter for considerable debate. Undoubtedly some of the ideas go back to medieval and possibly to ancient times.[8] The model of English involvement in Ireland was certainly the most direct and practical both in the development of leadership and in the evolution of attitudes.[9] But in its early years, English promotional literature for America consisted primarily of translations from the writings of foreign authors, and particularly from those of Spanish authors. Thus it was the Spanish experience, as embodied in the works produced by Richard Eden, John Frampton, Thomas Nicholas, and by or at the instigation of Richard Hakluyt, that became a principal factor in determining English thinking on the New World in general and the Amerindian in particular. Very few of these translations did much to place the Indian in a favourable light or to excite sympathy for him. For the most part, this was the result of the nature and purpose of the original Spanish writings. Unlike the English propagandists who tried to make practical use of their works, the Spanish authors were little interested in encouraging potential investors and settlers. Theirs was another purpose: the glorification of the Spanish conquest. In order to make that glory seem the greater, their theme was Spanish victory achieved in the face of overwhelming hardship and continual disaster. And the most important factor in this hardship and disaster, the rock on which the Spanish attempts at

---

7. Jennings, *Invasion*, pp. 12–31.

8. C. Verlinden, *The Beginnings of Modern Colonization*, trans. Y. Freccero (Ithaca, N.Y., 1970), *passim*, but especially pp. x–xvi and 3–32; Jones, 'Origins of the colonial idea' in his *Ideas in America* (Cambridge, Mass., 1944), pp. 45–48 (hereafter cited as Jones, 'Origins'); Jones, *New World*, pp. 1–34.

9. E. P. Cheyney, 'Some English conditions surrounding the settlement of Virginia', *American Historical Review*, xxii (1907), 515–22; Jones, 'Origins', pp. 49–62 and nn. 242–8; Jones, *New World*, pp. 167–79. On the connection of Ireland and America in regard to persons involved, see A. L. Rowse, *The Expansion of Elizabethan England* (New York, 1955), pp. 126–57 (hereafter cited as Rowse, *Expansion*). For D. B. Quinn's assessment of the connection between Irish and American colonization, see his *The Elizabethans and the Irish* (Ithaca, N.Y., 1966); Quinn, 'Sir Thomas Smith (1513–1577) and the beginnings of English colonial theory', *American Philosophical Society Proceedings*, lxxxix (1945), 543–60; and Quinn (ed.), *The Voyages and Colonizing Enterprises of Sir Humphrey Gilbert* (London, 1940), pp. 16–17, 168–238. The best analysis of the effect of Irish experience on American settlement is N. P. Canny, 'The ideology of English colonization: from Ireland to America', *William and Mary Quarterly*, 3rd series, xxx (1973), 575–98.

conquest nearly foundered, was the treachery and barbarism of the American Indian. It is true that one can, from time to time, find in the Spanish works examples of native virtue, and even now and then a reference to the Amerindian as living in the Golden Age. It is also true that the Spanish writers gave a good deal of attention to conversion, and on occasion even condemned their countrymen for mistreatment of the natives. But for the most part, the Spanish authors whose works were translated into English before 1590—Peter Martyr, Gonzalo Fernández de Oviedo y Valdés, and Francisco López de Gómara, in particular—presented a nearly unrelieved picture of native savagery.[1] In setting forth an image of the Spaniard as the personification of Renaissance virtue, they succeeded in creating an anti-image of America and of its inhabitants.[2]

The reaction of the English colonial propagandists to these Spanish accounts of warfare and massacre is instructive. Many historians have held that the English were repelled by the Spanish attitude towards the natives and were inspired to undertake their conversion as a reaction to Spanish oppression; further it is often argued that this reaction was an important contributing factor to the anti-Spanish feeling prevalent in England during the Elizabethan era. In short, anti-Spain and pro-Indian represented opposite sides of the same coin when the English made extensive use of the 'Black Legend'. But the promotional literature of the period before 1590 indicates this was not the case. Far from being repelled by Spanish repression of the natives, English propagandists at first looked upon it as the model to be followed by their own countrymen. According to Richard Hakluyt, the greatest of the early English colonial editors, for all the Amerindians' 'faire and cunning speeches', they were not to be trusted. They were the greatest liars and dissemblers in the

1. For the English translations from the Spanish which dealt extensively with the Indians, see R. Eden, *A treatyse of the newe India* (London, 1553); Eden, *The Decades of the Newe Worlde or West India* (London, 1555); Eden and R. Willes, *The History of travayle in the West and East Indies* (London, 1577); J. Frampton, *A briefe description of the portes, creekes, bayes, and havens, of the Weast India* (London, 1578); T. Nicholas, *The pleasant historie of the conquest of Weast India* (London, 1578; another edition, London, 1596); and Nicholas, *The discoverie and conquest of the provinces of Peru* (London, 1581). A number of early translations from the French did little to improve the Amerindian's reputation: See J. Ribaut, *The whole and true discoverye of Terra Florida* (London, 1563); T. Hackett, *A true and perfect description of the last voyage or navigation, attempted by Capitaine John Rybaut* (London, 1566); Hackett, *The new found worlde, or Antarctike* (London, 1568); J. Florio, *A shorte and briefe narration of the two navigations and discoveries to the northweast partes called Newe Fraunce* (London, 1580); and especially R. Hakluyt, *A notable historie containing foure voyages made by certayne French captaynes unto Florida* (London, 1587).

2. Jones, *New World*, pp. 35–70, 114–61.

world, 'for which they often had their deserved paiments' from the Spaniards. To handle them gently would be the best policy, but if gentle policy would not serve, 'then we shall not want hammorours and rough masons enow, I mean our old soldiers trained up in the Netherlands, to square and prepare them for our Preachers hands'.[3] Hakluyt wrote this passage in 1609 after other English propagandists had shifted their ground, but he spoke as the representative of an earlier day and an earlier policy. Though a clergyman and a strong believer in the necessity of Amerindian conversion, Hakluyt never favoured a soft or sympathetic attitude towards the native.[4]

The view of the Amerindian as portrayed in the translations was not much improved by the native English colonial propaganda before 1590. The northwest passage literature of the Frobisher period gave little attention to the American natives, in this case chiefly the Eskimos. This was natural enough, considering that the object of the expeditions was Asia and that the natives encountered were few. Such opinions as were expressed were mixed, but tended to be unfavourable. Dionyse Settle, who wrote an account of the second Frobisher voyage, described the natives as cruel and crafty people, and probably cannibals.[5] George Best, whose work covered all three voyages, and who was somewhat moved by religious motives, still described them as 'those ravenous, bloudye and man eating people'.[6] Only that 'patriarch of sixteenth century hacks',[7] Thomas Churchyard, had much admiration for the American natives: 'they have no skill of submission, nor will not learn to knowe the courtezie of a conqueror which resolution in them (though barbarous it seeme)

3. *Virginia richly valued, by the description of the maine land of Florida, her next neighbour* (London, 1609; reprinted, *Tracts and Other Papers*, ed. P. Force [New York, 1947], i, no. 1), p. 6. The passage quoted is from Hakluyt's own introduction.

4. Hakluyt's pro-Amerindian (and definitely anti-Spanish) reputation stems chiefly from the extreme tone of his unpublished (until the nineteenth century) 'Particular discourse'. For examples of the heavy emphasis given to the 'discourse' by modern historians, see Wright, *Religion and Empire*, pp. 43–49; Rowse, *Expansion*, pp. 209–10; Rowse, *The Elizabethans and America* (New York, 1959), pp. 46–47; Nash, 'Image', pp. 202–3 and n. 22; P. W. Powell, *Tree of Hate: Propaganda and Prejudice affecting United States relations with the Hispanic World* (New York, 1971), pp. 75 and 177, n. 36; W. S. Maltby, *The Black Legend in England: The Development of Anti-Spanish Sentiment, 1558–1660* (Durham, N.C., 1971; hereafter cited as Maltby, *Black Legend*); and Jennings, *Invasion*, p. 76. G. B. Parks, *Richard Hakluyt and the English Voyages* (rev. edn, New York, 1961), sees the 'discourse' as primarily an economic document (pp. 87–98).

5. *A true reporte of the laste voyage into the west and northwest regions* (London, 1577), sigs Bv^v–Bvi^r, Bviii^v–Di^r.

6. *A true discourse of the late voyages of discoverie, for the finding of a passage to Chathaya, by the northweast* (London, 1578), p. 19.

7. Miller, *Writer*, pp. 116–25.

. . . utters a miraculous manliness to abound in that bruitish nation'.[8]

Of the three major promotional works connected with the English colonization attempts in North America in the 1580s, the Amerindian played a major role in two.[9] One was Thomas Harriot's famous first-hand account, *A briefe and true report of the new found land of Virginia.*[1] On the whole it was rather neutral in its view of the Indians, and was not so much intended to indicate any particular virtue in them as to reassure those interested 'that they in respect of troubling our inhabiting and planting, are not to be feared'.[2]

Few of the early English colonial writers could pass muster as philosophers; foremost among those who could was Sir George Peckham. Peckham was involved with the colonization plans of Sir Humphrey Gilbert; and in 1583, in connection with the attempt to plant a catholic colony in America, published one of the best statements of English colonial thought in the sixteenth century.[3] In it he combined the practical mercantile arguments of the day with a religious justification of colonization based chiefly on conversion. For Peckham English–Amerindian relations could be founded on four well-known premises of the law of nations: that the seas were free to all, that no violence should be offered ambassadors, that strangers should not be driven away from a land to which they had come in friendship, and that those taken in war should be slaves. If at all possible, Peckham intended there should be peace between the races, but if the natives should prove recalcitrant, the right to spread the Christian faith by force of arms would be sufficient warrant for English colonization.[4] He made it clear that he strongly approved the methods of the Spanish conquest, and he recommended his readers to examine the works of the Spanish authors as the best means of understanding the nature of the Amerindian and the exploits of their conquerors, whose glorious deeds 'hath since awakened out of dreames thousands of soules to know theyr creator, being thereof before that time altogether ignoraunt'.[5]

8. *A prayse and reporte of Maister Martyn Forboishers voyage to Meta Incognita* (London, 1578), sig. Bii.

9. C. Carleill's *A discourse upon the intended voyage to the hethermoste partes of America* (n.p., c. 1583) was primarily mercantile in outlook, though it assumed the natives would be friendly. For the other two pamphlets, see below.

1. T. Harriot, *A briefe and true report of the new found land of Virginia* (London, 1588).

2. Ibid., sig. E1. See also sigs E1^r–E2^v, E4^r–F3^v. Harriot's view of the Amerindian was essentially negative, according to Pierce, *Savages*, pp. 5–6.

3. *A true reporte, of the late discoveries, and possession, taken in the right of the Crowne of England, of the New-found Landes* (London, 1583).

4. Ibid., sigs Ci^v–Diii^v.

5. Ibid., sig. Biii^v. See also sigs Gi^v–Hi^r.

Perhaps the best proof that most English propagandists for America before 1590 favoured a repressive native policy based on the supposed model of Spain is a negative one. Had the English propagandists been interested in polemics against Spanish oppression of the Amerindians, they had available to them the best possible source: the *Brevissima relacion de la destruycion de las Indias* of Bartolomé de las Casas.[6] Las Casas's work created a sensation on the Continent and was reprinted there innumerable times.[7] But except for a few scattered references it was virtually ignored by the English colonial writers for nearly seventy years,[8] and this in an era when these propagandists were making wide use of Spanish accounts of the New World. One edition of Las Casas's work did appear in England in 1583,[9] and has frequently been cited for its supposed effect on the English colonial propagandists.[1] But it remains to be shown that it had any direct connection with the English colonial movement. Its only preface, taken from the French edition from which the work was translated, indicates that its purpose was to encourage support for the Low Countries in their revolt against Spain.[2] The little regard of the colonial writers for Las Casas may be judged from the two editions of Richard Hakluyt's *Principal Navigations*. The first edition contained no mention of Las Casas while the second mentioned him directly only twice.[3] Hakluyt, together with the other promotional writers, may well have recognized that Las Casas's insistence on the possibility of conversion without conquest implied a view of native rights that no nation about to embark on colonial ventures could possibly accept.

6. (Seville, 1552).

7. J. Sabin *et al.* (eds), *A Dictionary of Books relating to America* (Amsterdam, 1965), iii. 391–401. For the view that these editions of Las Casas generally had little or nothing to do with the imperial motive of the countries in which they were published, and were frequently tempered with introductory remarks in praise of Spain, see B. Keen, 'The black legend revisited: assumptions and realities', *Hispanic-American Historical Review*, xlix (1969), 14–19; J. Friede and B. Keen (eds), *Bartolomé de las Casas in History: Toward an Understanding of the Man and his Work* (De Kalb, Ill., 1971), especially pp. 8–18, and the contribution by V. Afansiev, 'The literary heritage of Bartolomé de las Casas', pp. 539–78.

8. The first extensive and direct use of Las Casas by an English colonial writer was by Samuel Purchas in his *Hakluytus Posthumus or Purchas his Pilgrimes* (20 vols, Glasgow, 1906), xviii. 80–180.

9. M.M.S. (trans.), *The Spanish colonie* (London, 1583).

1. For examples, see W. F. Craven, *The Southern Colonies in the Seventeenth Century* (Baton Rouge, La., 1949), p. 77; R. R. Cawley, *The Voyagers and Elizabethan Drama* (Boston, 1938), pp. 381–7; Wright, *Religion and Empire*, p. 85; L. Hanke, *Bartolomé de las Casas: Bookman, Scholar and Propagandist* (Philadelphia, 1952), pp. 52–57, and 104, n. 41; and Maltby, *Black Legend*, pp. 12–20, 62–71. None of these works cites more than two or three instances of the use of Las Casas in the English colonial literature.

2. M.M.S., *Spanish colonie*, sigs q2r–qqr.

3. R. Hakluyt, *The Principal Navigations* (12 vols, Glasgow, 1903–5), vii. 52–53; ix. 496

Before 1590, then, English publications on America followed the model of the Spanish literature of conquest. This was manifest in the choice of translations, while original English works took the same line as the Spanish, at least in attitudes to Amerindians. But from about 1590 English promotional literature began to undergo fundamental alterations, one of which was that the use of translations as propaganda virtually ceased. The promotional writers apparently came to realize that these translations, emphasizing as they did the hardships of America rather than its opportunities, were quite ill-suited to the ends the propagandists had in mind. Such few translations as were used after this time tended to be much more optimistic about the prospects of America, and nowhere was this optimism more fully expressed than in regard to the American native. The best example is Edward Grimston's work of 1604, *The naturall and morall historie of the East and West Indies*,[4] drawn from the works of the Spanish Jesuit, José de Acosta. Acosta's object, as reflected in Grimston's translation, was to controvert the widely held belief that the Amerindians were a worthless and savage race:

And the subject of the Indians [he wrote] is not onely pleasant and agreeable, but also profitable, especially to such as have the charge to rule and govern them; for the knowledge of their acts invites us to give credit, and doth partely teach how they ought to be intreated: yea it takes away much of the common and foolish contempt they of Europe holde them, supposing that those Nations have no feeling of reason. For in truth we cannot cleare this error better, than by a true report of acts and deedes of this people.[5]

In a close examination of the Amerindian background, life, and religious institutions, Acosta portrayed a highly cultured and near-civilized people whose only fault was a lack of Christianity, a lack which had caused them to fall into savagery in a few instances, and from which the coming of the Spaniards had rescued them—Acosta was no Las Casas.[6] Grimston's was the first translation from the Spanish to English promotional literature that made the Indian an argument for colonization, rather than a hindrance or a menace.

The most favourable interpretation of the Amerindians to emerge from the translations came originally not from a Spanish but from a French writer, Marc Lescarbot, the lawyer who had served with Samuel de

---

4. E. Grimston, *The naturall and morall historie of the East and West Indies* (London, 1604).
5. Ibid., p. 496. See also sig. A3 and pp. 431–3, 495–7.
6. Ibid., pp. 343–7, 388–428, 433–6, 452–91, 562, 579–80.

Champlain. Part of Lescarbot's work was translated into English in 1609 by Pierre Erondelle, as propaganda for the Virginia Company of London.[7] In Lescarbot, the Amerindian came close to the idealistic view of the noble savage and his virtues seemed to place him in the Golden Age. The natives lived everywhere in common, and had that mutual charity 'which hath been taken away from us since mine and thine came into the world'. They took no care for the commodities of this life, and their lack of ambition was a positive virtue. 'Happy people! Yea a thousand times more happy than they which in these partes make themselves to be worshipped, if they had the knowledge of God and their salvation.'[8] Lescarbot's method throughout was to compare the Amerindian to the ancient European, and quite to the detriment of the latter.[9] Yet even this most favourable description had its dark side. Certain tribes, notably those of Brazil, were beyond hope of civilization, while others were thievish and traitorous, and could be dealt with only by terror.[1] In spite of these reservations, the translation from Lescarbot, like that from Acosta, represented a considerable shift in the propaganda line as it concerned the American native.

This new view of the Amerindian became more evident after 1590 as colonial propaganda shifted increasingly to native English materials. A case in point is the promotional literature connected with English attempts to establish themselves in Guiana. Here for the first time the colonial interests of England and Spain were obviously in direct conflict, and here for the first time the colonial propaganda was consistently anti-Spanish. Conversely, nowhere in the early English promotional literature was there such an optimistic portrayal of the natives. Sir Walter Ralegh in his *The discoverie of the large, rich and bewtiful empire of Guiana* described them in this fashion:[2]

Notwithstanding the moistness of the aire in which they live, the hardnesse of their diet, and the great labors they suffer to hunt, fish, and foule for a living, in all my life either in the Indies, or in Europe, did I never behold a more goodlie or better favored people, or a more manlie.[3]

---

7. P. Erondelle (trans.), *Nova Francia: or the description of that part of New France, which is one continent with Virginia* (London, 1609; reprinted, ed. H. P. Biggar, London, 1928).

8. Ibid., pp. 101, 227, 242–3.

9. Ibid., pp. 151–4, 201–4, 206–20, 223–37, 262–3.

1. Ibid., pp. 3, 52–53, 103, 109–10, 164–8.

2. London, 1596; reprinted in *The discoverie of the large and bewtiful empire of Guiana*, ed. V. T. Harlow (London, 1928), pp. 1–85 (hereafter cited as Harlow, *Discoverie*).

3. Ibid., p. 39. See also pp. 38, 46–47.

Everywhere the natives had greeted Ralegh with perfect friendliness and full co-operation, without guile or treachery. This, he claimed, was the result of their oppression by the Spanish and their consequent belief that the English came as liberators. This role of liberator Ralegh played to the hilt.[4] In fact he may be termed the first and before Samuel Purchas the only English promotional writer to use Spanish maltreatment of the Amerindians as an important and direct argument for English activities in America.[5]

Ralegh's *Discoverie of Guiana* was anti-Spanish and pro-native, but the emphasis on these two themes was nothing compared to what it might have been. This is evident from another tract which Ralegh either wrote or had prepared for him.[6] It accused the Spanish of committing an illegal invasion of America, an invasion which had resulted in 'barbarous and exquisite massacres to the distruction of . . . 20 millions of reasonable creatures . . . whereby more fruitful land was layd waste and depopulated then is in all Europe and some part of Asia'. After setting forth in grue-some detail the means by which the Spanish had massacred the natives, it concluded that any reasonable man would recognize that the time had now come 'to scourge and plague that cursed nation, and to take the yoke of servitude from that distressed people, as free by nature as any Chris-tian'.[7] The writer went on to insist that no man had the right to take away the lands of the heathen. Instead of conquest, he proposed an alliance between the Crown of England and the supposed great kingdom of Manoa, whereby the two partners could effect the conquest of Peru. To make sure the Manoans would keep the alliance, he suggested the native chiefs be given English wives. The only obligation on the part of the natives was that they accept Christianity, for this was vital to bringing God to the support of the venture. As for the gold of Guiana, it was to be had through a tribute agreement and through trade, especially through selling the Manoans firearms.[8] Here was the type of anti-Spanish diatribe we might expect to be common in English propaganda for American colonization, but it is in fact notably rare. Ralegh never published this tract; it was prepared for private circulation and for the eyes of Elizabeth.

4. See, for example, Harlow, *Discoverie*, pp. 15, 49.
5. The anti-Spanish theme was echoed by Ralegh's lieutenant, Lawrence Kemys, in *A relation of the second voyage to Guiana* (London, 1596), sig. F2. He, too, thought the Amerin-dians would welcome the English. But he was not entirely sanguine in his expectation (sig. D3ᵛ).
6. The manuscript is printed in Harlow, *Discoverie*, pp. 138–49.
7. Ibid., p. 140.
8. Ibid., pp. 141–9.

And in spite of all the pro-native and anti-Spanish posturing in both the *Discoverie of Guiana* and in this unpublished tract, it is clear that Ralegh's advocacy of these policies was based more on expediency than principle, for in the *Discoverie of Guiana*, he still appealed directly to the spirit of the *conquistadores*:

The common soldier shall here fight for gold, and pay himselfe in steede of pence, with plates of halfe a foote brode. . . . Those commanders and Chief- taines, that shoote at honour, and abundance, shal find there more rich and bewtiful cities, more temples adorned with golden Images, more sepulchers filled with treasure, then either Cortez found in Mexico or Pazzarro in Peru; and the shining glorie of this conquest will eclipse all those so farre extended beames of the Spanish nation.[9]

The improving reputation of the American Indian which began with the promotional literature for Guiana was continued after the turn of the century in the manifold propaganda activities of the Virginia Company of London. As in the case of Guiana, it seems clear that the favourable view taken in the Virginia promotional literature towards the native and his possible conversion stemmed not entirely from sympathy or understand- ing but also from propaganda necessity. The Virginia promoters recog- nized that if they were to induce investment in the enterprise and migration to the colony, they could tolerate nothing in their promotional literature casting doubts on their chances of success. The optimistic tone and rosy hue that generally pervade their propaganda are strikingly present in its references to the Amerindian. After all, what person in his right mind could be induced to settle among savages who posed a con- tinual threat to his life and property. Settlers had to be convinced that they were going to a community, not to a military camp.

The encouragement of settlers was not the only factor demanding a favourable portrayal of the native; such a view had to be maintained if the Company's main philosophical argument for colonization, conversion, was not to fall to the ground. By this period the conversion argument was no longer novel, but none of the English propagandists used it so effectively or for so many purposes as did the Virginia promotional writers. In earlier promotional literature, conversion had been a nebulous aim floating

9. Harlow, *Discoverie*, p. 71. Ralegh was still talking in the same terms in 1618, see his *Newes of Sr. Walter Raleigh. With a true description of Guiana* (London, 1618), pp. 39, 41. Parker (*Books*, pp. 147–50) and Jones (*New World*, pp. 46–48) are among the few writers who have recognized that the Guiana literature spoke in terms of plunder rather than humanitarianism.

amidst a host of more telling strategic and economic arguments; only Sir George Peckham had fitted it into a comprehensive theory of colonization. But now conversion became the answer to all of Virginia's promotional needs.[1] It gave reason to hope that the hand of God was behind the venture and it provided a rationale suited to the logic of the age.[2] It was a means of establishing a public opinion favourable to the Company's activities, of answering much of the criticism, and, above all, of justifying the Company's acquisition of land. As the Company was proposing settlement and not simply trade, its problem was to link the Amerindian and the English settlers in a community of interest. This was the reason for the ludicrous crowning of Powhatan; the most expedient approach was to link him ostentatiously with the English cause. However, by 1609 the policy had shifted to one of destroying Powhatan's influence, making the natives directly tributary to the English, and fostering friendly relations with the outlying tribes for the purpose of overawing those near at hand.[3] In 1612 policy shifted again and became one of even more widespread settlement as the company gave over its attempts to secure large amounts of trade commodities from the natives and abandoned its efforts to use them as a work force.[4] But whatever policy the Company was following in its first years, the friendly native and his aptitude for conversion were two of the most important facets of the Company's propaganda. What the Virginia Company propagandists did was to adopt the Las Casas–Acosta view of the Amerindian; though he might be a barbarian as compared to the European, he was not ignorant, inhumane, or bestial. At the same time the Company was unable to accept the Las Casas contention that the American native might be converted without extensive settlement and conquest.

In its first years the Company made very little use of printed propa-

1. The statement appears to square with the opinion of Parker, who finds only a modicum of conversion argument in the promotional literature before 1609 (*Books*, pp. 1–192), but finds it of great importance after that date.

2. On the sincerity of this conversion argument, see P. Miller, 'The religious impulse in the founding of Virginia: religion and society in the early literature', *William and Mary Quarterly*, 3rd series, v (1948), 492–522; vi (1949), 22–41; and Parker, *Books*, p. 197. Jennings, on the other hand, argues that the Company's attitude, and by implication, its propaganda were completely hypocritical, *Invasion*, pp. 53–56.

3. Craven, 'Indian policy', pp. 69–71; Craven, *Southern Colonies in the Seventeenth Century*, pp. 79–81; and Craven, *White, Red and Black: The Seventeenth Century Virginian* (Charlottesville, Va., 1971), pp. 41–52. For a somewhat different view, see Nash, 'Image', pp. 212–13.

4. Ibid., p. 217; S. Diamond, 'From organization to society: Virginia in the seventeenth century', *American Journal of Sociology*, lxiii (1958), 460–2; and E. S. Morgan, 'The labor problem at Jamestown, 1607–18', *American Historical Review*, lxxvi (1971), 597–600.

ganda, but after the reorganization of 1609 it embarked on an all-out national campaign that continued, though sometimes haphazardly, until the time of its dissolution. It is indicative of the religious orientation of the Virginia propaganda that a number of its most important tracts were in the form of sermons by some of England's most prominent ministers.[5] All these tracts concerned themselves with conversion, both as a merit in itself and as a justification for the occupation of native lands. William Symonds, a clergyman, based the right to occupy Amerindian lands primarily on the argument that the English had the same right of conversion as the Apostles.

What wrong I pray you did the Apostles in going about to alter the lawes of nations, even against the expresse commandament of the princes, and to set up the throne of Christ. If your mouth be so foule as to charge them with wrong, as the Gentiles did, we have more need to provide you a medicine for a cankered mouth, and a stinking breath, then to make any answer at all.[6]

Symonds further based the right to take land on the biblical conquests of Jacob, Joshua, Joseph, David, and Solomon, and argued that those who claimed there was no right to conquer were in effect denying the right of James I to the throne of England, since he held it in direct descent from William I. But he insisted that the conquest of Virginia would be peaceable: 'are we Spaniards?'[7]

Robert Gray argued that the conquest of Virginia could be justified on the grounds that the natives did not possess the lands in a private sense and were making no proper use of them. Though he thought the Amerindians savage and incredibly unpolished in manners, he explained that they were basically loving and gentle, and therefore 'farre be it from the nature of the English to exercise any bloudie cruelty among these people'. Gray refused to believe that any people were barbarous and uncivil by nature; given the proper education they would rectify and correct their ways. It was every man's duty to venture either with his person or his purse to bring the Virginia savages to civil and Christian government 'rather than to destroy them or utterly roote them out . . . devastation and depopulation ought to be the last thing which Christians put in practice'.[8]

5. A general discussion of the Company's use of sermons as propaganda is contained in Wright, *Religion and Empire*, pp. 87–112; see also J. Parker's essay in the present volume.

6. W. Symonds, *A sermon preached at White-Chappel* (London, 1600), p. 14.

7. Ibid., pp. 10–15.

8. Gray, *A good speed to Virginia* (London, 1609), sigs B1, C2, C3ᵛ–C4ʳ.

In his *Good Newes from Virginia,* published in 1613, Alexander Whitaker, that Cambridge Apostle to the Indians, extolled the virtues and prospects of the native race. According to him the Indians recognized there was a good God; it was simply that they did not know how to seek Him, and were misled by their medicine men, who were in league with the devil. Whitaker questioned the common view that the natives were lacking in intelligence; to him they were an 'understanding generation, quick of apprehension, sudden in their dispatches, subtile in their dealings, exquisite in their inventions, and industrious in their labor'. And while it was true they had to be dealt with carefully, there was no doubt about the ease of their conversion.[9]

Among other ministerial propagandists for Virginia was the violently anti-catholic William Crashaw, who wrote two pamphlets for the Company.[1] Crashaw went so far as to argue that the natives actually desired English settlement, and that to withhold it was to deny them brotherhood with the whites, a position he found untenable. He admonished the English to remember that they had been converted from paganism to Christianity and that to undertake a similar conversion would redeem a considerable portion of the burden of sin resting on the English nation. Crashaw utterly rejected the proposition that land, or anything else, could be taken from the natives; everything must be purchased, and with native consent.[2] It must be said that none of the other Virginia Company writers were willing to go quite this far. Indeed, in the works of most there lurked in the background the plain threat of coercion, though such coercion would probably be unnecessary and was to be used only as a last resort.[3]

The favourable view of the Amerindian was not confined to the Company's clerical propagandists. Virginia's lay promotional writers used it as well. Indeed the most comprehensive statement of the conversion argument is to be found in a pamphlet published by the Company in 1610.[4] The anonymous author's purpose was to prove the colony lawful,

9. Whitaker, *Good news from Virginia* (London, 1613), pp. 23–25, 40.

1. The first of Crashaw's works was *A sermon preached in London* (London, 1610); the second was the second part of Whitaker's *Good newes from Virginia.*

2. Crashaw, *Sermon preached in London,* sigs C3, D3, K1r–K2v.

3. Other propaganda writings on Virginia by clergy included D. Price, *Sauls prohibition staide* (London, 1609); P. Copeland, *Virginia's God be thanked* (London, 1622); and J. Donne, *A sermon, upon the VIII. verse of the I chapter of the Apostles* (London, 1622). Virginia was also prominently mentioned in other sermons of the day, see Wright, *Religion and Empire,* pp. 96–99.

4. *A true declaration of the estate of the colony in Virginia* (London, 1610.)

possible, and profitable in such a way as 'to resolve the religious, encourage the personall, confirm the noble, and satisfy the timorous adventurer'. The lawfulness of the plantation could be proved by its principal aim: conversion. There were only three ways conversion could be carried out: apostolically, or through conquest, or, as the writer put it, 'mixidly', that is 'by the discoverie and trade of merchants, where all temporal means are used for defense and security, but none for offense and crueltie'. The first was impossible in America, for it was more likely to lead to martyrdom than conversion. As for the second, conquest, it was the method of Spain. How was it possible, asked the writer, 'to set their soules at liberty, when we have brought their bodies to slaverie? . . . Let the divines of Salamanca discuss the question how the possessor of the West Indies first destroied and then instructed.' But by the third method, 'we doe buy of them the pearles of the earth and sell to them the pearles of heaven'. This could only be accomplished by settlement, for 'if we ever hope to convert them, it must be by daily conversation'. Thus colonization was not just one means of conversion, but the only possible legitimate method.[5]

There was only one important dissenter to the view of the Amerindian the Virginia propagandists were attempting to foster, and it is significant that the Company never permitted his works to appear under its imprint, even though he was one of its most important members. The dissenter was Captain John Smith. There were a number of reasons why the Company did not approve of his writings, but not the least of these was his attitude towards the natives. His view, which he maintained in varying degrees from his first pamphlet of 1608 up to the publication in 1624 of his *Generall historie of Virginia, New England, and the Summer Isles*, was that the Indians were not friendly, that they neither understood nor appreciated kind or paternalistic treatment and that the only way to handle them was by a show of superior force.[6] While Captain Smith never advocated

5. Ibid., pp. 5–6. For other lay pamphlets encouraging a favourable view of the natives see R. Johnson, *Nova Britannia. Offering most excellent fruites by planting in Virginia* (London, 1609; reprinted in *Tracts and Other Papers*, ed. Force, i, no. 6), pp. 7–8, 13–14; and R. Hamor, *A true discourse of the present estate of Virginia* (London, 1615), sigs A2ᵛ–A4ʳ, pp. 2, 3, 11, 16, 43–44, 46, 49–50, 61–68.
6. J. Smith, *A true relation of such occurrences and accidents of noate as hath hapned in Virginia since the first planting of the collony* (London, 1608, reprinted in E. Arber and A. C. Bradley (eds), *The Travels and Works of Captain John Smith*, 2 vols, Edinburgh, 1910), i. 5, 8–9, 11, 32–39; Smith, *A map of Virginia* (Oxford, 1612, as reprinted in *Travels*), i. 65–66, 72–73, 77, 91–92, 101–3, 106–7, 113, 124, 139–48; and Smith, *The generall historie of Virginia, New England, and the Summer Isles* (London, 1624, also reprinted in *Travels*), i. 272–382; ii. 385–784. The *Generall historie* included a lengthy attack on the now former Amerindian policy of the Company, see especially ii. 562–4, 572–87, 600.

extermination, he did espouse what he believed was the policy of Spain.[7] But this opinion did not make good propaganda, so the Company ignored Smith as far as it could.[8]

From its reorganization in 1609 until 1622 the Virginia Company maintained the optimistic view of the Amerindian as one of its most useful propaganda assets. All this came to an end on Good Friday, 22 March 1622, the day of the Virginia massacre. For some weeks after word of the tragedy arrived in England, the Company maintained a studied silence. Finally it realized the pressing necessity of stating its case to the public, and in August it published a pamphlet prepared by Edward Waterhouse, one of its chief officials.[9] In a complete reversal of previous Virginia promotional literature the principal rationale for settlement in Virginia—the Amerindian—now became the chief scapegoat for all the difficulties of the colony and the Company. Waterhouse made it his business to show that the massacre had been accomplished not through any strength of the natives, but through treachery. Only a month or two before the massacre, Waterhouse wrote, letters had arrived in London from Governor Francis Wyatt assuring the Company that the colonists and the natives were living in such perfect amity, mutually beneficial to both sides, that 'there was seldome or never a sword worne, and a Peece [i.e. gun] seldomer . . . the houses generally set open to the Savages, who were always friendly entertained at the tables of the English, and commonly lodged in their bed-chambers'.[1] The way seemed to be clear for conversion to proceed apace. Then came the attack, in which 'these miscreants . . . put off not only all humanity, but put on a worse and more unnatural brutishnesse', for they refused to content themselves with the murder of 347 men, women, and children, but fell to fresh slaughter, defacing and mangling the bodies and carrying the pieces away in derision and triumph.[2]

---

7. Nash, 'Image', p. 218, argues that Smith did advocate extermination. This is simply not correct. See Smith, *Generall historie*, ed. Arber and Bradley, ii. 579; P. L. Barbour, *The Three Worlds of Captain John Smith* (Boston, 1964), pp. 57–58, 135, 180–4, 190, 197–8, 261, 277, 352–3; K. Glenn, 'Captain John Smith and the Indians', *Virginia Magazine of History and Biography*, lii (1944), 231–48; and A. T. Vaughan, *American Genesis: Captain John Smith and the Founding of Virginia* (Boston, 1975), especially pp. 58–59.

8. H. T. Lefler, 'Promotional literature of the southern colonies', *Journal of Southern History*, xxxiii (1967), 10, correctly sees Smith's Virginia writings as 'demotional'.

9. E. Waterhouse, *A declaration of the state of the colony and affaires in Virginia* (London, 1622).

1. Ibid., pp. 11–13.

2. Ibid., pp. 14–15.

This clear exposition of treachery and brutality was a necessary prelude to the new propaganda line which Waterhouse now presented. Whereas the colonists' hands had been tied by the policy of gentleness and fair usage, the Indian attack had released them, and the English were now entitled by right of war and the law of nations to invade the country and 'destroy them who sought to destroy us', thereby 'turning the laborious Mattocke into the victorious Sword (wherein there is more both ease, benefit and glory)'.[3] This new posture toward the natives by no means meant that hope of civilizing and Christianizing them was to be given up. Though the devil had been responsible for the massacre, the miraculous preservation of so many English was obviously the hand of God, who had so wrought that the English would now see the necessity for a complete change in Amerindian policy, 'God almighty making way for severitie there, where a fayre gentlenesse would not take place'. As the natives were a rude, barbarous, and naked people scattered in small companies, conquest would be a simple matter accomplished in a few quick strokes.

Victorie of them may be gained in many waies: by force, by surprize, by famine in burning their Corne, by destroying and burning their Boats, Canoes, and Houses, by breaking their fishing Weares, by assailing them in their huntings ... by pursuing and chasing them with our hourses, and blood-Hounds to draw after them, and Mastives to tear them, which take this naked, tanned, deformed Savages for no other than wild beasts.[4]

In short what Waterhouse and, since he was the chosen spokesman in this situation, what the Virginia Company was now proposing was that England adopt the attitudes and methods of the early *conquistadores*, the very approach the Virginia propagandists of the previous two decades had been condemning. This was made more manifest by Waterhouse's repeated favourable allusions to the Spaniards and their policy.[5] Thus did the view of the Amerindian in English promotional literature come full circle. The campaign for the peaceful conversion of the Amerindians was by no means over, but it had to be seriously modified as the theoretical

3. Ibid., pp. 22–23.
4. Ibid., p. 24. The statement in Nash, 'Image', p. 219, that Waterhouse was advocating genocide is too strong; Waterhouse was certainly justifying almost any policy short of that, but he was still talking in terms of conversion.
5. Waterhouse, *Declaration of the state of the colony and affaires in Virginia*, pp. 21–22, 25–26, 27–30. The last promotional work issued by the company, J. Bonœil's *His Majesties gracious letter to the Earle of Southampton* (London, 1622), on p. 85, seconds the opinion of Waterhouse, and refers the reader to that work.

framework for colonization which the propagandists had so laboriously built up over twenty years crashed to the ground in a single day.

From this brief review of English promotional literature in the period 1575–1625 it seems clear that the English attitudes towards the American Indian represented no long-standing or deep-seated philosophical commitment, and certainly no reaction against the supposed repressive policies of Spain. In the years to 1590, when we might have expected to find such a reaction, the activities of Spain in the New World were more approved than condemned. When a change in this view did take place after 1590, it represented more the practical necessities of colonial promotion than reaction against Spain. And when this newer propaganda line itself became untenable after 1622, the next change was essentially a reversion to the attitudes of the sixteenth century.

10

Images of the New World:
Jacques Le Moyne de Morgues
and John White

PAUL HULTON

It would have been remarkable if drawings had not been produced along with the written records of the new discoveries. If skilful enough they might have expressed more accurately than words the appearance of new landscapes and the men, animals, and plants native to them. Yet very little original graphic work has come down to us from the earliest voyages. This is partly because such material as was produced was made for use rather than for preservation and must have been passed from hand to hand until worn out or lost. But it is doubtful whether professional artists were ever employed on these voyages. Graphic records might have been made by the captain of the ship or by the pilot, if the ship carried one, who would have a rudimentary knowledge of draughtsmanship, enough to enable him to draw his landmarks, harbours, or coastal profiles. Or an unofficial recorder on board might include some graphic work in his record as did Antonio Pigafetta in his journal of the voyage with Magellan round the world (1519–22).[1] As the impetus for discovery increased so the advantages of pictorial evidence seem generally to have become recognized and it is likely that by the later sixteenth century the employment of artists on voyages of exploration had become general. Certainly Jacques Le Moyne de Morgues, the artist who sailed with Laudonnière to Florida in 1564, was personally recruited in order 'to chart the sea coast and observe the situation of the towns and the depth and course of the rivers, and also the harbours, the houses of the people, and anything new there might be'.[2]

1. J. A. Robertson (ed.), *Magellan's Voyage round the World* (Cleveland, 1906), i, p. 16, pl. at p. 89; ii, pl. at p. 115.
2. T. de Bry (ed.), *Brevis narratio eorum quae in Florida Americae provincia Gallis acciderunt* (Francoforti, 1591), p. 6 (hereafter cited as De Bry, *America*, pt ii); translated in P. Hulton, *The Work of Jacques Le Moyne de Morgues, a Huguenot Artist in France, Florida and England* (2 vols, London, 1977), i. 119.

But realistic representation, as we think of it today, was not always required of the artist in Le Moyne's time, still less earlier in the sixteenth century, and was in fact much more the exception than the rule. Stylistic conventions and other preconceptions (made up of ignorance, fantasy, and a few scraps of genuine knowledge) were powerful influences on the way the artist portrayed the new discoveries and even on the way he actually saw them. These inhibiting factors have to be kept in mind when we attempt to evaluate the earliest records.

For reasons already touched on these are scanty and very variable in quality. Fragmentary graphic information first came from Brazil and Mexico, eventually to be preserved in published engravings or in finely produced maps intended as permanent repositories of the new knowledge. The so-called Miller Atlas (*c.* 1519; Bibliothèque Nationale),[3] the Rotz Atlas (1542, British Library)[4] and several other distinguished collections of maps dating from the earlier sixteenth century include illuminations of Indians of the Spanish and Portuguese American territories, of which the Tupinambas of Brazil are the most frequently and convincingly portrayed. So far as North America is concerned the earliest image which has survived is the picture plan of the Aztec capital Tenochtitlán, drawn, copied, and finally cut in wood by an engraver who misunderstood some of the details.[5] In the few instances where highly qualified artists were involved the results are quite distinct from the general run of crude illustration. Hans Burgkmair of Augsburg introduced Tupinambas into his woodcuts of the *Triumph of Maximilian* (1519).[6] Their dress and artefacts are impressively portrayed, less so their physical characteristics. He based his work on miniature paintings, but the original portrayer of these Indians is unknown. Christoph Weiditz of Augsburg was able in 1529 to make life studies in Spain of Aztecs brought over from Mexico to the Imperial court and these he engraved.[7] They are the most accurate records

3. Reproduced with descriptions in A. Cortesão and A. Teixeira da Mota (eds), *Portugaliae Monumenta cartographica*, i (Lisboa, 1960), 55–61, pls 19, 22, 24.

4. B.L., Royal MS. 20 E ix.

5. First published in *Praeclare Ferdinandi Cortesii de Nova maris oceani Hyspania Narratio . . . Carolo Romanorum Imperatori* (Norimberga, 1524); see I. Marquina, *El templo mayor de Mexico* (Mexico City, 1960), pp. 25–26, fig. 1. For this and other early graphic records of the American Indian I have drawn on William C. Sturtevant, 'First visual images of native America', in F. Chiappelli (ed.), *First Images of America: The Impact of the New World on the Old* (Los Angeles and London, 1976).

6. Reproduced in S. Appelbaum, *The Triumph of Maximilian I; 137 Woodcuts by Hans Burgkmair and Others* (New York, 1964), pp. 18, 19, pls 129, 131.

7. The illustrations described in H. F. Cline, 'Hernando Cortés and the Aztec Indians in Spain', *Quarterly Journal of the Library of Congress*, xxvi (Washington, D.C., 1969), 70–90.

of American Indians so far published though obviously limited in scope, cut off as these Aztecs were from their native land. Gonzalo Fernández de Oviedo, the chronicler of the Spanish American lands, showed a new awareness of the necessity to illustrate their ethnology and natural resources. In a *cri de coeur* he expressed his longing for an artist of the stature of Leonardo or Mantegna whom he had known in Italy. For want of a better hand he made his own rather crude but entirely adequate illustrations: at least twenty-one ethnographical drawings and rather fewer botanical and zoological ones relating to the West Indies, Columbia, and Panama.[8] They have never been completely published. By contrast Hans Staden of Hamburg, a prisoner of the Tupinambas of coastal Brazil in 1553–4, published his adventures in forty-two woodcuts showing a range of Indian activities with a strong emphasis on cannibalism.[9] Perhaps because of their subject matter some of these images became permanently embedded in the European consciousness of savage America and strongly influenced later artist recorders.

Thus far the graphic records which survived reflect almost exclusively Spanish or Portuguese expansion in the New World. The earliest French discoveries in North America are very sparsely illustrated, with almost no element of scientific realism. But out of Villegaignon's expedition to Brazil in 1555–6 came the first significant illustrations produced by Frenchmen. They were published in the works of André Thevet and Jean de Léry, both of whom were with Villegaignon.[1] Some of them have considerable ethnological interest, in particular the woodcuts in De Léry's history of the expedition. He is very conscious of the difficulties of drawing Indians, saying that 'by reason of their diverse gestures and behaviours, utterly different from ours, it is a very difficult matter to express their true proportion either in writing or painting'.[2] Yet these

8. Formerly in Oviedo's manuscript now in the Real Academia de la Historia, Madrid, the text not fully published until 1851–5 in J. Amador de los Rios (ed.), *Historia general y natural de las Indias* (4 vols, Madrid) with the illustrations excessively modernized. A manuscript version of part of this work is in the Huntington Library with nine ethnographic drawings, three of them reproduced in A. M. Josephy, Jr (ed.), *The American Heritage Book of Indians* (New York, 1961), pp. 81, 99.

9. Hans Staden, *Warhaftige Historia und Beschreibung eyner Landschafft der wilden, nacketen, grimmigen menschfresser Leuten, in der Newenwelt America gelegen* (Marburg, 1557). The woodcuts reproduced and described in Juan Staden, *Vera Historia y Descripción de un Pais de las Salvages*, ed. E. Wernicke (Museo Etnográfico, Universidad de Buenos Aires, Biblioteca de Fuentes, 1944).

1. André Thevet, *La Cosmographie universelle* (Paris, 1575), i, especially ff. 917, 922, 926, 927, 929, 930, 935, 938, 942, 943, 945, 946, 950, 952, 953.

2. Jean de Léry, *Histoire d'un voyage fait en la terre du Bresil* (La Rochelle, 1578), p. 129.

few illustrations give a clear and reasonably accurate picture of the dress and artefacts and some of the customs of the Indians they encountered. Much more was now being expected of the recording artist than to project preconceived images of the American savage. Jacques Le Moyne and John White were familiar with the growing volume of graphic material emerging from the new discoveries. What so distinguishes their contributions from those of their predecessors is the extensiveness of their records and the new and vivid way they were published by Theodor de Bry in large-scale, expertly (and accurately) engraved illustrations with explanatory notes. The image had at last become as important as the text and more memorable.

The work of White is by now well-known and has been investigated in detail.[3] He has the advantage of his elder contemporary Le Moyne in that a useful proportion of his original American record survives. As against more than sixty drawings of Eskimo, Caribbean, oceanic, and 'Virginian' subjects by White only a single original by Le Moyne is known, the miniature of Athore, son of the Timucuan chief of the St Johns River area of Florida, pointing out to Laudonnière the column set up by Ribault in 1562.[4] Apart from this, Le Moyne's graphic record can only be judged indirectly through the engravings of De Bry which he published with the artist's narrative of the Florida venture in *America*, part ii (1591). The purpose of this essay is not primarily to consider the value of Le Moyne's record as against White's, but rather to discuss the exchange of ideas between the two artists, which was more extensive than has previously been supposed. Before considering that rather involved subject, it might be useful to trace in outline the curiously parallel careers of the two men and to examine the recent history of White studies which led directly to the study of Le Moyne.

Both artists emerge into the historical limelight from almost complete obscurity. Research has so far failed to reveal anything of their origin and family background, though we know for certain that Le Moyne was a Dieppois and may conclude with less certainty that White was of West Country descent. Nothing is known of their training though both used miniature techniques and are likely to have been apprenticed to some miniaturist master. Their abilities certainly impressed the leaders or promoters of their respective expeditions, men like Laudonnière and

3. P. Hulton and D. B. Quinn, *The American Drawings of John White, 1577–1590* (2 vols London and Chapel Hill, 1964; hereafter cited as Hulton and Quinn, *White*).
4. New York Public Library, James Hazen Hyde Bequest.

Ralegh, who evidently judged them qualified to make the kind of detailed graphic survey already indicated for Le Moyne. In other words they were thought to be sufficiently able cartographers, portraitists, and natural history draughtsmen to cope with a wide range of new visual experiences.

Before White sailed as artist-recorder of Grenville's expedition of 1585 his presence on two earlier voyages may be deduced from circumstantial evidence. It is likely that he was with Frobisher in his search for a north-west passage in 1577, for one of a group of Eskimo drawings in the British Museum shows a seascape with ice floes and a boatload of Englishmen firing arquebuses at Eskimos who are discharging arrows at them from a cliff top. There are kayaks on the water and tents on a headland. The details of Eskimo costume, weapons, and equipment could only have been drawn from life. The scene depicted agrees so closely with the account by Dionyse Settle and George Best of a skirmish between Englishmen and Eskimos at Frobisher Inlet, Baffin Island, on Frobisher's second voyage,[5] that we are forced to the conclusion that White must have been there, for his ultimate authorship of the drawing is not in doubt. The drawing in question is a copy but an early and good one and is entirely characteristic of White if not quite so accomplished. Probably these Eskimo studies were known to the promoters of the 'Roanoke' voyages and convinced them that White could successfully undertake a similar role in 'Virginia'. In addition White may well have been with Amadas and Barlowe on their reconnaissance of the North American coast in 1584 and it is possible that some of his surviving work had its origin then.[6]

Le Moyne reached the coast of Florida with Laudonnière towards the end of June 1564; White the island of Wococon in the Carolina Outer Banks in June 1585, making drawings en route in Puerto Rico and at other points in the Spanish West Indies. (So perhaps did Le Moyne, who took much the same route, though no records have survived to enlighten us.)

Le Moyne spent fifteen months in Florida based at Fort Caroline on the St Johns. Naturally enough, but to us frustratingly, his account mentions nothing of his artistic activities. Clearly his illustrations were meant to speak for themselves. White spent about a year in Ralegh's Virginia, based on the Roanoke Island fort. He had the inestimable advantage of

5. See R. Collinson (ed.), *The Three Voyages of Martin Frobisher* (London, 1867), p. 142 and R. Hakluyt, *Principal Navigations* (12 vols, Glasgow, 1903–5), vii. 211–42.

6. White in 1593, in his account to Hakluyt of his last voyage of 1590, calls it his fifth voyage. Four voyages are well documented, the fifth can only be that of Amadas and Barlowe in 1584. See D. B. Quinn (ed.), *The Roanoke Voyages*, 2 vols (London, 1955), ii. 598 (hereafter cited as *Roanoke Voyages*).

working with Thomas Harriot. Together they made a formidable team, Harriot surveying the newly explored territory (parts of modern North Carolina and Virginia), observing the Indians and their way of life, systematically describing the fauna and flora they encountered, and White matching this activity with sketch maps and studies of human and natural life intended to be used later in finished compositions. The extent of their survey may be judged by such occasional clues found in Harriot's *Briefe and true Report* as 'Of al sorts of fowle I have the names in the countrie language of forescore and sixe of which number besides those that be named, we have . . . the pictures as they were there drawne . . .'.[7] The intention seems to have been to publish the Indian and natural history material with illustrations, though in the event only some of the Indian drawings were engraved by De Bry to illustrate Harriot's *Report* (1590). White returned on Drake's ship with the rest of the colonists in June 1586, probably bringing out the bulk of his drawings intact, though some may have been lost in their hurried departure from Roanoke Island.

There is no evidence to show that a survey of the Harriot–White type was undertaken in Florida. The episodic character of the Le Moyne illustrations in *America*, part ii, is misleading. Le Moyne's record, like White's, must have been of the same documentary kind though almost certainly not as systematic. The reason why the engravings do not generally reflect this is that the main part of Le Moyne's record perished in the disaster that overwhelmed the Frenchmen in September 1565. Le Moyne has left an account of his escape from Fort Caroline after the surprise attack of the Spaniards. In the melée he rushed out through an embrasure. It seems impossible that in the circumstances he could have managed to rescue any of his drawings. Yet there are some details in the Florida engravings which appear to be based on direct observation. In addition there are the two drawings of Indians of Florida by John White (Plates 1 and 2), copied directly from Le Moyne, which are more convincing ethnographically than any of the engravings after him and show that at least a small part of the Florida record was somehow got out, probably by ship before the final catastrophe.

On his return to France early in 1566 Le Moyne hurried to report to Charles IX at Moulins and certainly had something of his Florida record to show him. The king seemed impressed and advised him to put

7. Thomas Harriot, *A briefe and true Report of the new found Land of Virginia* (London [Robert Robinson], 1588), 'Of foule', sig. D2ᵛ.

Of Florida.

Of Florida.

2 *John White after Jacques Le Moyne.*
Indian Woman of Florida. Watercolour.

1 *John White after Jacques Le Moyne.*
Indian Man of Florida. Watercolour.

3 *Theodor de Bry after Jacques Le Moyne.*
   Chief Satouriwa's Wife. Detail of plate 39 of *America*, part II. Engraving.
   Reproduced by courtesy of the British Library Board.

4   *Theodor de Bry after John White or Jacques Le Moyne.*
    The 'Idol Kivvasa'. Detail of plate 21 of *America*, part I. Engraving.
    Reproduced by courtesy of the British Library Board.

(Overleaf)

5   *Theodor de Bry after Jacques Le Moyne.*
    The French reach Port Royal. Plate 5 of *America*, part II. Engraving.
    Reproduced by courtesy of the British Library Board.

6   *Theodor de Bry after John White.*
    The arrival of the Englishmen in Virginia. Plate 2 of *America*, part I. Engraving.
    Reproduced by courtesy of the British Library Board.

5

Prom̄ lupi

Portus Regalis, ſiue F.S.Helenæ.

6

SECOTAN

Pasquenoke

Dasamonquepeuc

WEAPEMEOC

Roanoac

Hatorasck

Trinety harbor

T.B. 2

together an illustrated account of the colony.[8] It seems likely that Le Moyne had reconstructed some scenes while his memory remained fresh, perhaps on board ship, but the compositions engraved by De Bry were probably drawn much later when he came under the patronage of Ralegh in England.

For both artists the failure of the attempt to establish a colony on American soil marked the end of their duties as recorders of the American scene. White changed his role from artist to organizer and leader. His return to Roanoke Island as governor in 1587 must have left him little time to depict the Indian and natural life he encountered. From that moment he became obsessively involved in efforts to supply the colony and was forced to leave at short notice. His dramatic failure to get help to the settlers is well-known. He is last heard of in 1593 when he wrote to Hakluyt from Newtown in Kilmore, County Cork, about the ill-success of the 1590 expedition.

Le Moyne's career in France after his meeting with Charles IX, is entirely obscure and nothing whatever is known of him until he settled in the parish of St Anne's, Blackfriars, 'for religion', in or about 1580. He was granted letters of denization on 12 May 1581.[9] When he came within the circle of English colonizing interests is not known, but it was presumably by 1584, when Ralegh sent out his first expedition to reconnoitre the American coastline to the north of Florida. It would be surprising if an artist with his experience of an area close to Ralegh's Virginia was not consulted. Hakluyt makes his first allusion to Le Moyne in the preface to his translation (1587) of Laudonnière's *L'Histoire notable de la Floride* (Paris, 1586). In the epistle addressed to Ralegh he writes of 'things of chiefest importance liuely drawn in coulours at your no smale charges by the skilfull painter Iames Morgues'.[1] Information of Le Moyne's work (as of White's) was given to De Bry by Hakluyt when the former visited England in 1587 and he attempted to secure Le Moyne's illustrated narrative for publication. He was unsuccessful, perhaps because Le Moyne or Ralegh had other ideas for publication in England. Le Moyne had already published at Blackfriars in 1586 *La Clef des Champs*—his own pattern book of woodcuts of birds, beasts, and plants—and dedicated it to Lady Mary Sidney. His creative interests had shifted from his American experiences,

8. 'De Autore' in De Bry, *America*, pt ii.

9. R. E. G. Kirk and E. F. Kirk (eds), *Return of Aliens, pt 2, 1571–1597* (Aberdeen, Huguenot Society of London, 1902), p. 354.

1. R. de Laudonnière, *A notable Historie containing foure Voyages made by certayne French Captaynes unto Florida* (tr. R. Hakluyt, London, 1587), f. iv.

now more than twenty years behind him, to the depiction of European plants. On a second visit in 1588 De Bry tried once again to obtain the Le Moyne material. In May of that year the artist had died and his widow Jeane, probably in need of money, sold her husband's American collection to the publisher. He also took some of White's American record, then or perhaps the previous year, back to Frankfurt. No doubt Hakluyt had a considerable say in the way both artists were presented and in the decision to publish White, not Le Moyne, as the first volume of De Bry's monumental series on the discoveries in the New World. And he translated for the English version (it was also issued in Latin, French, and German) Harriot's Latin captions to White's illustrations.[2]

No original work by Le Moyne was discovered until the beginning of this century.[3] On the other hand all the known White originals and the volume of early copies had long been available for study in the British Museum. The copies came with the Sloane bequest (Sloane MS. 5270) in 1753. There is an inscription on the flyleaf in Sloane's hand that these are 'the originall draughts by Mr. John White' and the assumption was a natural one since the only evidence of White's work before their appearance was the series of engravings after him in De Bry, *America*, part i. Sloane had purchased the copies from White's descendants.[4] They vary between excellent and rather feeble and are evidently by more than one hand. They include three Eskimo drawings besides the skirmish already mentioned, twenty-six sheets of Indians of Ralegh's Virginia, and West Indian and oceanic fauna and flora, all, apart from two Eskimo subjects, with counterparts among the original drawings which came to the museum much later. There are also fifty-eight sheets of European plants copied from various sources still not fully identified, and perhaps of most significance, forty-four drawings of birds, fish, and reptiles of 'Virginia'. This last group of fauna are not found among the originals; all have Indian names and indication of size. These copies alone, particularly the last group, give some idea, not fully realized until comparatively recently, of the range of the White–Harriot survey. What is missing is the concentrated precision and awareness of colours and texture shown by White in

---

2. See the second title-page to the De Bry edition of Harriot's *A Briefe and true Report* (Francoforti ad Moenvm, 1590), hereafter cited as De Bry, *America*, pt i.

3. The single miniature known by Le Moyne and already mentioned above (p. 198), was discovered in 1900 at the Château de Courance. See E. T. Hamy, 'Sur une miniature de Jacques Le Moyne de Morgues', *Académie des Inscriptions et Belles-Lettres, Comptes rendus des Séances de l'année 1901* (Paris, 1901), pp. 6, 8–17.

4. See Hulton and Quinn, *White*, p. 27.

the originals. It is with the rediscovery of these in 1865 that the scholarly evaluation of White's work really began.

Henry Stevens of Vermont holds a special place in White studies. 'The pictures of sondry things collected and counterfeited according to the truth in the voyage made by Sir Walter Raleigh, Knight, for the discouery of La Virginea . . .'[5] re-emerged to public view in the rooms of Sotheby, Wilkinson, and Hodge with the library of the third Earl of Charlemont in 1865. Awaiting sale the drawings barely escaped destruction by fire, the edges of the sheets being scorched and the whole volume lying saturated and under pressure for three weeks. As a result the colours offset on the blank sheets which lay between the drawings. The damage was severe and is still visible today in the water stains and confusing offsets which appear on the larger (folded) drawings, though the colours remain surprisingly strong. Stevens was concentrating his energies at this period on his catalogue of American books in the British Museum. Because of his knowledge of the De Bry plates and the Sloane volume of copies he immediately realized the significance of the White originals, purchased them in their damaged condition and put them in good order. He had the original sheets rebound, unfortunately discarding the old binding without recording any information about it, and made a separate volume of the offsets. Commendably he persuaded Panizzi, Principal Librarian, that the British Museum should buy both.[6] Here he also showed an acute business sense for he sold them for 225 guineas, almost double the price he had given little more than seven months before.

The drawings consisted of sixty-two subjects, including two maps, connected with the voyage of 1585–6 (and possibly that of 1584) to Ralegh's Virginia, a man and a woman of Florida, two European birds, a man and a woman Eskimo, six 'Picts' and 'Ancient Britons', and five costume studies of Middle Eastern and Oriental men and women. There is no evidence that Stevens carried out any detailed research on this material though he seems to have begun work on the identity of White without following it through. In spite of the unique survival of drawings so closely related to the earliest English efforts to explore and settle in North America, White studies did not significantly advance until the present century.

In 1907 appeared the fourth volume of Laurence Binyon's *Catalogue of*

5. White's autograph title to this set of drawings.
6. See H. Stevens, *Recollections of James Lenox*, ed. V. H. Paltsits (New York, 1951), p. 112, and Henry Stevens' Letterbooks, William L. Clements Library, University of Michigan.

Drawings by British Artists ... in the British Museum. Sidney Colvin, Keeper of Prints and Drawings, writes in his preface: 'the volume contains no more interesting section than that which describes (for the first time fully and accurately) the famous albums of drawings connected with the name of the Elizabethan traveller and explorer John White, the lieutenant of Raleigh in more than one of his colonising missions on the North American coast'.[7] The words 'fully and accurately' used in connection with Binyon's catalogue cannot today be accepted at their face value. His brief notice of the artist which heads the catalogue contains the deduction, without supporting evidence, that 'White probably made earlier journeys to the East of Europe'. Binyon clearly treated the costume drawings as original studies, not as the derivatives they have since been found to be, and on the same level as the North American drawings. On the other hand he perceptively remarks on the two natives of Florida: 'apparently drawn from the life, but possibly copied from drawings by Jacques Le Moyne'.[8] He also sees in the Eskimo material, both originals and copies, reason to suppose that White was with Frobisher on one of the three voyages to the northwest, 1576–8.[9] He correctly gauges the subsidiary artistic status of the Sloane volume as derivatives but does not fully realize their documentary significance. His catalogue descriptions are by present-day standards cursory, yet Binyon had begun to look at the drawings in their historical context, as witness his introductory notes to the volume of originals and to the Sloane volume of copies.[1]

Binyon provided a much fuller historical framework to White's record in an article published in 1925, where nine of the drawings were reproduced in collotype monochrome together with the Sloane copy of the skirmish with the Eskimos.[2] His account of White's career shows his familiarity with the documents in Hakluyt and with De Bry's *America*, parts i and ii. He begins by stating: 'The paramount interest of these drawings is not artistic: they are documents invaluable for the ethnologist and the historian. But English drawings of the sixteenth century are so rare and these betray so sensitive a hand, that they deserve a modest place in the history of English art.' In his attempt to dispel the obscurity sur-

7. L. Binyon, *Catalogue of Drawings by British Artists ... in the British Museum* (4 vols London, 1898–1907), iv, p. iv.
8. Ibid. iv. 330, nos 23–24.
9. Ibid. iv. 327.
1. Ibid. iv. 326–7, 334.
2. L. Binyon, 'The drawings of John White', *Thirteenth Volume of the Walpole Society 1924–25* (Oxford, 1925), pp. 19–24, pls xxiv–xxx.

rounding White's earlier career he is the first to suggest the probability that the artist sailed with Amadas and Barlowe in their reconnoitring expedition of 1584. Strangely, his earlier suggestion that White's Indians of Florida were copies of Le Moyne is abandoned for the theory that they could have been portrayed when 'Grenville's ships touched on the coast of Florida on the way to Wococon'. However, he does not attempt to support this statement and in fact none of the Roanoke voyagers except Drake made landings on the Florida coast. In spite of some unsupported suppositions Binyon succeeded in giving a wider and more accurate picture of the historical background of the White drawings than any previously obtainable. He was the first to be concerned at the same time with their artistic, historical, and scientific validity. The way was now open for the full publication of White's record and the detailed analysis which these convincing images called for.

Following Binyon, a new interest in White began to emerge on both sides of the Atlantic. Scholarly articles on White's identity and on scientific aspects of his Virginia record appeared in the United States.[3] The British Museum decided to publish all White's North American drawings in colour facsimile, in their original size, with an introduction and catalogue by Binyon and notes by ethnologists, natural scientists, cartographic and other specialists. A prospectus and skeleton catalogue with two-colour facsimiles were issued in 1936 but in the aftermath of the depression failed to attract sufficient support and the project was abandoned. The war postponed any such publication for a generation.

The success in the United States of Lorant's book on White and Le Moyne issued in 1946 showed the appetite in that country for early narrative and illustrative material on North American exploration.[4] More scholarly publications were slower to appear. In the early 1950s David Beers Quinn was compiling his monumental *Roanoke Voyages* for the Hakluyt Society. His visits to the Print Room to study the White drawings coincided with the preparation of a new catalogue of British drawings to supersede Binyon. I was concerned with the White drawings and we exchanged ideas and information over a long period. The White

3. W. J. Holland, 'The first picture of an American butterfly', *Scientific Monthly*, xxix (New York, 1929), 45–49; R. G. Adams, 'An effort to identify John White', *American Historical Review*, xli (1935–6), 87–91; W. P. Cumming, 'The identity of John White governor of Virginia and John White the artist', *North Carolina Historical Review*, xv (1938), 197–203.

4. S. Lorant, *The New World, the First Pictures of America made by John White and Jacques Le Moyne and Engraved by Theodor de Bry* (New York, 1946; London, 1954; revised American edn, 1965).

material—original drawings, copies, and engravings—poses certain questions about the relationship between the De Bry engravings and the original drawings, for the engravings are not taken directly from them, showing many variations, including added landscape backgrounds and back views of Indian portrait figures. There is also the question of the connection between the Sloane copies and the originals, where they exist, for they are mostly not direct copies. In *Roanoke Voyages* Quinn attempted to answer these and other questions for the first time by grouping the extant and lost White material into a sort of family tree.[5]

He supposed a lost archetype, White's basic collection, from which all others, both lost and surviving, were descended. From this the artist would have made a number of sets of finished drawings differing in complexity, and to a minor extent in detail, for different individuals and purposes: one for Thomas Harriot, we can be sure, now lost; one now in the British Museum possibly intended for presentation to a powerful patron and giving little detail beyond the basic composition; one certainly for De Bry to engrave, now lost, which, to judge from the engravings, was more elaborate and included at least four American subjects not in the Museum collection; and others for Thomas Penny, the entomologist, and Richard Hakluyt, probably less numerous. The Sloane volume of copies may be thought of as a third generation, reflecting no doubt something of the variety and range of the lost archetypal White collection and made up of drawings different from but closely connected with surviving originals, for example the Eskimo subjects, including the skirmish drawing. The Indian drawings among them are familiar from the originals but show significant variations, and there are others, for example the fishes, reptiles, and birds, not connected with any known originals, but which must have constituted a significant element of the Harriot–White survey in Virginia.

Nothing has happened since 1955 to upset Quinn's groupings. He then went on to arrange this material in historical sequence as documents with associated texts in order to provide 'though naturally with many gaps, a visual commentary on the course of Grenville's expedition through the West Indies to Ralegh's Virginia in 1585, and on the history of the first colony maintained at Roanoke Island during the following year'.[6] So we have first the drawings of the profiles of the islands of Dominica and Santa Cruz (probably not by White), followed by those connected

5. *Roanoke Voyages*, i. 392–8. 6. Ibid. i. 390.

with Puerto Rico, including a group of fauna and flora, among which were the outstanding drawing of the flamingo and the studies of the banana. Then follow the oceanic birds and fishes probably encountered between Hispaniola and the North American coast. The arrival of the colonists at the Outer Banks is illustrated by a De Bry engraving only, since the original is lost. Next we have the Indian village of Pomeiooc, probably drawn on 12 July 1585, and associated drawings; followed by neighbour-ing Secoton, visited on 15–16 July, again with connected drawings, some of them individual studies of scenes shown in miniature in the drawings of that village. The succeeding items are not documented in the accounts but are of Indians and natural life found on Roanoke or on expeditions into the interior of the mainland, such as the large group of fauna in the Sloane volume. Finally come the manuscript maps—of Ralegh's Virginia and the smaller scale map of eastern North America—composed probably last of all. The maps, both manuscript and printed, were excellently reproduced and analysed in detail. In this way the White material was brought into the body of documentary evidence, and the light it throws on the new world encountered by Grenville's expedition was focused to advantage.

It was inevitable that the *Catalogue of British Drawings*[7] followed virtually the same arrangement though it was to concern itself more with the media of the drawings and stylistic considerations; ten items were reproduced in colour and twenty-three in monochrome. By now it had become plain that nothing less than the reproduction of all the White material was called for, originals and derivatives, and that this should be accompanied by a catalogue and studies in depth of its historical and scientific content, particularly in the field of ethnology. It was clear too that David Quinn and I were best placed to undertake such a book. *The American Drawings of John White* appeared in 1964. All the original draw-ings were reproduced in colour facsimile at great trouble (and unfor-tunately at very great expense) and the derivative and associated graphic material in monochrome. We discovered little new biographical material on White, but a more precise identification of the North American fauna and flora was made by British and American natural scientists. Most productive of all the research embodied in the book was W. C. Sturte-vant's analysis of the ethnographical content of the drawings and what it

---

7. E. Croft-Murray and P. Hulton, *Catalogue of British Drawings* (2 vols, London, 1960), i, pp. 26–86; ii, pls 18–40.

revealed of the long extinct culture of the Carolina Algonquians.[8] He showed how, in spite of White's own artistic conditioning, his Indian drawings in general are remarkably true (for that period) to the facts of archaeological evidence. It was considered necessary to include a full description of Le Moyne's own extant miniature painting in order to make clear the differences and similarities in the approach of the two artists to the problem of portraying Indians. These factors had also to be taken into account in describing the drawings of the Indians of Florida by White after Le Moyne and two engravings of De Bry after Le Moyne from *America,* part ii. The latter were included as having elements in common with the drawings of the Florida Indians.[9] Thus the close consideration of White necessitated some investigation of Le Moyne.

By a curious chance, when the monograph on White was nearing completion, there appeared on the market a hitherto unknown collection of fifty-nine plant drawings by Le Moyne. In 1962 they were purchased by the British Museum. It was clear that now a similarly detailed study of Le Moyne must follow. This has now been undertaken and was published in 1977.[1]

Any comparison of the American records of Le Moyne and White must be to the disadvantage of Le Moyne in almost every way. Where White with Harriot's descriptions gives a clear if limited picture of the Carolina Algonquians and their way of life, Le Moyne's picture of the Timucua of northeastern Florida is blurred and often misleading. We have to look hard before we find in the single miniature and the De Bry engravings even a few details which can be considered valid representations. Many of the supposed Indian artefacts are based on European models—for example most of the agricultural tools and baskets. In portraying the Indians themselves Le Moyne often goes wrong in depicting features and postures. One glaring example is the blond hair of the Indian women and the cherry-coloured conventionalized lips of all the Indians. The stance of the chief Athore is also more the product of European sixteenth-century Mannerism than of observation. These examples can be multiplied extensively. Again in his map of Florida as engraved by De Bry his inaccuracies, or wilful distortions, are very marked, even for the area near the mouth of the St Johns River in the vicinity of the fort which the

8. Hulton and Quinn, *White,* i. 37–43 and notes to catalogue nos 34–54.
9. Ibid. i, catalogue nos 112, 113.
1. P. Hulton (ed.), *The Works of Jacques Le Moyne de Morgues, a Huguenot Artist in France, Florida and England* (2 vols, London, 1977, hereafter cited as Hulton, *Le Moyne*).

French knew so well. The estuary is seen to extend from the coast many miles northwest, whereas the river rises far to the south and runs north, only turning east to the sea comparatively close to the coast near the modern Jacksonville.[2] By comparison the accuracy of White's large-scale map of the coastal area of the Carolina Outer Banks is impressive. Yet we also know how accurately Le Moyne could observe and depict plant and insect life from the numerous examples of his work now available. Is it then possible that Le Moyne, though a more gifted and sophisticated artist than White, was conditioned by his training and less able to provide 'straight' graphic evidence, free from artistic preconceptions? We may well conclude that White was more workmanlike if less talented and, under the scientific influence of Harriot, better able to transmit a convincing record. But such a comparison is probably false. We are judging Le Moyne on one original miniature and forty-two engravings after him, all almost certainly derived from compositions reconstructed long after the events they illustrate and largely from memory. The White record on the other hand was derived from studies made from the life and put together at the most only a few years after the studies were first drawn.

It is likely that White spent some time with the older artist after his return from the first colonizing expedition in 1586, when he would have a great deal of new American material to show him; by now both enjoyed the patronage of Ralegh. Le Moyne must have given White access to his own collection, for the portraits of the Indian man and woman of Florida (Plates 1 and 2) do not exist in their original form but only in the copies made by White. The style and use of brush and colours are unmistakably White's, the content as certainly Le Moyne's. The originals of these studies must have formed part of what can be assumed to be the small amount of Le Moyne's original work to come out of Florida, perhaps sent back to France by ship in 1564 or in the earlier part of 1565. There is no reason to suppose that White made any significant alterations either to the features, dress, or artefacts. If this is accepted, and copyists usually copied closely, we have here a near approach to the field studies which Le Moyne must have made in considerable numbers. The features of these Timucuan Indians are more convincing than Athore's or those of the other Indians in Le Moyne's one surviving miniature. The tattooed patterns and painting on the faces and bodies of both man and woman are

2. The distortions are discussed at length by Quinn, 'The attempted colonization of Florida by the French, 1562–1565', in Hulton, *Le Moyne*, pp. 37–44.

supported by contemporary accounts, while the pendants hanging from the man's belt are similar to ones of stone and shell found archaeologically in the northeastern area of Florida. Again, the blue garment worn by the woman is certainly the fringe of Spanish moss mentioned in early accounts, though the strength of the colour is exaggerated. The ear ornaments of both, the bowl held by the woman, and to some degree the bow and arrow of the man, are more or less acceptable forms for this area of Florida.

In other words the drawings are in the same class ethnographically as the White drawings proper and that can only be the result of Le Moyne's powers of observation and graphic ability. There must have been many such studies as the lost originals of these copies in his portfolio. Satouriwa in plate 39 of *America,* part ii, was surely taken from a portrait study of the same kind; of the Indian chiefs he was the nearest and best-known to the French settlers. In the same plate is his 'queen' (Plate 3), clearly based on the original of the Florida woman but startlingly transformed. Her pose is sinuous and Mannerist instead of foursquare; her hair is long and curly, in accord with the European idea of beauty, rather than lank and merely shoulder length; the garment of Spanish moss just preserves the decencies whereas it makes no pretence of so doing in White's copy, but, curiously, the moss is more realistic in the engraving than in the drawing. The obvious question arises: who was responsible for the transformation, Le Moyne or the engraver? The changes made by De Bry in the Indian figures engraved after White in *America,* part i, are precisely known because of the existing originals. The engraver keeps closely to his models, though the features are often Europeanized and the poses somewhat modified to accord more with the fashion of European Mannerism; the hair length is not altered and for the woman made only slightly more wavy. Thus the changes may be said to be minor, perhaps the minimum thought necessary to make these exotic beings acceptable to De Bry's European readership. The conclusion must be that Le Moyne departed further from his original study than did De Bry from the Le Moyne drawing he engraved. It is reasonable to suppose that the length of time which elapsed between the studies made by Le Moyne in Florida and the time when he completed his elaborate compositions for the engraver largely accounted for the extent of these changes. The Florida man is also transmuted into the central figure of the three chiefs shown in the foreground of plate 14 in *America,* part ii, illustrating Outina's forces on the march. But the changes are not so forced. He is further embellished, but many of the items of dress and adornment remain the same, and though he is in movement something still persists of his original standing posture. There is reason to suppose that had his Florida experiences been fresher in Le Moyne's memory and had he been able to turn to a whole body of studies made from the life he could have provided De Bry with a record as convincing and consistent as White's.

In curious contrast to the sober engravings of Indians in *America*, part i, is the separate section of five flamboyant figures of 'Pictes which in the Olde tyme dyd habite one part of the great Bretainne'. De Bry's note on the title-page of this sub-section explains that White was the author and that De Bry himself decided to add these figures 'to show how that the Inhabitants of the great Bretannie haue bin in times past as sauuage as those of Virginia'. But not only their content differentiates them from the Indians; they are distinct in another way. The original drawings of 'Picts' by White in the British Museum are not as closely related to the engravings as are the Indians to theirs. One has no counterpart and two are modified considerably. And one engraving of 'a yonge doughter of the Pictes' has no counterpart among the drawings. In 1967 there appeared in the sale room a hitherto unknown miniature on vellum of precisely this subject. The quality of the painting, the precision and delicacy of the flowers which covered the woman's body confirmed that a new Le Moyne had come to light, the original of the *Young Daughter of the Picts*.[3] The pose of the figure and the details of the landscape background are exactly repeated in the engraving. Only the face has been modified to give it a more classical appearance. The flowers evidently proved too difficult for the engraver and have been replaced by a simpler floral pattern. If Le Moyne was the author of this figure it seems likely that the other four engraved 'Picts' were also taken from his work. De Bry says that the figures were found in an old English chronicle and Le Moyne and White may well have used such a source to produce their own versions of these primitive British islanders. When De Bry returned to Frankfurt after his second visit to London in 1588 he must have had at his disposal a large collection of drawings by Le Moyne and White containing not only the North American material but also their 'Picts'. It would not be surprising if he confused the artists when he decided to provide his readers with this piece of comparative ethnology.

Comparing the Indian plates after Le Moyne and White in *America*,

3. Now in the collection of Mr and Mrs Paul Mellon, Upperville, Virginia.

parts i and ii, we are struck by the similarity of many of the small details and some of the compositions. De Bry and his fellow engravers, as we have seen, normally followed the original accurately when engraving the main elements of a composition. This is not to say that they did not add inessential details to the backgrounds and foregrounds when it was thought necessary to provide the right context. The many glimpses of the lagoons in the backgrounds of the White–De Bry plates showing Indians canoeing and fishing or hunting on the mainland behind could have been added by De Bry from material at hand and would not necessarily have been provided by White. De Bry may have gone further by using details found in the work of one artist in his engravings of the other's. Thus the same plants (none identifiable) are sometimes shown in the foregrounds of both the Le Moyne and White plates of De Bry. There is, for example, a flowering plant seen on a bank in the right foreground of the Le Moyne miniature, *Young Daughter of the Picts*, which reappears as we might expect in the engraving after it, but is also unmistakably recognizable on the foreshore in the engraving of the fishing-scene after White (De Bry, plate 3). The original of the latter has a rather different kind of plant in that position. In addition the same grapes and pumpkins appearing in Le Moyne (De Bry, plate 5, here Plate 5) are found in White (De Bry, plates 2 and 20); and there are other examples of this kind of interchange.

Apart from such minor details there is at least some evidence that the two artists may have worked up their compositions for the engraver together or that each was aware of what the other was doing, and on occasions borrowed from him. If we compare White–De Bry plate 2 (*The Arrival of the Englishmen in Virginia*, here Plate 6), with plates 3, 4, and particularly 5 (*The French reach Port Royal*, here Plate 5) of Le Moyne–De Bry, it is difficult not to believe that the one artist was influenced by the other. There is precisely the same kind of half map, half bird's-eye view treatment of a section of coastline with ships at anchor or sailing up river estuaries. Sea-monsters are indicated in the same way and the exploring pinnaces are drawn so similarly as to be interchangeable, as are many of the background trees. The only distinction is the introduction of certain details in the White–De Bry plates such as the names and symbols for Indian villages mapped on the expedition of 1585–6. Apart from the general similarity of these particular plates there are major elements in other plates after White which echo parts of Le Moyne compositions. For example there is the barbecue of White (De Bry, plate 14), which is seen at exactly the same angle and in basically the same form as the one in Le

Moyne (De Bry, plate 24).[4] Again there is the canoe in White (De Bry, plate 12) seen at the same angle and with the same texture of knotted wood as the canoes in plates 22 and 42 after Le Moyne. Though the canoe in White's original of Indians fishing is rather differently drawn with curved ends, the men paddling it are reminiscent of the paddlers in the Le Moyne compositions. White must certainly have made a number of studies of the dug-out canoe, a form of boat used everywhere in the vicinity of Roanoke Island and the shallow waters of the lagoons, whereas we are much less aware of the canoe in the more land-locked illustrations of Le Moyne. It is conceivable that here Le Moyne borrowed from White rather than vice-versa.

A much more surprising and foreign element appears in the engraving after White of the 'Idol Kivvasa' (De Bry, plate 21, here Plate 4). Harriot describes it as having a 'heade like the heades of the people of Florida' and indeed the head with its top-knot is entirely Timucuan and must have been based on a study by Le Moyne. The beads too, which hang in four strings round its neck, can be matched only in the Le Moyne illustration of the sacrifice of the first born (De Bry, plate 34), where the chief is shown wearing the same pattern of three round beads strung between each long one. If we dismiss the possibility that De Bry invented the figure (he would have had to invent the description as well) what is the explanation? Can it be that the idol in fact had some feature that seemed reminiscent to White and Harriot of the Timucua of Florida (only after they had become familiar with Le Moyne's Timucuan material) and, having a not very satisfactory study of the idol to hand, White felt justified in using a source of Le Moyne's? The theory may seem far-fetched, but perhaps no more so than the appearance of this Timucuan element in White's otherwise consistently Algonquian material.

The question of White's debt to Le Moyne in compiling his general map of southeastern North America is problematical.[5] This manuscript map, not engraved by De Bry, shows the Florida peninsula in marked contrast to the parts of modern Virginia and North Carolina which the English explored and White and Harriot mapped at first hand. Whereas the latter areas are delineated in geographic detail of the kind to be found

4. It has been suggested, in an unpublished thesis by J. R. McPhail (Department of Anthropology, University of Florida), that a number of Hans Staden's images (see p. 197 above) may lie behind some of the details of De Bry's engravings of both Le Moyne and White, for example, the barbecue scene.

5. The problem is discussed in detail by R. A. Skelton, 'The Le Moyne–De Bry map', in Hulton, *Le Moyne*, pp. 45–54.

in White's large-scale map of the Outer Banks area, the coastline to the south has more the appearance of a sea-chart with generally only the mouths of rivers and headlands shown and named in French. Clearly these features imply a French source. But if we compare this area with Le Moyne's map of Florida as engraved by De Bry there are many differences. One is the appearance on White's map of French names along the Gulf of Mexico which do not appear on Le Moyne's map, and the lack in White's map of the details around the estuary of the St Johns River (Ribault's *R. de Maie*), which the French settlers knew so well. On the other hand there are features common to both maps, for example the incorrect location of *C. des Francoys* south instead of north of the *R. des Daufins*, which indicates a common prototype from which both derived. It seems likely that at some early stage the French names and some details of geographical configuration came to White through Le Moyne but that for some reason White did not have access to other sources later available to Le Moyne. Here, even more than for his Indian material, the precise nature of White's debt to Le Moyne remains speculative.

White's North American record then is not based so entirely on his own observations as we might suppose, and the influence of Le Moyne, if not considerable, must be taken into account. Le Moyne in his turn may have derived something from White. Failing the discovery of new original material by these artists it is unlikely that we shall get much further in assessing their mutual indebtedness. But whatever they owed to one another, the images so strongly engraved after them by De Bry had a European currency for many generations. The De Bry versions of White's Algonquians long remained the accepted type of the North American Indian even when the tribe they portrayed had become extinct.

II

The transfer of
English law to Virginia
1606-50

WARREN M. BILLINGS

One consequence of England's westward enterprise in the seventeenth century was the transfer of English law and its supporting institutions to the New World. From the beginning, promoters of colonial undertakings recognized the need to provide the means of maintaining order and stability in their plantations. Without laws to govern colonial conduct these outposts of English culture would degenerate into chaos, thereby jeopardizing their chances of success. Practical considerations were not the only impulses that led the English to transplant their legal system to a new setting. Along with their other intellectual belongings, colonial Englishmen carried to America a centuries-old legal tradition founded upon the belief that the conduct of civilized society was governed by rules, and that every man, irrespective of his station, was obliged to obey the laws of the realm. That tradition sharpened the colonists' concern about the necessity of providing laws for frontier communities, because the colonies were planted in a place where, by English reckoning, no shred of civilization existed. Creating viable laws for their colonies was therefore a paramount concern for backer and settler alike.

Even though they sprang from common origins, no two groups of colonists saw the problems of law and order in the same light. The motives for erecting colonies varied with the founders, and out of that variety arose differing views of what laws were necessary and to what ends they should be applied. Moreover, the colonists drew from their knowledge of a richly diverse legal heritage only those portions which they felt best met their particular requirements. Until they had actually begun living in their new settlements no one could say what parts of the mother country's law were suitable; time for experimentation was required to discover what worked. Their judgement of what was suitable, because it often rested upon an imperfect understanding of England's legal customs, was frequently faulty. At times, their deliberate dissent from past or contemporary legal practices at home ensured that they enjoyed wider rights before the bar than did their countrymen in England. Further, because they encountered situations for which the past was no guide at all, reality compelled them to strike beyond the bounds of tradition to create new bodies of law. These reasons account for the different manifestations of English law in colonial North America, and in the end, they account for why the process of adaptation was gradual and occasionally painful.

As England's first permanent colony, Virginia provides the earliest examples of how English law was adapted to colonial needs. Between 1606 and 1618 the London Company made several false starts in its efforts to create a viable legal system for Virginia. Beyond guaranteeing the colonists the same rights as homebound Englishmen, the charter of 1606 made no provision for a set of laws for the colony.[1] It is clear, though, that both the Crown and Company officials expected the settlers to follow familiar practices because the supplemental instructions which the Londoners prepared for the colonial council obliged the members to govern 'as neere to the Common Lawe [of] England, and the equity thereof as may be'.[2] These expectations were never to be realized fully because of the troubles that plagued the colonists from the moment of their arrival in the New World. Faulty information, dissension among the leaders, disease, and famine quickly reduced the venture to a desperate struggle for survival. By 1609 the Virginia operation was in such serious difficulty that in order to salvage it, the Company's backers proposed to reorganize their undertaking. As part of the reorganization, Company officials modified the colony's government. To that end, they solicited James I for a new charter, and on 23 May 1609, the King responded favourably by issuing the letters patent.[3]

Like its predecessor, the charter of 1609 contained a guarantee of traditional legal rights, but it too lacked any specific instruction as to

1. 'Letters patent to Sir Thomas Gates and others', 10 April 1606, in P. L. Barbour (ed.), *The Jamestown Voyages under the First Charter, 1606–1609*, 2 vols, Hakluyt Society, 2nd series (Cambridge, 1969), i. 31. For an elaborate discussion of the planting of Jamestown and its early history, see W. F. Craven, *The Southern Colonies in the Seventeenth Century, 1607–1689* (Baton Rouge, La., 1949), chaps 3 and 4.

2. 'Instructions for government', 20 November 1606, in Barbour, *Jamestown Voyages*, i. 35–36.

3. A text of the charter is in S. M. Bemiss (ed.), *The Three Charters of the Virginia Company of London, with Seven Related Documents, 1606–1621*, Jamestown 350th Anniversary Historical Booklet 4 (Williamsburg, Va., 1957), pp. 27–55.

what parts of English law should be used to bring order to the struggling colony. It did however make an important change in the form of government: where the old charter had constituted the council president, who had little power independent of the council, as the colony's chief executive officer, the new instrument provided for a governor who was to be responsible for stabilizing conditions in Virginia. Accordingly, the governor received substantial powers to 'correct and punishe, pardon, governe and rule all such the subjects of us . . . as shall from time to time adventure themselves . . . thither', and he was empowered to impose martial law in instances of mutiny or rebellion. The exercise of this broad authority was subject only to limitations imposed by such laws as the Company should adopt and, in their absence, 'the lawes, statutes, government and pollicie of this our realme of England'.[4]

These revisions in the charter indicate the Londoners' awareness that traditional modes of legal administration were ill-suited to a virtually all-male frontier settlement that lacked even the rudiments of English society. That realization was prompted by a belief that an insufficiency of discipline among the settlers was a key reason for the lack of the colony's success. To remedy the defect Virginia's backers decided to reorganize the operation along military lines in the hope that martial regulation would stabilize the situation.[5] The Company therefore chose Thomas, Lord de la Ware, and Sir Thomas Gates, both experienced soldiers, to be Virginia's governor and deputy-governor. And to reinforce the military character of the new administration, Sir Thomas Dale was designated marshal for the colony. Like his counterpart in the English army, after whom his office was patterned, Dale was responsible for maintaining discipline.

Although the timely appearance of Lord de la Ware in 1610 saved the colony from extinction, Virginia proved too inhospitable a place for his delicate health, and after being sick 'upon the point to leave the world', de la Ware fled back to England, leaving the government to Sir Thomas Gates.[6] Even before he replaced de la Ware, Gates had already begun, at the Company's instruction, to institute a series of regulations subjecting the colonists to martial law.[7] Upon his arrival in the spring of 1611, Sir

---

4. Ibid., p. 52.

5. S. Diamond, 'From organization to society: Virginia in the seventeenth century', *American Journal of Sociology*, lxiii (1957–8), 457–75.

6. 'The relation of the Lord de-la-Ware, 1611', in L. G. Tyler (ed.), *Narratives of Early Virginia, 1606–1625* (New York, 1907), p. 210.

7. 'Instructions Orders and Constitutions . . . to Sir Thomas Gates . . .', in S. M. Kingsbury (ed.), *Records of the Virginia Company of London* (Washington, D.C., 1906–35), iii. 12–24.

Thomas Dale quickly added more laws and ordinances to Gates's regulations. Following their codification and publication by William Strachey in 1612, these severe laws became known as the *Lawes Divine, Morall and Martiall*.[8]

Sir Thomas Dale's rigorous execution of the *Lawes* produced the desired result: it brought order out of chaos, and during the time Dale and Gates ruled Virginia, the colony enjoyed a degree of stability that it had not previously known. Dale's code had little long-range effect upon the growth of law in the colony, however. It was possibly never intended to be a permanent solution to the problems of law and order. Then, too, the draconian character of the *Lawes*, plus the stringency with which Dale enforced them, invited loud complaints from colonists whose non-military backgrounds made them even more reluctant to accept such a system of law. In the end the colonists' grumbling bore fruit. When the London Company tried to revive its flagging fortunes in 1618, Company officials finally abandoned Dale's laws in favour of a more traditional form of legal administration.[9]

Whereas the Londoners had been uncertain about the organization of their colony in 1607, they were now committed to transforming it into an economically viable community. The success of that commitment rested upon the ability to attract to Virginia those kinds of settlers who could turn the land into profitable uses. Farmers, craftsmen, and their families would not make Virginia their permanent residence unless it took on the attributes of home. Not the least of these was of course a legal system that resembled English rather than martial law. The Company's move to supplant Dale's laws with some parts of common law marks a turning point in Virginia's legal history. It was the first positive step towards the creation of permanent legal institutions in the colony, and it stands out as one of the London Company's most enduring contributions towards the transportation of English culture to the New World.

After 1618 the colonists adapted large portions of English law to their use. In a little more than thirty years, they wrote an extensive body of law

8. D. H. Flaherty (ed.), *Lawes Divine, Morall and Martiall* (Charlottesville, Va., 1969): the introduction analyses the Company's decision to settle military discipline on the colony. See also D. B. Rutman, 'The Virginia company and its military regime', in Rutman (ed.), *The Old Dominion: Essays for Thomas Perkins Abernathy* (Charlottesville, Va., 1964), pp. 1–20. On Strachey's role in publishing the *Lawes*, see S. G. Culliford, *William Strachey, 1572–1621* (Charlottesville, Va., 1965), pp. 144–8.

9. W. F. Craven, *The Dissolution of the Virginia Company* (New York, 1932), pp. 47–81; Kingsbury, *Records of the Virginia Company*, iii. 98–109.

that touched most aspects of colonial life. In turn, these laws were enforced by a set of judicial institutions that bore an increasing resemblance to those of the homeland. And, as an indigenous jurisprudence evolved, the men charged with executing the law increased their understanding of its mysteries, as well as its uses.

The manner in which these developments happened conformed to no prearranged scheme. Rather, they occurred as colonial lawmakers responded eclectically to the requirements of an ever-growing colony. Problems of a given moment provided the impulse to borrow from the past, and once the desired legal solutions had been discovered, they became precedents for future appropriations of English law. Although the bending of their legal heritage to the colonists' needs was a haphazard process, its result was impressive. By 1650 the Virginians had erected the structural supports for the colony's entire legal system. How these foundations were laid down is revealed in an examination of the men who made colonial law, the judicial institutions which they erected, the kinds of English law which formed their models, and some of the statutes which they enacted between 1618 and mid century.

Until the dissolution of the London Company in 1624, Virginia's leaders came from the traditional ruling classes. The men whom the Company appointed to positions of leadership were well-versed in the mother country's legal customs. Possessing the advantages that accrued to individuals of their station, they had been trained at the universities or the Inns of Court, and they were close to the centres of power at court and in parliament.[1] But in spite of their endowments, these men had little effect upon the growth of Virginia law because of their inability to adjust to life in a wilderness and the uncertainties about the direction of the colony's future development. The major responsibility for the transfer of English law to the Virginia setting therefore fell to their successors.

Their replacements were men who were among the more successful of the immigrants who began to pour into Virginia in the 1630s.[2] Soon the number of colonists became so large that in 1634 the General Assembly was compelled to make a fundamental alteration in the colony's government, in order to cope with the increased demands upon Virginia's

1. B. Bailyn, 'Politics and social structure in colonial Virginia', in J. Smith (ed.), *Seventeenth-Century America: Essays in Colonial History* (Chapel Hill, N.C., 1957), pp. 92–94.

2. W. F. Craven, *White, Red, and Black: The Seventeenth Century Virginian* (Charlottesville, Va., 1971), pp. 1–39.

judicial system.[3] The assembly's creation of the county court form of local government opened the way to a further infusion of English law.

These new leaders were unlike their predecessors in that they did not come from the ruling classes. While some could claim genteel birth, most had previously engaged in mercantile or other skilled occupations. At the time they emigrated to Virginia, a majority had lived in London or Bristol, but of these many were of rural birth and as youths had gone to the cities in hopes of bettering themselves. Some had benefited from the formal education then available in England, but only a few had attended the Inns of Court or the universities.[4] The greater part had probably served apprenticeships or attended grammar schools and then rounded off their education with experience gained in the rough-and-tumble world of their respective callings. A final difference between these men and their forerunners in the Company period was their general lack of influence at court and their inexperience at ruling others.

To a degree these deficiencies were offset by other attributes which the post-Company lawmakers brought to their task. One was their belief in the law as the tie that bound themselves and their countrymen in society.[5] This presumption of the law's purpose had centuries of tradition behind it, and every generation of Englishmen learned to accept it almost from birth. Continually reinforced by the family, the community, the Church, and the State, this social value had been absorbed along with other cultural traits as part of their insinuation into the world of adult Englishmen. To men lacking in formal legal training, such a conception of the law's social purpose provided intellectual sustenance for the impulse to create law in Virginia.

Apart from the cultural exposure, seventeenth-century emigrants had formed other acquaintances with English law prior to their settlement in Virginia. Those engaged in commerce and manufacturing had had regular contacts with legal processes, since their business required a practical knowledge of how and when to use such legal documents as charter-parties, letters of attorney, indentures, and bills of exchange. Tradesmen

---

3. W. W. Hening (ed.), *The Statutes at Large: Being a Collection of all the Laws of Virginia, from the First Session of the Legislature, in the Year 1619* (Richmond, New York, and Philadelphia, 1809–23), i. 224 (hereafter cited as Hening, *Statutes at Large*).

4. L. B. Wright, *Middle Class Culture in Elizabethan England* (Chapel Hill, N.C., 1935), chap. 2; M. H. Quitt, 'From élite to aristocracy: the transformation of the Virginia ruling class' (unpublished paper read at the annual meeting of the Southern Historical Association, Houston, Texas, 1971), pp. 6–8.

5. William Fulbeck, *A direction or preparative to the study of the lawe* (London, 1600), chap. I.

and merchants also knew about moving lawsuits, taking and giving evidence, and performing the obligations of an attorney. In short, before they settled in Virginia, the novice lawmakers had been endowed with a working understanding of some parts of English law and procedure.

Their practical knowledge was supplemented by their drawing upon a great body of printed legal literature that had appeared in England since the 1480s. Books like Michael Dalton's *The Countrey Justice: Containing the Practice of Justices of the Peace out of their Sessions,* William Lambarde's *Eirenarcha: Or the Office of Justices of Peace . . .,* John Cowell's *The Interpreter: or Book Containing the Signification of Words . . .,* Henry Swineburne's *A briefe Treatise of Testaments and last Willes,* and William West's *Symboleographia, Which may be termed the Art, Description, or Image of Instruments, Covenants, Contracts, etc. . . .* enjoyed wide circulation in Virginia throughout the seventeenth century.

An investigation of the use made in Virginia of these law books, which dealt with the practical application of the law instead of its theoretical aspects, provides a key to understanding what parts of the mother country's legal traditions had the greatest influence in the colony throughout the seventeenth century. For men who lacked formal legal education, the crucial words 'the common law' signified something rather different from what they had for their predecessors. The officials who served the London Company appreciated the shades of meaning that legal scholars attached to the phrase. For them, common law could be employed to differentiate between English and continental law, as well as between the law and equity in England itself; it might also mean those laws that regulated the proceedings of King's Bench or Common Pleas; and it could distinguish the unwritten law of immemorial usage from statute law. To their successors, however, common law had a more restrictive meaning: it was perceived as *lex non scripta*. In actual practice 'unwritten law' usually meant for them that area of English law with which they had greater familiarity, local law and custom. Since the literature to which Virginians turned for guidance articulated the duties of local magistrates, it emphasized the significance of local traditions. That accent reminded the colonists of their own earlier acquaintance with English law and reinforced their notion that local tradition was the form of English law most applicable to the situation in Virginia.[6]

6. Z. Chaffee, Jr, 'Colonial courts and the common law', in D. H. Flaherty (ed.), *Essays in the History of Early American Law* (Chapel Hill, N.C., 1969), pp. 53–83; and J. Goebel, Jr, 'Kings law and local custom in seventeenth-century New England', *ibid.*, pp. 83–121.

One evidence of the impact that English local law had in Virginia is to be seen in the character of the colony's judicial institutions as they evolved through the years down to the 1650s. When the original method of entrusting the colony's management to a resident council and president proved unworkable, the London Company supplanted it with a governor and a council. For nearly a decade the governor, the councillors, and the marshal exercised all judicial authority in accordance with the broad grants of power given them by the charter of 1609 and subsequent instructions from London. The charter revisions of 1618 gave the colonists a degree of home rule through the addition of a general assembly whose purpose it was to represent the interests of the free settlers, and to assist the governor and council by adopting laws and functioning as a law court. Most of the responsibility for administering justice still resided with the chief executive and his council, but the charter did settle some powers of administration upon the four boroughs, Henrico, Charles City, James City, and Elizabeth City, which it created, and upon the proprietors of several private plantations that had been seated before 1618.

So long as Virginia's population remained small and mostly confined to the area along the lower James River basin this system was satisfactory because it could serve the needs of an infant colony. But the pattern of development soon dictated a demand for other arrangements. On the eve of the Indian massacre of 1622 the line of settlement extended up to the falls of the James and along some of its tributaries, over to the peninsula formed by the James and York rivers, and across the Chesapeake Bay to the lower Eastern Shore. The Indian attack momentarily disrupted further expansion. By the early 1620s, however, additional judicial duties were being assigned to the commanders of the private plantations, and in 1624 the General Assembly established another jurisdiction when it ordered that 'there shall be courts kept once a month in the corporations of Charles City and Elizabeth Citty'.[7] As more settlers moved to the colony, additional monthly courts were added, and by 1632 the number had risen to five.[8]

While the General Assembly's obvious intent was to extend judicial institutions to newly settled areas as fast as conditions warranted, the establishment of the monthly courts added confusion to an already chaotic situation. Dependence upon the private plantations, the monthly courts, and the governor and council, created a crazy quilt of often-overrunning

---

7. Hening, *Statutes at Large*, i. 125.   8. Ibid., pp. 168–70.

jurisdictions that slowed down the disposition of litigation. Responding to the need for change, in 1634 the assembly replaced this creaky system with the county court form of local government.[9] This action marked the beginning of a statutory distinction between provincial and local governments for Virginia. It also heralded the prospect of the future extension of a uniform mechanism for the administration of justice that would in time come to bear a striking resemblance to English local institutions.

Initially the assembly divided Virginia into eight counties, but within two years of their creation an increase in population necessitated the addition of a ninth county. In turn, that county was divided in 1637, and for more than a decade the number remained at ten. By 1652 the pressure of an increasing number of settlers caused the assembly to carve two more counties out of the Virginia wilderness.[1]

Each county court consisted of justices of the peace, a sheriff and a clerk, with deputies, and several lesser office-holders such as tithing-men and constables. The duties of these officers were similar to those of their English equivalents. Single justices collected depositions and settled petty quarrels; together at monthly sessions the full commission disposed of those criminal and civil causes that fell within the ambit of its competence. Sheriffs and their deputies policed their counties. They also collected taxes, served warrants, executed sentences upon criminal offenders, and conducted elections for the assembly. Clerks enrolled the record of judicial proceedings as well as land titles, business and commercial papers, wills, and even private correspondence.

Use of the county court as a place of record for such documents was a departure from English practice, as was the office of clerk itself. In England trial records were maintained by the *custos rotulorum*, himself a member of the bench, and his deputy, the clerk of the peace. A clerk in Virginia had no such judicial responsibility. Instead, his duty was basically that of a scrivener, and his office seems to have represented a merger of the record-keeping duties of the *custos* with those of the clerk of the peace.

9. Ibid., p. 224.
1. The eight original counties were Accomack, Charles City, Charles River, Elizabeth City, Henrico, James City, Warwick River, and Warrosquyoake. New Norfolk County was created in 1636, only to be divided into Upper and Lower Norfolk the following year. By 1637 Warrosquyoake became Nansemond, and Warwick River became Warwick. Reflecting the northeastward migration of settlers, the assembly in 1648 carved Northumberland County out of lands on the lower Potomac river basin. Surry Country, south of the James, was cut off from James City in 1652.

The bases of the county courts' power were set during the first two decades of their existence. In the courts' formative stages the assembly assigned them competence over only minor civil and criminal offences. But they soon gained the authority to regulate wide areas of colonial life. In the absence of an Anglican establishment, the courts gained control over many functions that had been within the traditional provinces of ecclesiastical jurisdictions. Principal among these were the right to probate wills, grant administrations upon a decedent's estate, care for minors, assist in the management of parochial church affairs, and punish breaches of public morals. To facilitate the dispatch of litigation and reduce the growing case-load on the governor and council, the courts were authorized in 1645 to try all cases at common law and in equity. Besides these responsibilities, they oversaw the maintenance of bridges and roads as well as a welter of other administrative matters. Occasionally they even served as courts of admiralty.

By mid century the county courts had therefore garnered a large measure of control over local affairs in Virginia. Not only were they well on the way towards being judicial entities that combined various English ecclesiastical, criminal, civil, administrative, and admiralty jurisdictions, but they were also fast becoming the keystone in Virginia's legal system. In this respect they were already close to duplicating the age-old nexus between local government and higher legal authority in England.[2]

At the provincial level a similar modification of roles can be noted in the evolution of the Council of State and the General Assembly. The growth of the county courts lessened the need for the council to involve itself in routine legal matters. Sitting as the Quarter Court, the governor and the councillors continued to try capital cases and certain civil suits. Because these actions were comparatively few in number, most of their time was spent in hearing appeals from county courts. Thus, after 1634 the Quarter Court increasingly assumed the function of a high court of appeal.

For its part the General Assembly evolved into an institution whose tasks were more purely legislative. Comprised of the governor, the councillors, and the burgesses, who represented local interests, it had been

2. W. M. Billings, 'The growth of political institutions in Virginia, 1634–1676', *William and Mary Quarterly*, 3rd series, xxxi (1974), 225–31 (hereafter cited as *WMQ*); Billings (ed.), *The Old Dominion in the Seventeenth Century: A Documentary History of Virginia, 1606–1689* (Chapel Hill, N.C., 1975), pp. 70–103; P. A. Bruce, *Institutional History of Virginia in the Seventeenth Century* (New York, 1910), i. 463–696; Craven, *The Southern Colonies in the Seventeenth Century*, pp. 169–72, 270–89.

originally conceived as an administrative, judicial, and legislative body. It seems never to have fulfilled its intended administrative purpose, and its importance as a court diminished as the county courts grew. It retained the right to act as a court of last resort down to the 1680s, but few colonists appear ever to have exercised this legal option. A threat to its existence appeared when the London Company fell and Charles I failed to provide for its continuation upon the Crown's assumption of the Virginia government in 1625. Thereafter the assembly remained in legal limbo until Charles finally legitimized it in 1639.

Despite the uncertainties of the early years, the members of the assembly moved cautiously towards the establishment of their legislative prerogatives. At its very first meeting in 1619 the assembly established a precedent for judging the qualifications of members when the burgesses ejected two of their own number whose credentials they deemed to be of questionable quality.[3] Throughout the 1620s other privileges were added. A statute of March 1623/4 freed members from arrest during sessions; another laid claim to the power to tax, and by the end of the decade some degree of control over expenditures had been established. When it ordered the colonists to arm themselves against the Indians, the assembly began to arrogate to itself the liberty to defend the colony from harm, a right which it would enlarge as the century progressed.[4] The assembly had laid down a precedent for its regulation of local affairs when it created the monthly courts. This prerogative was amplified throughout the period after 1634 when the assembly gradually enlarged the duties of the county courts. In these and other areas the burgesses slowly extended their superintending authority over colonial life, and by the 1650s there were few areas in which they did not feel competent to legislate. Of course, the right that undergirded all others was the General Assembly's power to make laws for Virginia. That right inhered in the assembly from its inception, and through its exercise the assemblymen slowly perfected the means by which usable English law could be transferred to Virginia.

How the General Assembly exercised its lawmaking power is largely obscured by the loss of its journals, but the outlines may be roughly sketched. The legislative impulse came from two sources. Representing first the London Company and then the Crown, the governor proposed laws to implement his instructions from England. As the colony's chief

---

3. John Pory, 'Proceedings of the Virginia Assembly, 1619', in Tyler, *Narratives of Early Virginia*, pp. 252–3.
4. Hening, *Statutes at Large*, i. 124–5, 127, 150.

executive, he also had the authority to suggest any legislation that would facilitate his governing of Virginia. The burgesses also possessed the right of initiation; a precedent for that prerogative had been established at their first sitting. But much more of the momentum shifted to the burgesses when the assembly began to devote its attention to the needs of a rapidly growing local government. Increasingly after 1634, burgesses were elected from the county benches, and so they possessed a knowledge of local affairs that surpassed the governor's. They were therefore in a better position to move legislation that touched county matters. Owing to the dearth of evidence, however, it is impossible to say how much of the right to initiate new laws they could claim exclusively by 1650.

There were several ways the assembly could change existing laws. Amending them was a frequent mode of alteration, but the procedure that the assembly employed was rather clumsy. Instead of writing the amendment as a separate piece of legislation, the members merely grafted the alteration on to the body of the law being amended, and then re-passed the altered version. Frequently the wording did not mesh, making the amended law difficult to interpret or enforce. Despite the difficulties which such a procedure imposed, the General Assembly continued its use until the eighteenth century. As a result confusion born of imperfectly drawn statutes persisted.

Of course the most thorough means of change was to rewrite all the laws, and down to the 1650s the assembly undertook three such revisions.[5] The first came in September 1632. More than a decade had elapsed since the assembly's founding, and in that interval the legislators had drafted a sizeable body of statutes which were, in the words of the revisal's preamble, 'found in some cases defective and inconvenient'. These deficiencies were attributable to the assemblymen's lack of legislative experience, as well as their ignorance of what sorts of laws were suitable in the wilderness. But the desire to make 'a cleerer explanation of some of them, as likewise some additions and alterations'[6] is positive evidence of the lawmakers' growing maturity. So too is the fact that the 1632 revisal represents the General Assembly's first attempt to codify existing Virginia statutes into a reasonably logical system of law. In that respect, it became the model after which later revisions were patterned.

Another ten years passed before the second revision occurred. During that span of years the tempo of legislative activity increased as the Vir-

5. Hening, *Statutes at Large*, i, pp. iv–vii.
6. Ibid., p. 179.

ginia legislature attempted to address the needs of an expanding colony.[7] Additions to the code of 1632 soon became more extensive than the code itself. By March 1642/3 the laws had to be reduced to a 'more exact method and order' to prevent 'mistakes and pretenses, which may arise from misinterpretation or ignorance of the law's [*sic*] in force'.[8]

In April 1652 the General Assembly rewrote the laws a third time. While the reasons for this revisal were similar to those of earlier times, there was in this instance a more compelling motive. Virginia had recently surrendered to Oliver Cromwell's authority, and that circumstance required certain modifications in the colony's government, since the processes of justice now had to run in the name of the commonwealth, not of the king. There was also the necessity of bringing Virginia more nearly in line with London's emerging colonial policies. In the long run, the political changes at home had comparatively little impact upon the development of Virginia law, because the revision of 1652 did nothing to reverse the trends of the preceding two decades.[9]

Even the briefest comparison of the revisals will show that this periodic process of rewriting codes taught Virginia's legislators much about the art of lawmaking. Statutes that date from the late 1640s and early 1650s regulated a wider range of human activities than did those of twenty or thirty years earlier. Their language, intent, and construction are much more explicit than is true of the older laws. While there was still considerable room for improvement, it is clear that colonial politicians were becoming competent lawmakers.

Seven categories of their handiwork may be singled out for examination: criminal law and procedure, civil law and procedure, equity, land law, labour law, church law, and defence legislation. These various laws show how the colonists perceived their legal heritage, and they serve as a

7. Much of the legislation that the General Assembly passed between September 1632 and March 1642/3 is now missing, and parts were unavailable in the early nineteenth century when William Waller Hening did his edition of the statutes. See 'Acts of the General Assembly, 6 Jan., 1639/40', *WMQ*, 2nd series, iv (1924), 16–35, 145–62; Jon Kukla (ed.), 'Nine acts of the Grand Assembly of Virginia, 1641' (unpublished typescript, Virginia State Library, Richmond), pp. 1–7; 'The Virginia Assembly of 1641–42. A list of Members and some of the Acts', *Virginia Magazine of History and Biography*, ix (1901–2), 50–59 (hereafter cited as *VMHB*). I am indebted to Jon Kukla for supplying me with a copy of his edition of the acts of January, 1640/1 (hereafter cited as Kukla, 'Nine acts').

8. Hening, *Statutes at Large*, i. 239–40.

9. Ibid., pp. 282–362; 'Acts, orders and resolutions of the General Assembly of Virginia at the sessions of March, 1643–46', *VMHB*, xxiii (1915), 223–55; W. M. Billings (ed.), 'Some acts not in Hening's *Statutes*: The acts of assembly, April 1652, November 1652, and July 1653', ibid. lxxxiii (1975), 22–72.

demonstration of the manner in which the lawmakers tried to translate those perceptions into reality. The statutes also reveal how the Virginians acquired legislative skills and how they sometimes struck out beyond the bounds of tradition to create new bodies of law.

Down to 1652 Virginia had no separate criminal code that was distinct from the rest of the colony's statute law, although there were laws that proscribed certain types of criminal behaviour. The number of such acts was small in comparison to those concerning other aspects of colonial life. There were no statutes to provide for the detection, trial, and punishment of felons. Nor were there many written rules to govern the procedure in criminal trials. The absence of such statutes does not mean that traditional felonies like treason, murder, larceny, or rape went unpunished, or that Virginians did not acknowledge the concept of due process. Instead it means that the colonists had made a wholesale appropriation of English criminal law. Thus, the criminal statutes that appear on the books after 1618 are indications of where colonial law was at variance with that of the homeland.

In some instances the assembly created new categories of crimes, reduced felonies to lesser offences, modified the intent of English criminal statutes to fit novel conditions, or altered the place where some crimes might be tried. For example, English criminal law did not comprehend the presence of Englishmen in the midst of Indians. In consequence, there were no precedents to guide the establishment of rules of conduct between the settlers and the Indians. However, because the natives posed a danger to the colony's survival, the assembly at one time or another declared criminal such practices as trading without special licence, selling arms and ammunition, casually killing Indians, or keeping Indian children.[1]

The colonial treatment of the crime of stealing and killing hogs illustrates how some acts were raised to felonies and then reduced to petty crimes. A law of February 1637 declared hog-stealing and 'killinge ould hoggs' capital offences. Reasoning that the 'said offences doe deserve exemplary punishment, but not soe high a nature', the assembly repealed that statute in January 1641, replacing it with one that made killing a tame hog by anyone other than its owner a felony.[2] That provision was

1. Tyler, *Narratives of Early Virginia*, pp. 269–70; Hening, *Statutes at Large*, i. 126, 167, 219, 255–6; 'Acts of assembly, 1641–42', *VMHB*, ix. 53–54; 'Acts of assembly, 1643–1646', ibid. xxiii. 236; Billings, 'Acts not in Hening's *Statutes*', ibid. lxxxiii. 64–65; 'Acts of assembly, 1639/40', *WMQ*, 2nd series, iv. 150.

2. No text of the act of February 1636/7 is now extant, but the statute of January 1640/1 proves its existence. See Kukla, 'Nine acts', p. 6.

retained in the revisal of March 1643, but it was eventually repealed. By 1647 both offences had been reduced to minor breaches of the peace, the reduction probably having resulted from lessening fears about possible food shortages.[3]

On other occasions, attempts to resolve situations that were peculiar to Virginia led to the alteration of English criminal statutes to fit a particular colonial need. English vagrancy and bigamy laws are good illustrations of that practice. As the number of servants increased, the incidence of runaway bondsmen became more frequent. The assemblymen tried to formulate a remedy for the problem when they rewrote the laws on servants in March 1643. To punish repeated offenders the General Assembly made them liable to the statute of incorrigible rogues. Passed by Parliament in the first year of James I's reign, that law authorized local authorities to declare habitual vagabonds, beggars, or other vagrants recidivous persons, to identify them as such by branding them on the shoulder with the letter *R*, and to send them back to their home parishes. If such an individual were subsequently arrested for vagrancy, he was automatically guilty of a felony offence.[4] The purpose of the English statute was the restraint of vagrants, not servants. Nevertheless, its provisions seemed serviceable to the Virginians, and they borrowed them intact. Their application of the statute changed its intent altogether, and so it became necessary to annex their modification of it to a general law that defined servants' conduct.

A decade later the assembly extended English bigamy statutes to Virginia. The timing of that extension suggests that the impetus may have come from the new parliamentary regime, but whatever the reason, the fact that bigamy cases would lie in secular courts was also a departure from tradition, thereby requiring a statutory recognition of the change.[5] This manoeuvre is but one of many examples of how the General Assembly used its legislative authority to blend complex Old World jurisdictions into a single system of local and appellate courts. It also represents the method by which colonial court procedures were delineated in criminal trials.

Historically English criminal law began to emerge in the thirteenth

---

3. Hening, *Statutes at Large*, i. 294, 350–1.

4. Ibid., pp. 254–5; *The compleat justice, being an exact and compendious collection out of such as have treated of the office of justices of the peace* . . . (7th edn, London, 1661), p. 284.

5. Michael Dalton, *The countrey justice: containing the practice of justices of the peace out of their sessions* (12th edn, London, 1677), p. 388 (hereafter cited as Dalton, *Countrey justice*); Billings, 'Acts not in Hening's *Statutes*', *VMHB*, lxxxiii. 32.

century, and in the four hundred years that preceded the founding of Virginia it slowly evolved into a separate branch of law that had its own rules and procedures. Its fundamental purpose was the restraint of those forms of human activity that threatened the peace and order of the kingdom. Gradually such acts were given statutory definition; by the 1600s a considerable number of criminal statutes was already in existence. It was to these laws that the Virginians turned for guidance in creating their own criminal law.[6]

In a similar fashion, the manner in which the state proceeded against a criminal suspect had become standardized by the seventeenth century. Before he could be punished for an offence, the suspect had to be arrested, examined, indicted, tried, convicted, and sentenced. Each of these steps constituted due process of law, but that concept meant something quite different to seventeenth-century Englishmen than it now does. An arrest was made for 'some just cause, or some lawful and just suspition, at the least', but nothing obliged the arresting officer to inform his prisoner of a right to silence, as American law now commands.[7] The suspect could not have an attorney present during his examination by the magistrate, and except for trial by jury in felony cases, he had few rights at the trial itself.

Prior to trial the accused was kept in close confinement. He did not see the evidence against him before standing trial, and when it was introduced, he had to defend himself without benefit of counsel. No rules of evidence, in the modern sense, were applied to the introduction of pertinent material. Defendants did not confront their accusers, and the confessions of accomplices or co-defendants were admitted as particularly cogent evidence. Generally, a defendant could not call witnesses in his own behalf. If he did, he had no means of compelling their attendance at court or of knowing to what they would testify. In short, the odds were against a defendant. Thus the purpose of a trial was to protect society against wrongdoers, not necessarily to guard against the infringement of an individual's rights by the State.[8]

Such were the ideas about criminal law that the English brought to Virginia. Unlike their counterparts in Massachusetts Bay, Virginia legislators evinced little concern about adding to or improving upon this

---

6. Theodore F. T. Plucknett, *A Concise History of the Common Law* (5th edn, London, 1956), pp. 59–88.

7. Dalton, *Countrey justice*, p. 467.

8. Sir James Fitz James Stephen, *History of the Criminal Law* (London, 1883), i. 350.

facet of their legal birthright. For them, defining due process did not carry the same urgency as it did for the puritan saints. Consequently, they never specified the rights belonging to criminal defendants. They were content instead to borrow directly from English practice.

From the colony's earliest days the governor and council, sitting in quarterly sessions, held the power to adjudicate all criminal matters. The Quarter Court patterned trial by jury, which had been extended to Virginia in the charter of 1606, and other procedures after the usages of English justices of the peace and the judges of king's bench. Guides to these practices were readily available in Dalton's *Countrey justice*, and William Stanford's *Pleas of Crown* or one of its many epitomes.[9] In fact, such guidebooks were the colonists' chief sources of knowledge about traditional criminal law.

Significant variations with the past occurred following the General Assembly's creation of the county court system. After 1634 the assembly assigned the trial of all non-capital offences to the county jurisdictions. By the middle of the century local courts tried a number of criminal acts that ranged from bastard bearing to petty thievery.[1] Indeed, by virtue of an act passed as part of the 1652 revisal, local courts even got limited jurisdiction in felony cases, but that was subsequently repealed.[2]

As the scope of local authority in criminal causes enlarged, certain of its procedures were fixed by statute. One was the requirement that county courts impanel grand juries 'to enquire of the breaches of all penal laws and other crimes and misdemeanors'. Another was the extension of jury trials to anyone who wished them.[3] The assembly probably passed the grand jury statute in response to two specific needs. Until its passage, local justices were passive actors in the detection and arraignment of defendants. Before they could try wrongdoers, they had to rely upon private citizens and other officials to present evidence of their fellow colonists' misdeeds. But the grand juries met at regular intervals for the express purpose of investigating possible criminal violations. Upon discovering such occurrences, they were empowered to initiate charges against defendants and to deliver their presentments to the county courts. By this device, the need for a prosecuting attorney to draw up an

9. Dalton, *Countrey justice*, pp. 406–16, 529–43.
1. Hening, *Statutes at Large*, i. 126, 167, 227, 240, 310.
2. Billings, 'Acts not in Hening's *Statutes*', *VMHB*, lxxxiii. 71; Hening, *Statutes at Large*, pp. 397–8.
3. Ibid., pp. 397–8.

indictment was circumvented, thus sparing the colonists the difficulties arising from the lack of trained lawyers in the colony.[4]

While the trial-by-jury statute may be seen as an improvement upon tradition, its effects were minimal. Most cases that came to trial after the act's passage in November 1645 continued to be judged without juries. An explanation for this phenomenon lies in the text of the act itself, as well as in the nature of the offences that the courts heard. The statute required anyone who used juries to pay their expenses. Servants charged with fornication or running away from their service could not afford to pay jurors. Similarly, freemen accused of swearing or drunkenness were unwilling to incur the costs of jury trials in such minor matters. In the minds of the Virginians, therefore, a trial by jury should be reserved for instances of serious crimes like murder or larceny, which rarely occurred, or for those cases that involved the possible loss of property through civil litigation.

When justices of the peace tried criminal cases, they were bound to follow no formal rules, save what they might have gleaned from a manual or their own common sense. If the defendant confessed his act, they immediately passed judgement, and the case was closed. If he did not, the judges called in witnesses or perused sworn depositions that had been taken before the court convened. Then, on the basis of the facts presented to them, the magistrates made their decision and sentenced the guilty to receive punishment at the hands of the sheriff. Punishment varied with the severity of the crime and the judges' whim, although some offences carried specific penalties. Bastard bearing, for example, required whipping the mother and fining the father. The only formality to the whole proceeding was the taking of testimony upon oath and enrolling the trial in the county court records.[5]

---

4. Although the result was the same, an indictment and a grand jury presentment were different means of initiating trial proceedings. An indictment is a specification of charges that is drawn up by a prosecuting attorney and presented to a grand jury along with supporting evidence. If the jurors find that the evidence is sufficient to warrant the allegations, they return a true bill, and the case proceeds to trial. A presentment is a statement of charges drawn up and presented to the court by the grand jurors themselves. Upon receiving the presentment, the court makes a determination as to the truth of the matters alleged. See John Cowell, *A law dictionary: or the interpreter of words and terms used either in the common or statute laws of Great Britain* (London, 1727; 1st edn, Cambridge, 1607), under 'indictment' and 'presentment'.

5. Northumberland County order book, 1650–2, f. 43; Lower Norfolk County order book, 1637–46 (transcript), ff. 30–31, 100–1, 120, 180. These and all other citations are to microfilm copies of Virginia county court records that are housed in the Virginia State Library, Richmond.

These arrangements favoured the community and its leaders over the individual and the commoner, and they were susceptible to abuse. In more recent centuries, recognition of these abuses has resulted in statutory assurance of the individual's right to due process. But the earliest Virginians seem to have been relatively unconcerned about a written guarantee of that right. Perhaps that was so because the colonists' way so closely resembled what had been done at home and it therefore seemed comfortable to them, or possibly the lack of concern resulted from a conviction that the magistrates discharged their duties well and with equanimity. But the likeliest explanation is that Virginia was comparatively free of crimes against person and property. Most miscreants simply breached the colony's standards of public morality. Even these violations of the peace were fairly infrequent when they are compared to the great volume of civil suits brought in colonial courts.[6]

As surviving county court records show, instead of continually deciding upon the guilt or innocence of suspected criminals, magistrates spent much of their time engaged in such chores as hearing debt suits, probating wills, passing upon the validity of land titles, and caring for minor children. These activities reveal that preserving 'the Amity, Confidence and Quiet that is between men' required more than the punishment of wickedness and vice, for in fact most of the disputes between colonists were civil, not criminal, in nature.[7] Given that circumstance, Virginia legislators were more determined to devise methods of disposing of civil suits than they were to perfect techniques for the suppression of crime. Not unexpectedly, then, they invested considerable time in providing local and provincial courts with the means of handling an immense variety of such litigation.

The civil side of English law was vast and complex. Actually it consisted of several sub-systems of law that often overlapped and sometimes competed with one another. In the centuries that preceded Virginia's settlement, English judges—whom Sir William Blackstone once described as 'the depositary [*sic*] of the laws; the living oracles, who must decide in all cases of doubt, ... who are bound by oath to decide according to the law of the land'[8]—devised the customs, rules, and procedures

---

6. Lower Norfolk County order book, 1637–46, *passim*; Lower Norfolk County order book, 1632–40, *passim*; Northampton County order book, 1640–5, *passim*.

7. Dalton, *Countrey justice*, p. 9.

8. Sir William Blackstone, *Commentaries on the laws of England* (5th edn, Dublin, 1795; referred to hereafter as Blackstone, *Commentaries*), i. 69.

that became the common law. Taken in this sense common law was judge-made law, which the justices refined through decisions rendered in innumerable cases that were transmitted to succeeding generations in the form of case reports. The ancient maxim *stare decisis* was the guiding principle, although judges were never hidebound in their adherence to precedents. Changing times and differing needs sometimes caused them to alter past practices to suit new conditions.

By the opening of the seventeenth century this slow evolutionary process had already given rise to an exceedingly intricate and complicated system of law. Its supporting structures, the grand jury, jury, writs, summonses, written pleadings, and oral testimony, bespoke some of that complexity. Moreover, the use of Latin in written processes and the reporting of cases in law French all but obscured the processes of justice from everyone save judges and lawyers. And, as evidenced by the puritan attempts at law reform during the Civil War period, obtaining justice in a common-law court was slow and difficult.

Common law, the king's law, did not encompass the whole of the English legal landscape. There were other customs and courts that covered local conditions, and there were other more formal legal systems. Equity, canon law, the law merchant, and Admiralty law all rivalled common law at one time or another, although most had been subordinated to it by the seventeenth century. In brief, English law was pluralistic and was without a single focus.

It was to this rich and varied tradition that Virginians turned for guidance, and as they fashioned their own version of their heritage, they made significant modifications. They transferred many of the basic structures more or less intact, but their tendency was to simplify. The manner in which they erected courts provides one example. In England, there was a myriad of jurisdictions, each with its own court, but in Virginia jurisdiction lay in only one system of inferior and appellate courts. The duties and obligations of those courts were fixed by statute, and thus their powers were matters of written law rather than the accretions of long-term usage.

Another illustration is provided by the colonial treatment of equity. Unlike common law, equity had jurisdiction over persons, not things. It could compel someone to perform or to abstain from an act which he had been, or might be, doing, and could then punish him if he did not obey. No such coercive authority inhered in common law; it could only enumerate rights or responsibilities. Equity came into existence to fill this gap. It had grown up in the Middle Ages, and it derived from the chancellor's power to act as the king's conscience. As such, the chancellor had authority to dispense with the rules and make a determination of the issues on the basis of what was fair and just. Eventually the exercise of this prerogative led to the emergence of chancery courts, whose own rules and procedures differed from their common-law counterparts. Their rules lacked the fixity of common law, although their *ad hoc* character had diminished by the seventeenth century. Procedurally, equity's development was shaped by the fact that medieval chancellors were churchmen. Their ecclesiastical background disposed them to follow the legalisms of the church which led to an intrusion of Roman law and practice. For example, juries were noticeably absent from equity proceedings.[9]

Despite the procedural differences and the rivalries that existed between these two species of English law, they complemented one another. Through its battery of remedies, such as an injunction, equity could supply relief where none was available at common law. This was what made it attractive to the Virginians. And while the controversy over equity's place in the mother country's legal system raged at home, the colonists assigned both common law and equity jurisdictions to the county courts. The enabling statute outlined a simple method by which a case might be removed from common law to equity. All a defendant had to do was file a petition with the justices before his case went to trial, requesting that it be heard in equity. If the court granted the request, it resolved itself into a chancery court, and its determination was final. If the judges found no just reason for the petition, the case was remitted back to common law.[1]

Aside from its utility, equity's informality appealed to colonial lawmakers because it comported with their goal of stripping the complexities of court procedures to bare essentials. That objective arose from the necessity for rendering judicial processes intelligible to men who lacked formal legal training. English replaced Latin as the language of court. Writs, summonses, and pleadings all found their way into colonial procedure, but with a difference: they were streamlined and divested of their jargon. Pleadings, for example, were seldom more than a few headings, or the merest outline of an argument.[2]

---

9. L. M. Friedman, *A History of American Law* (New York, 1973), pp. 17–23; Plucknett, *Concise History of the Common Law*, pp. 673–702.

1. Hening, *Statutes at Large*, i. 303–4.

2. Ibid., pp. 174, 256–7, 270–2, 306, 345–6.

At the local level procedure was simpler still. In debt litigation the debtor merely acknowledged his obligation, and the suit ended with a judgement and an order for execution to pass. For other matters plaintiffs usually commenced their actions by petition, but they seldom entered pleadings of any sort. Evidence was presented in sworn depositions or oral testimony. Because few lawyers settled in Virginia before 1650, parties to a suit either handled it themselves or left it to an attorney.[3] In fact, litigants frequently made no appearance at court, preferring to let their attorney handle matters. For their part, the justices seemed content to hear whatever relevant material the contending parties presented, without regard to the niceties and regularity of traditional common law procedure. Their first objective seems to have been to ensure speedy, inexpensive access to justice with a minimum of delay.[4]

Land and labour were two key elements in the transformation of Virginia from a quasi-military outpost into a settled community. The laws that governed these two species of property represent one more example of colonial attempts to take from the past what was useful and apply it to new or different problems. Virginia land law never reached the complexities of its English counterpart. Over the centuries the English laws of real property spun out a fine web of rules defining rights, tenures, descents, and a welter of other matters that related to the ownership of land. The reason for the development of such a complicated body of law is simple enough. In the island kingdom land was a scarce and precious commodity. Moreover, it was the immemorial badge of social distinction, and its possession was limited to a proportion of English families. Land law had developed to ensure that they always retained ownership.

Conditions in Virginia were different. Land was everywhere abundant; quite literally, it was there for the taking. Still, some means for its acquisition, possession, and transfer had to be perfected, and by the 1650s the basic outlines of colonial property law had been drawn. Theoretically all land belonged to the King, and the settlers were his tenants. This idea, which sprang from medieval soil, undergirded the whole concept of land

3. 'Lawyer' and 'attorney' were not synonymous terms in the seventeenth-century usage. 'Lawyer' denoted someone who had professional training, whereas an 'attorney' could be any person who represented the interest of another in a judicial proceeding. Failure to distinguish between the different uses of the two words has led to some misunderstanding about a statute adopted in 1645 that expelled 'mercenary attornies' from Virginia. Legal scholars have interpreted the act as being directed against lawyers. It was not, nor did it bar all attornies, only those that the act defined as 'mercenary'. See Hening, *Statutes at Large*, i. 302, and Friedman, *History of American Law*, p. 81.

4. Lower Norfolk County order book, 1637–46, f. 117.

tenures in English law. Despite its transfer to Virginia, it had little effect there, even though the Crown tried to enforce it through the collection of quitrents. Laws calling for the collection of such fees went on the books at an early date, but colonists rarely paid them. In the end, this and other archaic tenures failed for the lack of institutional buttresses and the constraints imposed by an island kingdom. Released from such restraining influences, the Virginians borrowed a few traditional tenures such as freehold and leasehold.[5]

For most of the seventeenth century the fifty-acre headright, which had been introduced as an inducement to settlement by the London Company in 1617, was the basic means of acquiring a title to land. Any settler who could prove that he had bought his own or someone else's way to Virginia could claim a headright. All he had to do was file a certificate testifying that he had transported himself or servants, and the governor issued a patent, or deed, for the requisite amount of acreage. A copy of the patent was recorded in the secretary of the colony's office for safety's sake and in order to keep an account of what land had been distributed.

After 1634 the task of certifying land claims fell to the county courts, and they issued the certificates that initiated the acquisition process. The courts also became the place of record for deeds and all other transactions relating to the land titles.[6] In fact, one apparent consideration which led the assembly to create the county court system in the first place was its desire to establish the colonists' clear and unquestioned right to their land. Registering a deed in the county court records proved its existence, thereby guaranteeing ownership and establishing precedence over any claim that was unrecorded.[7]

Before a settler received his patent, he had to present a survey of his tract to the secretary, along with the other supporting documents that validated his claim. To provide the surveys, the colony employed a number of surveyors, the first of whom arrived in Virginia as early as 1616. By the 1630s the office of surveyor-general had been established, with the incumbent responsible for appointing and overseeing local surveyors. Recognizing that prompt and accurate surveys could reduce

5. 'Acts of assembly, 6 Jan. 1639/40', *WMQ*, 2nd series, iv. 153–5; Beverley W. Bond, Jr, *The Quit-Rent System in the American Colonies* (New Haven, Conn., 1919), pp. 221–3; P. A. Bruce, *Economic History of Virginia in the Seventeenth Century* (New York, 1895), i. 487–572.

6. Bruce, *Economic History of Virginia, passim*; Northampton County order book, 1632–40, *passim*. An excellent study of land use is John F. Fausz, 'Patterns of settlement in the James river basin, 1607–1642' (unpublished M.A. thesis, College of William and Mary, 1971).

7. 'Acts of assembly, 6 Jan. 1639/40', *WMQ*, 2nd series, iv (1924), 149–50.

litigation arising from confusion over boundaries, the General Assembly as early as 1624 took steps to require every colonist to have his land surveyed. The statute became the precedent for future legislation governing surveys and surveyors. Despite these efforts, disputes arose. Perhaps they were inevitable because the seventeenth-century surveyor's equipment was untrustworthy, and his methods were primitive.[8]

Possession of land implies the right to deed it over to someone else, but few colonists appreciated the intricacies of conveyancing. Lacking such expertise, they drew upon common sense and their mercantile experience. Their simplest device for transferring a title was for a patentee to endorse his headright to a second party in the presence of witnesses.[9] Another means of conveyance was a modified version of the English deed form known as bargain and sale. Bargain and sale was a contract between two parties, in which, for a monetary consideration, the seller agreed to give the buyer land or other property. Its application in the market place probably accounts for the colonists' familiarity with the form.[1] Land was also rented, and of course it passed to succeeding generations by last will and testament.[2] By whatever means conveyances were made, a record of the transaction was filed with the county courts. Performing this vital record-keeping function and settling litigation involving land were among the more important responsibilities that the General Assembly assigned to the courts in the years after 1634.

So too was their control over labour. The chronic demand for labour was a characteristic of the Virginia scene throughout the entire seventeenth century. Over the course of the colony's first one hundred years Virginians relied upon indentured servitude and chattel slavery. The story of both these institutions is too well known to be recounted here. Suffice it to say that while both had Old World antecedents, they represent the building of unique institutions in response to New World situations for which few known precedents existed.[3] Although some form

8. Bruce, *Economic History of Virginia*, p. 532; Daphne S. Gentry (ed.), *Virginia Land Office Inventory* (Richmond, Va., n.d.), p. xii; Hening, *Statutes at Large*, i. 125, 173, 262–3, 365; Fausz, 'Patterns of settlement in the James river basin', pp. 18–20.

9. *Virginia Colonial Land Patent Book*, i, pt i, 1623–43, ff. 461–2 (microfilm copy, Virginia State Library, Richmond).

1. W. West, *Symboleographia* (London, 1590), pt i, bk ii, section 436; Northampton County order book, 1642–5, f. 52.

2. Northampton County order book, 1642–5, ff. 146–7.

3. The literature on servitude and slavery is enormous. For example, see Bruce, *Economic History of Virginia*, i. 572–634; ii. 1–57; Abbot E. Smith, *Colonists in Bondage: White Servitude and Convict Labor in America, 1607–1776* (Chapel Hill, N.C., 1947); Edmund S. Morgan,

of chattel slavery existed in the colony's early years, indentured servitude was the mainstay of the labour system. Beginning in 1619 the drafting of servant law became one of the main tasks of virtually every General Assembly that met down to mid-century.[4]

The law of servants fell into several categories. Some parts of it defined the contractual rights of both master and servant. Others forbade the servant to marry without the master's consent and punished him if he stole, ran off, or fornicated. Still others used the power of the colonial government to assist masters in restraining the servant's supposed vicious tendencies. On the whole these statutes were punitive, harsh, and heavily weighted in favour of the master and the community. That was in part because of the servant's value as a highly prized commodity. But it also resulted from a fear that arose out of the fact that bondsmen accounted for perhaps as much as half of the colony's population. Ever an unruly and potentially dangerous lot, this peculiar class of property posed a genuine menace to the peace and security of local communities.[5]

Enforcing these laws, along with the general oversight of labourers, fell to the county courts. Like any other property, servants were regularly bought and sold; these transactions were entered in the court records, as were indentures and releases from servitude. Local justices fixed the ages of youngsters put into service, and they listened to complaints from bondsmen and employers alike. Whenever masters proved incapable of maintaining discipline, the courts stepped in and imposed order. In these and other matters, local jurisdictions acted in accordance with the authority assigned to them by the General Assembly.[6]

Finally, those laws that governed the Church and defence are noteworthy because in each instance the newness of the colonial experience caused a sharp break with past legal practices. From the beginning, the cure of souls received attention from founder and colonist alike. An expressed aim for planting the colony was 'to preach and baptize into *Christian Religion,* and by propagation of the Gospell, to recover out of the Armes of

American Slavery, American Freedom: The Ordeal of Colonial Virginia (New York, 1975); Winthrop D. Jordan, *White over Black: American Attitudes towards the Negro, 1550–1812* (Chapel Hill, N.C., 1968), pp. 3–98.

4. W. F. Craven, 'Twenty negroes to Jamestown in 1619', *Virginia Quarterly Review,* xlvii (1971), 416–20; A. T. Vaughan, 'Blacks in Virginia: a note on the first decade', *WMQ,* 3rd series, xxix (1972), 469–78; Tyler, *Narratives of Early Virginia,* p. 273.

5. Hening, *Statutes at Large,* i. 252–5, 257, 274–5; Kukla, 'Nine acts', p. 5; Billings, 'Acts not in Hening's *Statutes', VMHB,* lxxxiii. 37–39, 41, 47.

6. Northampton County order book, 1640–5, ff. 94, 125, 137; Lower Norfolk County order book, 1646–51, f. 120.

the Divell, a number of poore and miserable soules, wrapt up unto death, in an almost *invincible ignorance*', and to further the Church of England.[7] Apart from the spiritual sustenance that it afforded, the church could be a vital force for stability in a frontier setting. Its teachings and its organization could reinforce traditional social and religious values. The colonists recognized these facts, and from an early date they tried to create the institutional foundations that would encourage the transfer of the Anglican establishment to Virginia. Indeed the location of laws governing church affairs at the beginning of the revisions of 1632, 1642/3, and 1652 signifies the weight that the law-makers ascribed to the necessity of creating a well-ordered religious establishment.[8]

It was already apparent by 1652, however, that these hopes were not to be realized fully. There was no bishop for Virginia; it remained under the jurisdiction of the Bishop of London until the Revolution. In fact, few clergymen of any sort could be induced to leave their livings for a life in the wilderness; and until the founding of the College of William and Mary in 1693, the colony had no school to train settlers who aspired to the priesthood. Moreover, there were no church courts to regulate family relations, to prosecute offences against public morals, or to probate wills.

Quite simply, the failure of the institutional church to develop led the laity and secular authorities to assume many ecclesiastical functions. Governors inducted ministers, whenever willing clergymen could be found, while the General Assembly drew parish boundaries and vested the county courts with the prosecutorial and administrative duties of church courts. Thus canon law with its Roman antecedents was not to enjoy in Virginia even the limited coexistence with common law it did in England. Furthermore, the parish vestry, which traditionally concerned itself with poor relief, became the instrument of control in local parishes. Laymen recruited rectors, voted parish taxes, built churches, presented offenders to the county courts, and generally watched over routine parochial affairs. In the long run, such developments opened the way to a greater secularization of life in Virginia and pointed towards the eventual separation of Church and State in fact and in law.

The General Assembly's constant attention to defence reflected anxiety about a real threat to the colonists' security. At no time before 1652 were

---

7. Billings, *The Old Dominion in the Seventeenth Century*, p. 14.
8. Hening, *Statutes at Large*, i. 122–4, 180–5, 240–3; Billings, 'Acts not in Hening's *Statutes*', *VMHB*, lxxxiii. 31–32.

the settlers able to move decisively against their native enemy. The Indian attack of 1622 nearly wiped out the settlements, and even though Opechancanough's men failed in that objective, they touched off a decade of war. An uneasy truce ensued, but the mounting pressure of increased English immigration ensured that it would be temporary. A second war broke out in 1644, and although the English defeated the Indians, victory came at a high price. Despite the magnitude of their losses, the natives remained a potent force with which to reckon. Another thirty years would pass before the colonists enjoyed the advantages that ultimately enabled them to remove forever what they saw as 'the Indian menace'.[9]

That lawmakers should in these circumstances write legislation to build forts, to maintain local militias, and to secure the stores of war is obvious enough. What is less apparent, however, is the effect that such acts had upon traditional values. The necessity of putting the colony on a martial footing to forestall the threat of attack changed attitudes to the possession and use of small arms. According to English laws in force at the beginning of the seventeenth century, guns were forbidden to anyone who owned less than £100 in lands, leases, or offices. Practically speaking, that restriction prevented most law-abiding citizens from owning firearms. But the situation was different in Virginia. Early on, Virginia-bound immigrants were admonished to take with them a musket, a 'bandaleere', 'twentie pound of Powder, and Sixtie pound of shot or lead'. The assembly required all free, male colonists to own a gun and a store of powder, or face a fine for their contempt of the law. In effect, such legislation put weapons in the household of every settler.[1]

The consequences of such a step were wide-ranging. No one can speak with assurance about the actual number of guns that Virginians owned at any one time in the seventeenth century, but whereas their use was confined to a small number of people in England, it was spread across the whole spectrum of Virginia society. Despite laws to the contrary, guns could be obtained by servants, slaves, or Indians, thereby making all three more dangerous. In times of stress, such as the expulsion of Sir John Harvey in 1635 or Bacon's Rebellion in 1676, it was all too easy for someone to pick up his gun and vent his feelings in a most violent way.

9. Craven, *White, Red and Black*, pp. 39–72.
1. Hening, *Statutes at Large*, i. 127, 150, 173, 174, 175, 263, 293–4, 315, 320, 326–7; 'Acts of assembly, March 1643–1646', *VMHB*, xxiii. 235; Billings, *The Old Dominion in the Seventeenth Century*, p. 16.

Besides their protective value and their potential for harm, firearms were effective devices for securing food. Quickly they came to be viewed as just another implement in the settler's arsenal of tools to tame the wilderness. Herein lies the origin of a unique American character trait, a fiercely stubborn attachment to gun ownership that now borders on the irrational.

Taken as a whole, the foregoing examples of the types of acts that the General Assembly passed between 1618 and 1652 reveal many of the colonial assumptions about the purposes of law in a frontier society. First of all, the willingness to enact wide-ranging legislation suggests a general belief that every colonist should be held answerable to an acceptable standard of moral, personal, and public behaviour. From that notion followed the idea that legislators were empowered to regulate the affairs of men at every level of existence. Indeed, failure to exercise this obligation was seen as a dereliction of a magistrate's solemn duty. In this respect the Virginians remained true to their heritage, for these beliefs were merely extensions of English thought. On a more practical plane, the statutes evidence concern for social imperatives that were especially poignant at times when sheer survival in the Virginia wilds was problematical.

The dependence upon statute law as the mechanism for resolving the problems of settlement points to another important premise made by colonial legislators: laws should be written down. There was to be no accumulation of case law before 1650. Statute, not the accretion of judicial opinion, became the tool with which some parts of English law were fashioned for use in Virginia.

On the face of it, this reliance upon statute seems curious in light of the Virginians' lack of formal legal education, but is explained by several facts. The new bodies of law, such as those on servants, that resulted from the peculiarities of the New World, all required statutory definition. Written laws were also essential because colonial magistrates maintained only an informal acquaintance with the motherland's legal customs, as well as their own. For the judges' edification the assembly required every clerk of court to keep on record a copy of all Virginia statutes. Without these as guides, members of the benches could not have administered justice uniformly throughout the colony. Beyond that, all of the modifications of English law had to be set down in writing so that there would be no mistaking what was and what was not law in Virginia.

The latter observation points towards another possible explanation.

Putting colonial law into statute was an attempt to relate it to English law. Throughout the colonial period the view prevailed that English law had no force in Virginia unless it specifically mentioned the colony by name. But the matter was far from settled by the middle of the seventeenth century. In England the closest thing to settled law on this point was the decision rendered in *Calvin's Case* in the year 1608. The judges who heard the case declared that any Scot born after James I's accession to the English throne was not an alien, and could therefore inherit land like any English subject.[2] What appeared to have relevance for Virginia was that portion of the opinion explaining how a monarch could acquire lands outside his kingdom. He might conquer the land of another Christian prince, in which case the laws of the land would prevail until the new king changed them. If he seized them from a heathen, the act of conquest automatically abrogated local law, and the territory immediately passed under royal jurisdiction. Also, lands might, as in James's case, devolve upon the king in right of descent. In that event, only Parliament could alter the law.[3]

The extent to which the doctrines set forth in *Calvin's Case* applied to Virginia was uncertain. Clearly Virginia had not come into the Crown's possession through any of the ways described in the opinion, although Englishmen long treated it as territory seized from infidels.[4] How many men who sat in the General Assembly prior to 1650 actually knew of *Calvin's Case* cannot be proven. At the very least, some of them recognized the uncertainties arising from the lack of clear-cut opinion. As their actions make manifest, they tried to clear the haze by means of the employment of statute. As long as they remained 'as near as may be to the laws of England', and for as long as no one inquired very deeply into the nature of the nexus, the matter stood in abeyance. In the end the issue was not resolved before 1776, and the colonists made the best of the situation by exploiting it to their own advantage.[5]

2. The opinion is reported in Sir Edward Coke, *The reports of Sir Edward Coke, knt. late lord chief justice of England and one of his Majesties council of state* . . . (London, 1658), pp. 583–613.

3. For a discussion of the application of *Calvin's Case* to colonial America, see George Dargo, *Roots of the Republic, a New Perspective on Early American Constitutionalism* (New York, 1974), pp. 53–57.

4. Indeed, that fiction persisted and became so ingrained in English legal thought that Sir William Blackstone proclaimed that 'the common law of England . . . [had] no allowance or authority in America'. See Blackstone, *Commentaries*, i. 107.

5. Henry Hartwell, James Blair, and Edward Chilton, *The Present State of Virginia and the College*, ed. by H. D. Farish (Williamsburg, Va., 1940), p. 40; R. B. Davis (ed.), *William Fitzhugh and his Chesapeake World, 1676–1701, the Fitzhugh Letters and other Documents* (Chapel Hill, N.C., 1963), pp. 107–8; Billings, *The Old Dominion in the Seventeenth Century*, p. 52.

Whatever the reason for choosing to rely upon statutes, the effect of that choice was considerable. The colonists succeeded in doing what their contemporaries at home had not accomplished: reducing their laws to a written code. More importantly, they planted the seeds of an idea which held broader implications for a later age in American history. Like their puritan brethren to the north, they believed that fundamental law should stand in writing. Ultimately, the lack of a written specification for the constitutional relationship between the mother country and the colonies contributed to revolution in 1776 and a constitutional convention in 1787. The written statement of a citizen's rights and guarantees became in the end a hallmark of the American legal system.

Throughout the first half of the seventeenth century Virginians slowly adapted their legal heritage to American conditions. By 1650 colonists no longer perished from famine, although disease and unhealthy living conditions still made Virginia a deadly place in which to live. The grosser characteristics of a colony founded upon a quest for profit also remained. Tobacco planters, who often cared more for gain than for human life, shamelessly misused their labourers. Insensitive to those whom they governed, these ambitious men pursued power ruthlessly and relentlessly, sometimes resorting to violence to attain it and not hesitating to bend the law to their advantage. The drive for riches had already begun to produce its most painful legacy the enslavement of Africans and the destruction of the Indians. Colonial laws mirrored the harshness of such brutal realities, but they also reflected the legislators' growing political sophistication and the increasing complexity of Virginia society. During the second half of the seventeenth century the law remained fluid and was still influenced primarily by English local customs. In the eighteenth century other aspects of English law predominated. By that time, legislators and judges had ceased to be laymen, and were professionals who knew the totality of English law better than their predecessors. But, like their ancestors, these men were ready to embrace change as an essential prerequisite for the achievement of their aims.

The colonists who moulded English law to Virginia's needs in the half century before 1650 left an enduring monument to their efforts. The knowledge, experiences, and habits which they willed to their successors were to become part of the foundations of the modern American legal system.

12

Religion and
the Virginia colony
1609–10

JOHN PARKER

Promoters of the Virginia colony in its earliest years easily reduced the requirements for the struggling colony to two items: men and money. Appeals were made to adventure 'in purse' or 'in person'. In Stuart England, adventuring one's life or one's fortune abroad was not a casual investment, yet in 1609 and 1610 the appeal to do so was made persuasive enough to bring forth sufficient men and money to enable the Virginia settlement to take root, establishing England's first successful American colony. That appeal was primarily religious. A secular age instinctively looks for secular motives concealed in religious and missionary activities, and often they are to be found. They are not entirely absent from the Virginia promotional literature of 1609 and 1610, the years in which that enterprise recovered from the failures of the 1606 charter. But to a degree never again equalled in the history of British overseas expansion the appeal was most forcefully made by preachers, with a message essentially religious. And the pronouncements of the Virginia Company itself were in much the same tone.

In discussing this propaganda, Louis Wright has considered it mainly from the standpoint of the relationship between the Virginia Company and the clergy, a relationship which was unquestionably close and to the Company's great advantage.[1] Perry Miller, on the other hand, found in these sermons and related literature in Virginia's founding years 'a set of principles for guiding not a mercantile investment but a medieval pilgrimage. The cosmos expounded . . . is one where the principal human

---

1. Louis B. Wright, *Religion and Empire: The Alliance between Piety and Commerce in English Expansion, 1558–1625* (New York, 1965), pp. 85–104.

concern is neither the rate of interest nor the discovery of gold, but the will of God.'[2]

The preachers and the Company, of course, had an urgent problem in 1609 and 1610: recruiting men and money to save the Virginia colony, saving it as an investment of men and money, as a commitment of national prestige and as the first hope of a religious mission in America. Their rhetoric had to be tuned to the mentality of the moment, both religious and secular. If we suspect insincerity in such propaganda we must not assume it was less suspected then. The propagandists of these years will tell us above all else what they believed was in the minds of their readers, what would be convincing to them.[3] It is, therefore, the practical problem of making a case for Virginia which would convince investors, and answer effectively the many objections that were being raised, that is my primary concern in this essay. Indeed, since the objectors published no sermons or pamphlets articulating their negative attitudes, the pro-Virginia responses are the best insights we have into the anti-Virginia points of view. Whether affirming the merits of the enterprise or responding to the critics, the most telling points are made from a religious position, with classical history rather than contemporary politics as a supporting factor.

Perhaps we should not be surprised at this. In James I's England, the Bible was the cornerstone of all thought, with Greek and Roman influence following. James was heir to two generations of English Reformation, the central theme of intellectual life in Tudor England, a movement which, however uncertain, 'could not but excite all good minds'.[4] If the Reformation provided intellectual excitement, the intellectuals turned loose posed a relentless threat to a nation which had defined its separation from Rome on no deep doctrinal lines, with a resultant pulling and hauling from puritans and Roman catholics that threatened the very fabric of nationhood. Elizabeth's Church had been on the defensive much of the time. The Paul's Cross sermons, as an indication of what was important to the Crown during her reign, show 'a singular preoccupation with . . . *security*, with the theme of unity and the power and happiness which attend unity and justify it'.[5]

2. Perry Miller, 'The religious impulse in the founding of Virginia: religion and society in the early literature', *William and Mary Quarterly*, 3rd series, v (1948), 492–522.

3. Loren E. Pennington, 'Religion and empire: the English experience, 1550–1630' (unpublished paper presented at the Northern Great Plains Historical Conference, Grand Forks, North Dakota, 1975), p. 2.

4. Wallace Notestein, *The English People on the Eve of Colonization, 1603–1630* (New York 1954), pp. 25–35 (hereafter cited as Notestein).

5. Millar Maclure, *The Paul's Cross Sermons, 1534–1642* (Toronto, 1958), p. 86.

James brought no healing balm to the nation's religious wounds. The Hampton Court Conference and the Gunpowder Plot dominated the first three years of his reign.[6] Both made old problems worse, raising the level of religious unrest and intolerance: puritans 'looking forward to complete the half-reformation of the Tudors by a full emancipation of the laity',[7] while Roman catholics 'could not live at peace in a community which reduced a whole section of that community to the level of second-class citizens, criticized, distrusted and, where occasion served, denounced by influential demagogues'.[8]

This would not appear to be a nation ready to set out to colonize, from a missionary motive, a distant and threatened part of the world. A financially impoverished church harassed by disgruntled catholics and chafing puritans was a weak vessel indeed for a challenge to the Jesuits in the mission field. Yet the propaganda of 1609–10 sought to rouse England to such an effort in Virginia, and by building a missionary motive into a commercial company, uttered the first serious proposal to carry England's religion to a non-Christian people abroad.

Indeed, the appeals on behalf of the Virginia Company of the second charter provided English readers with their first exposure to aggressive religious expansionism. Richard Hakluyt and the writers of his generation, for all their propagandizing, had never tried to equalize the conquest of souls with the honour of the nation or the 'commodity of our country' as a motive for the expansion overseas which they advocated. Theirs was, after all, primarily a time for information-gathering, rather than a time for consideration of actual projects. None of them had suggested competing with the Jesuits. There had been allusions without plans, words that carried little heat of conviction. Dionyse Settle, reporting on Frobisher's 1577 voyage, alludes to 'Gods good will and pleasure that they [the natives] should be instructed in his divine service and religion'. George Best in 1578 had looked back on Frobisher's voyages and found among the positive results 'Christ's name spred: the Gospell preached, Infidels like to be converted to Christianitie'. Thomas Nicholas in translating Gómara's history of the Spanish conquest in America did not doubt that God had intended England to be 'a meane that the name of Christ

6. D. H. Willson, *James VI and I* (London, 1956) discusses James's problems with the puritans, pp. 197–216; and the catholic question, pp. 217–42.

7. H. R. Trevor-Roper, 'Scotland and the puritan revolution', *Religion, the Reformation and Social Change* (London, 1961), p. 398.

8. Joel Hurstfield, 'Gunpowder Plot and the politics of dissent', in Howard S. Reinmuth (ed.), *Early Stuart Studies: Essays in Honor of David Harris Willson* (Minneapolis, 1970), p. 103.

may be knowen unto this Heathenish and Savage generation'.[9] When Thomas Harriot wrote of the Indians encountered by the first English settlers in America at the Roanoke colony, he observed, 'Some religion they have alreadie, which although it be farre from the truth, yet beyng as it is, there is hope that it may bee easier and sooner reformed'. But he made no indication that the Indians' conversion was an item of high priority in the colony's plans. Richard Hakluyt, in dedicating the second volume of the enlarged edition of his *Principal Navigations* to Robert Cecil, made only a nod towards the view that the conversion of the American Indians to Christianity was a motive the Crown could serve by forwarding the colonization of North America.[1]

This lack of a strong religious emphasis continued naturally into the first charter of the Virginia enterprise, an enterprise which saw itself in the tradition of the commercial company, of which England had produced many.[2] None of these had seen missionary activity as a concern of theirs. Yet in the 'Instructions for government' of 20 November 1606, there is some evidence that the Company was mindful of a religious opportunity in Virginia:

wee do hereby determine and ordaine that every person and persons being our subjects of every the said Colonies and Plantations shall from time to time well entreate those salvages in those parts, and use all good meanes to draw the salvages and heathen people of ye said several places . . . to the true service and knowledge of God, and that all just, kind and charitable courses shall be holden with such of them, as shall conforme themselves to any good and sociable traffique and dealing with ye subjects of us . . . whereby they may be ye sooner drawne to the true knowledge of God, and ye obedience of us . . .[3]

With only one preacher, Robert Hunt, sailing as pastor to the 1606 voyage, it was realistic to emphasize good dealings rather than conversion by more overt means as the way to bring the Indians to Christianity, and thereby to obedience. Yet preaching to them is mentioned in the 'Instructions': it is urged that 'the true word and service of God and Christian

9. John Parker, *Books to Build an Empire: A Bibliographical History of English Overseas Interests to 1620* (Amsterdam, 1965), pp. 70, 84, 87.

1. Thomas Hariot, *A briefe and true report of the new found land of Virginia* (London, 1588), ff. E3ᵛ–E4ʳ; Richard Hakluyt, *The Principal navigations, voyages, traffiques, and discoveries of the English nation* (London, 1598–1600), ff. *2–4.

2. Notestein, p. 258.

3. Philip L. Barbour, *The Jamestown Voyages under the First Charter* (Cambridge, 1969), p. 43 (hereafter cited as Barbour).

Faith be preached, planted and used, not only within every of the said several Colonies and Plantations, but alsoe as much as they may, amongst the salvage people'.[4] The letters patent of 1606 were low on specifics, but they did see the intended colony as 'soe noble a worke which may by the providence of Almightie God hereafter tende to the glorie of his divyne majestie in propagating of Christian religion to such people as yet live in darknesse and myserable ignorance of the true knowledge and worshippe of god and may in tyme bring the infidels and salvages lyving in those partes to human civilitie and to a setled and quiet govermente'.[5] Civility and quietness on the part of the Indians were not unnatural desires among the intending first settlers, and probably the best that could be hoped for in an organization that had made no provision for a missionary cadre among its members. In fact, some limits were placed upon religion in the 'Instructions for government', where provision was made for election of a president from among members of the council, the only requirement being that the person named be not 'the minister of Gods word'.[6] But when the king issued his 'Ordinance and Constitution' on 9 March 1607, enlarging the number of the council in order to create a more workable group for the management of Virginia, included among the twenty-six members was Mathew Sutcliffe, Doctor of Divinity, suggesting an interest in religious influence, but a muted interest.[7]

Observations on Virginia's beginnings under the 1606 charter by two outsiders are somewhat contradictory as to the importance of religion at that point. Spain's ambassador, Pedro de Zúñiga, writing to Philip III on 22 September 1607, saw Virginia as a threat, a base for pirates and an encroachment on Spanish claims in America, but he made no suggestion of a religious motive among the colony's promoters—that is, a desire to unsettle catholicism in the New World. The Dutchman, Emanuel Van Meteren, recording in 1608 Virginia's beginnings, noted that 'the King of Great Britain praised highly the initiative as a work that might in time greatly contribute to the honour and glory of God and the spreading of the Christian religion and bring the savage infidel people to knowledge and common civility'.[8] Patently what Van Meteren detected in the king's attitude was more hope than anticipation of success or a plan of action.

4. Ibid., pp. 36-37.
5. Ibid., p. 35.
6. Ibid., p. 36.
7. Ibid., p. 74.
8. Ibid., pp. 114-15, 271.

As for those who established the Virginia settlement in 1607, there is evidence of an inverse religious motive. A group of the colony's leaders wrote on 22 June 1607, 'we most humblie praie the heavenly Kings hand to bless our labours with such consails and helpes, as wee may further and stronger proceede in this our Kinges and Countries service'.⁹ God was being asked to help England. On the other hand, 'A relatyon . . . written . . . by a gent. of the colony' in May–June of 1607, possibly by Gabriel Archer, concludes, 'so that I hope in God as he hath miraculously preserved us hither from all dangers . . . he will make us authors of his holy will in converting them [the Indians] to our true Christian faith'.¹

All of these instructions, reports, opinions, hopes, testify to a state of mind that saw religion as a part of the Virginia enterprise, if not a major motive or a well-planned aspect of the undertaking. And all of these expressions were made within the Company. No published statement made public the Company's plans or intentions in 1606 or 1607. That changed in 1608 with Captain John Smith's *A true relation of such occurrences of noate, as hath hapned in Virginia*.² Here was a message from Virginia for the concerned public. Or rather two messages. The first was in an introduction written very probably by John Healey, which recommends the Virginia enterprise thus: 'the action most honorable, and the end to the high glory of God, to the erecting of true religion among Infidells, to the overthrow of superstition and idolatrie, to the winning of many thousands of wandring sheepe, unto Christs fold, who now, and till now have strayed in the unknowne paths of Paganisme, Idolatrie, and superstition . . .'.³ If Healey was indeed the author of these words, they represent a deep conviction, for he went to Virginia and died there before the end of 1610. The second message is in contrast to the first. Smith's appraisal of the faltering effort in Virginia includes reference to an Indian king's curiosity about 'our God' but offers no suggestion of capitalizing on it. Smith presents a considerable account of the Indian's religion, but without comment. In general his narrative of events and the statement of his attitudes carry a deep distrust of the Indians, with clear implications that nothing but force could be the basis for a relationship with them.

The change that took place in the administration of the Virginia

9. Barbour, p. 80.

1. Ibid., p. 104.

2. John Smith, *A true relation of such occurrences and accidents of noate as hath hapned in Virginia since the first planting of that collony* . . . (London, 1608), reprinted in Barbour, pp. 165–208.

3. Barbour, pp. 167–8.

Company, from royal control to private direction under a charter, was accompanied by a change in approach with respect to the attempt to interest the public in the colony, and this was done through presenting the Company as the means of carrying England's religion abroad. It was not merely a public relations effort, for it was written into the new charter of 23 May 1609. 'The principall effect which we can desier or expect of this action is the conversion and reduccion of the people in those parts unto the true worshipp of God and Christian religion.'[4] Before the charter came into effect, the Company began its efforts to raise money and men for a massive new supply. Ambassador Zúñiga reported home on 15 March that 'they have collected in 20 days an amount of money for this voyage that frightens me'. Fourteen earls and barons had given 40,000 ducats, he reported, and merchants were even more generous. The whole public was showing great interest.[5] Was the new religious emphasis having an effect? Apparently so, for on 12 April Zúñiga reported that 'they have seen to it that the ministers, in their sermons, stress the importance of filling the world with their religion . . . In this way a good sum of money is being collected.'[6] It did not occur to Zúñiga that the preachers had found in the Virginia Colony a great hope of their own.

If investors in Virginia, moved by religious considerations, wished to know details of how the church was to accomplish its objectives there, they could be given some assurance. The Bishop of London, George Abbott, would be the overseer of the church in America, and he was one of the Virginia grantees.[7] Furthermore, the 'Instruccions orders and constitutions' to Sir Thomas Gates, issued in May 1609, preparatory to his sailing with a supply to Virginia, stated: 'you shall with all propensenes and diligence endeavour the conversion of the natives to the knowledge and worship of the true God and their reedeemer Christ Jesus, as the most pious and noble end of this plantacion'.[8] There was even a programme for commencing the work of conversion, for Gates was instructed, 'you must procure from them some convenient number of their children to be brought up in your language and manners'.[9] Children thus reformed

4. Samuel M. Bemiss, *The Three Charters of the Virginia Company of London* (Williamsburg, 1957), p. 54 (hereafter cited as Bemiss).
5. Barbour, p. 256.
6. Ibid., p. 259.
7. A. L. Cross, *The Anglican Episcopate and the American Colonies* (New York, 1902), p. 10 (hereafter cited as Cross).
8. Bemiss, p. 57.
9. Ibid., p. 57.

would thereafter be the agents of conversion to their people. Lord de la Ware, later in 1609 or early in 1610, was to have similar instructions, with the added suggestion, 'in case they shalbe willful and obstinate then send over some three or foure of them into England, we may endeavour theire conversion here'.[1]

The shallowness of these plans compared to the loudly trumpeted importance of missionizing Virginia may well have brought criticism, and as the preachers went about London an important part of their message was the refutation of a variety of criticisms made of the entire undertaking.

The first publication to carry the Company's appeal to the public was *Nova Britannia*, licensed by the Company of Stationers on 18 February 1609. It was dedicated to Sir Thomas Smith, treasurer of the Virginia Company, by Robert Johnson, chaplain to the Bishop of Lincoln and a vigorous anti-puritan, who called it 'the summe of a private speech or discourse . . . uttered not long since in London . . .'. If the speaker was not Johnson himself, then it was surely another involved preacher. First addressing himself to what was apparently a persistent objection, the issue of England's right to Virginia in the face of the papal donation of America, the speaker compares this grant to the Donation of Constantine, 'whereby the Pope himselfe doth hold and claime, the Citie of Rome and all the Westerne Empire, a thing that . . . crosseth all Histories of truth and sound Antiquitie'. The later donation by the pope to temporal rulers he calls 'a new toye most idle and ridiculous'.[2]

England's rights in America thus affirmed from the protestant point of view, Johnson's speaker then calls his readers 'Cheerfully to adventure and joyntly take in hand this high and acceptable work, tending to advance and spread the kingdome of God, and the knowledge of his truth among so many Millions of men and women, savage and blinde . . . to enlighten their mindes and confort their soules'.[3] He acknowledges the additional motives of honour to the king and succour for those already in Virginia, and he accepts the doubts of those who contend that the private profit of the adventurers is the Company's dominant motive. 'Me thinkes this objection comes in due time, and doth well admonish us, how to rectifie our harts, and ground our meditations before we begin . . . both in

1. Bemiss, p. 73.
2. Robert Johnson, *Nova Britannia. Offring most excellent fruites by planting in Virginia. Exciting all such as be well affected to further the same* (London, 1609), f. A4ᵛ.
3. Ibid., f. B1ʳ.

respect of God and the publike good.'[4] He is aware of the possibility of religion merely putting a good face on the project. 'But wee must beware, that under this pretence, that bitter roote of gready gaine be not so setled in our harts . . . if it fal not out presently to our expectation, we slinke away with discontent, and draw our purses from the charge.' He does not say that it is to be an adventure without hope of financial reward, but he counsels, 'look it not be chiefe in our thoughts, God will give the blessing'.[5]

A second objection, and a persistent one, that the Indians were being 'supplanted' in their own country, found a response based in religious motivation also. 'Our intrusion into their possessions shall tend to their great good . . . to bring them from their base condition to a farre better: First in regard of God the Creator, and of Jesus Christ their Redeemer, if they will beleeve in him: and secondly, in respect of earthly blessings . . .' The objectors are assured, 'we require nothing at their hands, but a quiet residence to us and ours that by our owne labour and toyle, we may worke this good unto them'. This opportunity is seen as a divine plan that in the last age of the world this remnant of souls unconverted should 'be wonne and recovered by our means'. Such a partnership with God implies a heavy burden upon the objectors, 'of whom so many as obstinately refuse to unite themselves unto us, or shall maligne or disturbe our plantation . . . shall be held and reputed recusant . . . and shall be dealth with as enemies of the Commonwealth of their country'.[6]

The theme of alliance between religion and state is carried forward in the second motive, honour to the king, for the reality of such honour is based on 'Divine testimonies' of the Old Testament conquests of David and the 'ample reigne' of Solomon which brought the Twelve Tribes together and neighbours under tribute, 'whereby they had the better meanes to beleeve and know God'. And from Daniel came the assurance 'that for this conquest, of turning many unto righteousnesse, he shall shine as the starres for ever and ever'.[7] Likewise, the supplying of Virginia's hard-pressed settlers found an Old Testament justification. Virginia is likened to Canaan, and the first settlers to those Old Testament explorers who had spied out the land and found it good. Canaan had not wanted for detractors among the Jews, and so also with Virginia. It was

---

4. Ibid., f. C1^r.
5. Ibid.
6. Ibid., f. C2^r.
7. Ibid.

necessary 'to rescue our enterprise from malicious ignorance, and still their murmurings with reproofe', but to do it in a meek and humble spirit as Caleb and Joshua had done with Canaan's nay-sayers. The objections must have been many and varied, for Johnson's speaker urged Virginia's friends not to try answering all of them. 'It is but our weaknesse to stumble at strawes, and a baseness to gnaw upon every bone that is cast in our way . . .'[8]

The case was thus established for giving Virginia a specific religious purpose. Other preachers would follow this approach in general, with elaboration on individual arguments, as we shall see. But there was also a set of domestic problems with moral and religious implications which were addressed by Virginia's promoters. Chief among these was over-population: 'swarmes of idle persons which . . . doe likewise swarme in lewd and naughtie practizes, so that if we seeke not some waies for their forraine employment, we must provide shortly more persons, and corrections for their bad conditions . . .'.[9] This was not to say that Virginia was to be merely a dumping ground for England's criminal element, since 'honest, wise and painefull men' were required also. As for the troublemakers in England who were to be excluded from Virginia, religion was the primary criterion. Dishonest persons and 'Evill affected Magistrates' were to be powerfully discouraged, but the door was most firmly barred to 'Papists, professed or Recusant, of which I would not one, seasoned with the least taint of that leaven, to be settled in our plantation'. Citing examples of their conduct and beliefs the speaker concludes, 'if they grow so bold and desparate in a mighty settled state, howe much more dangerous in the birth and infancy of yours'. If Virginia would admit papists and atheists, 'then looke for no blessing nor assistance from God'.[1]

With the Virginia Company setting forth its religious purpose, it received assistance from preachers whose primary concerns were not with colonizing America, but who saw in the enterprise a reason to rejoice. Such was the case of Richard Crakanthorpe, chaplain to the Bishop of London, who on 14 March 1608 preached *A sermon solemnizing of the happie inauguration of our most gracious and religious soveraigne King James*. The sermon was delivered from Paul's Cross, and its announced purpose was to prove that the sovereignty of kings is from God and from no other authority. It is vigorously anti-papal throughout, and to a less belligerent

8. Johnson, *Nova Britannia*, f. C3r.
9. Ibid., f. D1r–v.
1. Ibid., f. D2v.

extent anti-puritan. Celebrating James's great wisdom in steering England's church between these destructive forces, Crakanthorpe portrays his much-admired king as a champion who 'himselfe holds forth a glorious Lampe of Piety, and true Religion unto all Christian Kings and kingdomes ...'. And beyond that, 'let the honourable expedition now happily intended for Virginia be a witnesse: enterprised ... by the most wise and religious direction and protection of our chiefest Pilot, seconded by so many honourable and worthy personages'. He alludes briefly to the population problem to be solved, but the 'happie and glorious worke' is carrying religion to the Virginians. 'This being the Religious and honourable intendment of the enterprise, what glory shall heereby re-dound unto God? What Honour to our Soveraigne? What comfort to those his Subjects, who shall be the meanes and furtherers of so happy a worke ...'[2] This was no appeal for men and money, no defence of the enterprise, but a commendation of it as a religious effort.

In contrast, Robert Gray, rector of St Bennet Sherehog in Cheapward, laboured the Company's cause openly in *A good speed to Virginia*, which was licensed for publication on 3 May 1609. Gray's message gives no specific evidence of having been a pulpit-preached sermon, but a sermon it was nevertheless. He dedicated it to the 'Adventurers for the plantation of Virginea' and he praised them as God's 'instruments for the inlarging of his church militant heere upon earth' and promised 'the same God (shall) make you members of his Church triumphant in Heaven'. Gray grounds his message on Joshua 17:14, 'Then the children of Joseph spake unto Joshua, saying, why hast thou given me but one lot, and one portion to inherite, seeing I am a great people?' To which Joshua had replied, 'If thou beest much people get thee up to the wood, and cut trees for thyself in the land of the Perizzites, and of the Giants, if mount Ephraim be too narrow for thee.' Gray sees a larger part of mankind—perhaps of the English especially—as unworthy of the bounty God had provided, 'so improvident and irrespective is man that he had rather live like a drone, and feede uppon the fruites of other mens labors ... then looke out and flie abroad ...'. Thus it is that, while the earth was given to man by God, much of it remains unused, 'wrongfully usurped by wild beasts, and unreasonable creatures, or by brutish savages'. England had missed an opportunity by failing to support Columbus, in a time of ample supplies

2. Richard Crakanthorpe, *A sermon solemnizing the happie inauguration of our most gracious and religious soveraigne King James ... Preached at Paules Crosse, the 14 of March last, 1608* (London, 1609), f. D2ʳ⁻ᵛ.

and small population, but like the children of Joseph 'nowe God hath prospered us with the blessings of the wombe' and 'we are a great people and the lande is too narrow for us'.[3] Virginia obviously was the answer to this problem, which Gray viewed as the nation's greatest danger. Like the herdsman or the bee-keeper who move their charges to new locations for greater productivity, so too, he wrote, crowded nations should colonize, rather than make war, as a means of keeping the land and its people in balance. The opportunity was available; 'many valiaunt and couragious men, many rich and wealthie men adventure . . . towards the accomplishing of so godly and memorable a designe . . .' but they are confronted by those who prefer 'intemperancie, incontenancie, and other their luxurious and riotous courses . . .'.[4]

Joshua's command to Joseph's heirs to take over the territory of the Perizzites and giants by force involved Gray in defining prospective relations with the American Indians. He found adequate Old Testament justification for slaying idolaters, yet despite its acceptability in the sight of God, reclaiming a soul would be far better. Hence the 'loving and gentle' Indians who were 'desirous to imbrace a better condition' gave England her opportunity to enter this New World Canaan, and it was to be done peacefully, giving no occasion 'that the holy name of God, should be dishonoured among the Infidels . . .'. Only self-preservation would justify violence against the Indians.[5]

That problem solved, Gray moved on to the objectors who, like those in the tribe of Joseph after Joshua gave his orders, had found reasons to delay. The issue was England's rights to the Indians' lands, an issue already discussed in *Nova Britannia*. Gray's reply is more expansive than his predecessor's. The Indians, he writes, have no individual titles to the land, 'but only a general residencie there, as wild beasts have in a forest', and he finds no intention by the settlers to take large tracts of land. Indeed, the Indians had offered far more than was needed. There was, of course, Gray added, a general agreement among political authors, including St Augustine, that if necessary 'a Christian King may lawfullie make warre upon barbarous and Savage people'.[6] By peace or war, therefore, Christian teaching justified the English presence in Virginia.

Others who would delay England's mission to Virginia harped on the

---

3. Robert Gray, *A good speed to Virginia* (London, 1609), f. B2^v.
4. Ibid., f. B4^v.
5. Ibid., f. C2^r.
6. Ibid., f. C4^r.

lack of progress there since Ralegh's colony was begun. These Gray dismissed as irrelevant, 'indeed most childish . . . for neither was the end of the first attempt the same . . . nor the managing of the meanes', a clear statement of change in expansionist plans and policies. A further objection, that 'this age will see no profit', Gray bludgeoned with a statement of man's duty to posterity. 'We sow, we set, we plant, we build, not so much for ourselves as for posteritie', just as godliness is practised for rewards beyond this life. Finally, objectors to the high cost were denounced for their willingness to invest for less worthy purposes—to engross a commodity, 'to take their Neighbors house over his head', or for usury. The designs of the wicked, according to Gray, were always well financed. Virginia offered a way to invest for good works, and those who stood in the way through delays and excuses were in 'opposition against God, the King, the Church, and the Commonwealth', a larger set of adversaries than *Nova Britannia* had postulated.[7]

As for administering Virginia, Gray echoed *Nova Britannia*: keep out papists in the interest of unity. But he went beyond into the realm of social ethics, proposing to keep out guilds which he believed were based on 'deceit and fraud' and thereby could produce no good in a new society. And he believed in the doctrine of hard work. The 'sweat of thy brow' message was for Virginia 'an Evangelicall precept that they which will not labour must not eate'.[8]

The flurry of preaching on behalf of Virginia noted by Ambassador Zúñiga in the spring of 1609 included *Virginia, a sermon preached at White-Chappel, in the presence of many, honourable and worshipfull, the adventurers and planters for Virginia*. The preacher on this occasion, 25 April, was William Symonds of St Saviour's, Southwark, and the sermon, obviously Company-sponsored, was entered for publication with the Company of Stationers on 8 May. The lesson was from Genesis 12:1–3, 'For the Lord had said unto Abram, Get thee out of thy countrey, and from thy kindred, and from thy fathers house, unto the land that I will shew thee, and I will make thee a great nation, and I will blesse them also that blesse thee, and curse them that curse thee, and in thee shall all the families of the earth be blessed.' It was a magnificent promise for those who would hear the call, and Symonds, who later went to Virginia himself, had a broad theological reason for making it heard. God, he said, had made man in His image and intended him to rule over all other creatures in all the

7. Ibid., f. D2ʳ.   8. Ibid., f. D3ᵛ.

earth, because God's manifold creation could not be praised but by the presence of man in all places to do so. 'His Saints must be witnesses of all his workes, in all Climates . . .' And beyond that, he said, it was the duty of those who knew God to spread the knowledge of Him, citing Ezekiel 38: 23: 'I will be magnified, and sanctified, and knowne in the eyes of many nations.' How could there be any doubt 'that the Lord that called Abraham into another Countrey doeth also . . . call you to goe and carry the Gospell to a Nation that never heard of Christ'.[9]

Symonds is at greater pains than his predecessors to refute the arguments of the anti-Virginia element, whom he identifies only as objectors 'that come dropping out of some Anabaptist Spicery'. The Anabaptists were hardly a threat to the church in England from the standpoint of numbers, but their radical views of the relationship between church and state made them much hated by the crown and by ministers of the established church. In this instance they were accused of encouraging the nation to be timid, and Symonds brought history, scripture, and national consciousness against them: 'Come foorth ye great Princes, and Monarkes, of Assyria, Persia, Media, Greece and Rome, with your greatest counsellors . . . For your stories . . . your wisedom, your magnificence, and your great justice, are now arraigned and must be found guiltie.' Symonds scorns those who would 'nurture princes, as petties: telling them they must not make offensive warres', citing Cyrus, Joshua, and David as examples of warriors blessed of God. Yet he refers to Samson among the Philistines, and Jacob and Joseph in Egypt, as types more akin to the intending settlers of Virginia who would live at peace with their neighbours there.[1] Why, he asks, are such well-praised actions from the past 'so vile and odious among us'? And very close to home: 'If our objector bee descended of Noble Saxons bloud, Let him take heede lest while he cast a stone at us, he wounds his father, that first brought him in his loynes from forraigne parts into this happie Isle.'[2] As for delayers in general, and those who preferred the New Testament to the Old, Symonds had a verse from Luke ready at hand: 'And Jesus saide, No man that putteth his hand to the plough and looketh back, is apt to the kingdome of God.'[3]

9. William Symonds, *Virginia. A Sermon preached at White-Chappel, in the presence of many, honourable and worshipfull, the adventurers and planters for Virginia. 25. April. 1609. Published for the benefit and use of the colony, planted, and to bee planted there, and for the advancement of their Christian purpose* (London, 1609), p. 9.
1. Ibid., p. 13.
2. Ibid., p. 15.
3. Ibid., p. 18.

God's call to Abraham, and to Englishmen, required that they leave their homes; and in Symonds's comparison of the situations of the two, the English come off much the worse. In addition to atheists and papists who 'have sowed so much cockell among our wheate' that no one was safe from their mischief, even among one's own family, he adds a catalogue of agrarian social ills, finding 'the mightier like old strong bees thrust out the weaker'. Townships once well populated are reduced 'to a shepheard and his dog'. The honest farmers who had long supplied income to the crown, soldiers for the army, and saints for the church, had in many places been reduced to the status of labourers, hardly above vagrants. Similarly, merchants engrossed food supplies; the metal worker 'can hardly keepe himselfe from the almes box'; and the working mother, 'her candle goeth not out by night', singing sadly to her children as she plies her needle so that the hearer 'doth with pittie praise God, that hath given such meanes to mock hunger with, and give patience'. The conclusion to this populist message is to 'Take the opportunity, good honest labourers which indeede bring all the hony to the hive, God may so blesse you, that the proverbe may be true of you, that a May swarme is worth a king's ransome'.4

Continuing the comparison between Abraham and England, Symonds presents England's opportunity as much the greater. Abraham was being directed to an unknown land. Virginia was proved fruitful, its people no formidable enemy, 'a Land more like the garden of Eden . . . then any part else of all the earth'.5 As for the favours God promised Abraham, they were equally offered to England. Being made 'a great nation', meaning a populous one, is 'promised to all that are of his faith and obedience', but this carried with it from Abraham's time a stricture against marrying outside that faith, a clear warning to Virginia against disunity. 'The breaking of this rule, may breake the neck of all good successe of this voyage.'6 God's promise to bless Abraham was taken as assurance that 'such as transplant at God's commandment' would have God's promise, 'I will not leave thee nor forsake thee'. However, that blessing was dependent upon hard work and good conduct: 'You must not with Idleness, inforce God to worke myracles of mercie on the wilfully sinfull.'7 The promise of a 'great name' and the chance to be 'a blessing' were not to be wasted.

---

4. Ibid., pp. 21–22.
5. Ibid., p. 26.
6. Ibid., p. 35.
7. Ibid., p. 37.

'How tender ought your care to be, to gaine the reputation of a blessing among this people in Virginia . . . While we have time, let us doe good to all men . . . So the blessing of God shall be upon us, and we shall be a blessing wherever we goe.'[8]

The assurance given Abraham that 'the Lord will blesse them that blesse thee' is accepted by Symonds as a promise of God's assistance against enemies, an offer of alliance against papists who 'come to curse with Bell, Booke, and Candle, and the Divell and all: but remember this, God will curse them that curse Abram'.[9] With such assurance of success Symonds finds intolerable the lethargy of many among the clergy who choose 'to mind unprofitable questions at home', leaving the field to the enemy, 'Jesuits and Friers, that accompany every ship . . . to destroy soules'. But he concludes 'notwithstanding the snorting idleness of the ministry, suspect not the blessing of God'.[1]

It is not possible to know how many sermons touching the Virginia colony were preached in 1609, for publishers probably ignored all but the better-known preachers and the sermons patronized by the Virginia Company. Yet the issue of Virginia found expression from pulpits with no visible relationship to the Company, and in sermons like Crakanthorpe's which were primarily concerned with some other issue. Robert Tynley, Doctor of Divinity and Archdeacon of Ely, preaching on 17 April 1609, at St Mary's Spittle, moved with both scholarship and passion through a long diatribe against the idolatry of the Roman catholic church and its claims to miracles. England's church, he said, had miracles also. Its very emergence and survival was a miracle, 'the Lord's doing, and it is wonderfull in our eies'. And also, 'Witnesse abroad the planting intended, or rather already happily begun of our English Colonie in Virginia . . . for the gaining and winning to Christ . . . of so many thousands of those sillie, brutish, and ignorant soules . . . the principall scope of this businesse'. Dr Tynley is brief in his remarks on Virginia because he says it has been 'at sundry times and places, by divers of more abilitie and liesure, commended to your godly consideration'.[2]

Other such spokesmen were indeed at work, two of them in May from

8. Symonds, *Virginia*, pp. 37–38.
9. Ibid., p. 44.
1. Ibid., p. 54.
2. Robert Tynley. *Two learned sermons. The one, of the mischievous subtiltie and barbarous crueltie, the other of the false doctrines, and refined heresies of the Romish synagogue. Preached, the one at Paules Crosse the 5. of November, 1608. The other at the Spittle the 17th of Aprill. 1609* (London, 1609), pp. 67–68.

Paul's Cross, uttering praise for Virginia. George Benson, a Fellow of Queen's College, Oxford, preaching on 7 May, exhorted his hearers to a more zealous religious life as a means of banishing vanities from the mind and of overcoming a vast range of sins besetting the English people, in preparation for the end of the world which was near at hand. It was in this context that he came to the end of a ninety-three-page sermon with a commendation of Virginia as 'one of the most pregnant, most fresh' examples of the prophecy of the Gospel being published over the earth. Here was an opportunity for good, not to emulate the Spaniards who had used cruelly the helpless Indians, 'that scandall was given unto the name of Christ, the name of Christianity grew odious unto them'. Benson hoped that 'our English are of that metall, that having in their hands the key to the kingdome of God, they will not keep those weake ones out, but rather make way for the Gospell . . . by their gentle and humane dealing'.[3]

Tynley and Benson give no indication of any interest in Virginia beyond their desire that it be a successful missionary effort. They leave promoting the enterprise to others. Daniel Price, chaplain in ordinary to the Prince, preaching at Paul's Cross on 28 May, also brought Virginia into his sermon towards its end, giving it less prominence than the sermon's title would indicate. *Sauls prohibition staide . . . with a reproofe of those that traduce the honourable plantation of Virginia* was less a promotion piece than a threat to Virginia's critics. From his text 'Saul, Saul, why persecutest thou me?' (Acts 9:4), Price launches into a compilation of the wrongs and evils abroad in England, and these evils are likened unto Saul 'that had his hand in so many murthers, in so many bloody, tragicall, barbarous executions, against whome the bloud of the Martyrs cryed out for vengeance . . .'.[4] Yet God had merely admonished Saul. The lesson is God's forgiving nature, the purpose of which is 'onely to draw us to repentance'.[5] Contradicting Benson, who had endorsed zealousness in prayer and in action, Price said zeal, by God's example, even against evil, must be mitigated by knowledge, temperance, and love. But he found zeal abroad in the land against God in the form of 'oppressors, maligners, murtherers, persecutors, Barrowists, Brownists, Humorists, atheists,

---

3. George Benson, *A sermon preached at Paules Crosse the seaventh of May*, MDCIX (London, 1609), p. 92.
4. Daniel Price, *Sauls prohibition staide. Or the apprehension and examination of Saule. And the inditement of all that persecute Christ, with a reproofe of those that traduce the honourable plantation of Virginia. Preached in a sermon commaunded at Pauls Crosse, upon Rogation Sunday, being the 28. of May. 1609* (London, 1609), f. B4r (hereafter cited as Price).
5. Ibid., f. C4v.

Divels' (a list Benson would have endorsed), and these imitators of Saul were committing a wide variety of sins—pride, usury, dissension, disobedience, lies, lusts, drunkenness, profaneness, apostasy, popery—to which Price adds another, 'the lying speeches that have injuriously vilified and traduced . . . the Plantation of Virginia'.[6]

In such detractors Price finds the perverse spirit of those in an earlier generation who had lost for England the opportunity offered by Columbus. Virginia now offered a new chance to supply England with the goods she needed and would reward her with '. . . Pietie, in converting so many thousand soules'. And still 'our own lasie, drousie, yet barking countrimen traduce it'. We search in vain for any clear identity of the traducers. Price refers to them as 'Scepticall Humorists', which suggests actors satirizing Virginia from the stage.[7] He cites the 'fearefull woe denounced against those that came not to assist Deborah . . . wheresoever they be that purposely withstand or confront this most Christian, most Honourable Voyage, let him read that place and feare'. But those who lend support 'will make a Savadge country to become a sanctifyed Country; you will obtain their best commodities, they will obtain the saving of their Soules, you will enlarge the boundes of this Kingdome, nay the bounds of heaven . . .'.[8]

The 'May swarme' that William Symonds had called for did indeed materialize, and on 2 June 1609, Sir Thomas Gates with nine ships and 600 colonists sailed from Plymouth. Investments had poured in from individuals and from London's merchant companies: Mercers, Grocers, Fishmongers, Merchant-Taylors, Ironmongers, Clothworkers, Stationers.[9] It would be too much to say that all of the adventurers had been moved by the words of preachers, and yet if what was published is an index of what was being said in favour of Virginia and in response to its critics, then surely the religious motive must be credited as the dominant factor, even as the 1609 charter had said the conversion of the Indians was the most desirable outcome.

The spring of 1609 saw the publication of two other promotion pieces

6. Price, *Sauls prohibition staide*, f. F2r.

7. Ibid., f. F2v. The play *Eastward Ho!* (London, 1605) by George Chapman, Ben Jonson, and John Marston satirized Virginia, but there do not appear to have been other plays of this type published in 1609. That is not to say that there were not other plays performed which ridiculed the Virginia colony. Crashaw's remarks in his sermon (see p. 267 below) leave no doubt that the stage was critical of Virginia, and of course preachers and actors had no lack of grounds for mutual criticism.

8. Price, f. F3r.

9. Alexander Brown, *The Genesis of the United States* (2 vols, New York, 1964), i. 250.

for Virginia, both put forward by Richard Hakluyt, which provide an interesting contrast to the sermons of that season. *Nova Francia,* a translation of portions of Marc Lescarbot's *Histoire de la Nouvelle France* describing the lands to the north of Virginia and the French experience in colonizing them, was brought into English by Pierre Erondelle, a French Huguenot living in London. He catches some of the spirit of 1609 in encouraging 'that generous and godly action for the benefit of this land, too much pestred with over many people', an action which would 'bring the Naturals [of Virginia] . . . to civilitie and right knowledge of God'.[1] But the piece is addressed to royal rather than popular interests, and it lacks the urgency of the preachers' messages. Similarly informative, but even more lacking in religious appeal, was Hakluyt's *Virginia richly valued,* a translation of the Portuguese account of De Soto's exploration of lands to the south of Virginia.[2] Dated 15 April 1609, Hakluyt's dedication shows more interest in gold than in souls, and he dwells on the passage to the South Sea as a motive of importance, in short diminishing the importance of Virginia in favour of a route through it to the Pacific Ocean. The Spanish example of hard treatment to bring the Indians to order was starkly out of keeping with the message of Hakluyt's colleagues in the clergy who were promoting a missionary effort in Virginia. Both Hakluyt's motives and his method—the translation of continental authors—were out of tune with the mood of the 1609 sermons. The sermons were more idealistic and yet more aggressive than the publications of the Elizabethan age, when Hakluyt had held the centre of the stage as the proponent of overseas expansion.

One might believe that the preachers rested as England awaited news of the Virginia Company's fleet in the summer and autumn of 1609, for no sermons were registered for publication in those months. When news arrived in November it was shattering. It told of a storm that had carried off the *Sea Venture* with the colony's leaders, Sir Thomas Gates, Sir George Somers, and Captain Christopher Newport. Their survival on Bermuda was not yet known, so there was nothing but disappointment arising from this, England's first missionary effort. Yet plans had been made and were well advanced to send Lord de la Ware out to Virginia with a new supply. Virginia had to be defended again, and the Company

1. Marc Lescarbot, *Nova Francia: or the description of that part of New France, which is one continent with Virginia* (London, [1609]), f." r–v.
2. Hernando de Soto, *Virginia richly valued, by the description of the maine land of Florida, her next neighbour* (London, 1609).

rushed into print with *A true and sincere declaration of the purpose and ends of the plantation begun in Virginia.* It was licensed by the Company of Stationers on 14 December 1609.

This was no sermon. It was the Virginia management defending its colony and calling for 'the constant and patient prosecution therof'. But its tone remained distinctly religious as it sought 'to deliver roundly and clearely, our *endes* and *wayes*' and to counter 'the imputations and aspertions with which ignorant rumor, virulent envy, or impious subtilty, daily callumniateth our industries'.[3] The purposes of the colony were declared the same: to preach, baptize, propagate the Gospel, rescue souls from the Devil. National honour and private gain followed. As for rumours of distress in Virginia, 'of which though the noise have exceeded the truth, yet we doe confesse a great part of it'.[4] But it was due to idleness on the part of some settlers, and the lack of government as a result of the absence of Gates and Somers because of the storm, and 'who can avoid the hand of God, or dispute with him?' But possibly God was trying their intentions, 'whither Pyety or Covetousnesse carryed us swifter'.[5] The problem now was to hold adventurers to their pledges as the de la Ware expedition was being made ready; and they were reminded, 'remember that what was at first but Conveniency, and for Honor, is now become a case of necessity and of piety . . . that they have encouraged and exposed . . . 600 . . . Christians of one faith, and one Baptisme to a miserable and un-evitable death. Let not any man flatter himself that it concerns not him.' Backsliders were asked to look inward and to 'disperse that clowd of avarice which darkened [their] spiritual sight'. If all such appeals to piety, honour, profit, and conscience failed there was yet one appeal to be made, prayer 'unto that mercifull and tender God . . . that it would please him to blesse and water these feeble beginnings'.[6] The doubts, disillusionment, and continuing needs of the Company did not cause a lowering of standards. The Company's defence concluded with an appeal for settlers, but it specified 'no idle and wicked person . . . no man that cannot bring or render some good testimony of his religion to God, and

3. *A true and sincere declaration of the purpose and ends of the plantation begun in Virginia, of the degrees which it hath received; and meanes by which it hath beene advanced: and the resolution and conclusion of His Majesties Council of that colony, for the constant and patient prosecution thereof, untill by the mercies of God it shall retribute a fruitful harvest to the kingdome of heaven, and this common-wealth. Sett forth by the authority of the Governors and Councellors established for that plantation* (London, 1610), p. 2.

4. Ibid., p. 10.

5. Ibid., p. 15.

6. Ibid., pp. 22–24.

civill manners and behaviour to his neighbors'.[7] It was an appeal seldom repeated, a standard not often emulated.

The Virginia adventurers were held to the course, and when Lord de la Ware was ready to sail with new colonists and a year's supply of provisions he was preached on his way by William Crashaw, a vigorous anti-papist and puritan-type moralist who was at that time preacher at the Inner Temple, in a sermon delivered on 21 February 1610. Some ninety pages long, Crashaw's message is in large part a rebuttal to the 'discouragements' that were being advanced against Virginia. His lesson was from Luke 22:32, 'But I have praied for thee, that thy faith fails not: therefore when thou art converted strengthen thy brethren'.[8] These words spoken to Peter, according to Crashaw were not spoken 'as he was an Apostle, but as he was an ordinary Christian and a child of God'.[9] The implication for all Christians is obvious, in spite of Satan's desires, indeed because of them, which were appearing in the form of 'slanders, false reports, backwardnesse of some, baseness of others, by raising objections and divising doubts . . .'. What was the root of this negative stance? It was because 'the greater part of men are unconverted and unsanctified . . . and seeke merely the world and themselves and no farther'. Crashaw observes no difficulty in finding adventurers for strictly commercial voyages, 'but this . . . because it yields not present profit, it must seeke them . . . tell them of planting a Church, of converting 10000 soules to God, they are as senseless as stones'.[1] Virginia, as Crashaw sees it, calls Englishmen first to be converted themselves and then to labour for the conversion of the Virginians, who in God's sight were the equal of all men, only awaiting their more fortunate brethren who have the knowledge of Christ. Had not God done likewise with the ancient uncivilized English, sending 'some to make us civill, others to make us christians'?[2] Who among the converted were thus obligated? Everyone, except those without funds—but to those who might think of pleading poverty Crashaw brings a puritan's measurement: 'Consider how much thou hast abroad at Interest . . . in other adventures . . . how much thou spendest in sports and other vanities . . . in plaine superfluities of apparell, furniture, building or diet . . .'[3]

    7. Ibid., p. 25.
    8. William Crashaw, *A sermon preached in London before the right honorable the Lord Lawarre, Lord Governour and Captaine Generall of Virginea . . . at the said Lord Generall his leave taking of England . . . and departure for Virginea, Febr. 21, 1609* (London, 1610), f. A1ʳ.
    9. Ibid., f. A3ʳ.
    1. Ibid., ff. A4ʳ, C2ʳ.
    2. Ibid., f. C4ᵛ.
    3. Ibid., f. D2ʳ.

He then with great pains attacks the seven major 'discouragements' offered against Virginia, ploughing more deeply some of the ground gone over by his predecessors. The first discouragement remained the lawfulness of settling Virginia, which he said troubled many of good conscience. To the usual argument that no harm would be done to the Indians he adds a comment on the temporal benefits they would have from English technology. 'For he that hath 1000 acres, and being a civill and sociable man knowes how to use it, is richer than he that hath 2000 and being a savage cannot plow, till, plant or set . . . When they are civilized, and see what they have received from us, I dare say they will never make this objection against us as these men now doe.'⁴ The second discouragement, the distance and difficulty of the voyage, is disposed of by pointing to the new, more northerly route pioneered by Samuel Argall, without any dangers in it, 'as though God himselfe had built a bridge for men to passe from England to Virginea'.⁵ To the third discouragement, Virginia's poor beginnings, both in terms of the quality and quantity of settlers, Crashaw offers the example of Israel, seventy souls that in two centuries became 600,000, and Rome which from mean beginnings became 'Mistresse of the World'. As for allegations that the settlers were 'rakte up out of the refuse', he saw them as neither better nor worse than Englishmen in general, surely no worse than the objectors and mockers who held back the effort. Nehemiah, he recalls, had taken a much-scorned crew to restore Jerusalem; David had built his following from among debtors and men in trouble; the Church itself, 'was it not begun by twelve poore men . . . taken most of them from base, and some from bad occupations?'⁶ Why then should not Virginia, with God's blessing, grow from its humble beginnings 'to be as an host of God'?⁷

A fourth discouragement was that negative reports had been made on Virginia. So, says Crashaw, had ten out of twelve Israelites downgraded Canaan, and God had seen to their punishment while rewarding Joshua and Caleb who had told the truth. The slanderers of Virginia and their followers he found not hard to understand, 'For how can they speake good things when themselves are evill?'⁸ Closely related was the fifth discouragement, the reports of hard living conditions in Virginia. This

4. Crashaw, *A sermon preached in London*, f. D4ʳ.
5. Ibid., f. E1ᵛ.
6. Ibid., ff. E1ᵛ–E4ʳ.
7. Ibid., f. F2ʳ.
8. Ibid., f. F3ᵛ.

provoked a harsh rebuke. The early Britons had built their country in times of cold and storms and rain, showing a stamina that had unhappily been replaced by 'tendernesse and effeminatenesse', from which Crashaw hoped the nation would rally 'to more hardnesse' through a life of 'obedience under sharper discipline'.[9]

Of all the discouragements none was so base in Crashaw's eyes as the uncertainty of profit, which he saw in no way attuned to the first motives of the undertaking. No one, he states, should ever have come in with quick profit in mind. 'If the propagation of the Gospell, and inlarging the kingdom of Jesus Christ, be not inducements strong enough to bring them into this business, it is a pitie they be in at all.'[1] This was not to deny the profit motive or its ultimate reward, but only to affirm that profits would come as a blessing from God if the first motive was faithfully acted upon.

The final discouragement was the threat to Virginia from enemies. Who were they? Certainly not Spain, as alleged, for Spain and England were allied. The pope? He had no power to give any part of America away. The French had no cause to rival England in Virginia, and the Indians were inviting the English to settle, not resisting them. But enemies there were, and Crashaw turned on them. First, the Devil, 'for we goe to disherit him of his ancient freehold', and God would give the victory. Secondly, papists who 'have filled all corners of this kingdome with base reports and slanders of this action'. Let them curse it, says Crashaw, this will guarantee God's blessing on it. And finally, 'players', that is, satirists who attack all sorts of respectable things, including Virginia, 'because we resolve to suffer no Idle persons in Virginea'.[2] With God, His angels, and the prayers of the church allied against such foes, the triumph of Virginia was assured.

In his final exhortation Crashaw urged the Council to persist in the face of all obstacles 'till there be a church of God established in Virginea'. To the settlers he said, 'goe forward in the name of God . . . to eternize your owne names both heere at home and among the Virginians (whose Apostles you are)'. And to Lord de la Ware, 'Remember thou art a Generall of English men, nay a Generall of Christian men: therefore principally looke to religion. You goe to commend it to the heathen; practise it your selves. . . .'[3]

9. Ibid., f. G1[v].
1. Ibid., f. G2[v].
2. Ibid., ff. H1[v]–H4[r].
3. Ibid., f. L1[r].

Thus admonished, Lord de la Ware sailed for Virginia on 1 April 1610, arriving there in mid-May, just in time to intercept Sir Thomas Gates, who had already embarked the entire colony, tired and depressed, to return to England. The survival of the *Sea Venture*'s people on Bermuda, their arrival in Virginia, and now the timely arrival of de la Ware with new settlers and supplies, provided a mighty testimony to believers that God would not let their colony fail.

Such was the assurance given towards the end of 1610 by the Council for the Virginia Company, countering its critics, in *A true declaration of the estate of the Colonie of Virginia,* in which readers were shown 'how God inclineth all casual events, to worke the necessary helpe of his Saints'.[4] But not all the news from Virginia was good. Unfavourable reports had come back with deserters, so it became necessary to consider the 'great distance, betwixt the vulgar opinions of vulgar men, and the judicious apprehension of wise men', for the goodness of Virginia 'is being eclipsed by the interposition of clamorous and tragicall narrations'.[5] There is little that is new in the Company's defence of the colony, although the balance is shifting noticeably toward mercantile interests. The missionizing, it is explained, must be done 'mixtly, by discoveries, and trade of merchants', so that 'by way of marchandizing and trade [we] doe buy of them the pearles of earth, and sell to them the pearles of heaven'.[6]

What is different about this tract is the greater detail it exhibits in describing the 'pearles of earth', seven pages of appeal to the commercially minded, in addition to the familiar topic of over-population in England and the concern for a supply of shipbuilding materials to maintain 'our wooden wals'.[7] But the religious theme is by no means abandoned: 'Let Religion be the first aim of your hopes . . . and other things will come unto you . . . If God have scattered his blessings upon you as snow, will you return no tributary acknowledgement of his goodnesse? If you will, can you select a more excellent subject then to cast downe the altars of Divels, that you may raise up the Altar of Christ . . .'[8]

Virginia survived. But in the light of subsequent history—even in 1620

---

4. *A true declaration of the estate of the colonie in Virginia, with a confutation of such scandalous reports as have tended to the disgrace of so worthy an enterprise. Published by advise and direction of the Councell of Virginia* (London, 1610), p. 46.

5. Ibid., pp. 1–2.

6. Ibid., p. 9.

7. Ibid., p. 63.

8. Ibid., pp. 66–67.

the colony had only five clergymen[9]—it is easy for a secular age to see in the religious appeals of 1609–10 a degree of hypocrisy, the appeals lending sanctity to common commercial enterprise. Nothing in the 1609 charter, or in the church records that have been examined, points to any administrative structure designed to support a maior missionary effort. When the Company, in its *True and sincere declaration*, called for certain skilled types needed in the colony 'Foure honest and learned Ministers' were placed at the head of the list. But in number they were equal to pitch-boilers, sturgeon-dressers, and turners.

In the partnership between state, church, and merchants which supported the settlement of Virginia, the church was the weakest partner. Impoverished, divided, on the defensive, it had not the means to build, as the Jesuits were doing, a missionary empire abroad. Yet the more aggressive elements within the church were not less interested in doing so, fully aware that protestantism was being outdistanced by their hated rivals. The Virginia colony was their opportunity, their chance to carry 'true' Christianity abroad. This was no official church effort, so there was no organization to lay extensive plans for the mission, no budget, no call to crusade from the church hierarchy. The motivation existed without the machinery to implement it. But the message of the moment, 'God will give the blessing', was an acceptable one to many people in an emerging world power, and not least to those who could see the hand of Providence in the nation's successes against catholic Spain. Religion's defence of Virginia was the only idealistic argument capable of countering the idealists of other persuasions who saw the invasion of Virginia as an immoral act. The alliance of these churchmen with the Virginia Company was therefore a natural one, for each needed the other, and there is no reason to believe that many in the Company took less seriously the preachers' message than did many of those to whom the sermons and company propaganda were addressed. If this was somewhat other than a medieval pilgrimage which churchmen were undertaking, it was not less devout in its intentions. By no means was it a mere façade for the merchants' ambitions.

But the vision faded quickly. In the decade after 1610 Virginia took on the appearance of a permanent settlement, yet it had a precarious and troubled survival, the realities of which left no doubt that the hoped-for harvest of souls would have to await other more material harvests. The

9. Cross, p. 10.

Company's third charter, dated 12 March 1612, is elaborate in its plans for the civil government of the colony, but utterly silent about religion in Virginia.[1] The preachers did not cease to proclaim Virginia's holy purpose, but they spoke more occasionally and more softly. Robert Johnson's *The new life of Virginea*, published in 1612, was less militantly missionistic than *Nova Britannia* had been. The very success of recruiting settlers in 1609 had made the problem of their behaviour a concern of high priority for him.[2] William Symonds, in *The proceeding of the English Colonie in Virginia*, abandoned preaching and instead edited accounts of the colony favourable to Captain John Smith.[3] Alexander Whitaker, a preacher of the 1609 school, wrote from Virginia of the 'miserable covetous men' in the colony whose lack of faith in God was a drawback to Virginia's real mission.[4]

Thus the great crusade of 1609–10 bogged down in problems of management and mere survival. There would be other calls to do God's work among the Indians of North America. But never again would there be anything like this brief, enthusiastic hour in English and American history, when religion spoke more loudly for empire than either the state or the merchant community.

1. Bemiss, pp. 76–94.
2. Robert Johnson, *The new life of Virginea: declaring the former successe and present estate of that plantation* . . . (London, 1612).
3. William Symonds, *The proceedings of the English colonie in Virginia* (Oxford, 1612).
4. Alexander Whitaker, *Good newes from Virginia* (London, 1613).

13

Experiments holy
and unholy
1630-1

RICHARD S. DUNN

On 22 March 1630 John Winthrop of Groton, Suffolk, boarded the ship
Arbella at Southampton in order to emigrate to New England. On 29
March, expecting his ship to embark that morning, he began to keep a
journal in order to record the experiences of his voyage for the information of family and friends still in England who would be sailing on later
ships to join him in America. Fourteen months later, and fifty miles
further west, on 22 May 1631 an Essex gentleman named Sir Henry Colt
boarded the ship *Alexander* at Weymouth in Dorset to plant in the Caribbean. That day, as his ship set sail, he too began to keep a journal for the
instruction of his son at home, since he hoped that this youth would be
coming out to the islands shortly to join him. John Winthrop and his
journal are of course very famous. As the first governor of the Massachusetts Bay Company and the chief figure in his colony during its first
two decades, Winthrop has become the embodiment of New England
puritan orthodoxy. The journal begun in 1630 he kept more or less
regularly until his final illness in 1649; it has been recognized ever since
as the prime source for early New England history.[1] Posterity has been
less kind to Sir Henry Colt. He closed his journal on 20 August 1631,
just one month after he began to farm in St Christopher. Nothing much
more is known about him, except that by 1635 he was reported to be

---

1. The edition of Winthrop's *Journal* used in this essay is edited by J. K. Hosmer (2 vols,
New York, 1908), and is hereafter cited as Winthrop. I have also drawn upon Winthrop's
correspondence, edited by A. B. Forbes, *Winthrop Papers* (5 vols, Boston, 1929–47, hereafter
cited as *WP*). For a biography of Winthrop see Edmund S. Morgan, *The Puritan Dilemma*
(Boston, 1958). For a study of the Winthrop family, see my *Puritans and Yankees* (Princeton,
1962).

dead. The journal itself was forgotten until it was published in 1925.[2] Yet Colt's description of his voyage and his first impressions of tropical America are at least as informative as Winthrop's report; together they provide the two best accounts we have of what it was like to start a plantation in the New World around 1630.

The date is important, for Winthrop and Colt were early participants in the great migration of the 1630s that gave the English a secure footing in America for the first time. When Winthrop set sail, hardly more than 5,000 Englishmen were living in the New World: half of them in Virginia, and the rest precariously scattered in New England, Bermuda, Barbados, and the Leeward Islands. During the decade of the 1630s, at least 50,000 passengers embarked from British ports for America. We have the names of 4,890 people who sailed from London in the single year 1635, and London was far from being the only port of embarkation.[3] Many of these people died quickly, like Colt, and many others returned home. But thanks to the great migration, the population of the English colonies in America increased roughly eight-fold during these ten years; it stood at about 40,000 in 1640. Virginia, still a struggling plantation in 1630, trebled its population in this short time. But the two areas of heaviest immigration were New England and the Caribbean islands. By 1640 some 15,000 Britons inhabited each region.[4] Thus Winthrop and Colt recorded the start of the take-off process in two highly successful areas of English overseas settlement.

Even at this opening stage, the New England and Caribbean colonists had sharply different characteristics. Winthrop and his associates were animated by religious zeal; Colt and his associates were looking primarily for adventure and profit. Winthrop and a dozen other officers of the Massachusetts Bay Company were carrying their royal charter with them in order to establish a self-governing Bible commonwealth. The day before he sailed, Winthrop signed a public letter, the *Humble Request* of the Governor and Company of Massachusetts Bay, which asked all Anglicans (however suspicious of this puritan hegira) to pray for the success of the

2. 'The voyage of Sir Henry Colt' is printed by V. T. Harlow in *Colonising Expeditions to the West Indies and Guiana 1623–1667* (London, 1925), pp. 54–102 (hereafter cited as Colt). I have discussed Colt's place in Caribbean settlement in my *Sugar and Slaves* (London, 1973), chap. 1.

3. The London port register of 1635 is printed by J. C. Hotten in *Original Lists of Persons . . . who went from Great Britain to the American Plantations 1600–1700* (London, 1874), pp. 33–145 (hereafter cited as Hotten).

4. For discussion of the migration of the 1630s, see Carl Bridenbaugh, *Vexed and Troubled Englishmen 1590–1642* (New York, 1968), chaps 11–12.

new plantation. But Winthrop was leaving England in protest against the corrupt character of Church and State, and he entertained no doubt that God was opening a better life for His chosen people in America.[5] Colt, on the other hand, was a free-spirited gambler, drawn to the West Indies because this corner of the New World was a famous stage for daring deeds. Here the Spanish had found great wealth, and the English had come after them to search for El Dorado, or to trade with the Spaniards, or to capture their ships and plunder their settlements. To be sure, Sir Henry was ostensibly coming out as a mere farmer, to start a tobacco plantation in St Christopher. But as his narrative shows, he quickly dropped this prosaic goal, 'that we might proceed to greater exploits'.[6]

In literary style the two journalists express their contrasting personalities. Winthrop writes tersely, soberly, drily; Colt writes with verve and panache. Consider how each writer sets his opening scene. First, Winthrop:

Anno Domini 1630, March 29, Monday. Easter Monday. Riding at the Cowes, near the Isle of Wight, in the *Arbella*, a ship of three hundred and fifty tons. . . . About ten of the clock we weighed anchor and set sail, with the wind at N., and came to an anchor again over against Yarmouth, and the *Talbot* weighed likewise, and came and anchored by us.[7]

Next, Colt:

Upon Sunday morning the 22 May 1631 I arrived by post to Weymouth . . . and immediately quitted the town, took our boat, and went to our ship then riding in Portland road. Now are we all met, our joy not to be expressed, . . . but aboard we are. Neither do we lose time, for we presently weigh anchor, hoise up our sails, putting ourselves to sea, taking our course south south west alongst our English Channel.[8]

But before we follow Colt and Winthrop across the Atlantic, it is worth noticing the character of their fellow passengers. Winthrop headed a large, carefully organized migration. He had worked hard to recruit a congenial body of like-minded emigrants who paid £5 apiece for their

5. For background on the Massachusetts migration, see C. M. Andrews, *The Colonial Period of American History* (4 vols, New Haven, 1934–8), i. 344–99; and Perry Miller, *Orthodoxy in Massachusetts* (Cambridge, Mass., 1933), chaps 4–5.

6. Colt, p. 91. For background on the Caribbean migration, see A. P. Newton, *The European Nations in the West Indies* (London, 1933), chaps 7–11; and Carl and Robert Bridenbaugh, *No Peace beyond the Line* (New York, 1972), chap. 1.

7. Winthrop, i. 23–24.

8. Colt, p. 54. I have modernized Colt's spelling in this passage, to conform with Hosmer's modernization of Winthrop's text.

passage and £4 for each ton of goods they brought. By January 1630 Winthrop's ship was fully booked, and in March at Southampton 700 passengers with 240 cows and 60 horses boarded a fleet of eleven vessels. We do not have a passenger list for this fleet, but Charles Edward Banks has searched out the names of 537 people he thinks were on board. While Banks's findings are probably somewhat inaccurate, they are certainly of interest. According to him, about a hundred of the passengers came from villages within a ten-mile radius of Winthrop's estate at Groton, Suffolk. About 80 per cent came from Suffolk, Essex, or London. Another pertinent point is that 70 per cent of them travelled as family groups. Half of the adult males came with their wives, and many with young children. It appears that about 40 per cent of the passengers in 1630 were female and 25 per cent children. A few wealthy emigrants like Winthrop brought servants: he had three sons and eight servants in his entourage, with the rest of the family following in 1631. But most of the passengers seem to have been independent farmers and artisans. Banks's picture for 1630 is confirmed by the numerous passenger lists we have for ships bound to New England in the mid-1630s. Consistently these people came over in families. Consistently 40 per cent or more of the passengers were females, and, on lists where ages are given, a third were young people under the age of 15. Not many old people joined up; only about 2 per cent were over the age of 50. But plenty of married couples in their 30s and 40s came over with children and servants; these were people in mid-career who had pulled up stakes and intended to stay in America.[9]

How does the picture vary for emigrants to the Caribbean? Again, unfortunately, we have no passenger list for the *Alexander* in 1631, and given the paucity of early island records there is no way to replicate Banks's genealogical research. Colt himself was taking over a party of servants: probably fifteen or twenty men and boys, though he lists only a few by name. Some of his fellow passengers were bound for Barbados, others for St Christopher. Colt says there were 'divers captaynes and gentlemen of note' on board, and 'very many' women and children. It was, however, unusual for women and children to emigrate to the islands. The seventy-four colonists who first settled Barbados in 1627 were all males, and when Colt's ship, the *Alexander*, carried 162 passengers to

9. C. E. Banks, *The Winthrop Fleet of 1630* (Boston, 1930), *passim*; Hotten, pp. 33–145, 277–300. For an interesting analysis of 273 migrants to New England in 1637, see T. H. Breen and Stephen Foster, 'Moving to the New World', *William and Mary Quarterly*, 3rd series, xxx (1973), 189–222.

Barbados on a later voyage in 1635, only nineteen were women and seven were children under the age of 15.[1] Nearly twenty passenger lists for Caribbean-bound ships survive from the mid 1630s, and they show a sex and age distribution radically different from the New England lists. The overwhelming majority of the passengers on these ships were single males in their teens or 20s. Over 70 per cent were between 15 and 24 years old; less than 10 per cent were females. Few people over the age of 40 came over, scarcely any married couples, and almost no children below working age. Some of these young people were coming out to set up for themselves, but the great majority were hired labourers. They were indentured servants—like the gang Colt brought over in 1631—who bound themselves to four or five years of labour in the tropics for the adventure of it, with little expectation that they would stay once they had served their time.[2]

By 1630 the English had been sailing to America for seventy years, and they had been attempting to colonize for fifty, so the emigrants to New England and the Caribbean had plenty of experience to draw upon. On the whole, Winthrop and Colt equipped themselves in similar ways for the Atlantic crossing. The most important point was assembling provisions. We have the bills for food Winthrop ordered in London, and a list of provisions stored in the *Arbella*, but it is not clear how much of this was for the voyage and how much was for the first months in New England. If the *Arbella* stores were all for the voyage, and if—as seems likely—this ship carried about two hundred passengers and crew, the daily ration was half a gallon of beer per person, a pint of water, half a pound of salt meat, and half a pound of biscuit, supplemented by dried peas, oatmeal, butter, and mustard seed for flavouring. Fresh fruit and vegetables, and lemon juice to counter scurvy, were conspicuously missing. The galley was stocked with only 100 platters, 156 wooden spoons, and 78 drinking cans, so the passengers on the *Arbella* either shared utensils or supplied their own. On the *Alexander*, Colt's captain fixed the rations to be distributed among passengers and crew at every mess, to make sure he saved enough for the return voyage. Colt and his men ate a monotonous diet of broth, pudding, and boiled biscuit, embellished by pepper, raisins, and cheese to check diarrhoea. They had a little fresh and salted meat, but ate

1. This was definitely the same ship Colt sailed on, with Captain Burch in command, see Hotten, pp. 73–75. For a list of the settlers in 1627, see N. Darnell Davis, *Cavaliers and Roundheads of Barbados* (Georgetown, British Guiana, 1887), pp. 42–43.
2. Hotten, pp. 33–145, 296–8.

more sparingly of it than Winthrop's company. Both Colt and Winthrop wished that they had brought more supplementary provisions of eggs, meal, butter, fruit, and cheese. Both brought their own wine, which Colt stored in double-casked barrels to prevent the sailors from tapping them.[3]

Winthrop furnished his party on the *Arbella* with flock beds, bolsters, cushions, rugs, a bedpan, and close stool. The governor himself perhaps slept in the 'French Beadstead' that he bought for £2 12*s*. One week after boarding ship, he reported to his wife that their young sons 'lye both with me, and sleepe as soundly in a rugge (for we use no sheets heer) as ever they did at Groton, and so I doe my selfe (I prayse God)'. Colt tried sleeping in a hammock in the *Alexander*, but got too cold and could not roll over, so he too used a flock bed. He furnished his cabin with table linen, wax lights, eating utensils, a stewing pan, and a chamber pot. Since Colt was headed for the tropics and Winthrop for the North Atlantic, they dressed somewhat differently. Colt discarded his quilted doublet, because it was too warm, but he wore plenty of clothes: a long-sleeved shirt reaching to the knees, a sleeveless jerkin and puffed knee-breeches, a handkerchief around the throat, a feathered hat, beads, boot hose, stockings, and shoes. At sea he wore a stomacher—the seventeenth-century equivalent of a sweater—to protect against the wind. Winthrop does not describe his costume, but he warned his wife to dress very warmly on shipboard.[4] The servants sent to New England the previous year by the Massachusetts Bay Company were given heavier clothing than Colt wore: two suits of doublet and breeches apiece, including one made of leather, as well as girdles, waistcoats, shirts, neckbands, hats and caps, shoes and stockings.[5]

As they embarked, both the *Arbella* and the *Alexander* prepared for military combat against unfriendly vessels. England was at war with Spain when Winthrop sailed, and though the two countries made peace in November 1630, America lay outside the territorial limits of European treaties. On the high seas and in the New World, might made right. The *Arbella* was a relatively large ship of 350 tons; she carried twenty-eight guns, was manned by fifty-two seamen, and sailed in convoy with three other ships chartered by the Massachusetts Bay Company. The masters of these four vessels signed formal articles of consortship, by which it was

3. *WP*, ii. 171–2, 216–18, 274–5, 278, 303–4, 314; Colt, pp. 56–57, 99–100.
4. *WP*, ii. 208, 216, 224; Colt, pp. 99–101.
5. N. B. Shurtleff (ed.), *Records of the Governor and Company of the Massachusetts Bay*, (Boston, 1853–4), i. 23–24 (hereafter cited as *Mass. Rec.*).

agreed that Captain Milborne, the master of the *Arbella*, was admiral of the fleet; Mr Beecher of the *Talbot*, who had taken his ship to New England in 1629, was vice-admiral; the masters of the other two ships were rear-admiral and captain. These preparations immediately proved useful. On the second day at sea, eight ships that seemed to be Dunkirk privateers bore down on Winthrop's fleet. Captain Milborne cleared the *Arbella*'s gun-deck for action, dismantled passenger cabins that were in the way, took down hammocks, threw flammable bedding into the sea, armed twenty-five of the passengers with muskets, and called the company to prayer on the upper deck. The Lord answered their call, for the Dunkirk privateers turned out to be friendly merchant and fishing ships. Winthrop encountered no further scares of this sort, meeting only five small ships during the rest of his voyage.[6]

Colt had considerably more reason to worry, since the *Alexander* was sailing without escort into Spanish waters. This ship was perhaps as large as the *Arbella*—large enough, in any case, to carry 200 tons of cargo back to England, and on a later voyage 162 passengers—but she was more lightly armed, with only sixteen guns. Colt says that Captain Burch's first care as they set sail was to assign twenty-nine of his seamen to man the guns, and to form sixty of the male passengers into squads of musketeers. During their Atlantic crossing they sighted only three small ships. But when they reached the islands and were sailing from Barbados to St Christopher, they were surprised near Guadeloupe by a fleet of twenty or more Spanish vessels bearing down on them in full sail. The *Alexander* ran for her life to open sea. The two closest Spanish ships kept up the pursuit and, having the wind, soon overtook Colt's ship. Both sides prepared to fight. As on the *Arbella*, Captain Burch had to knock down passenger cabins and toss cargo overboard in order to clear his gun-deck for action. Meanwhile, Sir Henry 'bestowed two great bottles full of hott water [spirituous liquor] amongst our men'. The Spanish fired first, and the English replied with seven guns at close range, doing enough damage to the leading ship so that both of the Spaniards fell off. But the danger had been great, the *Alexander* was leaking badly and far off course, and Colt felt vastly relieved when he finally reached St Christopher five days later.[7]

Captain Burch ran a tight ship, with public prayers held three times daily, at 10 in the morning, 4 in the afternoon, and 8 at night before

6. Winthrop, i. 23–24, 27–28.   7. Colt, pp. 55–56, 77–82.

setting the watch. The godly, disciplined atmosphere on board the *Alexander* sounds surprisingly similar to Winthrop's portrait of his voyage. As Colt put it, they ordered their ship 'towards the service of God from whose divine power and providence we must expect all our securitye and happinesse in this our voyage'. Needless to say, Winthrop also ordered his ship toward the service of God. The Reverend George Phillips of Boxsted, Essex, future minister of the church in Watertown, Massachusetts, was a passenger on the *Arbella*; he preached every Sunday when he was not feeling too seasick, and catechized the ship's company every Tuesday and Wednesday. In times of crisis, as during the worst storms and fog, Phillips appealed to the Lord for help by exercising the passengers in day-long fasts. And when the weather cleared, he held thanksgiving. Captain Milborne had his sailors join in these fasts; after the voyage Winthrop wrote: 'I founde that love and respect from Capt. Milburne our master, as I may not forgett.' Passengers and sailors who were caught stealing liquor and food, or who breached discipline by fighting or by disrespectful speech, were placed in irons, or stood in disgrace with weights about the neck. Nor was Phillips the only preacher on board the *Arbella*. Winthrop composed his famous lay sermon, 'A Modell of Christian Charity', during the voyage, and he presumably delivered it to his fellow passengers, inspiring them to behave as a covenanted 'company professing our selves fellow members of Christ', knit together by the bond of love, to serve God 'as a Citty upon a Hill', with the eyes of all people upon them.[8]

Winthrop's and Colt's sea journals are sufficiently detailed so that their transatlantic routes can be traced with some accuracy.[9] Winthrop had to endure an exceptionally lengthy and rough crossing. After boarding ship on 22 March 1630, he was held at the Isle of Wight for seventeen days by contrary winds. Setting sail at last on 8 April, he took his last sight of England on the third day out, passing the Lizard in Cornwall. One week out, during the first big storm, the *Arbella* lost touch with the *Talbot*, vice-admiral of the fleet, and did not see her again until she straggled into Charlestown three weeks after the other three ships, with fourteen of her passengers dead. During the first three weeks the *Arbella* worked her way 900 miles west to the longitude of the Azores, and 6 degrees south to

8. Colt, p. 57; Winthrop, i. 25, 29–31, 36–37, 40, 42, 46; *WP*, ii. 228, 230, 282–95, 305.
9. See H. E. Ware, 'Winthrop's course across the Atlantic', *Colonial Society of Massachusetts Publications*, xii (1908–9), 191–203; xx (1917–19), 278–9; also S. E. Morison, 'The course of the *Arbella* from Cape Sable to Salem', ibid. xxvii (1927–30), 285–306.

the latitude of the Maine coast. For the rest of the voyage Captain Milborne tried to hold to a due westerly course, following a well-established sea route that skirted the Grand Bank, passed south of Sable Island, and made landfall at Cape Sable, Nova Scotia. Unfortunately for Milborne, he was constantly having to fight west winds, tempestuous seas, fierce rain, and thick fog. The manuscript of Winthrop's journal in the Massachusetts Historical Society bears mute witness to this stormy weather, for on the worst days the governor's crabbed handwriting danced crazily across the pages of his notebook. In a thick fog off the Nova Scotian coast, the three remaining ships in the Winthrop fleet became separated, not to rejoin until they reached Salem. At last, on the fifty-ninth day of the voyage, 'the mist then breaking up, we saw the shore to the N. about five or six leagues off, and were (as we supposed) to S.W. of Cape Sable'. Having made landfall, Captain Milborne headed straight west across the Gulf of Maine, fearing that if he steered southwest toward Massachusetts, the Arctic current would carry him on to the treacherous Georges Bank off Cape Cod. But he miscalculated and touched the Maine Coast at Mount Desert Island, sixty miles further up the coast than he wanted to be. It took five more days to work south past Penobscot Bay, Cape Porpoise, the Isles of Shoals, and Cape Ann. During this last week of the voyage they put out their fishing lines and feasted on fresh codfish and mackerel. 'We had now fair sunshine weather,' wrote Winthrop gratefully, 'and so pleasant a sweet air as did much refresh us, and there came a smell off the shore like the smell of a garden.' On 12 June, after sixty-six days at sea, they anchored in Salem harbour.[1]

When Sir Henry Colt sailed to the Caribbean the following year, he had a much quicker and easier passage. Not that he found the voyage short. 'Suerly the Journye is great,' he protested in mid-passage, 'and further by a 1000 miles then ever I supposed itt to be.' The sea route to the Caribbean was indeed longer than to New England, but sailing ships generally covered the distance more rapidly because they took advantage of the constant trade wind blowing to the Indies. The *Alexander* followed the route first charted by Christopher Columbus. Leaving Weymouth on 22 May 1631, Colt's ship sighted the Lizard on the second day out, and bore south across the Bay of Biscay, past Portugal, Madeira, and the Canaries. At the end of three weeks she had travelled about 1,500 miles—much further than the *Arbella* in the same time—and stood 300 miles

1. Winthrop, i. 32, 37, 45–49.

west of the Canaries in the latitude of central Florida. Here the *Alexander* picked up the trade wind and headed west by southwest across the Atlantic. Colt complained of feeble breezes, 'like the languishinge motions of a dyinge man', but when the wind blew strong they ran ten leagues a watch, or 180 miles a day. When they reached the latitude of Barbados, their first port of call, they had difficulty in reckoning their exact longitude—a problem also on the *Arbella*, because the instruments of observation used by sailors in the 1630s were so crude. Captain Burch knew that he must be near Barbados, but since this island has a low silhouette, it was easy to sail past by mistake, and once to the leeward of any Caribbean island a sailing ship had much difficulty in beating back against the wind. As Colt put it, Barbados is 'like sixpence throwne downe uppon newmarkett heath'. Thus the *Alexander* tacked cautiously for several days. In the small hours of the morning on 1 July, a lookout in the forecastle cried 'Land!' Colt saw nothing in the darkness and longed for daylight like 'the woman with childe for her good howre'. When day broke he was surprised to see a white line of breakers, sand, and rocks less than a mile away with wooded land rising steeply beyond. It was the craggy eastern coast of Barbados. Only forty days had passed since they embarked from Weymouth, and not one passenger sick, thanks to God's gracious favour. 'You alone art able to walke uppon the waves of the seas and givest limitts to the waters therof,' wrote Colt gratefully, 'to the glory and prayse of [your] holy name for ever.'[2]

Once they reached America, Winthrop and Colt encountered radically different situations—alarming situations, in both cases, that quickly tested the new settlers' resourcefulness and courage. To read Winthrop's journal, one might suppose he had a cheerful arrival at Salem. John Ende-cott, who had been managing the advance settlement for the Massachusetts Bay Company since 1628, and the Reverend Samuel Skelton, pastor of Salem church, came aboard to escort the new governor ashore to a supper of 'good venison pasty and good beer', while other passengers gathered wild strawberries on Cape Ann. But then Winthrop reports that he returned to his ship and stayed aboard all the next day, which was Sunday. Why did this land-starved puritan gentleman avoid attending Salem church service? The reason is that Skelton told him he was excluded from communion until he subscribed to the covenant of a gathered New England church—doubtless quite a shock to the spokesman for a city

2. Colt, pp. 59–60, 62–65.

on a hill, and a startling testimonial to the new religious practices already evolving in New England.[3] But this was far from the greatest shock. Winthrop never mentioned it in his journal, but he found on arrival that eighty of the three hundred colonists previously sent to Salem had died, and the others were sick and nearly out of food. The servants sent ahead by the Massachusetts Bay Company in 1628–9 had failed to build houses or to produce crops for the hundreds of new colonists arriving in 1630. Since these servants could not be fed, they had to be released from their indentures at great loss to the Company.[4] Skelton might be good at organizing a new church, but Endecott was certainly poor at managing a labour force. Now, in late June, the growing season for 1630 was nearly half over, and the passengers from the *Arbella* and the other ships were weakened by scurvy and sea fever, and had little food. Winthrop faced a grave situation. Since Salem could not accommodate so many newcomers, he and his colleagues must quickly decide where else to settle, in order to clear fields and build lodgings before winter.

Unfortunately, Winthrop was far too busy during the next desperate months to keep a proper journal. His entries became maddeningly irregular and brief. Five days after arriving, on 17 June 1630, he noted: 'We went to Mattachusetts, to find out a place for our sitting down. We went up Mistick River about six miles.' These two sentences are among the most tantalizing in the whole journal. By *Mattachusetts* he meant the environs of Boston harbour, inhabited at this time by a handful of Englishmen. Charlestown was the only collective settlement, with one house and a few wigwams. Winthrop and the other new colonists were clearly bent on finding 'a place' to settle in this region. But how literally should we interpret 'a place'? Did Winthrop intend that all of the incoming settlers should congregate in a single community—a considerably larger town than the average seventeenth-century English village?[5] Or did he intend the *Arbella* passengers to form one community expecting that later shiploads would form into other communities? This seems to me far more plausible. Two weeks before Winthrop arrived, a shipload of 140 colonists from the west of England had landed on the south side of

3. Winthrop, i. 49–50. See Larzer Ziff, *The Career of John Cotton* (Princeton, 1962), pp. 59–60, 74–76.

4. See Deputy Governor Dudley's letter to the Countess of Lincoln, 12 March 1631, in Alexander Young (ed.), *Chronicles of the First Planters of the Colony of Massachusetts Bay* (Boston, 1846), pp. 311–12.

5. This is the argument of Darrett Rutman, *Winthrop's Boston* (Chapel Hill, N.C., 1965), pp. 23–28, 280–3.

Boston harbour at Mattapan, and they founded their own town of Dorchester. Meanwhile, the *Arbella* colonists argued over the best site for settlement. Winthrop favoured the Mystic River, while Deputy Governor Dudley favoured the Charles River. During late June, when there is a two-week gap in Winthrop's journal, the newly arrived planters were ferrying their goods from Salem to the Boston harbour area. Most of the ships arriving in July and August landed at Charlestown, at the confluence of the Charles and Mystic rivers. By 14 July, the date of his first letter to England, Winthrop was living in Charlestown, occupying one of the few houses built by Company servants the previous year. In October, together with a good many other colonists, he moved across the Charles River to Boston. Meanwhile other newcomers were founding Watertown on the Charles, Medford on the Mystic, Roxbury, west of Boston, and Weymouth, south of Dorchester. Within three months of arrival the new settlers had grouped themselves into seven little nucleated towns, ringing Boston harbour.[6]

In other ways the colonists very rapidly organized a highly distinctive society. In July, covenanted churches of self-nominated saints were gathered in three of the new towns, along the lines of the Salem church. On 30 July, Winthrop was the first signatory of the covenant forming the Charlestown church, soon to be transferred to Boston. One month later the congregation of this church ordained the Reverend John Wilson as their teacher, using the imposition of hands as a sign of election and confirmation. Winthrop protested that this was 'not of any intent that Mr. Wilson should renounce his ministry he received in England', but in practical fact Winthrop's gathered congregation was renouncing the national, episcopal, liturgical establishment at home.[7] When Winthrop presided over the first meeting of the Massachusetts Bay Company in August, the initial item on the agenda was to provide maintenance for Wilson and Phillips, the Charlestown and Watertown ministers. At the second company meeting in September, Winthrop and his fellow magistrates dealt with a Massachusetts settler who clearly did not fit into their scheme of things: Thomas Morton, who had set up a maypole at Merrymount and had sold liquor and firearms to the Indians. They burned his

6. Winthrop, i. 50–53; *WP*, ii. 301; Young, *Chronicles of the First Planters*, p. 312; J. F. X. Davoren (ed.), *Historical Data relating to Counties, Cities and Towns in Massachusetts* (Boston 1966), pp. 14, 44, 69, 77–78, 87, 91.

7. Winthrop, i. 51–52; H. F. Worthley (ed.), *An Inventory of the Records of the Particular (Congregational) Churches of Massachusetts gathered 1620–1805, Proceedings of the Unitarian Historical Society*, xvi (Cambridge, Mass., 1970), 53, 91–92, 644.

house down, threw him in prison, and sent him to England on the first ship willing to carry him. And to block people like Morton from settling in the colony, they ruled that no colonist could henceforth plant within the limits of Massachusetts unless he had permission from the Company officers. Finally, in October, Winthrop and his fellow magistrates staged the first open meeting of the Company in America. Here they took the names of 109 men—probably just about every household head in the colony—who desired admission as freemen of the Company, but got all present to agree 'by the generall vote of the people, and erection of hands', that freemen would only elect the Company officers and not otherwise participate in the decision-making process. Thus in just a few months Winthrop had laid down the main lines of a system under which the Massachusetts colonists would live for the rest of the century.[8]

But the immediate question was: how could the colonists survive the first year? Seventeen ships brought a thousand people to Massachusetts in 1630; many of them arrived in a starving condition, and most of their livestock died in transit. Since the advance settlers at Salem were likewise weak and short of food, there was nothing for it but to trade with the Indians for corn and fish, to cultivate quick garden crops, and to cut hay from the meadowlands to support the remaining livestock through the coming winter. Winthrop took special care during his opening months in America to keep on good terms with the Indians. He sent a pinnace to Cape Cod to buy eighty bushels of corn from the Indians, and he dispatched the ship *Lyon* to Bristol for emergency provisions. He reported home that the New England diet of peas, puddings, Indian corn, and fish was wholesome enough, though coarse. But soon the newcomers began to sicken and die. On 30 July the colony held a fast day because so many people were falling victim to dysentery and scurvy. Winthrop himself suffered terrible losses. His 22-year-old son Henry drowned immediately after arrival. Eleven other 'members of my family'—that is, servants and associates from his Groton, Suffolk, neighbourhood—were dead by November. And then, as winter came on, new problems arose. Some colonists were still living in tents, and they suffered extremely from the cold. At least eight planters who built houses during the summer and autumn of 1630 lost these buildings in fires during the winter of 1630–1. Some of the houses were Indian-style wigwams; others were English-style, with wattle and daub chimneys and thatched roofs; all were highly

8. *Mass. Rec.*, i. 73–80.

flammable. The fire hazard was especially great because the colonists were burning their fields to clear out undergrowth preparatory to planting corn. When these winter brush fires ran out of control, they frequently burned down haystacks and sometimes ignited houses. Furthermore, when winter came many planters had not yet built barns or pens, and so lost their calves to the wolves and their cows and goats to the freezing weather. Caught in a December storm, six Bostonians in a small boat were driven ashore on Cape Cod, and four of them froze to death. Not surprisingly, these blows discouraged many people. Among the Company officers, two died in 1630 and five returned to England within a year, leaving only seven magistrates to manage the colony by the spring of 1631. Among the colonists at large, the loss was almost as bad: some two hundred of the thousand immigrants died within the first year, and another two hundred returned home.[9]

But Winthrop was not discouraged, for he saw the opening disasters as God's mode of testing the colonists' corrupt hearts. At the peak of mortality he insisted to his wife that he did not repent coming, and would not alter his course 'though I had foreseene all these Afflictions: I never fared better in my life, never slept better, never had more content of minde'. Doubtless Winthrop's stubborn buoyancy helped to keep the colony going. In February 1631 the *Lyon* returned from Bristol with £300 worth of desperately needed provisions: fifty-three hogsheads of wheat meal, peas, and oatmeal, smaller quantities of beef, pork, suet, cheese and butter, and lemon juice to cure the scurvy. Sickness was checked after this, and though goods remained scarce, the survival crisis was over. Only six ships arrived during 1631, bringing some ninety passengers—a tremendous decrease from the previous year. But the colonists harvested a plentiful crop, and when the governor's wife and three children landed in November 1631 with thirty-five tons of provisions and household goods, there was a great celebration. 'At their landing,' wrote Winthrop, 'most of the people, of the near plantations, came to welcome them, and brought and sent, for divers days, great store of provisions, as fat hogs, kids, venison, poultry, geese, partridges, etc., so as the like joy and manifestation of love had never been seen in New England.'[1]

To move south from Winthrop's New England to Sir Henry Colt's Caribbean is to enter an altogether different environment—a lushly

---

9. Winthrop, i. 51–59, 67; *WP*, ii. 302–3, 305, 309, 320. For a fuller discussion of Winthrop's first months in Massachusetts, see Rutman, *Winthrop's Boston*, chap. 2.

1. Winthrop, i. 57–71; *WP*, ii. 313, 318; iii. 41–49.

tropical world with its own brand of danger. Colt gives us vignettes of planter life on the little islands of Barbados and St Christopher. He stayed the first two weeks of July 1631 in Barbados, while his ship took on some passengers and a cargo of dyewood and tobacco. The English had occupied this island for only four years when Colt arrived, and as yet it bore little resemblance to the rich and crowded slave-based sugar-making society that would take shape in the 1640s and 1650s. The population of Barbados was probably under a thousand in 1631. Only the coastal land along the leeward shore was as yet under cultivation, since the island was covered with rain forest which was very hard to clear. The 250 planters who held land patents in 1631 raised tobacco and cotton for export, but the tobacco was of poor quality and the planters made small profit. Colt does not mention seeing any black slaves, though there probably were a few, since the first settlers brought Negroes with them in 1627. Mainly the labour force consisted of white indentured servants. Political control was in the hands of an absentee proprietor, the Earl of Carlisle, whose chief concern was the collection of quitrents. Management of the island was relegated to his governor, Henry Hawley, who dined on board the *Alexander* during Colt's visit. Sir Henry found Hawley modest and temperate, but very young. Among the Barbados planters and servants, he found no sign of the social discipline that Winthrop was building in Massachusetts.

In many respects Barbados was a perfect spot for colonization. It was extremely fertile, and uninhabited by Indians. Being the easternmost island in the Antilles, it became the first port of call for provision ships from Europe or slave ships from Africa. Barbados was the only English West Indian island in the seventeenth century to escape invasion by the Spanish or French. In 1631 it seemed to be a healthy place with no evidence as yet of the yellow fever that caused such terrible mortality later in the century. Certainly there was no danger of starvation, unlike the position in Massachusetts, for food crops grew year round and ripened very quickly. Colt was delighted with the natural beauty of the island, and spent most of his space describing the exotic tropical vegetation, and the strange birds, insects, reptiles, and fish he saw. But he was highly critical of the English planters. 'You are all younge men,' he said of the Barbadians, 'and of good desert, if you would but bridle the excesse of drinkinge, together with the quarrelsome conditions of your fyery spiritts.' In Colt's opinion, the planters were so busy drinking and quarrelling that they kept no control over their servants. The *Alexander* was continually pestered by servants who came on board hoping to escape from the island or at least to avoid working in the fields. During his stay, forty servants stole away from the island in a Dutch pinnace, and when Captain Burch tried to set sail, it took him a full day to clear all the unwanted visitors off his ship. Colt claims that in two weeks he never saw any man at work in Barbados. The planters cleared their land pretty much as the New Englanders did, by slashing and burning, and it shocked Colt to see charred tree trunks, weeds, brush, and desolate stumps six feet high standing or lying in the fields. A Barbadian plantation looked 'like the ruines of some village lately burned'. He also complained that the planters spread so dispersedly along the coast that they could not pool together in case of enemy attack. They had a fort and a watch house, but no militia.[2]

As Colt saw it, Barbados's basic problem was its lazy and undisciplined work force. We may readily sympathize with the servants on Barbados: they were young men, thoroughly sex-starved, who saw little point in labouring hard for others in the hot sun far from home. The problem was scarcely confined to Barbados. In Virginia, indentured servants were also the backbone of the labour force, and always unreliable—the 'terrible young men' in Edmund Morgan's phrase who kept that colony in a state of social unrest throughout the seventeenth century.[3] And in Massachusetts the servants sent over by the Company almost wrecked the colony, until the families of self-employed farmers and artisans in Winthrop's fleet took over the task of settlement in 1630.

As it turned out, Colt was a poor prognosticator about Barbados. Strong defence against Spanish and Indian attacks proved to be unnecessary, while the jungled terrain proved—once the rich soil of the interior valleys and the central upland was cleared and cultivated—to be magnificent sugar country. Had Colt patented several hundred acres in Barbados rather than in St Christopher, and cleared it with the servants he brought over, he would have joined a group of pioneers who were already staking out ambitious estates in the 1630s. These people formed the nucleus of the planter class that switched from tobacco and cotton to sugar in the 1640s, and as they profited from the sugar bonanza, these planters bought black slaves to replace their white indentured labourers. By 1660 the Barbados sugar magnates had established a highly exploitive,

2. Colt, pp. 65–75. For fuller discussion of early Barbados, see J. A. Williamson, *The Caribbee Islands under the Proprietary Patents* (Oxford, 1926), chaps 2–3, 5–7; V. T. Harlow, *A History of Barbados 1625–1685* (Oxford, 1926), chap. 1; and my *Sugar and Slaves*, chap. 2.

3. See Edmund S. Morgan, *American Slavery, American Freedom: The Ordeal of Colonial Virginia* (New York, 1975), especially chaps 6, 11.

rigidly disciplined sugar production system—as cohesive in its own fashion as Winthrop's Massachusetts. But such developments lay in the future. In 1631 Colt visited the plantations of two chief Barbadians. James Futter served him a feast of pigs, chickens, turkey, corn, cassava, and palm cabbage, boasting that he could entertain at the same rate every day of the year. James Holdip seemed to Colt 'the beautye, hands, eyes, feet, of all other planters'; ten years later Holdip would be the first Barbadian to experiment with sugar cane.[4]

From Barbados Colt sailed three hundred miles northwest to St Christopher. The English had been planting on this island since 1624, three years longer than on Barbados, and accordingly Colt saw more cleared fields and a better settled appearance. He found less drinking, quarrelling, and idleness than on Barbados, and he admired the strong leadership of the Earl of Carlisle's governor, Sir Thomas Warner, who was a Suffolk friend and neighbour of John Winthrop. Colt noticed immediately that Warner provided for the defence of the island, trained the militia, appointed a court of guards, set forth sentinels, 'and with great care and diligence visitts them day and night'. Strict military discipline was essential at St Christopher, for the planters were surrounded by potential enemies. The English shared the island with French colonists, while fierce Carib Indians from Dominica and other Antillean islands could easily stage raids, and the Dutch occupied neighbouring St Martin. The French had come to St Christopher in 1625, and Warner felt so weak that he agreed to partition the island with them, the French taking the two ends and the English the middle. The two parties drew up a partition treaty, binding themselves to share highways, roadsteads, and salt ponds, and to pool forces in case of attack. This treaty had done no good in 1629 when a large Spanish squadron attacked St Christopher and neighbouring Nevis. On the appearance of the Spaniards, the English servants on Nevis had thrown away their guns, crying 'Liberty, joyfull Liberty', and some had swum to the Spanish ships to tell the enemy where the English hid their possessions. The Spanish quickly overcame Anglo-French resistance, destroyed the buildings and crops, and shipped as many people as they could catch back home. But some of the English and French hid away and were soon back rebuilding their ruined plantations. In 1631, it looked as though the Spanish were on the attack again. As we have seen, Colt's ship narrowly escaped capture by another large Spanish squadron at

4. Colt, pp. 75–76; Dunn, *Sugar and Slaves*, pp. 57–67.

Guadeloupe. But when the *Alexander* moored in the roadstead before the English fort on 21 July 1631, welcomed by volleys of shot from planters up and down the shore, Colt could see that the Spaniards had not come back.

The St Christopher planters were, however, excited and tense. A few days after Colt's arrival, one man killed another in a brawl. In mid-August, seven or eight Caribs shot arrows at an English fishing party at the salt flats, wounding one of them and setting off a general alarm. Sir Henry suspected that the Indians were really naked Frenchmen daubed with red annatto dye. Such incidents and such suspicions were a staple feature of life on this island, for the Anglo-French partition worked poorly. St Christopher was as much a garrison as an agricultural settlement in 1631. Colt found breastworks erected at strategic points throughout the English sector. His field labourers were requisitioned for guard duty, and he stationed sentinels while he slept at night. Sir Henry thought the devil must have special power in America. 'Who is he that cann live long in quiett in these parts?' he asked. 'For all men are heer made subject to the power of this Infernall Spiritt. And fight they must, although it be with ther owne frends.' The English and French were certainly not friends. Throughout the century the settlers on St Christopher found themselves in the centre of Anglo-French conflict. Eventually, the island would change hands between the two sides seven times, with the French sacking the English sector three times, and the English sacking the French sector twice, before the French finally surrendered their claims in 1713.[5]

Sir Henry soon found that starting a new plantation was much harder work than he had supposed. First he pitched a tent and stored his goods by the seaside, then he set his servants to work clearing land and building a house on a mountainside lot he had chosen half a mile from the sea. Colt had brought only one axe, and his men spent half of their first work day making an axe handle before they could start to chop. Once they had their axe in working order, they had a terrible time trying to cut through the jungle growth and root out the vines. Formerly the Indians had planted sugar cane and annatto plants on this land, but now everything was overgrown. Tiring of his slow progress, Sir Henry decided to buy a house with cleared land at Palmetto Point near the French quarter, and set his men to work planting peas, potatoes, and wheat for provisions. Meanwhile, the *Alexander* was at St Martin lading salt as ballast for the

5. Colt, pp. 71, 73, 86–98. For a fuller discussion of early St Christopher (St Kitts), see my *Sugar and Slaves,* chap. 4.

homeward journey, when suddenly a freak tropical storm struck. The sailors were up in the rigging, trying to furl her sails. A lightning bolt, striking the mainmast, flung six of the sailors dead into the sea, tossed the master and boatswain overboard, and slammed Captain Burch and the others down on to the deck. The mainmast was shivered, the sails burned, and Captain Burch not only had to repair his ship but to sign up new men for the voyage home.

Colt wrote home for four horses, two cows, and forty additional servants to man his 'great plantation' at Palmetto Point, but already he was looking for fresh adventures. He commissioned Captain Burch to buy him a forty-ton pinnace mounted with six guns, which Colt intended to sail in 1632 from St Christopher to the Spanish Main so that he could trade with the Indians there, in open violation of Spanish territorial rights. Colt wanted the Spanish to know that he was affronted by their attack on the *Alexander*, and he was deliberately planning to invade their territory and offend them in recompense. A few months in America had filled Sir Henry with the infernal fighting spirit. 'For rest we will nott,' he said, 'untell we have doone some thinges worthy of ourselves, or dye in the attempt.'

Irrepressible as ever, Sir Henry Colt ended his journal on 20 August 1631, writing from his tent at St Christopher, with greetings and blessings to all the members of his family. 'Your mother I have alreadye sent two letters,' he told his son George; 'I will send noe moor untell our shipp returnes, for I love her nott.'[6] John Winthrop had stopped writing letters to his wife for another reason. In late August 1631, within a few days of the closing entry in Colt's journal, Margaret Winthrop set sail from England to join her husband in Massachusetts. The Winthrops, a family willing to take great risks, had come to America on a godly mission. Sir Henry Colt, a godly man, had come to America for the lure of risky enterprise. The difference may seem slight, but in conjunction with the geographical contrast between rock-ribbed New England and the palm-fringed Antilles, and the institutional contrast between the Massachusetts Bay Company and Carlisle's absentee proprietorship, and the character of the labour force drawn to the two regions, the difference turned out to be great indeed. Even in 1630–1 the contrasting experiences of Winthrop and Colt suggest some of the ways by which the New England and Caribbean planters came to be polar opposites, who represented the outer limits of English social expression in the seventeenth century.

6. Colt, pp. 90–91, 94–96, 101–2.

14

The problem of
perspective in the history
of colonial America

HUGH KEARNEY

Nationalist assumptions in English and American historiography are still strong on both sides of the Atlantic.[1] Many English historians show surprisingly little interest in what happened north of the Tweed or west of Offa's Dyke and even less if it occurred on the other side of the Irish sea or the Atlantic. Even the Puritan Revolution, which once did imply the existence of an ideological horizon stretching as far as Geneva, has now shrunk to something called 'the English Revolution'. Such attitudes are paralleled in the United States, where there is still considerable stress upon the uniqueness of the American Experience, a judgement which the celebrations of the bicentennial year have done little to weaken.[2] In the world of historical research few have emulated the transoceanic approach of D. B. Quinn. Readers of the *English Historical Review* and the *William and Mary Quarterly* go their separate ways.

To say this, is, of course, to exaggerate. Alongside the nationalism exemplified in the tradition of Frederick Jackson Turner and the work of Daniel Boorstin, broader attitudes have survived and in recent years perhaps displayed signs of an eventual blossoming. The work of Charles McLean Andrews, Lawrence Harper, and the imperial school of American colonial historians, though at times out of fashion, has never been lost sight of.[3] In the 1950s and 1960s, scholars such as Caroline Robbins,

1. I am greatly indebted to my friends Alan Day, History Department, University of Edinburgh, and Van Beck Hall, History Department, University of Pittsburgh, for criticizing a draft of this paper and making a number of valuable comments.
2. See for example Daniel Boorstin, *The Americans: The Colonial Experience* (New York, 1958).
3. C. M. Andrews, *The Colonial Period of American History* (New York, 1958); L. A. Harper, *The English Navigation Laws: A Seventeenth Century Experiment in Social Engineering* (New York, 1939).

Bernard Bailyn, and John Pocock demonstrated what advantages could be gained from adopting Anglo-American perspectives in the history of political ideology. Studies by Philip Greven and Kenneth Lockridge may also be mentioned as examples of a similar trend in the field of demography.[4]

One of the earliest attempts at a broader approach was Bernard Bailyn's brilliant bibliographical study, *Education in the Forming of American Society* (1959). In it, Bailyn took as a target for criticism the history of American education which, he felt, had been discussed in too narrow a context by professional educators. In the interests of more profound historiography, he pressed for a social approach to American educational history, which would take note of English as well as American experiences. Bailyn's book has been widely read in the universities, though it has yet to have its fullest impact on the history of education. It is the aim of the present essay to take up some of the points raised by Bailyn and consider their implications for Anglo-American historiography dealing with the colonial period, as well as for the history of education in particular. Bailyn is surely correct in pressing for a cross-cultural approach. The question is whether, in dealing with the problems raised, he has been influenced by assumptions embedded in American historiography. The problem of perspective is all-important.[5]

In his essay, Bailyn argued that the role of formal education in colonial America was radically different from its role in the mother country. In the traditional society which Bailyn saw existing in England, the main burden of transmitting cultural values was carried by three institutions: the family, the church, and the community. Of these, the family—the extended family in Bailyn's view—was the most important, organized as a patriarchal society in which 'the conjugal unit was only the nucleus of a broad kinship community'. Beyond the family lay the community, which Bailyn described in somewhat emotional terms as 'the soil of stable, slowly changing village and town communities in which intermarriage among the same groups had taken place generation after generation'. It was the

4. Caroline Robbins, *The Eighteenth Century Commonwealthman* (Cambridge, Mass., 1959); Bernard Bailyn, *The Ideological Origins of the American Revolution* (Cambridge, Mass., 1967); J. G. A. Pocock, *The Machiavellian Moment* (Princeton, 1975); S. N. Katz, *Newcastle's New York, Anglo-American Politics 1732–1753* (Cambridge, Mass., 1958); Philip Greven, *Four Generations* (Ithaca, N.Y., 1970); Kenneth Lockridge, *A New England Town* (New York, 1970).

5. Bernard Bailyn, *Education in the Forming of American Society* (Chapel Hill, N.C., 1960); see also 'The educational response to the American wilderness', appendix A in Kenneth Lockridge, *Literacy in Colonial New England* (New York, 1974).

role of community to introduce the younger generation to the duties of public life. The third institution—the church—completed the picture, by providing the sanction for morality, by introducing the images and symbols of the culture, and by exercising 'a powerful unifying influence'. The church was also responsible for supporting schools, but one of Bailyn's main points is that formal pedagogy played only a small part in the over-all process by which the English cultural heritage was transmitted. 'Education' as such was basically a utilitarian training for well-defined roles. In all this the state played little part.

Bailyn then drew a contrast between the role of formal education in this traditional society of Tudor and Stuart England and in colonial America. The crux of the contrast lay in the effect of the wilderness upon the early settlers. In Bailyn's judgement, it had proved to be impossible for them to maintain the three main traditional institutions in anything like the same form as in England. The extended family was replaced by the isolated conjugal unit. Partible inheritance replaced primogeniture. The community was also placed under the stress of the constant mobility and instability of frontier life, and as a consequence the traditional link between family and community tended to disappear. He argued finally that the response of the New England puritans to the challenge of their new environment was to turn to formal education and to lay a much greater emphasis on the school and schooling than had ever been the case in the Old World. Laws were passed in Massachusetts and Connecticut, ordering towns to set up schools and fining those who did not. The puritans demonstrated a zeal for formal education which survived the revolution of 1776.

Before the significance of this interpretation is discussed more fully, one general point may be made. The name of Frederick Jackson Turner is not mentioned by Bailyn but the influence of the 'Frontier Thesis' is apparent. Bailyn speaks of the threat from the environment, from barbarism and from the intense social changes forced upon the settlers. There is here a sharp contrast between early Bailyn and later Bailyn, between the author of the nationalist *Education in the Forming of American Society* and the Anglo-American *Ideological Origins of the American Revolution*. Bailyn's views on education are nationalist in their stress upon the uniqueness of American developments. But he is also a New England nationalist. 'New England', he believes, 'carried into the national period a faith in the benefits of formal schooling, and a willingness to perpetuate and enrich it, that has not yet been dissipated' (p. 27). He speaks of the 'veritable frenzy of [New England] parental concern lest they and their children succumb to a savage environment'. The southern and middle colonies do not enter his picture.

The essay is a remarkable *tour de force*. Future historians will turn to it for inspiration, as well as to Eggleston's *Transit of Civilization*, which Bailyn argued should be rescued from obscurity. None the less, I do not think that his interpretation stands without need of modification after fifteen years.

Criticism may be first directed towards his contrast between the traditional Old World and the changing New World. Research pursued in the 1960s (i.e. after Bailyn's essay had been published) raises some doubt as to whether this contrast can be sustained along the lines which Bailyn suggested. In the first place, as Peter Laslett, in his recent book on the family has shown, there is little evidence for the existence of the extended family in the early modern period.[6] The European family model indeed seems to have been the conjugal unit. If this is the case, it raises a question mark against Bailyn's description of traditional society in England. Secondly, it appears from the researches of Joan Thirsk and others, that partible inheritance, far from being an American breakaway from Old World patterns, was common in many parts of England, suggesting that patriarchal concern to retain control of the family unit was weak in such areas.[7] Bailyn's model of the English village community is also open to criticism. It is all too good to be true—the merging of family into communal harmony over the generations. Recent research in Britain suggests that price rises and population pressure brought considerable social change. Dr Margaret Spufford's study of three Cambridgeshire villages shows that a good deal of emigration and immigration took place. In one village, for example, two-thirds of the family names disappeared between 1575 and 1720, a figure which does not include the landless labourers, who were even more obviously exposed to the shifts of economic climate.[8] Bailyn's 'slowly changing and stable' village, if it ever existed, was subjected in the south and east of England to challenges deriving from rural industrialization and the growing food market of London.

Thirdly, the role which Bailyn ascribes to the church in pre-reformation England no longer seems as clear cut as it did when he wrote. As the

6. Peter Laslett (ed.), *Household and Family in Past Time* (Cambridge, 1972), p. 703.

7. Joan Thirsk (ed.), *The Agrarian History of England and Wales, vol. iv, 1500–1640* (Cambridge, 1967), p. 902, and also under 'inheritance customs'; Margaret Spufford, *Contrasting Communities* (Cambridge, 1974), pp. 87, 106, 159.

8. Ibid., pp. 21–22.

work of John Bossy and others has shown, the medieval church was much less of an organized institution than historians have maintained.[9] Parochial organization as such seems scarcely to have existed. Indeed the parish as described by Bailyn seems to be an institution which came into existence as a result of the administrative exigencies of the Elizabethan state. In other words, it was a 'modern' rather than a 'traditional' institution and was strongest in those areas which were most exposed to the 'modernizing' practices of Tudor administration.

To find the type of traditional society which Bailyn describes, one would need to turn to the Celtic-speaking areas of Ireland, the Scottish Highlands, and Wales or to the remoter areas of England—precisely those areas where emigration did not take place. It was in East Anglia, as the work of Alan Macfarlane has shown, that witchcraft persecution was particularly intense, suggesting that the social world from which so many of the puritan colonists emerged was far from being as idyllically unchanging as Bailyn's thesis implies.[1]

Indeed, Tudor and Stuart England cannot be termed a traditional society without serious qualification. The period witnessed, as Lawrence Stone has argued, an 'educational revolution' marked by greatly increased literacy.[2] It also witnessed, in many areas, an 'agricultural revolution' marked by technical innovation as well as by enclosure for pasture. Peter Laslett has noted the extraordinarily high rate of mobility of the population in the villages, admittedly few, which he and his colleagues have studied.[3] The work of Peter Clark on the mobility of artisans in Kent reinforces this picture of a mobile society.[4] Complaints made to the Privy Council about industrial unemployment in East Anglia also suggest that a cloth industry catering for foreign markets was a central feature of the rural economies from which emigration took place.[5]

If we, for the moment, accept this picture of a literate, innovative, and mobile English society, what of New England, or to be more specific, Massachusetts? R. R. Seward in a recent article used a number of modern

9. John Bossy, 'Blood and baptism', in D. Baker (ed.), *Sanctity and Secularity: The Church and the World* (London, 1973), p. 142.

1. Alan Macfarlane, *Witchcraft in Tudor and Stuart England* (London, 1970).

2. Lawrence Stone, 'The educational revolution', *Past and Present*, xxviii (1964), 41–80.

3. Peter Laslett and J. Harrison, 'Clayworth and Cogenhoe', in H. E. Bell and E. L. Ollard (eds), *Historical Essays, 1660–1750, presented to David Ogg* (London, 1963).

4. Peter Clark, 'The migrant in Kentish towns, 1580–1640', in P. Clark and P. Slack (eds), *Crisis and Order in English Towns, 1500–1700* (London, 1972).

5. Joan Thirsk and J. P. Cooper (eds), *Seventeenth Century Economic Documents* (Oxford, 1972), p. 32.

studies to show that the nuclear family was the rule rather than the exception in the colonies.[6] In one of these studies, that of Philip Greven dealing with Andover, the suggestion is made that, by the eighteenth century, families in this area were becoming more patriarchal in character. Greven argues that the need to maintain the family holding undivided (i.e. to avoid the disadvantages of partible inheritance) was becoming a prime consideration and he even uses for purposes of comparison the patriarchal family structure of modern Ireland noted by Arensberg and Kimball in their classic study of county Clare.[7] Thus in this case at least, family structure, regarded by Bailyn as crucial for the transmission of values, was becoming more, not less, traditional.

The work of Greven and other scholars also brings into question Bailyn's view that the sense of community was breaking down in New England. Sumner Powell, in his study *Puritan Village*, describes the four Massachusetts villages of Watertown, Dedham, Sudbury, and Marlborough.[8] These differed markedly in their economic organization, Watertown being an open field village and Marlborough one of individual farms. But in all four cases a tightly organized community existed. Though the hiving off of dissident groups seems to have been due to what was regarded as excessive communal control, the dissidents in their turn established equally closely knit communities of their own. Zuckerman in his study of so-called 'peaceable kingdoms' argues for the existence of such communities well into the eighteenth century.[9] The detailed researches of these scholars suggest what might have been expected, namely that a hostile environment tended to enjoin interdependence between neighbours. In short, it is precisely to colonial Massachusetts that we must look for the strong community sense that Bailyn regards as characteristic of traditional society.

Evidence drawn from the crisis over the Half Way Covenant tends to reinforce this conclusion. The puritan family in its second or third generation was being asked to choose between spiritual kinship based on the covenant and the physical kinship of the family. Indeed, the crisis over church membership may have arisen largely because kinship ties were so

6. R. R. Seward, 'The colonial family in America: toward a socio-historical restoration of its character', *Journal of Marriage and the Family*, xxv (1963), 58–70.

7. P. Greven, *Four Generations*, p. 136.

8. S. C. Powell, *Puritan Village, the Formation of a New England Town* (Middletown, Conn., 1963).

9. Michael Zuckerman, *Peaceable Kingdoms: New England Towns in the Eighteenth Century* (New York, 1970).

strong. The work of Pope on the 'Half Way Covenant' illustrates how much variation existed in the decisions arrived at by local communities but he shows how for most the issue was a crucial one, which unmistakably demonstrated their wish to maintain ideological unity over the generations.[1]

Thus, if we look at Bailyn's model in the light of research done since 1959, his contrast between the traditional Old World and the changing New World seems to have lost its sharpness of outline. It is tempting to go further and argue that the Bailyn model should be stood on its head. If we do so, it would seem that it was 'Old England' far more than New England which experienced rapid social change during the two centuries of the first colonial empire. At the central point of much of this social change was the city of London. As E. A. Wrigley has argued, 'if it is fair to assume that one adult in six in England in this period had had direct experience of London life it is probably also fair to assume that this must have acted as a powerful solvent of the customs, prejudices and modes of action of traditional rural England'.[2] Here was a really new society—in the teeming streets of London—which in its patterns of consumption created an expanding market in agriculture, consumer goods, coal, and the like. The experience of urbanization broke down rural attitudes, which still survived in the towns (perhaps more correctly termed villages) of New England.

What then are we to make of the undoubted zeal for education displayed in Massachusetts during the seventeenth century? Bailyn's answer to this is clearcut. The school replaced the family, the community, and the church, the three traditional institutions, which succumbed rapidly to the pressures of a savage environment. If what has been said so far in criticism of Bailyn's thesis is correct, however, any suggested explanation must take a different form. The physical dangers of the frontier, after all, were common to all the mainland colonies. What was distinctive about Massachusetts was not its natural environment but the way in which the community, under the guidance of its élite, came to regard itself. Massachusetts from the beginning was committed to a specific ideology and, as will be argued in a moment, it seems to have been the threat to the purity of the ideology and not 'the savage environ-

---

1. R. G. Pope, *The Half-Way Covenant: Church Membership in Puritan New England* (Princeton, 1969).
2. E. A. Wrigley, 'A simple model of London's importance in changing English society and economy', *Past and Present*, xxxvii (1967), 50.

ment' which aroused most anxiety. From the sense of crisis at the internal dangers facing the colony was derived, it will be argued, the passionate concern for education, as a bulwark against the enemy within. The college and the school joined family, church, and community in the fight against Satan.

A sense of crisis could well have been predicted before the colonists set sail. A well-grounded historiographical tradition leads us to regard colonial America as a brave new world, but so far as Massachusetts is concerned, this description is couched in terms far too relaxed and optimistic. Whatever may have been the attitude of the great majority of settlers, the ministers (that is, the intellectuals of the community) saw the fate of the colony in millenarian terms. They found the key to history in the Book of Daniel and the Song of Solomon, the latter a source which John Cotton felt needed much heavenly love to 'extinguish base kitchin lust'.[3] For John Winthrop the new colony itself was a sign of the latter days, along with such other signs as the appearance of Anti-Christ in the person of the Jesuits.[4] The colonists left England in an atmosphere of crisis and the feeling of anxiety was maintained after they arrived in the New World.

The sense of crisis among the saints owed its existence in part to the ambivalence and ambiguity of the highly charged imagery of the Book of Daniel and the Book of Revelation. In Thomas Shephard's view, which became the orthodoxy of the colony, the task of the saints was to maintain themselves during the latter days, however long this period might be. Others, notably Mistress Ann Hutchinson and Roger Williams, wished to tread a more adventurous path.[5] In the bitter conflict of 1635-7 victory went to the orthodox, but the problem was how to ensure the victory would be a lasting one. For a church governed by bishop or presbytery, the solution was obvious. For one which placed its emphasis upon independent congregations as Massachusetts did, the problem was more difficult. One method of counteracting potentially centrifugal tendencies which independency might lead to was to encourage informal consultation between ministers. Another was to ensure that the supply of learned ministers came solely from an institution of orthodox doctrine. For such reasons, it may be argued, Harvard College was founded in

3. J. Rosenmeir, 'The teacher and the witness: John Cotton and Roger Williams', *William and Mary Quarterly*, 3rd series, xxv (1968), 425.

4. John Winthrop, 'Reasons . . . justifying . . . the plantation in New England', reprinted J. P. Greene (ed.), *Settlements to Society, 1584–1763* (New York, 1966), pp. 62–63.

5. E. Battis, *Saints and Sectaries* (Chapel Hill, 1962).

1636 with a function similar to that of certain colleges in England and Ireland. From Harvard, as from Emmanuel College, Cambridge, and Trinity College, Dublin, came a supply of ministers upon whose orthodoxy puritan gentry could rely.[6]

It was not the savage environment which supplied the threat to orthodoxy but the dangers of unlicensed, uncontrolled theological debate, which carried within it the seeds of social disturbance. As was pointed out later in the seventeenth century, 'the ruling class would have been subjected to mechanic cobblers and tailors; the gentry would have been overwhelmed by lewd fellows of the baser sort, sewage of Rome, the dregs of the illiterate plebs'.[7] The foundation of Harvard College in the 1630s was followed by the passing of School Laws of the 1640s, which obliged town governments to establish schools. Looked at in the context of the internal history of the colony, the School Laws appear as a response to a continuing ideological crisis, one of the major issues at stake being the role of learning in relation to godliness. For the sectaries in England, the two did not go well together and they criticized the principle of a learned ministry openly during the 1640s. They saw the universities, and the education provided therein, as the basis of an intellectual monopoly from which true godly professors, though unlearned, were excluded. The Leveller William Walwyn declared that the clergy 'made it a difficult thing to be a minister and so have engrossed the trade to themselves and left other men by reason of their professions in an incapacity from being such in their sense'.[8]

The Massachusetts School Law made the same point, though in this case from the point of view of the authorities. Those who drew up the law saw it as a defence of truth against the 'ould deluder Satan' who in former times had plotted to keep men from knowledge of the Scriptures but now in the 1640s had shifted his point of assault by persuading some misguided men that knowledge of the ancient languages, indeed learning itself, was no longer necessary for the study of the scriptures, 'in these latter times by persuading them from the use of tongues that so at least the true sense and meaning of the original might be clouded by the glosses of saint seeming deceivers'.[9] The anxiety of the visible saints about the proliferation of 'saint seeming deceivers' was to be relieved by setting up

6. H. F. Kearney, *Scholars and Gentlemen* (London, 1970), pp. 67–70.
7. Ibid., p. 116.
8. Ibid., p. 111.
9. Greene, *Settlements to Society*, p. 119.

a system of sponsored education to reinforce the protection offered by the establishment of Harvard College a decade earlier.

Early in the eighteenth century the foundation of Yale in the traditionally minded area of Davenport's New Haven colony was another example of an attempt to meet ideological threats by erecting educational bulwarks. In God's good time the foundation of Yale would work towards the furtherance of liberal education. In the immediate circumstances of 1701 it must surely be seen as part of the conservative response to an ideological crisis. The Saybrook Platform was an attempt similar to that set forth in the Cambridge Platform to tighten up the religious defences of this least commercial of the New England colonies. Interestingly enough, Saybrook was chosen as the original site for Yale College before the decision to move it to New Haven. At Yale, the *Medulla Theologiae* of the Jacobean theologian William Ames, with its exposition of traditional ethics, was recommended as a staple text, along with the Bible. Samuel Sewall wrote to Thomas Buckingham, minister of Saybrook in 1701, 'the end of all learning is to fit men to search the Scriptures that thereby they may come to the saving knowledge of God in Christ'.[1]

Similar traditional attitudes could be found in other parts of the British Empire, most notably perhaps among the small farmers of Presbyterian Ulster, which resembled Massachusetts in so many ways, for example in the emphasis on the covenanting community and on the traditional ethic with its suspicion of commerce. Education, so far from transforming this traditional world, was reinforcing its traditional assumptions.

In contrast, drastic social change was taking place in areas which in the early seventeenth century had been as traditional as Massachusetts—in the south and east of Ireland and in the lowlands of Scotland, where during the eighteenth century the consolidation and improvement of large estates organized for production and profit took place. But the sectors of the Empire in which men and land were most clearly organized for large-scale production of specialized commodities for the European market were the West Indies and the southern mainland colonies.

On the other hand, much of Massachusetts and Connecticut remained traditional in character. There was a sharp division between the commercial urban areas of Boston, Salem, Newbury, etc., and the inland villages. It was precisely in the developing sections of Massachusetts

1. F. B. Dexter, *Documentary History of Yale University, 1701–1740* (New Haven, 1916), p. 16; for more recent histories of Yale see R. Warch, *School of the Prophets: Yale College, 1701–1740* (New Haven, 1973); B. M. Kelley, *Yale: A History* (New Haven, 1974).

that most diversity in matters of religion and culture existed. The less Puritan, the more Yankee. Economic growth and literacy did not necessarily go together.

Somehow, the implications of this for the over-all colonial picture tend to be lost sight of. As a result of that historical accident we call the American Revolution, the history of the West Indies has come to be treated in a separate compartment under the auspices of British historians. However, distinct though the southern colonies and the West Indies may have been in the nineteenth century, the links between them in the eighteenth century (and the late seventeenth century) were very close. Eugene Sirmans and more recently Richard Dunn in his book *Sugar and Slaves* have shown how South Carolina began as a colony of Barbados and Jamaica.[2] In social structure and in life style 'the South' resembled the West Indies more than it did the north-east. The history of the south, however, has been dealt with by the historians of colonial America. The economic decline of the West Indies in the nineteenth century, coupled with the aftermath of the American Civil War, has sanctified a historiographical divorce which did not exist before 1776.

It is this, in essence, which has led to our 'problem of perspective'. The cultural prestige of New England in the nineteenth century, associated with the intellectual dominance of Harvard and Yale, has led to the importance of New England in the period before 1776 being grossly exaggerated. Puritanism has been associated with the rise of capitalism, not with its absence. The southern colonies, in which, along with the West Indies and Ireland, capital investment and economic exploitation set the tone of society, have been largely ignored. And of course, puritanism was never a dominant feature either of the south or the West Indies. Dunn, for example, contrasts the reading matter of a West Indian planter, poetry and other such frivolous works, with the New England diet of sermons and tracts.[3] In short, the educational barriers erected by the early puritans against social and intellectual change proved to be almost too successful in creating a conservative-minded Bible Belt.

Any explanation of the rapid economic acceleration which marks off the eighteenth-century Atlantic economy from that of the seventeenth must take account of the booming staples of tobacco, sugar, and rice of the

---

2. R. S. Dunn, *Sugar and Slaves: The Rise of the Planter Class in the English West Indies, 1624–1713* (Chapel Hill, 1972); M. E. Sirmans, *Colonial South Carolina: A Political History, 1663–1763* (Chapel Hill, 1966).

3. Dunn, *Sugar and Slaves*, p. 271; and see his essay in this volume.

southern colonies and the West Indies. The slave trade itself was a vital, if hideous, ingredient in this economic expansion. Looked at over-all, the growth of the middle colony ports such as Philadelphia and New York was also a central feature. In contrast, much of puritan New England languished in a rural backwater. Those areas of the northern colonies which developed substantial trades in produce and foodstuffs depended upon the West Indies for their market. Even so, Boston lost ground to Philadelphia, New York, and other ports.

The implications of this for English history must also be considered. Perhaps the current interpretation of English puritanism as 'forward looking' and 'commercial' needs to be looked at more critically. Far too much seems to have been made of the link between puritanism and trade. As the most recent study of puritan lectureships has shown, puritanism was not dominant in London, nor indeed were puritan merchants. The assumption that puritanism and capitalism went together has led, as a consequence, to an exaggeration of the commercial activities of the New England merchants in the seventeenth century, indeed to a general overestimate of the significance of the colonies generally. The capital invested in the Massachusetts Bay Company was minute compared to that invested in giants like the East India, Levant, and Eastland companies.[4] Few of the merchants involved in these enterprises were puritan and in general they were too closely linked to the court via government finance to have much truck with radicalism. Nor were their virtues the traditional virtues of thrift and prudence. These were the merchants who eventually made hay while the re-export sun shone in Restoration England, and from whose ranks the banking and financial groups known as 'the City' eventually emerged. In contrast the puritan merchants were few in number and their scale of operations was small.

Such a shift in perspective affects our view of the great puritan migration in the 1630s. John Winthrop spoke of the growth of poverty in England, the shortage of land and the increase of conspicuous consumption of which he disapproved. The type of society which the first emigrants set up in Massachusetts seems to have been based on an idealized version of the gentry-cum-yeoman society which they had seen disappearing in England. Certainly the society which Chilton Powell describes in *Puritan Village* was one in which yeoman size holdings were the norm. Hence came too the emphasis upon the just price and the control of

4. T. K. Rabb, *Enterprise and Empire: Merchant and Gentry Investment in the Expansion of England, 1575–1630* (Cambridge, Mass., 1967), pp. 58, 65.

craftsmen's wages. There was not much encouragement here for the commercial ethic or the making of large fortunes.

It is, of course, possible to go too far and to dismiss New England as a figment of Perry Miller's imagination. But, exaggeration apart, it does seem that New England occupies a distortingly central position in American historiography. An alternative approach would at least suggest that the real challenges to social cohesion were experienced not on the New England frontier so much as in the industrializing and urbanizing areas of England and in the slave-owning societies of the southern colonies and the West Indies where formal education had little role to play.

The explanation for this long-term historiographical trend is a simple one. It lies in the intellectual dominance of New England (and its educational preserve of Harvard) in the nineteenth century, which in turn is bound up with such phenomena as the Unitarian conscience and with the response of certain white puritan Anglo-Saxons to immigration. Edmund Morgan in his article 'Historians of early New England'[5] has traced its development from the enthusiasm of early amateur historians in organizing the Massachusetts Historical Society to the sustained power and style of such Harvard historians as Samuel Eliot Morison and Perry Miller. Whatever the reasons are, the fact remains that the strength of the New England myth has increased, is increasing, and ought to be diminished.

5. Edmund S. Morgan, 'Historians of early New England', in R. A. Billington (ed.), *The Re-interpretation of Early American History* (New York, 1968), pp. 41–64.

15

The writings of D. B. Quinn

A bibliography of publications up to mid-1976
compiled by Alison M. Quinn and P. E. H. Hair

Starred items have been collected together in the volume *England and the Discovery of America 1481–1620* (1974).

'An early Irish settlement at Malone, Belfast', *Proceedings and Reports of the Belfast Natural History and Philosophical Society 1930–1931* (1932), 46–49.

'Descriptions of Ards Peninsula by William Montgomery of Rosemount in 1683 and 1701', *The Irish Booklover*, xx (1932), 28–32.

'Irish records, 1920–1933: a survey', *Bulletin of the Institute of Historical Research*, xi (1933), 99–104.

'MSS in Lough Fea Library catalogue of 1872', *The Irish Booklover*, xxi (1933), 12–13.

'Anglo-Irish Ulster in the early sixteenth century', *Proceedings and Reports of the Belfast Natural History and Philosophical Society 1933–1934* (1935), 28–42; reprinted separately as *Ulster 1460–1550* (Belfast, 1935), 23 pp.

'The Irish parliamentary subsidy in the fifteenth and sixteenth centuries', *Proceedings of the Royal Irish Academy*, xlii (1935), sect. C, no. 11, 219–46.

'Edward IV and exploration', *The Mariner's Mirror*, xxi (1935), 275–84.

'Henry, Duke of Richmond and his connexion with Ireland, 1529–1530', *Bulletin of the Institute of Historical Research*, xii (1935), 175–7.

'Ormond Papers, 1480–1535', in *Calendar of Ormond Deeds*, ed. E. Curtis, vol. iv (Dublin, 1937), 307–80.

The Port Books or Local Customs Accounts of Southampton, 1468–1481, 2 vols, Southampton Record Society, nos 37–38 (1937, 1938), xix, xlii, 222 pp.

'Anglo-Irish local government, 1485–1534', *Irish Historical Studies*, i (1939), 354–81.

'Revolutionary army' [review of A. S. P. Woodhouse, 'Puritanism and Liberty'], *The Modern Quarterly*, 2/2 (April 1939), 205–11.

The Voyages and Colonising Enterprises of Sir Humphrey Gilbert, 2 vols, Hakluyt Society, 2nd series, nos 83–84 (London, 1940; Nendeln, 1967), xxix, xiii, 534 pp. (index by Alison Quinn).

(With Oliver Davies), 'The Irish Pipe Roll of 14 John, 1211–1212', *Ulster Journal of Archaeology*, 3rd series, iv (1941), supplement, 1–76.

'Guide to English financial records for Irish history, 1461–1558', *Analecta Hibernica*, x (1941), 1–69.

'Bills and statutes of the Irish parliaments of Henry VII and Henry VIII', ibid. x (1941), 71–169.

'The early interpretation of Poynings' Law, 1494–1534', *Irish Historical Studies*, ii (1941), 241–54.

'Parliaments and Great Councils in Ireland, 1461–1586', ibid. iii (1942), 60–77.

' "A discourse of Ireland" (*circa* 1599): a sidelight on English colonial policy', *Proceedings of the Royal Irish Academy*, xlvii (1942), sect. C, no. 3, 151–66.

'Information about Dublin printers, 1556–1573, in English financial records', *The Irish Booklover*, xxviii (1942), 112–14.

'Government printing and the publication of the Irish statutes in the sixteenth century', *Proceedings of the Royal Irish Academy*, xlix (1943), sect. C, no. 2, 45–129.

'Agenda for Irish history: Ireland from 1461 to 1603', *Irish Historical Studies*, iv (1945), 258–69.

'Sir Thomas Smith (1513–1577) and the beginnings of English colonial theory', *Proceedings of the American Philosophical Society*, lxxxix (1945), 543–60.

Raleigh and the British Empire (London, 1947, 1962, 1973; New York, 1949, enlarged 1962), xiii, 284 pp. [Note: *Ralegh* in later editions.]

'Edward Walshe's "Conjectures" concerning the state of Ireland, [1552]', *Irish Historical Studies*, v (1947), 303–22.

★ 'The failure of Raleigh's American colonies', in *Essays in British and Irish History in Honour of J. E. Todd*, ed. H. A. Cronne, T. W. Moody, and D. B. Quinn (London, 1949), 61–85.

'Preparations for the 1585 Virginia voyage', *William and Mary Quarterly*, 3rd series, vi (1949), 208–36.

'Ireland, History [from 1171]', *Chambers's Encyclopaedia* (London [1950], and subsequent editions), 7, 725–35 and 741–2.

'The expansion of Europe to 1783', *Annual Bulletin of Historical Literature*, Historical Association (London, 1950 annually to 1959, and 1960 with A. N. Ryan).

★ 'Some Spanish reactions to Elizabethan colonial enterprises', *Transactions of the Royal Historical Society*, 5th series, i (1951), 1–23.

'Christopher Newport in 1590', *North Carolina Historical Review*, xxix (1952), 305–16.

Preface to *Black Gown and Redskins: Adventures and Travels of the Early Jesuit Missionaries in North America (1610–1791)*, ed. E. Kenton (New York, 1954; London, 1956), iii–xi.

The Roanoke Voyages, 1584–1590: Documents to Illustrate the English Voyages to North America under the Patent granted to Walter Raleigh in 1584, 2 vols, Hakluyt Society, 2nd series, nos 104–5 (London, 1955; Nendeln, 1967), xxvi, vi, 1004 pp. (index by Alison Quinn).

'The library as the Arts Faculty's laboratory', *23rd Conference of Library Authorities in Wales and Monmouthshire, Newport 1956* (Swansea, 1956), 14–18.

'A merchant's long memory', *Gower*, ix (1956), 8–11.

'Local history in perspective', *Morgannwg*, ii (1958), 3–8.

'Ireland and sixteenth century European expansion', in *Historical Studies, I: Papers Read before the Second Irish Conference of Historians*, ed. T. Desmond Williams (London, 1958), 22–32; reprinted with corrections (Tralee, [1959]), 15 pp.

'Die Anfänge des britischen Weltreiches bis zum Ende der Napoleonischen Kriege', in *Historia Mundi: eine Handbuch der Weltgeschichte*, viii (1959), 455–95.

'Notes by a pious colonial investor, 1608–1610', *William and Mary Quarterly*, 3rd series, xvi (1959), 551–5.

(With Jacques Rousseau) 'Hakluyt et le mot "Esquimau"', *Revue de l'histoire de l'Amérique française*, xii (1959), 597–601.

★ 'Edward Hayes, Liverpool colonial pioneer', *Transactions of the Historic Society of Lancashire and Cheshire*, cxi (1960), 25–45.

'Henry the Navigator', *The Listener*, 27 October 1960, 736–8.

★ 'Simão Fernandes, a Portuguese pilot in the English service, circa 1573–1588', in *Actas, Congresso internacional de história dos Descobrimentos*, iii (Lisbon, 1961), 449–65.

★ 'The argument for the English discovery of America between 1480 and 1494', *Geographical Journal*, cxxvii (1961), 277–85.

'Henry VIII and Ireland, 1509–1534', *Irish Historical Studies*, xii (1961), 318–44.

'The voyage of Étienne Bellenger to the Maritimes in 1584; a new document', *Canadian Historical Review*, xliii (1962), 328–43.

(With Paul H. Hulton) 'John White and the English naturalists', *History Today*, xiii (1963), 310–20.

(With Paul H. Hulton) *The American Drawings of John White*, 2 vols (London and Chapel Hill, 1964), xvii ,179, ix pp., 160 plates.

★ 'Sailors and the sea', in *Shakespeare Survey 17*, ed. Allardyce Nicoll (Cambridge, 1964; reprinted 1976), 21–36, 242–5.

(With R. A. Skelton) *Richard Hakluyt, The Principall Navigations, Voiages and Discoveries of the English Nation: a facsimile of the edition of 1589, with an introduction by D. B. Quinn and R. A. Skelton and with a new index by Alison Quinn*, 2 vols, Hakluyt Society, extra series, 39 (Cambridge, 1965), lx, 975 pp.

The New Found Land: the English contribution to the discovery and settlement of North America, An address . . . together with a catalogue of the exhibition (John Carter Brown Library, Providence, 1964), 45 pp.

'Étienne Bellenger', 'Thomas Bradley', 'Richard Clarke', 'Thomas Croft', 'Sir Bernard Drake', 'Hugh Eliot', 'Richard Fisher', 'Sir Humphrey Gilbert', 'Edward Hayes', 'Richard Hore', 'David Ingram', 'John Jay', 'George Johnson', 'La Court de Pré-Ravillon et de Grandpré', 'Charles Leigh', 'Madoc', 'Anthony Parkhurst', 'Stephanus Parmenius', 'John Rastell', 'John Rut', 'Lancelot Thirkill', 'Robert Thorne', 'Silvester Wyet', in *Dictionary of Canadian Biography/Dictionnaire biographique du Canada, 1, 1000–1700*, eds G. W. Brown, Marcel Trudel, and André Vachon (Toronto and Quebec, 1965).

'Exploration and the expansion of Europe', *Rapports, 1, Comité international des sciences historiques, XIIᵉ Congrès international des sciences historiques* (Vienna, 1965), 45–60.

★ 'England and the St. Lawrence, 1577 to 1602', in *Merchants and Scholars*, ed. John Parker (Minneapolis, 1965), 117–44.

'Elizabethan birdman', *The Times Literary Supplement* (1 April 1965), 250.

The Elizabethans and the Irish (Folger Monographs on Tudor and Stuart Civilization, Ithaca, 1966), ix, 204 pp. (index by Alison Quinn).

★ 'The road to Jamestown', in *Shakespeare Celebrated*, ed. Louis B. Wright (Folger Library Publications, Ithaca, 1966), 31–60.

★ (With P. G. Foote) 'The Vinland Map', *Saga Book, Viking Society for Northern Research*, xvii (1966), 63–89.

'Advice for investors in Virginia, Bermuda, and Newfoundland, 1611', *William and Mary Quarterly*, 3rd series, xxiii (1966), 136–45.

★ 'The first Pilgrims', ibid. 3rd series, xxiii (1966), 359–90.

(With Jacques Rousseau), 'Les toponymes amérindiens du Canada chez les anciens voyageurs anglais, 1591–1602', *Cahiers de géographie de Québec*, x (1966), 263–78.

'The Munster plantation: problems and opportunities', *Journal of the Cork Historical and Archaeological Society*, lxxi (1966), 19–40.

'État présent des études sur la découverte de l'Amérique au XVᵉ siècle', *Journal de la Société des Américanistes*, lv (1966), 343–82.

Richard Hakluyt, Editor: with facsimiles of Richard Hakluyt, Divers Voyages Touching the Discoverie of America (1582), and A Journal of Several Voyages into New France (1580), 2 vols (Amsterdam, 1967), xi, 87, [208] pp. (index by Alison Quinn).

(Editor) *Observations Gathered out of 'A Discourse of the Plantation of the Southern Colony in Virginia by the English, 1606.' Written by that honorable gentleman, Master George Percy* (Charlottesville, 1967), xv, 27 pp.

'The English discovery of America', in *The Expansion of Europe*, ed. De Lamar Jensen (Boston, 1967), 47–51.

'John Cabot's *Matthew*', *The Times Literary Supplement* (8 June 1967), 517.

★ 'John Day and Columbus', *Geographical Journal*, cxxxiii (1967), 205–9.

★ (With Warner F. Gookin) 'Martin Pring at Provincetown in 1603?', *The New England Quarterly*, xl (1967), 79–91.

'Calendar of the Irish Council Book, 1 March 1581 to 1 July 1586', *Analecta Hibernica*, xxiv (1967), 93–180.

★ *Sebastian Cabot and Bristol Exploration*, Bristol Branch of the Historical Association, Local History Pamphlets, xxi (Bristol, 1968), 30.

'La contribution des Anglais à la découverte de l'Amérique du Nord au XVIᵉ siècle', in Manuel Ballesteros-Gaibrois *et al.*, *La Découverte de l'Amérique: esquisse d'une synthèse: conditions historiques et conséquences culturelles* (Paris, 1968), 61–76.

(With R. Dudley Edwards) 'Thirty years' work in Irish history (ii); sixteenth century Ireland, 1485–1603', *Irish Historical Studies*, xvi (1968), 15–32.

'Josias Crowe', 'Archibald Cumings', 'Samuel Gledhill', 'Arthur Holdsworth', 'Thomas Lloyd', 'William Pynne', 'James Smith', in *Dictionary of*

Canadian Biography/Dictionnaire biographique du Canada, 2, 1701–1740, eds David M. Hayne and André Vachon (Toronto and Quebec, 1969).

(With John W. Shirley) 'A contemporary list of Hariot references', *Renaissance Quarterly*, xxii (1969), 9–26.

(With A. C. Crombie, J. V. Pepper, J. W. Shirley, and R. C. H. Tanner) 'Thomas Harriot (1560–1621): an original practitioner in the scientific art', *The Times Literary Supplement* (23 October 1969), 1237–8.

'A list of books purchased for the Virginia Company', *Virginia Magazine of History and Biography*, lxxvii (1969), 347–60.

Jamestown Day Address, May 11, 1969, Association for the Preservation of Virginia Antiquities (Richmond, 1969), 29 pp.

'Additional Sidney State Papers, 1566–1570', *Analecta Hibernica*, xxvi (1970), 89–98.

★ ' "Virginians" on the Thames in 1603', *Terrae Incognitae*, ii (1970), 7–14.

★ 'Thomas Hariot and the Virginia voyages of 1602', *William and Mary Quarterly*, 3rd series, xxvii (1970), 268–81.

North American Discovery, circa 1000–1612 (New York and Columbia, S.C., 1971), xlvi, 324 pp.

(With W. P. Cumming and R. A. Skelton) *The Discovery of North America* (London and New York, 1971), 304 pp. (index by Mollie Skelton and Alison Quinn).

(With R. Dudley Edwards) 'Sixteenth century Ireland', in *Irish Historiography*, ed. T. W. Moody (Dublin, 1971), 23–42.

'The Voyage of *Triall*, 1606–1607: an abortive Virginia venture', *American Neptune*, xxxi (1971), 85–103.

'Raleigh Ashlin Skelton: his contributions to the history of Discovery', *Imago Mundi*, xxv (1971), 13–15.

'A Tempest allusion?', *Shakespeare Quarterly*, xxii (1971), 78.

(With Neil M. Cheshire) *The New Found Land of Stephen Parmenius* (Toronto, 1972), xii, 250 pp. (index by Alison Quinn).

'Richard Hakluyt and his successors', *Annual Report of the Hakluyt Society, 1972*, 1–11.

'William Montgomery and the description of the Ards', *Irish Booklore*, ii (1972), 29–43.

(With Alison M. Quinn) *Virginia Voyages from Hakluyt* (London, 1973), xxv, 195 pp.

England and the Discovery of America, 1481–1620 (London and New York, 1974), xxiv, 497, xviii pp. (index by Alison Quinn).

(Editor) *The Hakluyt Handbook*, 2 vols, Hakluyt Society, 2nd series, nos 144 and 145 (London, 1974), xxvi, xiii, 706 pp. (index by Alison Quinn).

'William Taverner', in *Dictionary of Canadian Biography/Dictionnaire biographique du Canada, 3, 1740–1770*, eds F. G. Halpenny *et al.* (Toronto and Quebec, 1974).

'Thomas Harriot and the New World', in *Thomas Harriot, Renaissance Scientist*, ed. John W. Shirley (Oxford, 1974), 36–53.

'Stephen Parmenius of Buda. The first Hungarian in North America', *New Hungarian Quarterly*, xiv (1974), 152–7.

'Budai Parmenius István: az elsö magyarutazó Eszak-Amerikában', *Irodalomtörteneti Közlemenyek*, ii (1974), 203–10.

(With W. P. Cumming *et al.*) *The Exploration of North America 1630–1776* (London, 1974), 272 pp.

'James I and the beginnings of empire in America', *Journal of Imperial and Commonwealth History*, ii (1974), 135–52.

'The Vinland map and the historian', *Geographical Journal*, cxl (1974), 194–9.

The Last Voyage of Thomas Cavendish 1591–1592 (Chicago and London, 1975), x, 166 pp. (index by Alison Quinn).

'An Anglo-French "Voyage of discovery" to North America in 1604–5, and its sequel', in *Miscellanea offerts à Charles Verlinden à l'occasion de ses trente ans de professorat*, 2 vols (Ghent, 1975), 513–34; also in *Bulletin de l'Institut Historique Belge de Rome*, xiv (1974), 513–34.

(With Selma Barkham), 'Privateering: the North American dimension (to 1625)', *Course et piraterie*, ed. M. Mollat, 2 vols (Paris, 1975), i. 360–86.

'The attempted colonization of Florida by the French, 1562–1565', in Paul Hulton, *The Work of Jacques Le Moyne de Morgues, a Huguenot Artist in France, Florida and England* (1976), 17–44.

'New geographical horizons: literature', in *First Images of America*, ed. F. Chiapelli, 2 vols (Los Angeles, 1976), ii. 635–58.

(With K. W. Nicholls) 'Ireland in 1534', in *A New History of Ireland*, eds T. W. Moody, F. X. Martin, and F. J. Byrne, iii (1976) (index by Alison Quinn), 1–38.

'Did Bristol sailors discover America?', *The Times* (30 April 1976), 17.

'Renaissance influences in English colonization', *Transactions of the Royal Historical Society*, 5th series, xxv (1976), 73–93.

INDEX

Note the general entries for 'Commodities', 'Merchants', and 'Authors, modern'. Page references are to the text (but the Preface is only lightly indexed) and to discussion in footnotes.

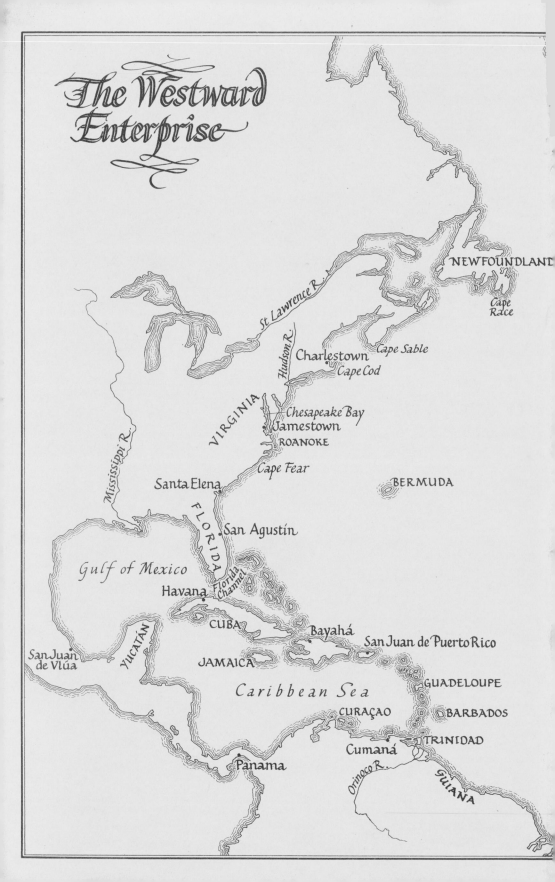

The Westward Enterprise

NEWFOUNDLAND

Cape Race

St Lawrence R.

Cape Sable

Charlestown

Cape Cod

Hudson R.

Chesapeake Bay

VIRGINIA

Jamestown

ROANOKE

Cape Fear

BERMUDA

Santa Elena

Mississippi R.

FLORIDA

San Agustín

Gulf of Mexico

Florida Channel

Havana

CUBA

Bayahá

San Juan de Puerto Rico

San Juan de Vlúa

YUCATÁN

JAMAICA

GUADELOUPE

Caribbean Sea

CURAÇAO

BARBADOS

TRINIDAD

Cumaná

Panama

Orinoco R.

GUIANA